WORKBOOK

STECK-VAUGHN

SCIENCE

TEST PREPARATION FOR THE 2014 GED® TEST

- Life Science
- Physical Science
- Earth and Space Science
- Science Practices

Harcourt

Ho
Mi
Ha

POWERE

PAX

Acknowledgments

For each of the selections and images listed below, grateful acknowledgment is made for permission to excerpt and/or reprint original or copyrighted material, as follows:

Text

31 Used with permission of Michigan Department of Natural Resources. **47** Used with permission of learn.genetics.utah.edu.

Images

Cover (bg) © Chen Ping-hung/E+/Getty Images; **cover (inset)** © Design Pics/John Short/Getty Images. **31** Oscar Warbach, Michigan Department of Natural Resources. **49** iStockphoto. **147** U.S. Geological Survey. **151 (1913 photo)** W. C. Alden, courtesy of U.S. Geological Survey Photographic Library. **151 (2005 photo)** Blase Reardon, courtesy of U.S. Geological Survey.

Science

Workbook

Table of Contents

About the GED® Test...iv–v
GED® Test on Computer...vi–vii
About *Steck-Vaughn*
Test Preparation for the 2014 GED® Test.................viii–ix
About the GED® Science Test x
About *Steck-Vaughn Test Preparation for the 2014*
GED® Test Science xi
Calculator Directions .... xii–xiii
Test-Taking Tips xiv
Study Skills xv

UNIT 1 *Life Science*
LESSON
1: Interpret Illustrations 2–5
2: Identify Main Idea and Details 6–9
3: Interpret Tables 10–13
4: Identify Cause and Effect 14–17
5: Interpret Graphs and Maps 18–21
6: Interpret Diagrams 22–25
7: Categorize and Classify 26–29
8: Generalize 30–33
9: Compare and Contrast.................................. 34–37
10: Relate Text and Visuals............................... 38–41
11: Understand Content-Based Tools................. 42–45
12: Use Context Clues 46–49
13: Understand Scientific Evidence................... 50–53
14: Make and Identify Inferences 54–57
15: Draw Conclusions 58–61

UNIT 2 *Physical Science*
LESSON
1: Understand Scientific Models......................... 62–65
2: Interpret Complex Visuals 66–69
3: Interpret Complex Tables 70–73
4: Understand Chemical Equations 74–77
5: Predict Outcomes 78–81
6: Calculate to Interpret Outcomes................... 82–85
7: Understand Vector Diagrams 86–89
8: Apply Scientific Laws 90–93
9: Access Prior Knowledge 94–97
10: Link Microscopic and Observable Events....98–101
11: Interpret Observations 102–105
12: Link Content from Varied Formats............. 106–109
13: Draw Conclusions from Mixed Sources......110–113
14: Understand Investigation Techniques 114–117
15: Evaluate Scientific Information................. 118–121

UNIT 3 *Earth and Space Science*
LESSON
1: Understand Scientific Theories 122–125
2: Summarize Complex Material 126–129
3: Understand Patterns in Science................. 130–133
4: Interpret Three-Dimensional Diagrams........ 134–137
5: Apply Science Concepts 138–141
6: Express Scientific Information.................... 142–145
7: Identify Problem and Solution.................... 146–149
8: Analyze and Present Arguments................ 150–153

ANSWER KEY 154–195
INDEX 196–203

About the GED® Test

Welcome to the first day of the rest of your life. Now that you've committed to study for your GED® credential, an array of possibilities and options—academic, career, and otherwise—awaits you. Each year, hundreds of thousands of people just like you decide to pursue a GED® credential. Like you, they left traditional school for one reason or another. Now, just like them, you've decided to continue your education by studying for and taking the GED® Test.

Today's GED® Test is very different from previous versions of the exam. Today's GED® Test is new, improved, and more rigorous, with content aligned to the Common Core State Standards. For the first time, the GED® Test serves both as a high-school equivalency credential and as a predictor of college and career readiness. The new GED® Test features four subject areas: Reasoning Through Language Arts (RLA), Mathematical Reasoning, Science, and Social Studies. Each subject area is delivered via a computer-based format and includes an array of technology-enhanced item types.

The four subject-area exams together comprise a testing time of seven hours. Preparation can take considerably longer. The payoff, however, is significant: more and better career options, higher earnings, and the sense of achievement that comes with a GED® credential. Employers, colleges, and universities alike accept the GED® credential as they would a high school diploma. On average, GED® graduates earn at least $8,400 more per year than those with an incomplete high school education.

The GED® Testing Service has constructed the GED® Test to mirror a high school experience. As such, you must answer a variety of questions within and across the four subject areas. For example, you may encounter a Social Studies passage on the Reasoning Through Language Arts Test, and vice versa. Also, you will encounter questions requiring varying levels of cognitive effort, or Depth of Knowledge (DOK) levels. The following table details the content areas, number of items, score points, DOK levels, and total testing time for each subject area.

Subject-Area Test	Content Areas	Items	Raw Score Points	DOK Level	Time
Reasoning Through Language Arts	**Informational Texts**—75% **Literary Texts**—25%	*51	65	80% of items at Level 2 or 3	150 minutes
Mathematical Reasoning	**Algebraic Problem Solving**—55% **Quantitative Problem Solving**—45%	*46	49	50% of items at Level 2	115 minutes
Science	**Life Science**—40% **Physical Science**—40% **Earth and Space Science**—20%	*34	40	80% of items at Level 2 or 3	90 minutes
Social Studies	**Civics/Government**—50% **U.S. History**—20% **Economics**—15% **Geography and the World**—15%	*35	44	80% of items at Level 2 or 3	90 minutes

*Number of items may vary slightly by test.

Because the demands of today's high school education and its relationship to workforce needs differ from those of a decade ago, the GED® Testing Service has moved to a computer-based format. Although multiple-choice questions remain the dominant type of item, the new GED® Test series includes a variety of technology-enhanced item types: drop-down, fill-in-the-blank, drag-and-drop, hot spot, short answer, and extended response items.

The table to the right identifies the various item types and their distribution on the new subject-area exams. As you can see, all four tests include multiple-choice, drop-down, fill-in-the-blank, and drag-and-drop items. Some variation occurs with hot spot, short answer, and extended response items.

2014 ITEM TYPES

	RLA	Math	Science	Social Studies
Multiple-choice	✓	✓	✓	✓
Drop-down	✓	✓	✓	✓
Fill-in-the-blank	✓	✓	✓	✓
Drag-and-drop	✓	✓	✓	✓
Hot spot		✓	✓	✓
Short answer			✓	
Extended response	✓			✓

Moreover, the new GED® Test relates to today's more demanding educational standards with items that align to appropriate assessment targets and varying DOK levels.

- **Content Topics/Assessment Targets** These topics and targets describe and detail the content on the GED® Test. They tie to the Common Core State Standards, as well as state standards for Texas and Virginia.
- **Content Practices** These practices describe the types of reasoning and modes of thinking required to answer specific items on the GED® Test.
- **Depth of Knowledge** The DOK model details the level of cognitive complexity and steps required to arrive at a correct answer on the test. The new GED® Test addresses three levels of DOK complexity.
  - **Level 1** You must recall, observe, question, or represent facts or simple skills. Typically, you will need to exhibit only a surface understanding of text and graphics.
  - **Level 2** You must process information beyond simple recall and observation to include summarizing, ordering, classifying, identifying patterns and relationships, and connecting ideas. You will need to scrutinize text and graphics.
  - **Level 3** You must explain, generalize, and connect ideas by inferring, elaborating, and predicting. For example, you may need to summarize from multiple sources and use that information to develop compositions with multiple paragraphs. Those paragraphs should feature a critical analysis of sources, include supporting positions from your own experiences, and reflect editing to ensure coherent, correct writing.

Approximately 80 percent of items across most content areas will be written to DOK Levels 2 and 3, with the remainder at Level 1. Writing portions, such as the extended response item in Social Studies (25 minutes) and Reasoning Through Language Arts (45 minutes), are considered DOK Level 3 items.

Now that you understand the basic structure of the GED® Test and the benefits of earning a GED® credential, you must prepare for the GED® Test. In the pages that follow, you will find a recipe of sorts that, if followed, will guide you toward successful completion of your GED® credential.

GED® Test on Computer

Along with new item types, the 2014 GED® Test also unveils a new, computer-based testing experience. The GED® Test will be available on computer and only at approved Pearson VUE Testing Centers. You will need content knowledge and the ability to read, think, and write critically, and you must perform basic computer functions—clicking, scrolling, and typing—to succeed on the test. The screen below closely resembles a screen that you will experience on the GED® Test.

The **INFORMATION** button contains material vital to the successful completion of the item. Here, by clicking the Information button, you would display a map about the American Revolution. On the Mathematical Reasoning exam, similar buttons for **FORMULA SHEET** and **CALCULATOR REFERENCE** provide information that will help you answer items that require use of formulas or the TI-30XS calculator. You may move a passage or graphic by clicking it and dragging it to a different part of the test screen.

Social Studies   Question 1 of 10

Information

DIRECTIONS: Study the map, read the question, and choose the best answer.

AMERICAN REVOLUTION 1776–1777

- American forces
- American victory
- British forces
- British victory

Hudson R.
NY
White Plains Oct. 28, 1776
CT
Long Island Sound
Fort Lee Nov. 19, 1776
Long Island
Morristown
Harlem Heights Sept. 16, 1776
NJ
Long Island Aug. 27, 1776
Staten Island
Princeton Jan. 3, 1777
ATLANTIC OCEAN
Trenton Dec. 26, 1776
PA
0   20   40 miles
0   20   40 kilometers

1. The New York–New Jersey military campaign marked a key turning point for the Colonial Army in the American Revolution. Based on the map, what were the first and last battle sites of the campaign?

- A. Harlem Heights and Princeton
- B. Fort Lee and Trenton
- C. Long Island and Princeton
- D. Harlem Heights and White Plains

← Previous | Next →

To select a response, click the button adjacent to the answer. If you wish to change your answer, click a different button, thereby clearing the previous selection.

Where a passage or graphic does not entirely fit in a window, scrolling is required. To scroll, click the scroll bar and drag it downward to display the part of the text or graphic. The light gray portion of the scroll bar shows the amount of text or graphic that you cannot presently see.

To return to the prior screen, click **PREVIOUS**. To advance to the next screen, click **NEXT**.

Some items on the new GED® Test, such as fill-in-the-blank, short answer, and extended response questions, will require you to type answers into an entry box. In some cases, the directions may specify the range of typing the system will accept. For example, a fill-in-the-blank item may allow you to type a number from 0 to 9, along with a decimal point or a slash, but nothing else. The system also will tell you keys to avoid pressing in certain situations. The annotated computer screen and keyboard below provide strategies for entering text and data for fill-in-the-blank, short answer, and extended response items.

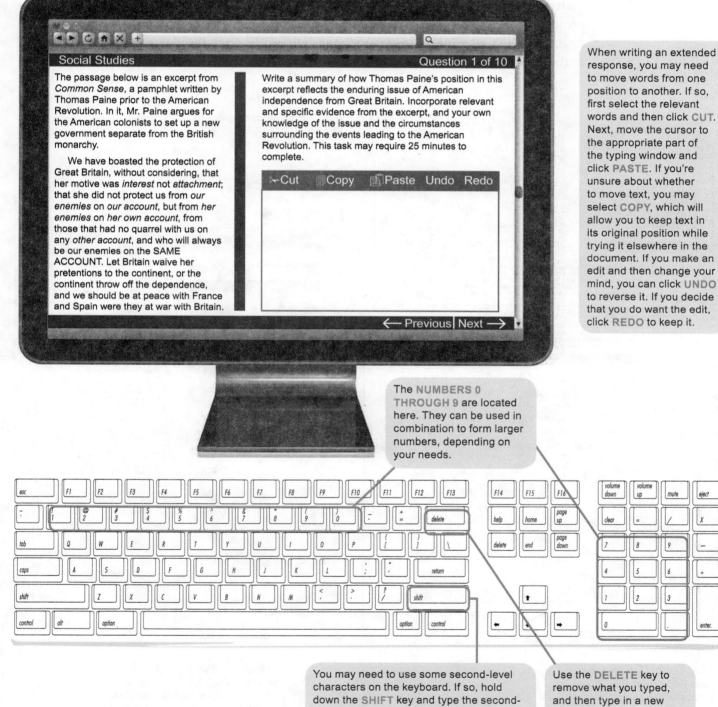

Social Studies — Question 1 of 10

The passage below is an excerpt from *Common Sense*, a pamphlet written by Thomas Paine prior to the American Revolution. In it, Mr. Paine argues for the American colonists to set up a new government separate from the British monarchy.

We have boasted the protection of Great Britain, without considering, that her motive was *interest* not *attachment*; that she did not protect us from *our enemies* on *our account*, but from *her enemies* on *her own account*, from those that had no quarrel with us on any *other account*, and who will always be our enemies on the SAME ACCOUNT. Let Britain waive her pretentions to the continent, or the continent throw off the dependence, and we should be at peace with France and Spain were they at war with Britain.

Write a summary of how Thomas Paine's position in this excerpt reflects the enduring issue of American independence from Great Britain. Incorporate relevant and specific evidence from the excerpt, and your own knowledge of the issue and the circumstances surrounding the events leading to the American Revolution. This task may require 25 minutes to complete.

Cut   Copy   Paste   Undo   Redo

← Previous | Next →

When writing an extended response, you may need to move words from one position to another. If so, first select the relevant words and then click CUT. Next, move the cursor to the appropriate part of the typing window and click PASTE. If you're unsure about whether to move text, you may select COPY, which will allow you to keep text in its original position while trying it elsewhere in the document. If you make an edit and then change your mind, you can click UNDO to reverse it. If you decide that you do want the edit, click REDO to keep it.

The NUMBERS 0 THROUGH 9 are located here. They can be used in combination to form larger numbers, depending on your needs.

You may need to use some second-level characters on the keyboard. If so, hold down the SHIFT key and type the second-level key, such as a question mark.

Use the DELETE key to remove what you typed, and then type in a new answer.

About *Steck-Vaughn Test Preparation for the 2014 GED® Test*

Along with choosing to pursue your GED® credential, you've made another smart decision by selecting *Steck-Vaughn Test Preparation for the 2014 GED® Test* as your main study and preparation tool. Our emphasis on the acquisition of key reading and thinking concepts equips you with the skills and strategies to succeed on the GED® Test.

Two-page micro-lessons in each student book provide focused and efficient instruction. For those who require additional support, the companion workbooks provide *twice* the support and practice exercises. Most lessons in the series include a *Spotlighted Item* feature that corresponds to one of the technology-enhanced item types that appear on the GED® Test.

The **REVIEW THE SKILL** section reteaches the skill.

Each lesson includes correlations to **ASSESSMENT TARGETS** that will help focus your studies.

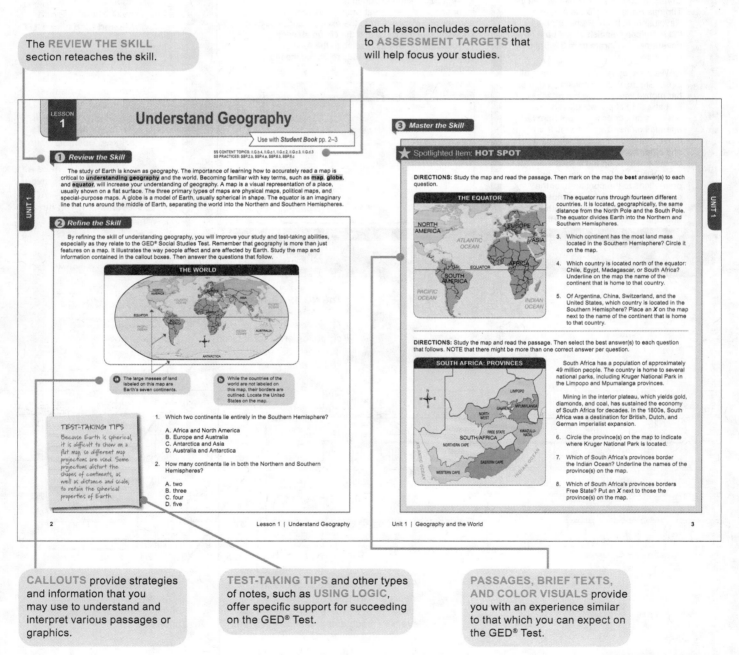

CALLOUTS provide strategies and information that you may use to understand and interpret various passages or graphics.

TEST-TAKING TIPS and other types of notes, such as **USING LOGIC**, offer specific support for succeeding on the GED® Test.

PASSAGES, BRIEF TEXTS, AND COLOR VISUALS provide you with an experience similar to that which you can expect on the GED® Test.

Student Book

Every unit in the student book opens with the feature GED® Journeys, a series of profiles of people who earned their GED® credential and used it as a springboard to success. From there, you receive intensive instruction and practice through a series of linked lessons, all of which tie to Content Topics/Assessment Targets, Content Practices (where applicable), and DOK levels.

Each unit closes with an eight-page review that includes a representative sampling of items, including technology-enhanced item types, from the lessons that comprise the unit. You may use each unit review as a posttest to gauge your mastery of content and skills and readiness for that aspect of the GED® Test.

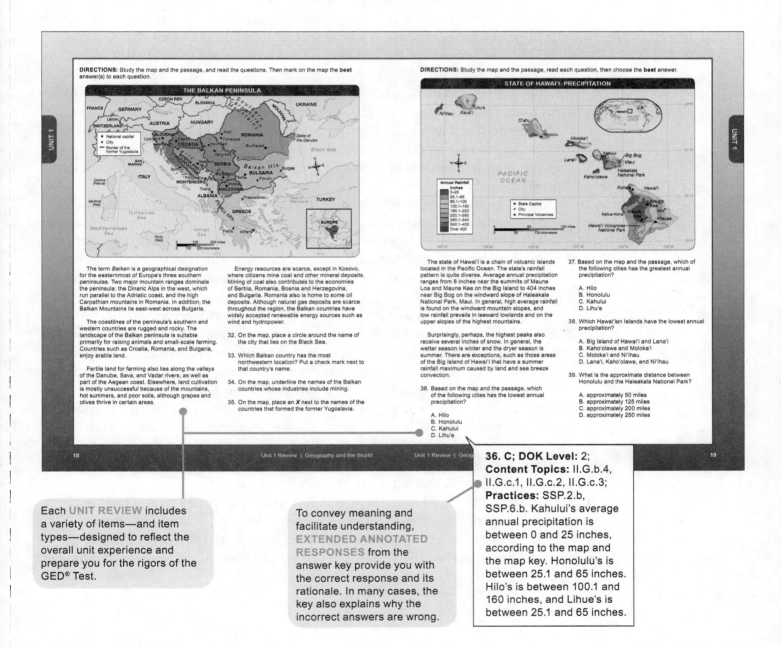

Each **UNIT REVIEW** includes a variety of items—and item types—designed to reflect the overall unit experience and prepare you for the rigors of the GED® Test.

To convey meaning and facilitate understanding, **EXTENDED ANNOTATED RESPONSES** from the answer key provide you with the correct response and its rationale. In many cases, the key also explains why the incorrect answers are wrong.

36. C; DOK Level: 2; **Content Topics:** II.G.b.4, II.G.c.1, II.G.c.2, II.G.c.3; **Practices:** SSP.2.b, SSP.6.b. Kahului's average annual precipitation is between 0 and 25 inches, according to the map and the map key. Honolulu's is between 25.1 and 65 inches. Hilo's is between 100.1 and 160 inches, and Lihue's is between 25.1 and 65 inches.

About the GED® Science Test

The new GED® Science Test is more than just a set of investigations and procedures. In fact, it reflects an attempt to increase the rigor of the GED® Test to better meet the demands of a 21st-century economy. To that end, the GED® Science Test features an array of technology-enhanced item types. All the items are delivered via computer-based testing. The items reflect the knowledge, skills, and abilities that a student would master in an equivalent high school experience.

Multiple-choice questions will remain the majority of items on the GED® Science Test. However, a number of technology-enhanced items, including drop-down, fill-in-the-blank, drag-and-drop, hot spot, and short answer questions, will challenge you to master and convey knowledge in deeper, fuller ways.

- Multiple-choice items assess virtually every content standard as either discrete items or as a series of items. Multiple-choice items on the new GED® Test include four answer options (rather than five), structured in an A./B./C./D. format.
- Drop-down items include pull-down menus of response choices, enabling you to complete statements on the GED® Science Test.
- Fill-in-the-blank items allow you to type in one-word or short answers. For example, you may be asked to describe in a word or a short phrase a trend on a graph or to demonstrate understanding of an idea or vocabulary term from a text passage.
- Drag-and-drop items involve interactive tasks that require you to move small images, words, or numerical expressions into designated drop zones on a computer screen. On the GED® Science Test, you may be asked to assemble data, compare and contrast, or sequence information. For example, you may be asked to place organisms in specific locations on a food web or sequence the steps in a scientific investigation.
- Hot spot items consist of a graphic with virtual sensors placed strategically within it. They allow you to demonstrate understanding of information presented visually or in text or relationships between data points in a passage or graphic. For example, a hot spot item could ask you to demonstrate your understanding of heredity by selecting offspring with a particular trait.
- Short answer items on the GED® Science Test feature two 10-minute tasks in which you compose brief responses to science content. Such responses may include providing a valid summary of a passage or model, creating and communicating a valid conclusion or hypothesis, or deriving evidence from a passage or graphic that supports a particular conclusion.

You will have a total of 90 minutes in which to answer about 34 items. The GED® Science Test is organized across three main content areas: life science (40 percent), physical science (40 percent), and Earth and space sciences (20 percent). All told, 80 percent of the items on the GED® Science Test will be written at Depth of Knowledge Level 2 or 3.

About *Steck-Vaughn Test Preparation for the 2014 GED® Test: Science*

Steck-Vaughn's student book and workbook help unlock the learning and deconstruct the different elements of the test by helping you build and develop core reading and thinking skills. The content of our books aligns to the new GED® science content standards and item distribution to provide you with a superior test preparation experience.

Our *Spotlighted Item* feature provides a deeper, richer treatment for each technology-enhanced item type. On initial introduction, a unique item type—such as drag-and-drop—receives a full page of example items in the student book lesson and three pages in the companion workbook lesson. The length of subsequent features may be shorter depending on the skill, lesson, and requirements.

A combination of targeted strategies, informational callouts, sample questions, assorted tips and hints, and ample assessment help focus study efforts in needed areas.

In addition to the book features, a highly detailed answer key provides the correct answer and the rationale for it so that you know exactly why an answer is correct. The *Science* student book and workbook are designed with an eye toward the end goal: success on the GED® Science Test.

Along with mastering key content and reading and thinking skills, you will build familiarity with alternate item types that mirror in print the nature and scope of the technology-enhanced items included on the GED® Test.

LESSON 15

Draw Conclusions

SCIENCE CONTENT TOPIC: L.f.3
SCIENCE PRACTICES: SP.1.a, SP.1.b, SP.1.c, SP.3.a, SP.3.b, SP.6.c, SP.7.a

UNIT 1

① Learn the Skill

A **conclusion** is a reasoned understanding of something. Often, a conclusion is based on a collection of inferences. Remember that an inference is a logical guess based on facts, evidence, experience, or observations. When you **draw a conclusion**, you make a statement that explains the overall meaning of various pieces of information and inferences you have made.

A valid conclusion conveys an idea that is supported by all available information and accurate inferences. Conclusions can be supported by information presented in text or information presented visually.

② Practice the Skill

By practicing the skill of drawing conclusions, you will improve your study and test-taking abilities, especially as they relate to the GED® Science Test. Read the passage below. Then answer the question that follows.

SELECTION PRESSURE, ADAPTATION, AND SPECIATION

ⓐ To draw a conclusion, make inferences. From this information and what you know, you can infer that selection pressures cause natural selection.

Selection pressures are features of an environment that affect an organism's ability to survive and reproduce in the environment over time. Changes in these pressures, such as climate changes, enable animals having traits suitable to the new environment to flourish and cause others to struggle and possibly even die off.

ⓑ From this information, you can infer that adaptations are passed from generation to generation.

Over time, selection pressures and natural selection lead to adaptation. Through adaptation, species develop traits that allow them to respond to certain features of their environment. These traits, or adaptations, can be physical or behavioral.

ⓒ From this information, you can infer that adaptation is related to evolution.

Biological evolution is a process of constant change over generations. Because adaptation is ongoing, species change over time. Sometimes populations of a species develop different adaptations in response to different selection pressures. These differences can be substantial enough that the populations eventually become separate species. Formation of a new species is called speciation.

USING LOGIC

Think carefully about what the question is asking. In this case, the question asks for a conclusion. Therefore, the correct answer will not be directly stated in the passage.

1. Which statement is a valid conclusion supported by the passage?

A. Over time, changing selection pressures affect a species' ability to survive and reproduce in its environment.

B. Species can develop adaptations that allow them to respond to features of their environments.

C. Evolution is the result of selection pressures, natural selection, and adaptation.

D. If populations of a species develop different adaptations, they always become separate species.

③ Apply the Skill

★ Spotlighted Item: **SHORT ANSWER**

DIRECTIONS: Read the passage, and study the table. Then read the question, and write your response on the lines. This task may take approximately 10 minutes to complete.

SIGNIFICANCE OF ADAPTATIONS IN REPTILES

Almost all amphibians must spend part of their lives in an aquatic habitat to survive. One reason is that they must be able to replenish water they lose through their thin, porous skin. Also, their eggs are laid in water and will dry out and die if they do not remain submerged. Reptiles do not lose much water through their skin, and they lay their eggs on land, sometimes in holes they dig. Despite these differences, scientists think that reptiles share a common amphibian ancestor. This ancestor probably lived more than 300 million years ago. Various adaptations arose in generations of reptile ancestors, allowing them to move to drier environments over time. The table contrasts the traits of amphibians and reptiles.

Group	Characteristics
Amphibians	Eggs lacking shells
	Development of lungs and legs following birth
	Moist skin
	Toes lacking claws
Reptiles	Eggs having fluid contained by leathery shells
	Born with lungs and legs
	Scaly skin
	Toes with claws

2. Draw a conclusion about how adaptation has resulted in the ability of reptiles to live in different environments than amphibians. Include support from the passage and table in your response.

Calculator Directions

Certain items on the GED® Mathematical Reasoning Test allow for the use of a calculator to aid in answering questions. That calculator, the TI-30XS, is embedded within the testing interface. Students may also bring their own TI- 30XS MultiView calculator to use on the test. The TI-30XS calculator will be available for most items on the GED® Mathematical Reasoning Test and for some items on the GED® Science Test. The TI-30XS calculator is shown below, along with callouts of some of its most important keys. A button that enables the calculator reference sheet is located in the upper right corner of the testing screen.

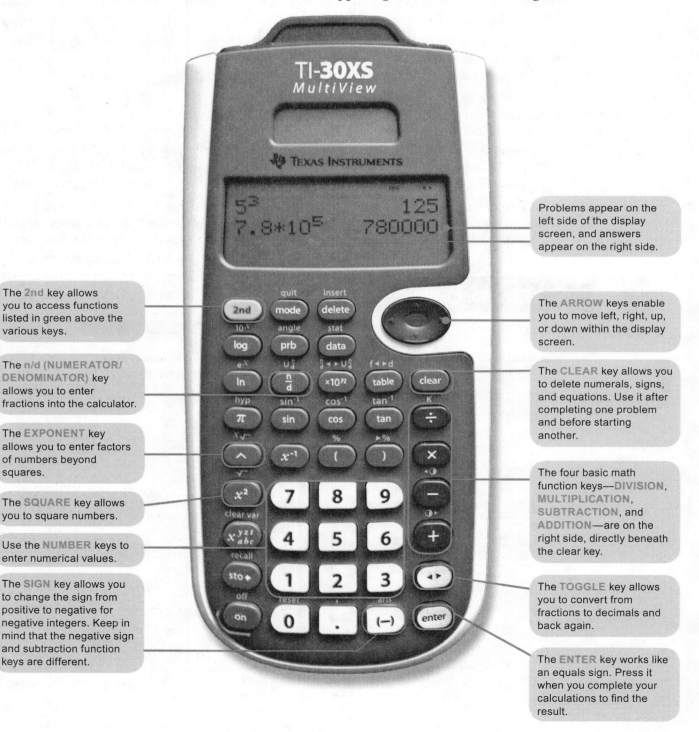

The 2nd key allows you to access functions listed in green above the various keys.

The n/d (NUMERATOR/ DENOMINATOR) key allows you to enter fractions into the calculator.

The EXPONENT key allows you to enter factors of numbers beyond squares.

The SQUARE key allows you to square numbers.

Use the NUMBER keys to enter numerical values.

The SIGN key allows you to change the sign from positive to negative for negative integers. Keep in mind that the negative sign and subtraction function keys are different.

Problems appear on the left side of the display screen, and answers appear on the right side.

The ARROW keys enable you to move left, right, up, or down within the display screen.

The CLEAR key allows you to delete numerals, signs, and equations. Use it after completing one problem and before starting another.

The four basic math function keys—DIVISION, MULTIPLICATION, SUBTRACTION, and ADDITION—are on the right side, directly beneath the clear key.

The TOGGLE key allows you to convert from fractions to decimals and back again.

The ENTER key works like an equals sign. Press it when you complete your calculations to find the result.

Getting Started

To enable the calculator for a question that allows it, click the upper left portion of the testing screen. If the calculator displays over the top of a problem, you may move it by clicking it and dragging it to another part of the screen. Once enabled, the calculator will be ready for use (no need to push the **on** key). The directions below are for using the calculator in *mathprint* mode. Classic mode can be used by pressing the **mode** key and selecting *classic*.

- Use the **clear** key to clear all numbers and operations from the screen.
- Use the **enter** key to complete all calculations.

2nd Key

The green **2nd** key is located in the upper left corner of the TI-30XS. The **2nd** key enables a second series of functions, which are located above the keys and noted in green type. To use the 2nd-level functions, click the **2nd** key, and then click the key with the 2nd-level function you need.

Fractions and Mixed Numbers

To enter fractions, such as $\frac{3}{4}$, click the **n/d (numerator/denominator)** key, followed by the numerator quantity [**3**]. Next, click the **down arrow** button (upper right corner of the calculator), followed by the denominator quantity [**4**]. To calculate with fractions, click the **right arrow** button and then the appropriate function key and other numerals in the equation.

To enter mixed numbers, such as $1\frac{3}{8}$, first enter the whole number quantity [**1**]. Next, click the **2nd** key and the **mixed number** key (1st level **n/d**). Then enter the fraction numerator [**3**], followed by the **down arrow** button and then the denominator [**8**]. If you click **enter**, the mixed number will convert to an improper fraction. To calculate with mixed numbers, click the **right arrow** button and then the appropriate function key and other numerals in the equation.

Negative Numbers

To enter a negative number, click the **negative sign** key (located directly below the number **3** on the calculator). Keep in mind that the **negative sign** key differs from the **subtraction** key, which is found in the far right column of keys, directly above the **addition (+)** key.

Squares, Square Roots, and Exponents

- **Squares:** The x^2 key squares numbers. The **exponent** key (^) raises numbers to powers higher than squares, such as cubes. For example, to find the answer to 5^3 on the calculator, first enter the base number [**5**], then click the exponent key (^), and follow by clicking the exponent number [**3**] and then the **enter** key.
- **Square Roots:** To find the square root of a number, such as 36, first click the **2nd** key, then click the **square root** key (1st-level x^2), then the number [**36**], and finally **enter**.
- **Cube Roots:** To find the cube root of a number, such as **125**, first enter the cube as a number [**3**], followed by the **2nd** key and **square root** key. Finally, enter the number for which you want to find the cube [**125**], followed by **enter**.
- **Exponents:** To perform calculations with numbers expressed in scientific notation, such as 7.8×10^9, first enter the base number [**7.8**]. Next, click the **scientific notation** key (located directly beneath the **data** key), followed by the exponent level [**9**]. You then have 7.8×10^9.

Test-Taking Tips

The new GED® Test includes more than 160 items across the four subject-area exams of Reasoning Through Language Arts, Mathematical Reasoning, Science, and Social Studies. The four subject-area exams represent a total test time of seven hours. Most items are multiple-choice questions, but a number are technology-enhanced items. These include drop-down, fill-in-the-blank, drag-and-drop, hot spot, short answer, and extended response items.

Throughout this book and others in the series, we help you build, develop, and apply core reading and thinking skills critical to success on the GED® Test. As part of an overall strategy, we suggest that you use the test-taking tips presented here and throughout the book to improve your performance on the GED® Test.

> **Always read directions thoroughly so that you know exactly what to do.** As we've noted, the 2014 GED® Test has an entirely new computer-based format that includes a variety of technology-enhanced items. If you are unclear of what to do or how to proceed, ask the test provider whether directions can be explained.

> **Read each question carefully so that you fully understand what it is asking.** For example, some passages and graphics may present information beyond what is necessary to correctly answer a specific question. Other questions may use boldfaced words for emphasis (for example, "Which statement represents the **most** appropriate revision for this hypothesis?").

> **Manage your time with each question.** Because the GED® Test is a series of timed exams, you want to spend enough time with each question, but not *too* much time. For example, on the GED® Mathematical Reasoning Test, you have 115 minutes in which to answer approximately 46 questions, or an average of about two minutes per question. Obviously, some items will require more time and others will require less, but you should remain aware of the overall number of items and amount of testing time. The new GED® Test interface may help you manage your time. It includes an on-screen clock in the upper right corner that provides the remaining time in which to complete a test.

Also, you may monitor your progress by viewing the **Question** line, which will give you the current question number, followed by the total number of questions on that subject-area exam.

> **Answer all questions**, **regardless of whether you know the answer or are guessing.** There is no benefit in leaving questions unanswered on the GED® Test. Keep in mind the time that you have for each test, and manage it accordingly. If you wish to review a specific item at the end of a test, click **Flag for Review** to mark the question. When you do, the flag will display in yellow. At the end of a test, you may have time to review questions you've marked.

> **Skim and scan.** You may save time by first reading each question and its answer options before reading or studying an accompanying passage or graphic. Once you understand what the question is asking, review the passage or visual for the appropriate information.

> **Note any unfamiliar words in questions.** First attempt to re-read the question by omitting any unfamiliar word. Next, try to use other words around the unfamiliar word to determine its meaning.

> **Narrow answer options by re-reading each question and re-examining the text or graphic that goes with it.** Although four answers are *possible* on multiple-choice items, keep in mind that only one is *correct*. You may be able to eliminate one answer immediately; you may need to take more time or use logic or make assumptions to eliminate others. In some cases, you may need to make your best guess between two options.

> **Go with your instinct when answering questions.** If your first instinct is to choose **A** in response to a question, it's best to stick with that answer unless you determine that it is incorrect. Usually, the first answer someone chooses is the correct one.

Study Skills

You've already made two very smart decisions in studying for your GED® credential and in purchasing *Steck-Vaughn Test Preparation for the 2014 GED® Test: Science* to help you do so. Following are additional strategies to help you optimize your possibilities for success on the GED® Test.

4 weeks out ...

➤ **Set a study schedule for the GED® Test.** Choose times in which you are most alert and places, such as a library, that provide the best study environment.

➤ **Thoroughly review all material in *Steck-Vaughn Test Preparation for the 2014 GED® Test: Science*.** Use the *Science* workbook to extend understanding of concepts in the *Science* student book.

➤ **Keep a notebook for each subject area that you are studying.** Folders with pockets are useful for storing loose papers.

➤ **When taking notes, restate thoughts or ideas in your own words rather than copy them directly from a book.** You can phrase these notes as complete sentences, as questions (with answers), or as fragments, provided you understand them.

2 weeks out ...

➤ **Review your performance on the unit reviews in the student book, note any troublesome areas.** Focus your remaining study around those areas. For additional test practice, you may also wish to take the GED Ready™ practice tests or the *Pretests and Posttests for the Steck-Vaughn Test Preparation for the 2014 GED® Test*.

The days before ...

➤ **Map out the route to the test center, and visit it a day or two before your scheduled exam.** If you plan to drive to the test center on the day of the test, find out where you will need to park.

➤ **Get a good night's sleep the night before the GED® Test.** Studies have shown that students with sufficient rest perform better in testing situations.

The day of ...

➤ **Eat a hearty breakfast high in protein.** As with the rest of your body, your brain needs ample energy to perform well.

➤ **Arrive 30 minutes early to the testing center.** Arriving early will allow sufficient time in the event of a room change.

➤ **Pack a sizeable lunch.** A hearty lunch is especially important if you plan to be at the testing center most of the day.

➤ **Remember to relax.** You've come this far and spent weeks preparing and studying for the GED® Test. Now it's your time to shine!

Interpret Illustrations

Use with *Student Book* pp. 2–3

SCIENCE CONTENT TOPICS: L.b.1, L.d.1, L.d.2, L.d.3
SCIENCE PRACTICES: SP.1.a, SP.1.b, SP.1.c, SP.7.a

UNIT 1

1 Review the Skill

Illustrations are important tools for explaining parts of a whole and how those parts fit together. Some illustrations show things that are not normally visible, such as the parts of a cell. Others may help you visualize what is happening in a complex process. When you **interpret illustrations**, you use visual elements and labels or other related text to understand the structure of an object, how something works, or how something happens.

Because much of science relates to objects or processes that cannot be observed directly, illustrations are important parts of scientific presentations. Viewing and interpreting illustrations helps you improve your understanding of science topics.

2 Refine the Skill

By refining the skill of interpreting illustrations, you will improve your study and test-taking abilities, especially as they relate to the GED® Science Test. Study the illustration below. Then answer the questions that follow.

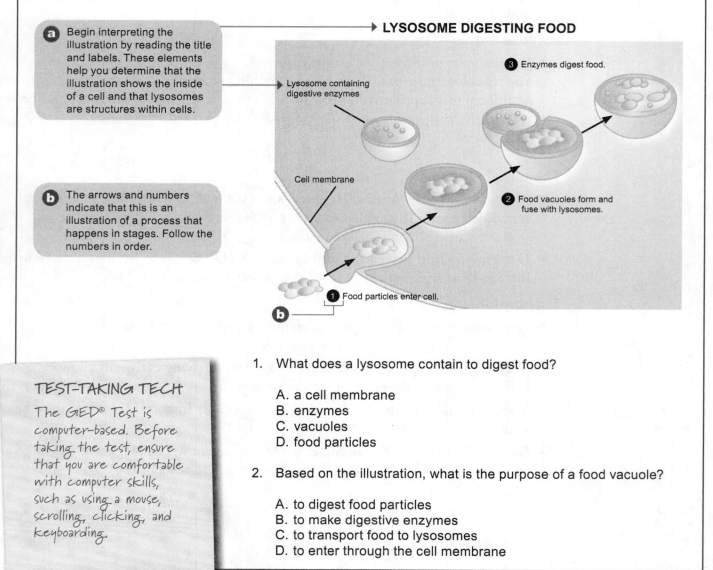

a Begin interpreting the illustration by reading the title and labels. These elements help you determine that the illustration shows the inside of a cell and that lysosomes are structures within cells.

b The arrows and numbers indicate that this is an illustration of a process that happens in stages. Follow the numbers in order.

LYSOSOME DIGESTING FOOD

3 Enzymes digest food.

Lysosome containing digestive enzymes

Cell membrane

2 Food vacuoles form and fuse with lysosomes.

1 Food particles enter cell.

1. What does a lysosome contain to digest food?

   A. a cell membrane
   B. enzymes
   C. vacuoles
   D. food particles

2. Based on the illustration, what is the purpose of a food vacuole?

   A. to digest food particles
   B. to make digestive enzymes
   C. to transport food to lysosomes
   D. to enter through the cell membrane

DIRECTIONS: Study the information and illustration, read each question, and choose the **best** answer.

MEIOSIS

Through mitosis, a cell divides to form two daughter cells that are the same as the parent cell. Cells also divide through meiosis. As with mitosis, a cell's nucleus divides after genetic, or hereditary, material in the cell replicates. During meiosis, however, the two daughter cells divide, without duplicating their genetic material. The result is four cells called gametes. Egg and sperm cells are gametes. Gametes join during sexual reproduction to form a single cell having the same number of chromosomes the original cell had before meiosis. The illustration shows what happens to the genetic material in a cell nucleus before and during meiosis.

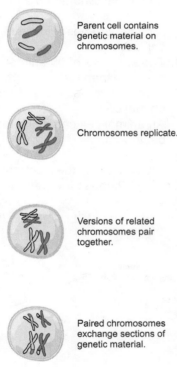

Parent cell contains genetic material on chromosomes.

Chromosomes replicate.

Versions of related chromosomes pair together.

Paired chromosomes exchange sections of genetic material.

Two daughter cells form.

Two daughter cells divide to form four new cells (gametes).

3. The parent cell in the illustration has four chromosomes. How many chromosomes does each gamete have at the end of meiosis?

   A. two
   B. four
   C. six
   D. eight

4. Of these events, which happens last during meiosis?

   A. The cell splits into two identical daughter cells.
   B. The chromosomes swap sections of genetic material.
   C. The two daughter cells split to form gametes.
   D. The chromosomes replicate.

5. Based on the illustration, what is produced when chromosomes swap sections of genetic material?

   A. gametes that cannot be damaged
   B. gametes having different numbers of chromosomes
   C. gametes that divide to form new cells
   D. gametes with unique genetic material

DIRECTIONS: Study the information and illustration, read the question, and choose the **best** answer.

CELL MEMBRANE

The cell membrane, which encloses the cell, is mostly made of lipids (fats) and proteins. It allows only substances that dissolve in lipids to move freely into and out of the cell. Oxygen is an example of a lipid-soluble substance. Water and water-soluble substances, such as glucose, need proteins to help move them across the cell membrane.

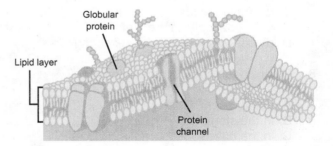

Globular protein

Lipid layer

Protein channel

6. What does the illustration show?

   A. the way that cells reproduce
   B. the nucleus of a cell
   C. the contents of a typical cell
   D. the structures of a cell membrane

DIRECTIONS: Study the information and illustration, read each question, and choose the **best** answer.

PHOTOSYNTHESIS

Plants use energy from sunlight to make their own food through the process of photosynthesis. During photosynthesis, a plant turns carbon dioxide gas (CO_2) from the air and water from the soil into glucose. Glucose is a simple sugar stored in the plant's tissues. Oxygen gas (O_2) is released during the process. Photosynthesis occurs in tiny structures called chloroplasts. Chloroplasts contain chlorophyll, a material that absorbs energy from sunlight and is necessary for changing light energy into the chemical energy the plant stores in its tissues.

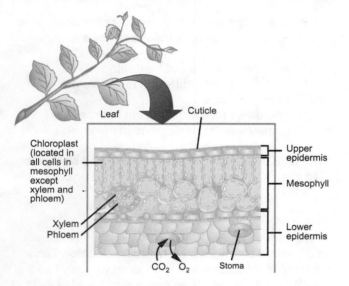

7. What are the upper epidermis, mesophyll, and lower epidermis?

   A. areas where photosynthesis occurs
   B. layers in the leaf's structure
   C. individual cells in the leaf
   D. places where gases are exchanged

8. Where does photosynthesis happen?

   A. in the xylem
   B. in the stoma
   C. in the cuticle
   D. in the mesophyll

9. What would be the **best** title for this illustration?

   A. Leaf Structure and Photosynthesis
   B. How Photosynthesis Works
   C. Composition of Chlorophyll
   D. Understanding Chloroplasts

DIRECTIONS: Study the illustration, read the question, and choose the **best** answer.

BACTERIUM CELL AND ANIMAL CELL

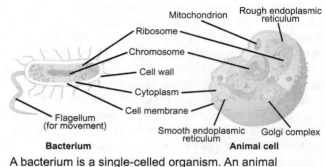

A bacterium is a single-celled organism. An animal is a multi-celled organism.

10. How do a bacterium and an animal cell differ?

    A. A bacterium has a nucleus, whereas an animal cell does not.
    B. The structure of an animal cell is more complex than the structure of a bacterium.
    C. A bacterium has more cytoplasm than an animal cell.
    D. An animal cell can move more easily than a bacterium.

DIRECTIONS: Study the illustration, read the question, and choose the **best** answer.

CELL NUCLEUS

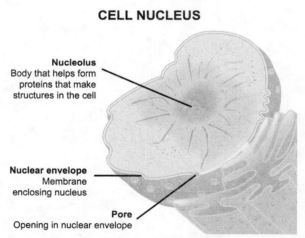

A cell's nucleus controls the functions of the cell and contains the cell's genetic material.

11. What is the **most likely** function of the pore?

    A. to let materials into and out of a nucleus
    B. to enclose genetic material within the nucleus
    C. to seal the nuclear envelope
    D. to help form proteins

DIRECTIONS: Study the information and illustration, read each question, and choose the **best** answer.

CELLULAR RESPIRATION

Cellular respiration is the process by which energy from food is released and made into energy that cells can use. Glucose is the main source of food for cells. During cellular respiration, glucose is turned into adenosine triphosphate, or ATP. ATP stored in cells is the energy source for many cellular processes. Cellular respiration may be aerobic, with oxygen, or anaerobic, without oxygen. Anaerobic respiration, sometimes called fermentation, produces less ATP than the citric acid cycle involved in aerobic respiration. However, anaerobic respiration is important in that it enables ATP to be produced without using oxygen.

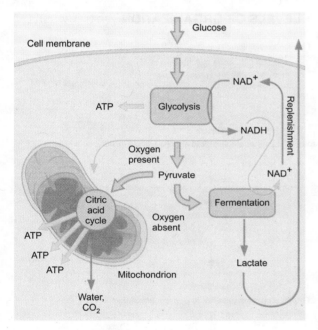

12. Which step in cellular respiration produces the most ATP?

   A. replenishment
   B. fermentation
   C. citric acid cycle
   D. glycolysis

13. Which substance is a product of fermentation?

   A. lactate
   B. water
   C. carbon dioxide
   D. pyruvate

14. Based on the illustration, how does fermentation result in the production of ATP?

   A. It provides NADH to enable the citric acid cycle to occur.
   B. It enables the cell to take in glucose through the cell membrane.
   C. It provides pyruvate for use in the citric acid cycle.
   D. It produces the chemical compound NAD^+, which is used in glycolysis.

DIRECTIONS: Study the illustration, read each question, and choose the **best** answer.

ANIMAL CELL MITOCHONDRION

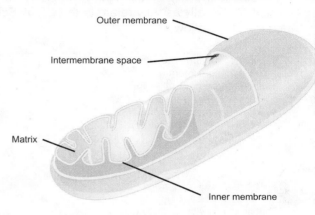

Mitochondria in animal cells release energy stored in compounds such as sugars.

15. What is the purpose of this illustration of an animal cell mitochondrion?

   A. to show how a mitochondrion changes over time
   B. to show the parts of a whole mitochondrion
   C. to show how materials move through cells
   D. to show the process of making energy

16. Based on the illustration, which statement describes the mitochondrion?

   A. It is the largest structure inside a cell.
   B. It has two membranes.
   C. It is part of the nucleolus.
   D. It can move easily into and out of a cell.

17. What information does the caption provide?

   A. the location of the matrix
   B. a purpose of the intermembrane space
   C. the size of the outer membrane
   D. a function of the mitochondrion

Identify Main Idea and Details

Use with *Student Book* pp. 4–5

SCIENCE CONTENT TOPICS: L.a.1, L.d.2
SCIENCE PRACTICES: SP.1.a, SP.1.b, SP.1.c, SP.7.a

① Review the Skill

The **main idea** is the most important part of an informational passage, an article, a paragraph, or even information presented visually. You can **identify the main idea** by looking for a statement or an idea that is supported by other information. This other information is conveyed through **supporting details**. Supporting details can be facts, statistics, data, descriptions, and explanations.

A main idea might be stated obviously in a sentence, or it might be implied. If a main idea is implied, you need to use logic and reasoning to determine what that main idea is, based on the supporting details.

② Refine the Skill

By refining the skill of identifying main idea and details, you will improve your study and test-taking abilities, especially as they relate to the GED® Science Test. Study the information below. Then answer the questions that follow.

a Like information presented in a passage, information presented in a visual element, or graphic, has a main idea. Titles, headings, and other text in a graphic can tell you that main idea.

b The main idea of a graphic may be implied. To identify an implied main idea, study the entire graphic and all the information to decide what main idea is supported.

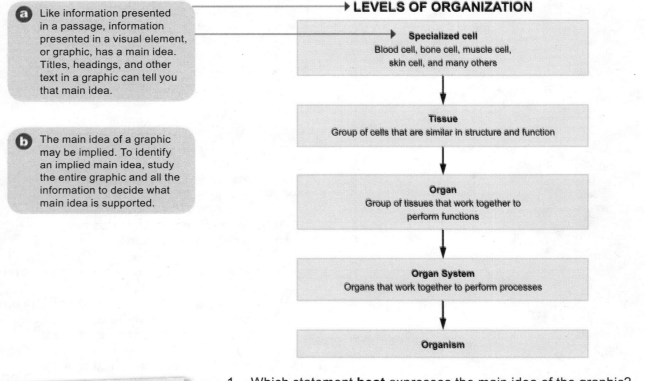

LEVELS OF ORGANIZATION

Specialized cell
Blood cell, bone cell, muscle cell, skin cell, and many others

Tissue
Group of cells that are similar in structure and function

Organ
Group of tissues that work together to perform functions

Organ System
Organs that work together to perform processes

Organism

CONTENT TOPICS

The human body has many organs, but its largest organ is the skin. The skin is made up of three layers. Each contains various tissues and cells. The skin is part of the integumentary system.

1. Which statement **best** expresses the main idea of the graphic?

   A. In a multicellular organism, cells are organized by function.
   B. Cells in a multicellular organism are organized by their size.
   C. The organs in a multicellular organism have different functions.
   D. A multicellular organism has more systems than organs.

2. Which sentence expresses a supporting detail of the graphic?

   A. The skin is made up of three layers.
   B. Cells are different shapes and sizes.
   C. Groups of similar cells form tissues.
   D. Muscles can be smooth, cardiac, or skeletal.

DIRECTIONS: Read the passage and question, and choose the **best** answer.

MOVING OXYGEN THROUGH THE BODY

The circulatory system carries oxygen to all the cells in the body through the blood. To do this, the circulatory system acts in conjunction with the respiratory system. Oxygen enters the blood and moves to the rest of the body through a cycle involving the heart, lungs, and blood vessels. Blood from the body's cells flows through blood vessels to the heart. This blood contains very little oxygen because the cells have used most of the available oxygen. The heart pumps the oxygen-poor blood to the lungs, where it flows through tiny blood vessels. Next, oxygen in the air in the lungs moves through the walls of the blood vessels and into the blood. Special cells in the blood absorb the oxygen. Then the blood moves through larger blood vessels back to the heart. The heart pumps the oxygen-rich blood through blood vessels to the rest of the body. As the blood moves through the body, the cells absorb oxygen from it. Finally, the oxygen-poor blood moves back to the heart, and the cycle repeats.

3. Which statement expresses the main idea of the passage?

   A. The circulatory system and respiratory system work together to get oxygen to cells.
   B. Blood moving from cells to the heart contains very little oxygen.
   C. The heart provides the power to pump the blood through the body.
   D. Oxygen is taken in by the lungs and moved to the blood.

DIRECTIONS: Read the passage and question, and choose the **best** answer.

BODY SYSTEMS WORKING TOGETHER

Some body systems work in tandem. For example, when nutrients are absorbed through the wall of the small intestine, parts of food that the body cannot digest are left behind as waste. The waste moves into and through the large intestine. There, most of the water in it is absorbed, making the waste very compact. The compact waste materials, which are known as feces, move into the rectum. The feces are stored in the rectum until they are eliminated from the body through the anus. So the large intestine is a part of both the digestive system and the excretory system.

4. Which detail **best** supports the main idea of the passage?

   A. Water is absorbed in the large intestine.
   B. Compact waste materials are called feces.
   C. Nutrients are absorbed through the wall of the small intestine.
   D. The large intestine is part of the digestive tract but also helps eliminate waste.

DIRECTIONS: Read the passage. Then read each question, and choose the **best** answer.

MUSCULAR SYSTEM

There are three main types of muscle. Skeletal muscle is the muscle that is attached to bone. This type of muscle controls the body's movements by contracting and relaxing. Each skeletal muscle fiber is a single muscle cell. Cardiac muscle, another muscle type, is known as heart muscle because it is found only in the heart. Cardiac muscle works with the circulatory system to circulate blood throughout the body. The third type of muscle is smooth muscle, which makes up the walls of internal organs. For example, the walls of the stomach and intestines are composed of smooth muscle. This muscle pushes food along through the digestive tract. Smooth muscle acts involuntarily; that is, it contracts and relaxes on its own.

5. Which statement expresses the main idea of the passage?

   A. Skeletal muscle fibers are made up of single muscle cells.
   B. Cardiac muscle works along with the circulatory system to circulate blood.
   C. The three types of muscle play different roles in the muscular system.
   D. Internal organs are lined with smooth muscle.

6. How do the details support the main idea of the passage?

   A. They identify data collected during an investigation of how muscles move.
   B They list all the ways in which skeletal muscles move the body.
   C. They explain how smooth muscles push food through the digestive tract.
   D. They describe each of the three types of muscle.

DIRECTIONS: Study the illustration and information, read each question, and choose the **best** answer.

NEURONS

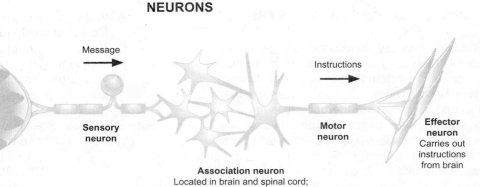

Receptor neuron
Translates what body
senses into nerve impulses

Sensory neuron

Association neuron
Located in brain and spinal cord;
determines meaning of message

Motor neuron

Effector neuron
Carries out
instructions
from brain

Message →

Instructions →

The nervous system includes many types of nerve cells, or neurons. They all have different functions. When someone sees a delicious-looking piece of chocolate cake, receptor neurons in the eyes recognize the cake. They send the image of the cake along sensory neurons to association neurons in the brain and spinal cord. In a fraction of a second, the brain decides how the body should respond. The brain may decide that the correct response is to reach for the cake. As a result, the brain sends this signal through the motor neurons to the effector neurons in the hand. The muscles in the person's hand move, and he or she grasps the plate that holds the cake.

7. Which statement expresses the main idea of the illustration and passage?

   A. Nerve impulses follow a specific path through different neurons to determine meaning and make the body react.
   B. Effector neurons carry out instructions from the brain.
   C. The brain and spinal cord are responsible for making sense of messages from sensory neurons.
   D. Motor neurons and sensory neurons deliver messages.

8. What detail does the illustration provide to support **most directly** the main idea of the illustration and passage?

   A. examples of the shapes of different types of neurons
   B. an explanation of the role of the brain and spinal cord
   C. descriptions of specific functions of three types of neurons
   D. an example of something the body senses

9. Which detail could be added to the passage to support the main idea of the illustration and passage?

   A. Neurons have a nucleus and genetic material like other cells.
   B. There are three classes of neurons, and each class includes hundreds of different types of neurons.
   C. Neurons are the longest cells in the body.
   D. Some brain diseases are caused by the unnatural death of neurons.

DIRECTIONS: Study the passage and illustration, read each question, and choose the **best** answer.

ENDOCRINE SYSTEM

The endocrine system is made up primarily of glands that secrete hormones, such as testosterone and estrogen. Hormones secreted by the endocrine system control growth, metabolism, sexual development, and other body functions.

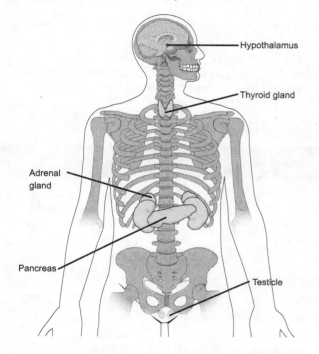

10. Which statement expresses the main idea of the passage?

   A. The endocrine system is centrally located in the body.
   B. The endocrine system comprises glands that make hormones to regulate body systems.
   C. The endocrine system keeps the body in a state of balance.
   D. The endocrine system controls sexual maturation.

11. Which detail could be added to the passage to support the main idea?

   A. The pituitary gland, a major part of the endocrine system, produces seven hormones.
   B. The pituitary gland has an anterior lobe and a posterior lobe.
   C. The pituitary gland is located in the brain near the hypothalamus.
   D. The pituitary gland is very tiny, about the size of a pea.

12. Which statement **best** expresses the main idea of the illustration?

   A. The pancreas is the largest endocrine gland.
   B. The thyroid gland is located in the neck.
   C. Endocrine glands affect sexual development.
   D. Glands throughout the body are part of the endocrine system.

DIRECTIONS: Study the passage and illustration, read the question, and choose the **best** answer.

HORMONE BALANCE

The endocrine system uses hormones, which are chemical messengers, to regulate the body's activities. The body needs just the right amount of each hormone to stay healthy and balanced. To provide the appropriate amount of each hormone, the endocrine system has feedback loops. These loops signal parts of the endocrine system to produce more or less of a certain hormone. The illustration shows feedback mechanisms involved in the production of growth hormone.

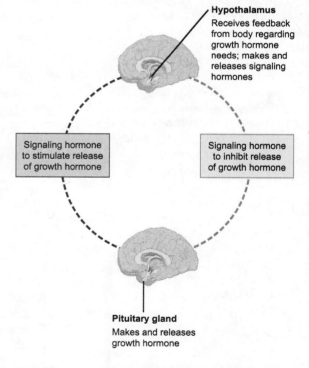

13. The title of an illustration often tells its main idea. Which title **best** expresses the main idea of this illustration?

   A. How Growth Hormone Is Inhibited
   B. Endocrine Feedback Loop
   C. Growth Hormone Regulation in the Body
   D. Monitoring of Growth in the Human Body

Interpret Tables

Use with **Student Book** pp. 6–7

UNIT 1

1 Review the Skill

SCIENCE CONTENT TOPIC: L.a.3
SCIENCE PRACTICES: SP.1.a, SP.1.b, SP.1.c, SP.3.b, SP.8.b

A **table** provides a way to organize information so that it can be presented clearly. A table's columns and rows present different but related information and show by their placement how the information is related. When you **interpret tables**, you can identify information quickly without having to read long text passages.

Even a simple table can contain several parts. For example, a typical table has a title and column headings. A table also may have a key to help you understand the information presented in the table or a source line to tell the origin of the information. To interpret a table correctly, you must study all its parts.

2 Refine the Skill

By refining the skill of interpreting tables, you will improve your study and test-taking abilities, especially as they relate to the GED® Science Test. Study the table below. Then answer the questions that follow.

a Information in columns of some tables may look similar. Read headings carefully. Here, there are four categories pertaining to sedentary and active males and females.

b This table has a key. Read the key to learn more about the information presented in the table.

RECOMMENDED DAILY CALORIC INTAKE

Age (Years)	*Sedentary Male	**Active Male	*Sedentary Female	**Active Female
10	1,600	2,200	1,400	2,000
20	2,600	3,000	2,000	2,400
30	2,400	3,000	1,800	2,400
40	2,400	2,800	1,800	2,200
50	2,200	2,800	1,800	2,200
60	2,200	2,600	1,600	2,200
70	2,000	2,600	1,600	2,000

b *Sedentary—participates in light physical activity associated with daily life
**Active—is physically active

Source: U.S. Department of Agriculture Center for Nutrition Policy and Promotion

c This table allows you to compare different types of data. For example, you can compare Calories needed by males and females of a certain age or Calories needed by males of different ages.

MAKING ASSUMPTIONS

Avoid making assumptions based on limited data in tables. From information provided in this table, you cannot assume that someone who is 80 needs fewer Calories than someone who is 70.

1. Which description **best** identifies the information in the table?

   A. Calories needed based on age, gender, and activity level
   B. Calories needed after periods of light or heavy physical activity
   C. average ages of males and females in relation to caloric intake
   D. differences in Calories males and females need at various ages

2. According to the table, at what age does the number of Calories recommended for an active male begin to decrease?

   A. 20
   B. 30
   C. 40
   D. 50

DIRECTIONS: Study the information and table, read each question, and choose the **best** answer.

IMPORTANCE OF VITAMINS AND MINERALS

Vitamins and minerals are vital to human health. The body uses these nutrients to strengthen bones and teeth, make blood, build cells, and carry oxygen, among other functions. Without sufficient vitamins and minerals, the body cannot function properly. The history of the discovery of vitamins supports this point. In the 1700s, a disease known as scurvy had been around for centuries, but no one knew its cause. Scurvy tended to be a problem in the winter months, when fruits and vegetables were scarce. Then a connection between diet and scurvy was discovered. When scurvy patients were given several doses of lemon juice, they were healed. Researchers later realized that scurvy was caused by a vitamin C deficiency.

Vitamin or Mineral	Why Do You Need It?	What Can You Eat to Get It?
Iron	Carries oxygen from lungs to cells throughout the body to maintain energy	Meat, fish, poultry, soybeans, lentils, beans
Calcium	Builds strong bones and teeth; keeps heart, nerves, and muscles working	Milk, cheese, yogurt
Sodium	Keeps pressure balanced in and out of cells	Milk, fresh vegetables, salt
Folic acid	Makes blood; builds cells	Dark leafy vegetables, whole grains, eggs, liver, nuts, cheese

3. Which diet would benefit someone who has a calcium deficiency?

   A. one rich in meat and beans
   B. one heavy in dairy products
   C. one with plenty of nuts
   D. one with increased amounts of salt

4. If a person feels weak and tired, which vitamin or mineral is he or she **most likely** lacking in an adequate amount?

   A. iron
   B. calcium
   C. sodium
   D. folic acid

DIRECTIONS: Study the table, read the question, and choose the **best** answer.

RECOMMENDED DAILY VALUES

Nutrient	Amount
Sodium	2,400 mg
Potassium	3,500 mg
Total carbohydrate	300 g
Dietary fiber	25 g
Protein	50 g
Vitamin A	5,000 IU
Vitamin C	60 mg
Calcium	1,000 mg
Iron	18 mg
Vitamin D	400 IU
Vitamin E	30 IU
Vitamin K	80 µg
Thiamin	1.5 mg
Riboflavin	1.7 mg
Niacin	20 mg
Vitamin B6	2 mg
Folate	400 µg
Vitamin B12	6 µg
Biotin	300 µg
Pantothenic acid	10 mg
Phosphorus	1,000 mg
Iodine	150 µg
Magnesium	400 mg
Zinc	15 mg
Selenium	70 µg
Copper	2 mg
Manganese	2 mg
Chromium	120 µg
Molybdenum	75 µg
Chloride	3,400 mg

g—grams
IU—international units
mg—milligrams
µg—micrograms

Source: U.S. Food and Drug Administration

5. Who is getting at least the recommended daily values of the identified nutrients?

   A. a person who gets 350 g carbohydrates, 80 µg vitamin K, and 500 mg phosphorus
   B. a person who gets 300 g carbohydrates, 100 µg vitamin K, and 1,200 mg phosphorus
   C. a person who gets 400 g carbohydrates, 50 µg vitamin K, and 900 mg phosphorus
   D. a person who gets 500 g carbohydrates, 40 µg vitamin K, and 1,300 mg phosphorus

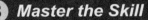

DIRECTIONS: Study the information and table, read each question, and choose the **best** answer.

WHAT IS A CALORIE?

You have likely heard the term *Calorie* in reference to how many Calories an amount of food has, but what exactly is a Calorie? It is a unit of heat energy. In relation to the human body, Calories are energy that our bodies need. The body breaks down food particles to release the energy stored in them. It then uses the energy it needs immediately and stores any leftover energy in the form of fat cells. When considering Calories, it is important to know what amount of food has a certain number of Calories. For example, 1 cup of yogurt has fewer Calories than 2 cups of yogurt. The table lists Calorie counts for some common foods.

Food	Number of Calories
1 medium apple	72
1 cup grapes	104
1 medium salmon fillet	403
1 large egg	77
1 slice whole-wheat bread	69
1 cup broccoli	30
1 slice colby cheese	112
1 oatmeal cookie	60
1 cup low-fat milk	102
1 10-ounce chocolate milkshake	366
1 ear of corn	96

6. According to the table, how many Calories does a slice of colby cheese have?

    A. 30
    B. 112
    C. 60
    D. 102

7. Which two items listed in the table have more than 200 Calories combined?

    A. a medium apple and a cup of low-fat milk
    B. a slice of whole-wheat bread and a cup of broccoli
    C. a slice of colby cheese and an ear of corn
    D. a large egg and an oatmeal cookie

8. What is the **main** purpose of the table?

    A. to encourage people to choose foods with fewer Calories
    B. to provide information for planning a weekly menu
    C. to compare and contrast Calories for different serving sizes of the same food
    D. to identify the number of Calories in servings of certain foods

DIRECTIONS: Study the table and information, read each question, and choose the **best** answer.

RECOMMENDED DAILY ALLOWANCE

Food Group	Amount
Grains	7 ounces
Vegetables	3 cups
Fruits	2 cups
Dairy products	3 cups
Proteins	6 ounces

Source: U.S. Department of Agriculture

RDA stands for "recommended daily allowance." The U.S. Department of Agriculture issues guidelines on RDA of foods from the main food groups. The RDA for an adult who consumes 2,200 Calories is shown in the table above.

9. How many more cups of vegetables than fruits should someone have if following the guidelines from the table?

    A. $\frac{1}{2}$ cup

    B. 1 cup

    C. $1\frac{1}{2}$ cups

    D. 2 cups

10. What is the **most likely** way that someone would use information from the table?

    A. to determine what to eat for breakfast
    B. to calculate his or her Calorie intake for a day
    C. to plan a healthful diet
    D. to find out how much protein is in a particular food

DIRECTIONS: Study the information and table, read each question, and choose the **best** answer.

MACRONUTRIENTS AND MICRONUTRIENTS

Like everything else in the universe, the human body is made up of various elements. Just four elements—oxygen, carbon, hydrogen, and nitrogen—make up 99 percent of the human body. The remaining 1 percent is made up of macronutrients and micronutrients. Both macronutrients and micronutrients are necessary for good health, but macronutrients are needed in much greater amounts. Even some elements that might be harmful at high levels, such as sodium, are necessary in small amounts for proper health. The table gives examples of macronutrients and micronutrients needed by the human body.

Element	Nutrient Type	Major Role in Body
Calcium	Macronutrient	Strengthening of teeth and bones; muscle contraction
Potassium	Macronutrient	Nerve function
Sodium	Macronutrient	Nerve and muscle function
Zinc	Micronutrient	Immune system function
Copper	Micronutrient	Nervous system development
Iodine	Micronutrient	Proper thyroid function; metabolism

11. Which idea about sodium is supported by the passage and the table?

    A. In the proper amount, sodium supports good muscle functioning.
    B. An unlimited sodium intake is beneficial to the body.
    C. Sodium serves many more functions in the body than iodine does.
    D. Sodium is the main macronutrient needed by the body.

12. Based on the table, a lack of which element in the diet affects muscles directly?

    A. zinc
    B. iodine
    C. potassium
    D. calcium

13. Based on the table, which statement accurately describes a relationship between macronutrients and micronutrients and the human body?

    A. All macronutrients and micronutrients support immune system function.
    B. Deficiencies in macronutrients or micronutrients can affect many body systems.
    C. The nervous system depends on macronutrients but not micronutrients for proper development.
    D. The body needs much smaller quantities of macronutrients than micronutrients.

DIRECTIONS: Study the information and table, read the question, and choose the **best** answer.

MEAL PLANNING

When planning a meal, it is important to consider the number of Calories and how well the meal incorporates different food groups. We do not need to meet all of our dietary needs in each meal, but we should strive to include all the food groups in our eating over the course of a day. The table provides dietary information for some sample meal items.

	1 Piece Vegetable Lasagna	1 Cup Cream of Tomato Soup	2 Slices Banana Nut Bread	1 Tuna Salad Sandwich
Grains (ounces)	$1\frac{1}{2}$	$\frac{1}{2}$	$2\frac{1}{2}$	2
Vegetables (cups)	$\frac{3}{4}$	1	0	$\frac{1}{4}$
Fruits (cups)	0	0	$\frac{1}{4}$	0
Dairy (cups)	$\frac{3}{4}$	$\frac{1}{2}$	0	0
Proteins (ounces)	0	0	$\frac{1}{2}$	2
Total Calories	320	135	430	290

14. Based on the table, which meal item provides the most protein for the least amount of Calories?

    A. vegetable lasagna
    B. cream of tomato soup
    C. banana nut bread
    D. tuna salad sandwich

Identify Cause and Effect

SCIENCE CONTENT TOPIC: L.a.2
SCIENCE PRACTICES: SP.1.a, SP.1.b, SP.1.c, SP.3.b, SP.7.a

UNIT 1

1 Review the Skill

Identifying cause and effect can help you understand how and why events happen. A **cause** is an action or object that makes something happen. The event that results is the **effect**. If a cold virus enters your body, you may experience a stuffy nose. The cold virus is the cause, and the stuffy nose is the effect. A cause can lead to more than one effect, and an effect may be the result of more than one cause. For example, a cold virus also could have the effect of producing a sore throat.

2 Refine the Skill

By refining the skill of identifying cause and effect, you will improve your study and test-taking abilities, especially as they relate to the GED® Science Test. Read the passage below. Then answer the questions that follow.

MAINTAINING APPROPRIATE BODY TEMPERATURE

Humans are warm-blooded animals, meaning that we maintain a near-constant body temperature between 97.7 and 99.5 degrees Fahrenheit. Body temperature is regulated by the hypothalamus region of the brain.

The hypothalamus is like a control center for temperature. Various temperature receptors exist throughout the body. Certain temperature receptors send signals to the hypothalamus that the body is too hot or too cold. When the hypothalamus receives signals that the body is hot, it begins a series of events that leads to perspiring to cool the body. When the hypothalamus receives information that the body is too cold, it signals the body to conserve heat. This type of event cycle is known as a feedback loop.

The body maintains balance by reacting constantly to feedback. However, the body can do only so much. Some external conditions are too extreme for the body's feedback mechanisms. For example, someone's body temperature can become too low to be raised by the typical feedback mechanisms. As a result, the person can die of hypothermia. **b**

a When trying to identify cause and effect, look for sequences of events. In many cases, one event in a sequence is caused by an earlier event.

b Look for signal words that can help you identify cause and effect. These include words such as *affect, as a result, because, cause, effect, lead to, since, so,* and *therefore.*

USING LOGIC

A cause must always happen or exist before the resulting effect. In a sequence of events, the cause must occur at an earlier stage than the effect.

1. What causes the hypothalamus to regulate the body's temperature?

    A. Sweat glands secrete perspiration.
    B. Temperature receptors send signals.
    C. The feedback loop starts working.
    D. Perspiration evaporates from the skin.

2. What is the **main** purpose of feedback loops in the body?

    A. to maintain balance
    B. to control the hypothalamus
    C. to receive signals
    D. to regulate temperature

★ Spotlighted Item: **DROP-DOWN**

DIRECTIONS: Read the passage titled "Homeostasis: The Body's Balancing Act," and study the illustration. Then read the incomplete passage that follows. Use information from the illustration to complete the passage. For each drop-down item, choose the option that **best** completes the sentence.

HOMEOSTASIS: THE BODY'S BALANCING ACT

Homeostasis is the ability to maintain balance in an internal environment while responding to changes in the external environment. The illustration shows how homeostasis regulates blood pressure.

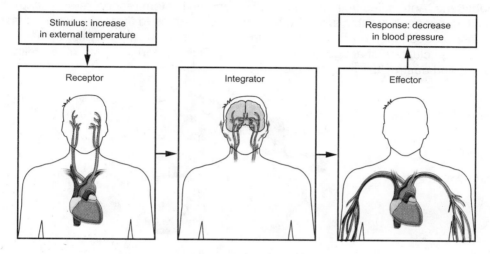

3. Homeostasis includes regulation of blood pressure. External changes cause fluctuations in blood pressure. One such external change, or stimulus, is 3. Drop-down 1 . This external change initially causes an increase in blood pressure. However, certain events occur to return the body to a balanced state. Receptors sense a change in blood pressure and send signals to the 3. Drop-down 2 . As a result, it processes the information and 3. Drop-down 3 the effector. The effector, or heart in this case, then acts to cause a response in the body. That is, the heart slows, causing blood pressure to 3. Drop-down 4 .

Drop-Down Answer Options

3.1 A. an irregular heartbeat
B. a higher temperature
C. lowered blood pressure
D. an imbalance of activities

3.2 A. integrator
B. response
C. stimulus
D. environment

3.3 A. shuts down
B. bypasses
C. inhibits
D. stimulates

3.4 A. remain the same
B. drop to nothing
C. lower
D. increase

3

Spotlighted Item: **DROP-DOWN**

DIRECTIONS: Read the passage titled "Role of Antibodies in the Immune System," and study the illustration. Then read the incomplete passage that follows. Use information from the first passage and the illustration to complete the second passage. For each drop-down item, choose the option that **best** completes the sentence.

ROLE OF ANTIBODIES IN THE IMMUNE SYSTEM

An antigen is any foreign substance that enters the body. Antibodies are proteins in the blood that attach to antigens. Antibodies help the cells of the immune system recognize and destroy harmful antigens. When antigen particles enter the body, antibodies bind to them. This binding action is specific. Antibodies are produced for specific antigens and, therefore, bind with only those antigens. The binding action forms large clusters of antigens and antibodies. This clustering allows other cells of the immune system to find and destroy the antigens more easily.

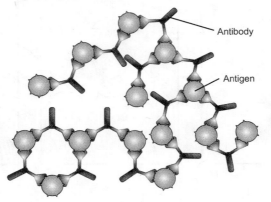

4. When a foreign substance, such as a cold virus, enters the body, the immune system springs into action to eliminate it. The presence of a virus, or any other foreign substance, causes the immune system to ⬚ 4. Drop-down 1 ⬚ . Soon these cold fighters are flowing through the blood with the goal of ⬚ 4. Drop-down 2 ⬚ antigens. The structure of an antibody is particularly helpful in bringing about this result. Each antibody has ⬚ 4. Drop-down 3 ⬚ binding sites for antigens. This configuration causes bound antibodies and antigens to ⬚ 4. Drop-down 4 ⬚ , making them easier for immune system cells to find.

Drop-Down Answer Options

4.1 A. form bonds with antigens
    B. send antibodies
    C. send antigens
    D. produce clusters

4.2 A. binding to
    B. collecting
    C. attacking
    D. destroying

4.3 A. zero
    B. two
    C. three
    D. five

4.4 A. speed up
    B. increase in size
    C. create long chains
    D. form large clusters

DIRECTIONS: Read the passage titled "Allergy: Product of an Overactive Immune System," and study the illustration. Then read the incomplete passage that follows. Use information from the first passage and the illustration to complete the second passage. For each drop-down item, choose the option that **best** completes the sentence.

ALLERGY: PRODUCT OF AN OVERACTIVE IMMUNE SYSTEM

Usually, the human immune system responds only to harmful substances. Sometimes, though, the immune system reacts in an extreme way to relatively harmless substances, such as pollen, molds, dust, or pet fur. These reactions are called allergies. Some allergic reactions are mild. Other allergic reactions are more severe. In people who have asthma (an illness of the lungs), allergic reactions can cause severe breathing problems.

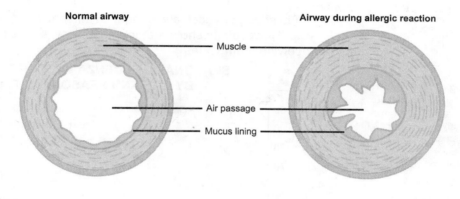

5. A person who has asthma may have extreme difficulty breathing during an asthma attack. A typical cause of an asthma attack is
    5. Drop-down 1 .

    When a person who has asthma is exposed to certain substances, those substances can cause air passages to
    5. Drop-down 2 . Exposure to the triggering substances also results in 5. Drop-down 3 . This series of events leads to 5. Drop-down 4 as the main symptom of an asthma attack.

Drop-Down Answer Options

5.1 A. dust or pollen
    B. muscle contractions
    C. sneezing and a runny nose
    D. antibodies in the blood

5.2 A. swell with air
    B. close, choking off all air
    C. narrow as muscles tighten
    D. fill completely with fluid

5.3 A. an increase in mucus
    B. air passage expansion
    C. muscle cramps
    D. relaxed breathing

5.4 A. headache
    B. joint pain
    C. upset stomach
    D. shortness of breath

Interpret Graphs and Maps

Use with *Student Book* pp. 10–11

SCIENCE CONTENT TOPIC: L.a.4
SCIENCE PRACTICES: SP.1.a, SP.1.b, SP.1.c, SP.3.a, SP.3.b, SP.3.c

UNIT 1

1 Review the Skill

Graphs and thematic **maps** present data in a visual way. To **interpret a graph or map**, you must study the title, labels, key, and format. Circle graphs show the parts of a whole. Bar graphs can be used to compare data. Both bar graphs and line graphs can show change over time. A thematic map shows data for a particular geographic area.

2 Refine the Skill

By refining the skill of interpreting graphs and maps, you will improve your study and test-taking abilities, especially as they relate to the GED® Science Test. Study the information and graph below. Then answer the questions that follow.

INFLUENZA VACCINATION

Flu shots, or vaccinations against influenza, are available every year. However, flu shots are not mandatory, so the number of people receiving them varies.

a Identifying exact values from a graph can be difficult. To determine an approximate value, study the values on the axes. Then estimate the value of a particular data point based on those values.

b The key gives information about what the lines show. Here, the yellow line represents children between 6 months and 17 years old, and the green line represents adults.

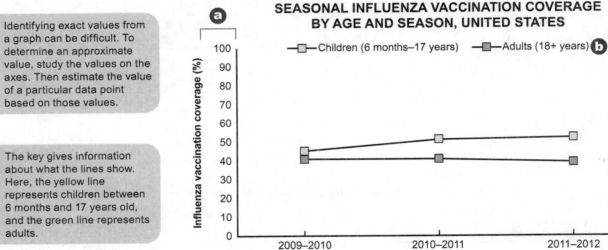

SEASONAL INFLUENZA VACCINATION COVERAGE BY AGE AND SEASON, UNITED STATES

Source: Centers for Disease Control and Prevention

MAKING ASSUMPTIONS

Labels on the axes of a graph give information about the kind of data shown on the graph. Here, you can assume that the numbers on the y-axis are percentages of the total population.

1. According to the graph, about what percentage of children were vaccinated during the 2010–2011 flu season?

   A. 30 percent
   B. 40 percent
   C. 50 percent
   D. 60 percent

2. Which statement is supported by the graph?

   A. About the same percentage of adults got flu shots each season.
   B. The highest percentage of children got flu shots in 2009–2010.
   C. A higher percentage of adults than children get flu shots.
   D. More than 60 percent of children got flu shots in 2011–2012.

DIRECTIONS: Study the information and graph, read each question, and choose the **best** answer.

IMPACT OF PLAGUES

During the 1300s, a plague called the Black Death killed one-third of the population of Europe. The plague is caused by the bacterium *Yersinia pestis*. Rats that carried fleas infected with the bacterium stowed away aboard ships, spreading the plague around the world. Neither the fleas nor the rats were affected by the bacterium, but when a flea bit a human, the result was deadly. The bacterium then could transfer from human to human. In some European towns, nearly every person died, often within a day of infection.

One way scientists have learned about plagues such as the Black Death is by excavating "catastrophe cemeteries." By studying remains, scientists are able to produce data such as those shown in the graph below. The graph represents the male and female distribution at the East Smithfield Black Death cemetery in London.

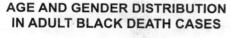

AGE AND GENDER DISTRIBUTION IN ADULT BLACK DEATH CASES

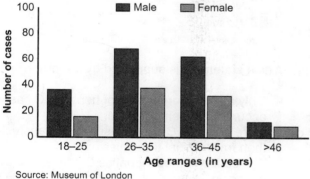

Source: Museum of London

3. According to the graph, the greatest number of adults killed by the Black Death in this community were

   A. males 18 to 25 years old.
   B. males 26 to 35 years old.
   C. females 36 to 45 years old.
   D. females over 46 years old.

4. In this community, about how many females over 46 years old died from the Black Death?

   A. fewer than 20
   B. between 20 and 40
   C. between 40 and 60
   D. between 60 and 80

DIRECTIONS: Study the graph and information, read each question, and choose the **best** answer.

PERCENTAGE OF POPULATION USING IMPROVED SANITATION

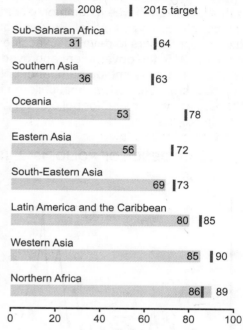

The above data are from the United Nations Millennium Development Goals. When setting the objectives, a main goal the United Nations hoped to meet was to reduce by half the number of people in the world who lack sustainable access to safe drinking water. The yellow bars show the percentage of people in each area having access to basic sanitation and safe water as of 2008. Blue lines show the targets for the percent of the population using improved sanitation.

5. Which statement is supported by the graph?

   A. No progress is being made in improving sanitation in the areas listed.
   B. By 2008, none of the areas had met its 2015 goal.
   C. Western Asia is at greatest risk for not meeting its 2015 goal.
   D. Sub-Saharan Africa needs to achieve the greatest change to meet its 2015 goal.

6. Based on the data, how many areas can you predict **most likely** will have reached their goals by 2015?

   A. one
   B. two
   C. four
   D. eight

DIRECTIONS: Study the information and graph, read each question, and choose the **best** answer.

SUCCESS OF THE POLIO VACCINE

Until the 1950s, polio was a common disease that left many people paralyzed. Jonas Salk and others worked for several years to develop a vaccine for the polio virus. In 1955, the government approved Salk's vaccine. From that point on, the number of polio vaccinations increased. Today, most children in the United States are vaccinated for polio at very young ages.

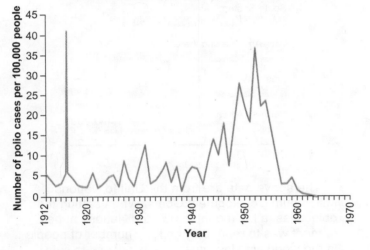

U.S. INCIDENCE OF POLIO, 1912–1970

7. In about what year did the incidence of polio peak, according to the graph?

   A. 1912
   B. 1916
   C. 1952
   D. 1963

8. The graph supports the statement in the passage that the rate of polio vaccination increased after government approval of the vaccine by showing

   A. an increase in the number of polio cases in vaccinated children.
   B. a decrease in the number of polio cases in the early 1950s.
   C. an increase in the number of young children in the United States.
   D. a decrease in the number of new polio cases after 1955.

DIRECTIONS: Study the information and graph, read each question, and choose the **best** answer.

HEPATITIS C

Hepatitis C is one of the most significant bloodborne infections in the United States. Hepatitis C was discovered in 1988. Many people who have it may not know they do because they do not show symptoms. However, chronic liver disease occurring 10 to 20 years after infection is a major concern.

HEPATITIS C INFECTION SOURCES

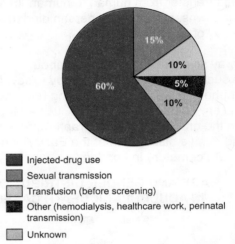

■ Injected-drug use
■ Sexual transmission
■ Transfusion (before screening)
■ Other (hemodialysis, healthcare work, perinatal transmission)
■ Unknown

Source: Centers for Disease Control and Prevention

9. Which statement is supported by the graph?

   A. Only a small percentage of hepatitis C cases occur due to hemodialysis.
   B. More hepatitis C cases result from transfusion than from sexual transmission.
   C. The cause of most hepatitis C cases is unknown.
   D. The fewest number of hepatitis C cases are caused by injected-drug use.

10. Which group is **most likely** at highest risk for contracting the hepatitis C virus?

    A. those who work in the healthcare industry
    B. those who engage in unprotected sex
    C. those who share needles while using drugs
    D. those who donate blood

DIRECTIONS: Read the passage titled "HIV and AIDS," and study the map. Then read the incomplete passage that follows. Use information from the map to complete the passage. For each drop-down item, choose the option that **best** completes the sentence.

HIV AND AIDS

HIV is a virus that can cause the body to develop acquired immune deficiency syndrome (AIDS). AIDS is a disease in which the immune system stops working as it should. As a result, the body becomes susceptible to various diseases and infections. Many of these diseases would have little or no effect on individuals with healthy immune systems. However, AIDS patients typically die from infections that their immune systems cannot fight.

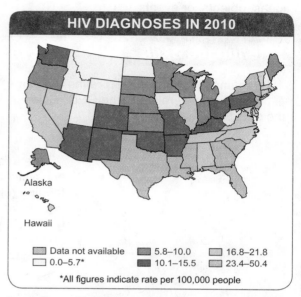

HIV DIAGNOSES IN 2010

Alaska

Hawaii

☐ Data not available   ☐ 5.8–10.0   ☐ 16.8–21.8
☐ 0.0–5.7*   ☐ 10.1–15.5   ☐ 23.4–50.4

*All figures indicate rate per 100,000 people

Source: Centers for Disease Control and Prevention

11. Even with education related to the transmission of HIV in the United States, new cases continue to be diagnosed each year. The highest rate of new cases are appearing in [11. Drop-down 1] . Here, the rate per 100,000 people is 23.4 to 50.4. In states with [11. Drop-down 2] diagnosis rates, the rate of diagnoses is 5.7 or fewer people per 100,000. According to separate data, the rate of diagnoses per 100,000 people in Texas in 2007 was 17.7 to 22.6. This statistic indicates that the number of diagnoses in Texas, shown in lighter green on the map, has [11. Drop-down 3] . Healthcare workers can use the available data to argue that greater [11. Drop-down 4] is still needed in certain areas of the United States.

Drop-Down Answer Options

11.1 A. the West
      B. the Northeast
      C. the Northwest
      D. the South

11.2 A. unavailable
      B. the highest
      C. the lowest
      D. the fastest changing

11.3 A. increased
      B. decreased
      C. doubled
      D. remained unchanged

11.4 A. access to medicines
      B. education about HIV transmission
      C. availability of medical care
      D. health insurance coverage

UNIT 1

Interpret Diagrams

Use with *Student Book* pp. 12–13

SCIENCE CONTENT TOPICS: L.c.1, L.c.2
SCIENCE PRACTICES: SP.1.a, SP.1.b, SP.1.c, SP.3.b, SP.3.d, SP.7.a

UNIT 1

1 Review the Skill

A **diagram** uses visual elements to show how things relate to one another. Often, a diagram can show relationships more simply than text can explain them. Some diagrams show the parts of something and how those parts interact. Some diagrams show an order of events. Other diagrams show how things are alike and different. When you **interpret diagrams**, you use their visual elements to understand relationships between ideas, objects, or events.

2 Refine the Skill

By refining the skill of interpreting diagrams, you will improve your study and test-taking abilities, especially as they relate to the GED® Science Test. Study the information and diagram below. Then answer the questions that follow.

FEEDING RELATIONSHIPS IN ECOSYSTEMS

Like a food chain, a food web shows feeding relationships in an ecosystem. However, a food web shows more than a single set of feeding relationships. It shows the feeding relationships among many organisms in an ecosystem. The diagram shows a food web for a grassland ecosystem.

a Diagrams can show simple or more complex relationships. To interpret a diagram that shows complex relationships, look carefully at parts of the diagram and at the diagram as a whole.

b Look at the relationships of the elements in the diagram. The arrows show the direction in which food moves from organism to organism. Also, each organism is connected by several arrows to other organisms.

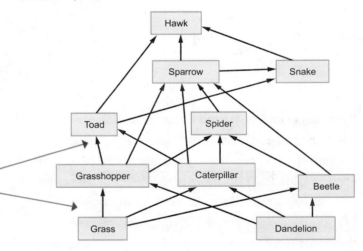

USING LOGIC

Diagrams represent something real. As you interpret a diagram, consider what you already know. If your interpretation disagrees with what you know, you may be misinterpreting the diagram.

1. Based on the information in the diagram, what do sparrows eat?

   A. grass
   B. dandelions and grasshoppers
   C. grasshoppers, caterpillars, spiders, and beetles
   D. hawks and snakes

2. Which statement describes feeding relationships in the grassland ecosystem represented by the diagram?

   A. Snakes have fewer food sources than spiders have.
   B. Each animal eats only one other kind of animal or plant.
   C. Hawks eat both plants and animals.
   D. Most living things in a grassland eat insects.

DIRECTIONS: Study the information and diagram, read each question, and choose the **best** answer.

TROPHIC LEVELS

Scientists group living things in an ecosystem based on where they get their energy. The groups are called trophic levels. Producers make up the first trophic level. Producers obtain energy by converting light energy from the sun into simple sugars. Plants are producers in most land-based ecosystems. Primary consumers make up the second trophic level. They get energy by eating producers. Secondary consumers, which make up the third trophic level, eat primary consumers. The grouping continues through the top level of feeding relationships in the ecosystem. The diagram shows examples of trophic levels in a desert ecosystem.

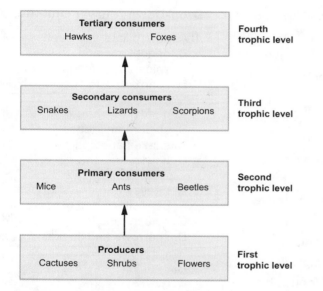

3. Based on the diagram, which statement identifies the trophic level of certain organisms in a desert ecosystem?

   A. Lizards and snakes are secondary consumers.
   B. Ants and beetles are in the first trophic level.
   C. Hawks and foxes are in the third trophic level.
   D. Flowers and shrubs are sometimes consumers.

4. Which statement describes how certain organisms get food in the desert ecosystem represented by the diagram?

   A. Plants get food from each other.
   B. Scorpions eat other animals.
   C. Ants eat both plants and animals.
   D. Snakes eat tertiary consumers.

DIRECTIONS: Study the information and diagram, read each question, and choose the **best** answer.

ENERGY TRANSFER WITHIN AN ECOSYSTEM

On average, an organism stores about 10 percent of the energy it gets from food. The rest of the energy is lost to the surroundings. Therefore, the amount of energy available at one trophic level is smaller than the amount available at the previous trophic level. The diagram shows an example of this energy transfer.

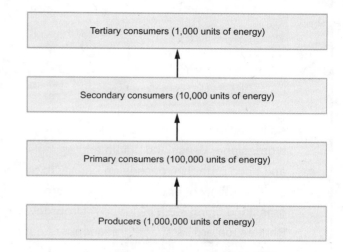

5. How much energy is lost during the energy transfer from primary consumers to secondary consumers in the ecosystem represented by the diagram?

   A. 900,000 units
   B. 100,000 units
   C. 10,000 units
   D. 90,000 units

6. How does the diagram support the idea that an ecosystem has fewer organisms at the fourth trophic level than at the first trophic level?

   A. The diagram shows that tertiary consumers are at the fourth trophic level and producers are at the first trophic level.
   B. The box sizes in the diagram indicate that an ecosystem has fewer organisms at the fourth trophic level than at the first trophic level.
   C. The diagram shows that less energy is available to support living things at the fourth trophic level than at the first trophic level.
   D. The shape of the diagram indicates that the number of organisms at the fourth trophic level is less than the number of organisms at the first trophic level.

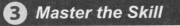

Master the Skill

Spotlighted Item: DROP-DOWN

DIRECTIONS: Study the diagram. Then read the incomplete passage that follows. Use information from the diagram to complete the passage. For each drop-down item, choose the option that **best** completes the sentence.

FLOW OF ENERGY IN A GRASSLAND ECOSYSTEM

7. As in any ecosystem, energy flows through the trophic levels of a grassland. Grassland plants and animals get energy from food, and each organism passes on energy to any organism that feeds on it. The flow of energy begins with producers. Producers in a grassland ecosystem include [7. Drop-down 1]. Beetles, caterpillars, and grasshoppers eat the producers and pass on energy to [7. Drop-down 2]. Hawks are at the top of a grassland energy pyramid. Their food consists of [7. Drop-down 3]. Living things use some of the energy they take in for movement, growth, and repair. However, most of it is lost to the environment. Consequently, organisms at one trophic level have less energy available to them than organisms at the trophic level below theirs. For example, in the grassland ecosystem, more energy is available for use by [7. Drop-down 4] than by spiders.

Drop-Down Answer Options

7.1 A. caterpillars and beetles
    B. dandelions and grasses
    C. spiders and toads
    D. sparrows and snakes

7.2 A. dandelions and grasses
    B. spiders and toads
    C. snakes and sparrows
    D. hawks

7.3 A. beetles and grasshoppers
    B. dandelions and grasses
    C. spiders and toads
    D. sparrows and snakes

7.4 A. beetles
    B. hawks
    C. snakes
    D. toads

DIRECTIONS: Study the diagram, read the question, and choose the **best** answer.

DIETS OF THREE FOREST ANIMALS

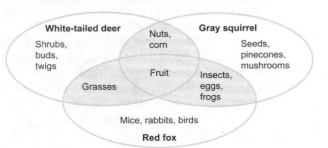

8. Which statement describes feeding relationships of animals identified in the diagram?

    A. White-tailed deer, gray squirrels, and red foxes are at different trophic levels.
    B. Red foxes eat only mice, rabbits, and birds.
    C. White-tailed deer and gray squirrels both eat nuts and corn.
    D. Gray squirrels and red foxes compete for all the same foods.

DIRECTIONS: Study the information and diagram, read each question, and choose the **best** answer.

DEEP-OCEAN ECOSYSTEM

In the 1970s, scientists traveled to the ocean floor to study the rocks and minerals there. They did not expect to find any life that deep in the ocean. Surprisingly, they discovered an entire ecosystem deep below the ocean's surface. Tiny bacteria form the basis of the ecosystem. These bacteria use chemicals from within Earth to make food. The diagram shows relationships between some living things in the ecosystem the scientists discovered.

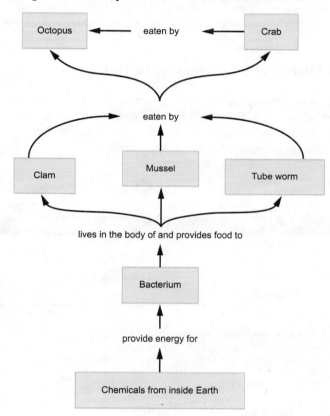

9. What is the ultimate source of energy for all the living things identified in the diagram?

   A. octopuses
   B. bacteria
   C. chemicals from within Earth
   D. sunlight

10. A type of large fish also lives in this ecosystem. It eats tube worms, clams, mussels, and crabs. Its position in the food web is **most similar** to that of which animal?

    A. crab
    B. mussel
    C. tube worm
    D. octopus

DIRECTIONS: Study the information and diagram, read the question, and choose the **best** answer.

ROLE OF DECOMPOSERS AND DETRITIVORES

Decomposers and detritivores are organisms that break down dead plants and animals. In doing so, they return nutrients to the soil. Some fungi and bacteria are decomposers. Millipedes and earthworms are examples of detritivores. The diagram shows how decomposers and detritivores fit into the nutrients cycle of an ecosystem.

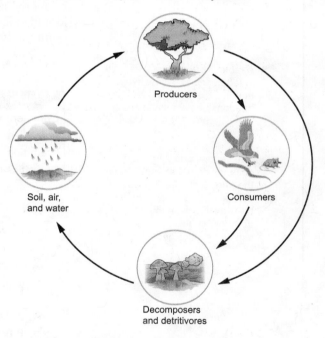

11. Which statement describes the importance of decomposers and detritivores in the nutrients cycle shown in the diagram?

    A. Plants use them as food.
    B. Both producers and consumers rely on them in the nutrients cycle.
    C. Dead animal matter cannot exist without them.
    D. Animals that eat plants also eat them.

Categorize and Classify

Use with *Student Book* pp. 14–15

SCIENCE CONTENT TOPIC: L.c.4
SCIENCE PRACTICES: SP.1.a, SP.1.b, SP.1.c, SP.3.a, SP.3.b, SP.6.c

1 Review the Skill

When you **categorize**, you identify groups you can use to organize things such as organisms, objects, or processes. Each category should be based on relationships between the things you want to organize or on features those things share. When you **classify**, you place specific things into categories that already exist.

Scientists use categorization and classification to organize aspects of the natural world. By categorizing and classifying, scientists and others who study science improve their understanding of relationships among objects, processes, systems, and so on.

2 Refine the Skill

By refining the skill of categorizing and classifying, you will improve your study and test-taking abilities, especially as they relate to the GED® Science Test. Study the information and table below. Then answer the questions that follow.

RELATIONSHIPS AMONG LIVING THINGS

A community contains many types of organisms. They live together, forming different relationships. For each species in a relationship, the relationship can be beneficial, neutral, or harmful. The table below identifies some of the major relationships among organisms in a community and the effects of those relationships.

a A table is often used in categorizing and classifying. In this table, categories of relationships are listed in the first column.

b The second and third columns of the table describe the effects of different types of relationships. You can use the information in the table to determine how relationships should be classified.

Relationship	Effect on Species A	Effect on Species B
Commensalism	Positive	No effect
Mutualism	Positive	Positive
Predation	Positive	Negative
Parasitism	Positive	Negative

c When considering a relationship between organisms, decide whether the effect on each species is positive or negative. Then classify the relationship accordingly.

MAKING ASSUMPTIONS

The table does not describe each type of relationship. It only tells the effects. From your own experience, though, you may know examples of how each type of relationship works.

1. Which relationship can be classified as mutualism?

   A. a flea living on a dog
   B. a mosquito biting a human
   C. a bee getting nectar from a flower and transferring pollen
   D. a bat capturing a moth in flight to eat

2. An animal unknowingly carries a burdock weed's seeds in its fur and then scatters the seeds as it moves from place to place. Which type of relationship do the burdock weed and the animal have?

   A. commensalism
   B. mutualism
   C. predation
   D. parasitism

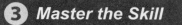
⭐ Spotlighted Item: **FILL-IN-THE-BLANK**

DIRECTIONS: Study the table. Then complete each statement by filling in the box.

TWO CATEGORIES OF SYMBIOTIC RELATIONSHIPS

Type of Relationship	Examples
Parasite-host	Tapeworms-humans Barber's pole worms-sheep Anchor worms-fish Bird mites-pigeons
Predator-prey	Sea otters-fish Salamanders-frog tadpoles Great horned owls-raccoons Cheetahs-wildebeests

3. Based on the information in the table, a sea otter, a salamander, a great horned owl, and a cheetah all can be classified as

.

4. A relationship that is classified as parasitic involves an organism that benefits, the parasite, and an organism that is harmed, the host. Examples of parasites are some worms and mites. Examples of hosts listed in the table are

.

DIRECTIONS: Read the scenario. Then read each question, and fill in your answer in the box.

CLASSIFYING RELATIONSHIPS

A scientist is preparing to classify symbiotic relationships between organisms into the categories of commensalism, mutualism, and parasitism. The scientist records the following notes:

White-winged doves and saguaro cacti The white-winged dove eats the fruit of the saguaro cactus, including the seeds. The bird flies off and deposits the seeds elsewhere.
Spider crabs and algae Spider crabs that live on the bottom of the ocean floor have greenish brown algae living on their backs, making the crabs blend in with their environment.
Bacteria and humans Bacteria living in the intestines of humans partly digest and use the food that humans are unable to digest. Once the food is partially digested, humans are able to continue the digestion process.

5. Into which category will the scientist place all three relationships?

6. Why do the examples the scientist noted all fit in this category?

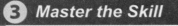
UNIT 1

DIRECTIONS: Read the passage, and study the illustration. Then complete each statement by filling in the box.

RHINOCEROSES AND OXPECKER BIRDS

Organisms can have different relationships with one another. One type of relationship is mutualism. In a mutualistic relationship, both organisms benefit. The illustration shows an example of a mutualistic relationship between a rhinoceros and oxpeckers. In this relationship, the oxpeckers eat insects off the rhinoceros. The birds get food, and the rhinoceros gets rid of biting insects.

7. If the oxpeckers harmed the rhinoceroses by eating insects off their bodies, the relationship would be classified as

_____ .

8. The relationship between the oxpeckers and the insects fits into the

_____ category.

DIRECTIONS: Read the passage, and study the illustration. Then read each item, and fill in your response in the box.

BARRACUDA AND CLEANING FISH

Tiny organisms live on the exteriors of barracuda. Barracuda are a species of fish considered to be predators. However, barracuda modify their behavior to meet different needs. At times, a barracuda positions itself in an unusual posture with its head up to signal to smaller cleaning fish that it will not eat them. When the cleaning fish see this sign, they know it is safe to approach the barracuda. The cleaning fish then eat the tiny organisms that live on the barracuda.

9. Classify the relationship between the barracuda and the cleaning fish.

_____

10. Classify the relationship between the organisms that live on a barracuda and the barracuda.

_____

11. How would the relationship between a barracuda and cleaning fish be classified when the barracuda is not in a heads-up posture?

_____

DIRECTIONS: Study the table. Then read each question, and fill in your answer in the box.

MUTUALISM AND COMMENSALISM

Mutualism (Both Organisms Benefit)	Commensalism (One Organism Benefits; Other Is Not Affected)
Honeybees-flowers	Orchids-tall trees
Leaf-cutting ants-fungi	Barnacles-humpback whales
Clown fish-sea anemones	Redwood sorrel plants-redwood trees
Humans-pets	Pearl fish-sea cucumbers

12. What characteristic must a relationship have to be classified as commensalism?

13. Suppose that the barnacles on a humpback whale are so numerous that they cause infection. What category could be added to the chart to fit this relationship?

14. Eagles eat fish. What category could be added to classify this relationship?

DIRECTIONS: Read the passage. Then read each question, and fill in your answer in the box.

ALLIGATOR HOLES

Some scientists consider alligator holes to be an example of mutualism. Using their feet and snouts, alligators clear mud and muck from the limestone bedrock to form holes they can use for shelter. The holes may be quite large, even the size of a small backyard pool. The holes are important to wetland ecosystems because they retain water during dry times of the year, and many animals drink from them. Because so many animals use the holes for water, the holes also are good places for certain other animals to find food.

15. What type of relationship exists between the animals that come to an alligator hole seeking food and the animals that come there for water?

16. In what category besides mutualism might scientists classify the relationship between alligators and the animals that use their holes, and why would scientists choose this category?

Generalize

Use with *Student Book* pp. 16–17

SCIENCE CONTENT TOPICS: L.c.3, L.c.4
SCIENCE PRACTICES: SP.1.a, SP.1.b, SP.1.c, SP.3.a, SP.3.b, SP.3.d

UNIT 1

1 Review the Skill

A generalization is a broad statement that applies to an entire group. You **generalize** based on information about objects, organisms, places, or events. A generalization can be valid or invalid. If it is supported with multiple facts and examples, it is valid. If it is supported by few or no facts, it is invalid.

When you generalize, consider information from passages, tables, graphs, and diagrams. All may contain information to help you make a valid generalization.

2 Refine the Skill

By refining the skill of generalizing, you will improve your study and test-taking abilities, especially as they relate to the GED® Science Test. Study the information and graph below. Then answer the questions that follow.

ST. MATTHEW ISLAND REINDEER

a Remember, generalizations may be valid or invalid. Look for facts that support a generalization to determine whether it is valid or invalid.

St. Matthew Island is a small island—about 125 square miles—in the Bering Sea. In 1944, the U.S. Coast Guard stocked St. Matthew Island with 29 reindeer. The island had much vegetation to provide food for the reindeer and no predators of the reindeer. Experts estimated that the island could support about 15 reindeer per square mile. So they calculated that the maximum population the island could support for a long period of time was about 2,000 reindeer. The graph shows the population of reindeer on St. Matthew Island from 1944 to 1966.

b When you use information from a table or graph to generalize, think of a broad statement you can make that expresses a "big picture" idea conveyed by the data.

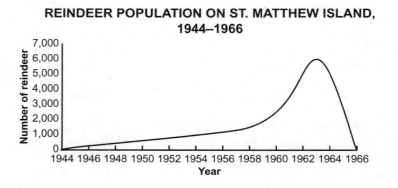

REINDEER POPULATION ON ST. MATTHEW ISLAND, 1944–1966

1. Based on the information, which statement is a valid generalization about populations in an ecosystem?

    A. Fluctuations in population size are due mostly to predation.
    B. Population size can change notably in a relatively short period.
    C. All populations remain stable for at least a hundred years.
    D. Population size continues to increase if resources are abundant.

2. An invalid generalization about the reindeer population is that it

    A. increased before it decreased.
    B. never exceeded 6,000.
    C. generally remained stable until 1958.
    D. decreased due to introduction of a new predator.

DIRECTIONS: Study the information and illustration, read the question, and choose the **best** answer.

CARRYING CAPACITY

The number of animals a given area of land or water can support over time is called that area's carrying capacity. Consider this illustration representing muskrats in a marsh. The barrel represents the marsh habitat—the amount of food, water, and cover for a fixed number of muskrats. The water in the barrel is the number of muskrats the habitat can support. The pipe pouring water into the barrel represents the new muskrats that are born in the marsh or wander in from other places. The water spilling out is the number of muskrats that die each year due to starvation, predators, disease, or other factors. The barrel can only hold so much water. That is, there is a limit to the number of muskrats that can survive here from year to year unless the habitat (the size of the barrel) is changed in some way. Every parcel of land has a different carrying capacity for every different kind of wildlife that lives there. A pristine cattail marsh would be a deep barrel for muskrats, while a dune forest would hold few, if any.

From Michigan Department of Natural Resources (DNR) via michigan.gov, accessed 2013
Original artwork by Oscar Warbach, Michigan DNR

3. Based on the information, which statement is an invalid generalization?

   A. Pollution has a negative effect on populations in an ecosystem.
   B. Conserving marsh areas will maintain the carrying capacity for muskrats.
   C. The number of muskrats an area can support is most influenced by disease.
   D. A population generally stays at its carrying capacity when population losses balance population gains.

DIRECTIONS: Read the passage. Then read each question, and choose the **best** answer.

GRAY WOLVES IN NORTH AMERICA

Gray wolves once were common across North America. However, to prevent wolves from attacking cattle, settlers killed many wolves. By the 1920s, gray wolves were gone from most of the Rocky Mountains. By 1950, few wolves were left in the United States. The 1973 Endangered Species Act helped protect the remaining wolf populations. In the following years, scientists made plans to reintroduce wolves in certain areas. In 1995, a new plan began to put wolves back into Yellowstone National Park and surrounding areas. In 2007, more than 1,500 wolves lived in the area around the Rocky Mountains.

4. Which idea from the passage supports the generalization that human activity can negatively affect a population of organisms?

   A. North America once had large numbers of gray wolves.
   B. The killing of gray wolves by settlers drastically reduced their numbers.
   C. The 1973 Endangered Species Act helped protect wolves.
   D. Scientists reintroduced wolves in certain areas.

5. Which is a valid generalization based on the information provided in the passage?

   A. Populations of endangered species can be rebuilt if appropriate actions occur.
   B. Changes in an ecosystem generally change the carrying capacities of the ecosystem.
   C. Survival of organisms often depends on predator-prey relationships.
   D. Competition for resources always leads to the steep decline of a population.

UNIT 1

DIRECTIONS: Study the information and graph, read each question, and choose the **best** answer.

PREDATION IN ECOSYSTEMS

Many relationships between species exist in an ecosystem. The relationship between some animals is a predator-prey relationship. The graph below shows the relationship between the populations of lynxes and hares in an ecosystem over time. In this ecosystem, the lynx is a predator, and the hare is its prey.

POPULATIONS OF HARES AND LYNXES, 1845–1935

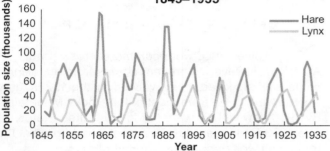

6. Which statement is a valid generalization based on the graph?

   A. Populations of predators and prey generally follow the same trends.
   B. As the population of prey increases, the population of predators typically decreases.
   C. A large number of predators leads to an increase in the number of prey.
   D. In populations of predators and their prey, the number of prey is always greater than the number of predators.

7. Which statement is an invalid generalization based on the graph?

   A. The total number of prey typically exceeds the total number of predators in a community.
   B. An increase in the prey population is usually followed by an increase in the predator population.
   C. Changes in the population of prey are due solely to changes in the population of the predator.
   D. Prey populations fluctuate more drastically than predator populations.

DIRECTIONS: Read the passage. Then read each question, and choose the **best** answer.

NONLIVING FEATURES OF ECOSYSTEMS

Ecosystems include not only living organisms but also nonliving features, such as water. All living things need water to survive, but different living things need different amounts of water. So the amount of rainfall that an ecosystem receives helps determine which organisms can live in the ecosystem and how large a population of each organism the ecosystem will support. Carrying capacity is the maximum number of individuals of a given species that an area's resources can sustain. The carrying capacities of an area can change based on factors such as rainfall. In addition, an ecosystem's amount of sunlight and temperature similarly limit the organisms that can live there. Most organisms survive best within a narrow range of conditions. Only a few kinds of organisms can survive in very hot, very cold, very dry, or very dark environments.

8. Which statement expresses a valid generalization made in the passage?

   A. Living things depend on nonliving things to survive.
   B. All organisms can live in all types of conditions.
   C. The amount of sunlight in an ecosystem affects the organisms that live there.
   D. Most organisms need specific environmental conditions to survive.

9. Which statement is a valid generalization based on the passage?

   A. Organisms require different amounts of sunlight to survive.
   B. The temperature range in an ecosystem affects which organisms live in the ecosystem.
   C. All living things need water to survive.
   D. Nonliving features typically have a significant impact on an ecosystem.

10. An invalid generalization based on the passage is that nonliving features of an ecosystem

   A. affect living things in the ecosystem.
   B. include only rainfall and sunlight.
   C. can have a significant impact on a population.
   D. contribute to the range of conditions present in the ecosystem.

EFFECTS OF HUMAN ACTIVITY

Humans have a tremendous impact on other populations. For example, hundreds of years ago, 30 million bison may have roamed the Great Plains. As a result of human activity, the bison nearly disappeared. The timelines show some major events in the interactions between humans and other populations in the United States.

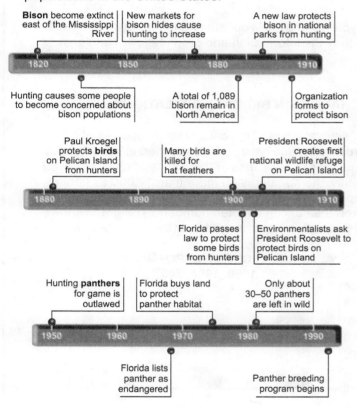

11. Which statement is a valid generalization about the relationship between humans and other populations in the United States?

A. Over time, people generally have become more concerned about their effect on other populations.
B. Population size is typically unchanged by human interaction in the United States.
C. People perceive any relationship with another population as a competition for resources.
D. Physical changes to U.S. ecosystems are as important as human impacts.

EXPONENTIAL POPULATION GROWTH

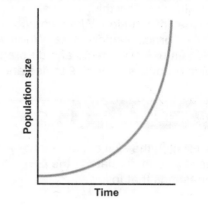

The graph shows exponential population growth. In the presence of unlimited resources, a population experiencing exponential growth would increase continuously.

12. Based on the information, what valid generalization can be made about exponential growth of populations?

A. Typically, exponential growth will continue beyond carrying capacity.
B. Rapid exponential growth of populations is always due to a decrease in predation.
C. During periods of exponential growth, populations are always inhibited by factors such as limited resources and competition.
D. In populations that are growing exponentially, reproduction usually is occurring constantly.

13. Exponential population growth cannot continue indefinitely because in general

A. unlimited resources are not a reality.
B. every species stops reproducing eventually.
C. a species in exponential population growth will prey on itself.
D. a catastrophic event will occur to eliminate the population.

UNIT 1

Compare and Contrast

Use with **Student Book** pp. 18–19

SCIENCE CONTENT TOPICS: L.c.2, L.c.5
SCIENCE PRACTICES: SP.1.a, SP.1.b, SP.1.c, SP.3.a, SP.6.a, SP.6.c

1 Review the Skill

Considering how things are alike and different can help you sort, analyze, and better understand written and visual information. When you **compare**, you identify ways in which organisms, objects, data, behaviors, events, or processes are alike. When you **contrast**, you look for ways in which such things are different.

You can use similarities and differences to group things you learn about while studying science topics. Graphic organizers such as tables and Venn diagrams can help you compare and contrast.

2 Refine the Skill

By refining the skill of comparing and contrasting, you will improve your study and test-taking abilities, especially as they relate to the GED® Science Test. Study the information and graph below. Then answer the questions that follow.

CHANGES IN BIG CAT POPULATIONS

Populations of several kinds of big cats, such as species of cheetahs, leopards, lions, and lynxes, have reached exceedingly low levels. At one time, for example, tens of thousands of cheetahs lived in the wild. Currently, the number is no more than 12,000 as habitat destruction, competition from larger predators, and persecution by humans have taken their toll on cheetah numbers. The graph shows how the cheetah population has changed over the years.

a A bar graph shows data in a form that helps you compare and contrast. The scale on the *y*-axis increases, so you can compare and contrast the heights of the bars to compare and contrast data.

b The categories for data that are being compared and contrasted on a bar graph are shown on the *x*-axis.

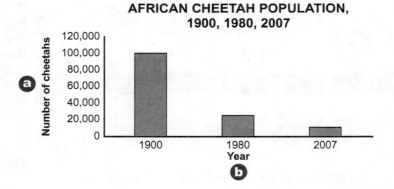

AFRICAN CHEETAH POPULATION, 1900, 1980, 2007

1. Compare the cats identified in the passage. How are they alike?

   A. Their populations have decreased over time.
   B. They all have populations of 12,000 or less.
   C. Their populations peaked in size in 1900.
   D. They are all native to Africa.

2. Contrast the cheetah population figures shown on the graph. Which statement correctly describes a difference in the figures?

   A. The population increased between 1900 and 1980.
   B. There were more cheetahs in 2007 than in 1980.
   C. The greatest number of cheetahs were living in 1900.
   D. There were fewer cheetahs in 1900 than in 2007.

★ Spotlighted Item: **DRAG-AND-DROP**

DIRECTIONS: Read the passage and question. Then use the drag-and-drop options to complete the table.

EFFECTS OF DESERTIFICATION

Disruptions to an ecosystem can be caused by natural events or human activities. Consider the example of desertification, which is caused primarily by human activity. Desertification is the changing of productive lands into desert. Ironically, the many human activities that lead to desertification are intended to make land more productive. For example, trees and forests are cut down to make land available for growing agricultural crops. At the time, using the land for crops is more productive for humans. Ultimately, however, the land could be damaged beyond recovery. The more exposed land becomes, the more at risk it is for soil erosion.

Desertification does not happen overnight. Rather, it progresses at very different rates depending on the environment and the activities causing it. A common misconception is that desertification is caused by drought. To be sure, an area that is being overgrazed by animals becomes less productive more quickly if a drought occurs. However, the reality is that although desertification can be sped up by drought, drought is not its cause. A healthy, balanced ecosystem has the ability to recover from drought. It may take years, but it can recover naturally. On the other hand, after desertification, there is little hope for recovery for an area unless human intervention occurs.

Human intervention to reduce and even reverse desertification is under way. New techniques for managing grazing herds are being explored. Soil conservation and water conservation are other factors that can help bring about change before it is too late.

3. Based on the passage, determine whether each drag-and-drop option is a characteristic an area has before or after desertification. Then record each characteristic in the appropriate column in the table.

Before Desertification	After Desertification

Drag-and-Drop Options

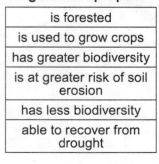

is forested
is used to grow crops
has greater biodiversity
is at greater risk of soil erosion
has less biodiversity
able to recover from drought

★ Spotlighted Item: **DRAG-AND-DROP**

DIRECTIONS: Read the passage and question. Then use the drag-and-drop options to complete the diagram.

FOOD WEB DISRUPTION

Food webs are fragile. Small changes in the population of one organism can have significant effects on the populations of other organisms. The sea otter food web provides an effective example of the fragility of food webs. The sea otter is often considered a keystone species, or one that plays a crucial role in the way an ecosystem functions. A reduction in numbers of a keystone species can start a domino effect that can lead to the disappearance of other species in the ecosystem and even the elimination of certain species.

In the 1990s, sea otter populations in western Alaskan coastal ecosystems were declining by about 25 percent every year. Researchers attributed the decline to a chain of events. They found that the main force behind the decline was that orca whales began hunting sea otters in larger numbers. They thought that this change was due to a decrease in the population of orca whales' usual prey—seals and sea lions. The seal and sea lion populations had been reduced because the populations of the fish they eat were low. Scientists think that overfishing or possibly increasing ocean temperatures may have caused the change in fish populations.

By examining the situation with the sea otters, it is not difficult to understand how all the populations involved in a food web are dependent on one another. In addition, the entire food web is dependent on external forces, such as climate change and human activity.

4. Based on the passage, identify ways in which the food web **most likely** would be different or the same after a drastic reduction in the sea otter population. Use the drag-and-drop options to show an increase (plus sign), a decrease (minus sign), or no change (equals sign) in populations shown on the food web. Record the appropriate symbol in the correct place to show the effect on kelps, algae, sea urchins, mussels, clams, and sea lions.

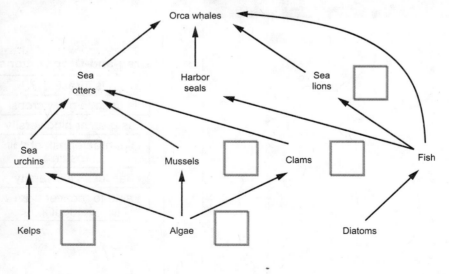

Drag-and-Drop Options

+
−
=

DIRECTIONS: Read the passage and question. Then use the drag-and-drop options to complete the diagram.

INVASIVE PLANTS VERSUS NATIVE PLANTS

Sometimes people introduce organisms from one ecosystem into another. The introduced species can become problematic in the new ecosystem. One example of such a problematic species is the kudzu vine. Kudzu is native to Japan. People first planted it in the southern United States to try to stop soil erosion. Although the vine did help reduce soil erosion, it had no restraints on its growth in the new environment. It began to grow out of control. Kudzu can grow up to a foot in a single day, and it is hard to kill. In only a few weeks or months, it can completely cover buildings and other structures, and can even kill trees. Although herbicides can kill kudzu, these chemicals also harm other plants. Today, kudzu grows wild in every state in the southeastern United States. It has spread as far north as New York and Massachusetts and as far west as Texas and Nebraska.

Alternatively, native plants are those that occur naturally in a particular region. In the United States, the plants that are considered native in particular areas are those that were here at the time Europeans arrived in North America. Native plants are well-suited for growing in the environment in which they live. They usually grow well and require little care. In contrast to invasive species, such as kudzu, they do not grow out of control. Native plants are important parts of an ecosystem. They provide animals with protective cover and food in the form of seeds, nuts, and fruits. Populations of native plants are also good for the soil. They prevent erosion and contribute to healthy soil.

5. Compare and contrast native and invasive plants. Based on the passage, determine whether each drag-and-drop option is a characteristic of a native plant, an invasive plant, or both. Then record each characteristic in the appropriate part of the Venn diagram.

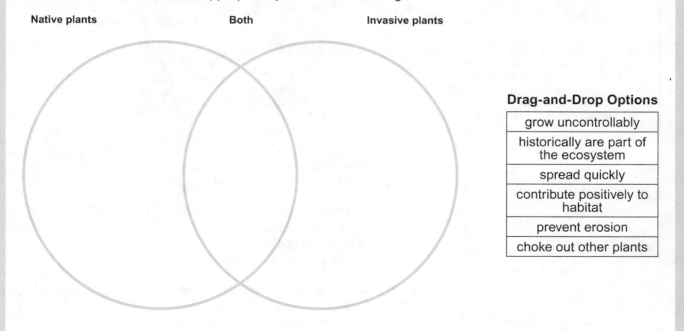

Native plants   **Both**   **Invasive plants**

Drag-and-Drop Options

grow uncontrollably
historically are part of the ecosystem
spread quickly
contribute positively to habitat
prevent erosion
choke out other plants

Relate Text and Visuals

Use with *Student Book* pp. 20–21

SCIENCE CONTENT TOPICS: L.d.3, L.e.1
SCIENCE PRACTICES: SP.1.a, SP.1.b, SP.1.c, SP.6.a, SP.6.c, SP.7.a, SP.8.b

UNIT 1

① Review the Skill

Often, text is accompanied by visual elements, such as illustrations, tables, and diagrams. Knowing how to **relate text and visuals** will help you fully understand the information presented. The text usually contains information that is not included in the visuals. Likewise, the visuals might present information not included in the text. Read the text and examine the visuals carefully to understand how the information goes together.

② Refine the Skill

By refining the skill of relating text and visuals, you will improve your study and test-taking abilities, especially as they relate to the GED® Science Test. Study the information and illustration below. Then answer the questions that follow.

PACKAGING OF DNA IN CELLS

The deoxyribonucleic acid, or DNA, in a cell is actually quite long—up to 2 meters long in a human cell. All this DNA and its genetic (hereditary) information has to be packaged together to fit into each cell. In organisms such as plants and animals, the DNA is wrapped around special proteins called histones. Together, the DNA and histones form chromatin. Chromatin is the material that makes up chromosomes. The chromosomes replicate just before a cell begins cell division, the part of the cell division process when the cell nucleus divides. Replication of a chromosome creates two identical parts called <u>chromatids</u>.

ⓐ When you see labels in an illustration, also look for those words in the text. The text may offer additional explanations that can help clarify the labels.

ⓑ When text and a visual occur together, both are often required to answer a question. The text tells what chromatids are, but you need to examine the illustration to see how they are joined.

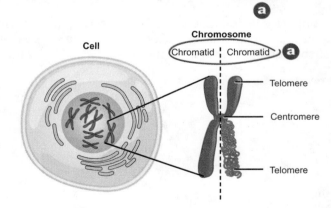

CONTENT PRACTICES

Understanding nontextual scientific presentations is an important content practice for the GED® Test. Relating text to visuals will help you with this task.

1. Based on information from the passage and illustration, which statement describes the cell shown in the illustration?

   A. It is a human cell.
   B. It is packaging DNA.
   C. It is beginning cell division.
   D. It is completing cell division.

2. The two parts of a chromosome created during replication are joined

   A. by a centromere.
   B. by a telomere.
   C. by another chromosome.
   D. by histones.

DIRECTIONS: Study the information and diagram, read each question, and choose the **best** answer.

CELL DIFFERENTIATION

Complex multicellular organisms are made up of a wide variety of cell types. For example, humans have muscle cells, skin cells, bone cells, liver cells, and so on. Cell division in humans, beginning with division of the fertilized egg cell, produces early embryonic cells that are all alike. As human development continues, cell division results in the formation of specialized cells. Differentiation is the process by which a cell divides to produce cells specialized to perform distinct functions.

Although cells in an organism contain the same DNA, cell types differ in structure and function due to gene expression. As depicted in the diagram, gene expression is the process by which information from certain genes is used to make certain proteins. Only a portion of the genes in a cell's DNA are expressed, or activated. The other genes are repressed, or left inactive. During an organism's development, genes are expressed and repressed in different patterns to cause cells to develop in specialized ways. For example, genes that code for, or provide instruction for, making proteins involved in detoxification are expressed in liver cells because the liver removes damaging substances from blood.

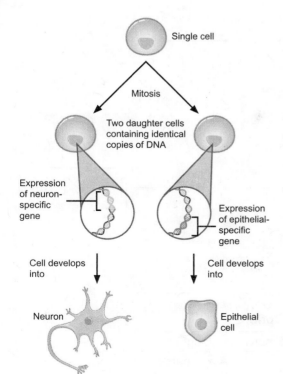

3. Neurons are nervous system cells. Based on the passage and diagram, which situation must be present for cell division to produce neurons?

   A. The correct genes must be activated in the cells that are produced.
   B. The correct genes must be present in existing neurons.
   C. The genes must code for the proteins involved in building bone.
   D. The neuron-specific genes in the cells must be repressed at the right time.

4. Based on the explanation of cell differentiation provided by the passage and diagram, which action can occur?

   A. Stomach cells may differentiate to form skin cells.
   B. An embryonic cell may differentiate to form liver cells.
   C. Muscle cells may differentiate to form white blood cells.
   D. White blood cells may differentiate to form red blood cells.

DIRECTIONS: Study the information and table, read the question, and choose the **best** answer.

EUKARYOTES AND PROKARYOTES

Organisms can be eukaryotes or prokaryotes, meaning that they are made of larger, more complex eukaryotic cells or smaller, less complex prokaryotic cells. In eukaryotes, most genetic material is contained in the nuclei of cells. Confining a cell's genetic material to the nucleus makes cell division more efficient.

Organism Type	Cell Type
Animal, plant, fungus	Eukaryotic
Bacterium	Prokaryotic

5. According to information from the passage and table, DNA is not contained in cell nuclei in

   A. animals.
   B. plants.
   C. fungi.
   D. bacteria.

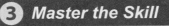

3 *Master the Skill*

★ Spotlighted Item: **DRAG-AND-DROP**

DIRECTIONS: Read the passage and question. Then use the drag-and-drop options to complete the diagram.

REPLICATION OF DNA THROUGH MITOSIS

Mitosis is one way in which cell nuclei divide during cell division. Cell development and replication via mitosis is a continual cycle of stages. Interphase is the period before mitosis. Prophase, metaphase, anaphase, and telophase are the active phases of mitosis. Cytokinesis, which happens at the end of mitosis, is the period when the cytoplasm divides to complete the cell division process.

When a cell divides via mitosis, it passes identical genetic information to two daughter cells. How does this happen? Chromosomes in the parent cell's nucleus carry most of the organism's DNA. The DNA contains genes that provide instructions for producing the organism's traits. Before a cell enters mitosis, the chromosomes replicate themselves, each creating two identical parts called chromatids. The replicated chromosomes are visible in the first phase of mitosis. During mitosis, the chromatids separate so that each daughter cell will have one copy of each chromosome.

6. Based on the passage and the completed parts of the diagram, determine where in the cell development and replication cycle each drag-and-drop option belongs. Then record each description in the appropriate place on the diagram.

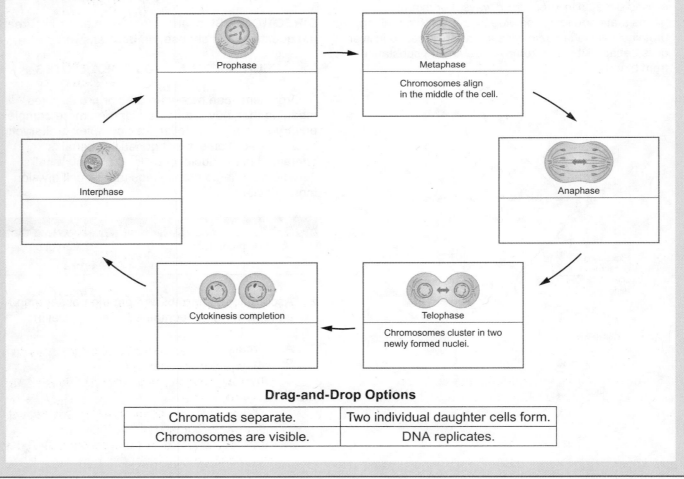

| Prophase | Metaphase |
| | Chromosomes align in the middle of the cell. |

| Interphase | Anaphase |

| Cytokinesis completion | Telophase |
| | Chromosomes cluster in two newly formed nuclei. |

Drag-and-Drop Options

Chromatids separate.	Two individual daughter cells form.
Chromosomes are visible.	DNA replicates.

GAMETES

The human body is made up of somatic cells, or body cells, and gametes, or sex cells. In humans and many other animals, the gametes are male sperm and female eggs. The somatic cells are all other cells in the body. Gametes form as the result of meiosis. Through this process, each daughter cell receives only one chromosome from each chromosome pair in the parent cell. The diagram indicates the number of chromosomes in each parent cell.

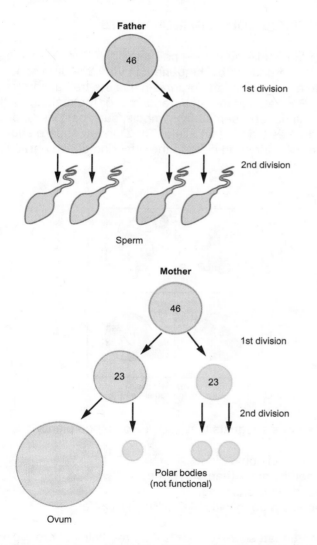

7. Based on the passage and diagram, how many chromosomes does each sperm or ovum have?

   A. 46
   B. 23
   C. 92
   D. 12

GENETIC RECOMBINATION

Cell division through mitosis produces two somatic cells that are identical to the parent cell. Cell division through meiosis produces four gametes that are genetically different from the parent cell and from each other. The genetic differences occur because genes are combined in new ways during meiosis. How does this genetic recombination come about? Genes occur in pairs because they are carried on chromosomes, which occur in pairs. Homologous chromosomes, which contain genes donated from the mother and father of an organism, line up next to each other during meiosis. When the chromosomes are next to each other, chromatids cross over one another. This crossing over leads to an exchange of genetic information.

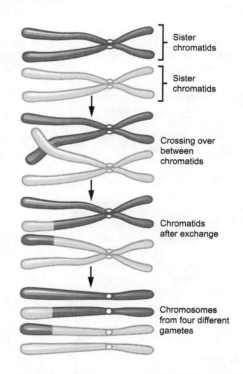

8. What do the passage and diagram suggest about genetic recombination?

   A. The two chromosomes involved in crossing over are nonhomologous.
   B. Crossing over happens after cell division has formed gametes.
   C. Swapping of genetic material occurs between nonsister chromatids.
   D. After crossing over occurs, two of the resulting chromosomes are identical.

Understand Content-Based Tools

Use with *Student Book* pp. 22–23

SCIENCE CONTENT TOPIC: L.e.2
SCIENCE PRACTICES: SP.1.a, SP.1.b, SP.1.c, SP.3.d, SP.8.b, SP.8.c

① Review the Skill

Some tools are related specifically to certain content areas. For example, Punnett squares and pedigree charts are critical for understanding topics in genetics but are not used in other areas of science. **Understanding content-based tools** will help you comprehend specific science content more clearly.

② Refine the Skill

By refining the skill of understanding content-based tools, you will improve your study and test-taking abilities, especially as they relate to the GED® Science Test. Study the information and Punnett square below. Then answer the questions that follow.

SEED COLOR IN PEA PLANTS

The two alleles that make up a gene pair can differ. When a gene's alleles differ, the trait produced by the gene can vary. If a dominant allele is present in an organism, the organism has the trait associated with that allele. In Punnett squares, the genotype, or the makeup of the alleles in a gene pair, is represented by symbols, such as *YY*, *Yy*, or *yy*. A capital letter indicates a dominant allele. The Punnett square shows the potential genotypes for seed color in the offspring of two particular pea plants.

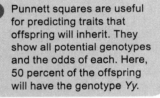

a Punnett squares are useful for predicting traits that offspring will inherit. They show all potential genotypes and the odds of each. Here, 50 percent of the offspring will have the genotype *Yy*.

b Larger Punnett squares show genotypes for two traits. For example, such a Punnett square may show offspring with the genotype *YyRr* for the traits of seed color (*Yy*) and seed texture (*Rr*).

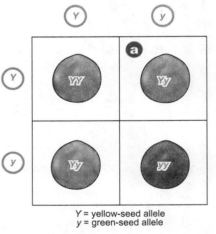

Y = yellow-seed allele
y = green-seed allele

CONTENT
PRACTICES

On the GED® Science test, you may be asked to determine the probability of events, as in question 2. A Punnett square can be considered a probability model.

1. The Punnett square suggests that seed color in pea plants

   A. is yellow-green in some plants.
   B. is determined by more than one gene.
   C. is not passed on to offspring.
   D. is controlled by a gene with alleles that can differ.

2. Based on the Punnett square, what is the probability of producing a plant with yellow seeds?

   A. 25 percent
   B. 50 percent
   C. 75 percent
   D. 100 percent

★ Spotlighted Item: **HOT SPOT**

DIRECTIONS: Read the passage and question. Then answer by marking the appropriate hot spot or hot spots.

GENOTYPE, PHENOTYPE, AND FRECKLES

Genotype is the genetic makeup of an individual. It can refer to the entire genetic makeup of an organism or, more commonly, to the makeup of alleles for a particular gene. A genotype having two identical alleles, such as *YY*, is homozygous. A genotype having two different alleles, such as *Yy*, is heterozygous.

Phenotype is the observable expression of a genotype; that is, the observable trait. The phenotype is controlled by the dominant allele of a gene. For example, in humans, freckled skin is a dominant trait, and nonfreckled skin is a recessive trait.

3. The incomplete Punnett square represents the offspring of two individuals and shows their genotypes for the trait of freckles. Mark an *X* on any offspring whose genotype for freckles is homozygous.

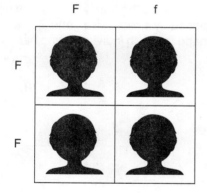

DIRECTIONS: Study the information and table. Then read the question, and answer by marking the appropriate hot spot.

SEED TEXTURE IN PEA PLANTS

In the mid-1800s, Gregor Mendel used pea plants to investigate heredity. One trait that Mendel studied was the texture of pea plant seeds. Some pea plants have smooth seeds, and others have wrinkled seeds. The smooth seeds phenotype is expressed by the dominant allele. The table identifies the phenotypes and genotypes of the parent plants in three investigations.

Investigation 1	Investigation 2	Investigation 3
Smooth (RR) × Smooth (Rr)	Wrinkled (rr) × Wrinkled (rr)	Smooth (RR) × Wrinkled (rr)

4. Punnett squares can be used to show the potential genotypes of the offspring from Mendel's investigations. Mark an *X* on the Punnett square below that represents Investigation 2.

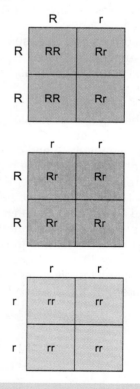

★ Spotlighted Item: **HOT SPOT**

DIRECTIONS: Read the passage and question. Then answer by marking the appropriate hot spot or hot spots.

TRACKING TRAITS IN FAMILIES

Because pedigree charts are useful for tracking traits through multiple generations, a pedigree chart can show the inheritance of a particular trait in a family's history. Also, scientists and others use pedigree charts to study patterns of inheritance in humans.

Various formats are used to develop pedigree charts. In many pedigree charts, males are represented by squares, and females are represented by circles. In some pedigree charts, color is used to provide information. For example, colored shapes represent individuals having a particular trait, and white shapes represent individuals not having the trait.

5. Assume that the trait tracked in this pedigree chart is controlled by the dominant allele. Mark an X on the shape for each individual who definitely has a homozygous genotype for the trait.

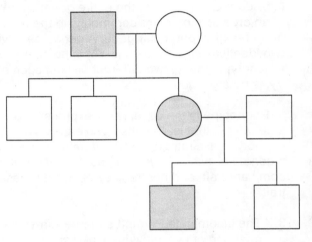

DIRECTIONS: Read the passage and question. Then answer by marking the appropriate hot spot or hot spots.

TRACKING INHERITABLE DISEASES

Many disorders and diseases are caused by recessive genes—that is, genes having two recessive alleles. Cystic fibrosis is an example of such a disease.

People having the recessive gene for cystic fibrosis have the disease. People having a gene with one dominant allele and one recessive allele do not have the disease but are carriers of it. Therefore, a child may inherit cystic fibrosis from his or her parents if each parent carries a recessive allele, even if neither parent has the disease. A child will not inherit the disease if one parent is a carrier and the other is not. Additionally, a child will be a carrier of the disease if one parent has the disease, even if the other parent neither has the disease nor is a carrier.

6. Pedigree charts showing genotypes can be used to track inheritable diseases. This pedigree chart shows the family history of a disease caused by a recessive gene. Mark an X on the shape for each individual who has this disease.

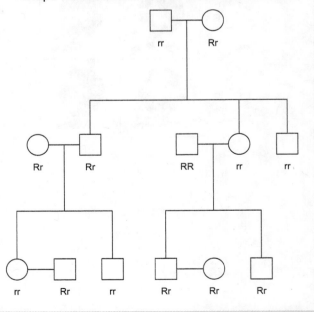

DIRECTIONS: Read the passage. Then read each question, and answer by marking the appropriate hot spot or hot spots.

IDENTIFYING GENOTYPIC AND PHENOTYPIC RATIOS

Punnett squares often are used to determine the percentage of offspring that likely will have a particular trait. They also can be used to predict ratios of genotypes and phenotypes in offspring.

A genotypic ratio expresses the number of offspring having homozygous dominant genotypes, then the number of offspring having heterozygous dominant genotypes, and finally the number of offspring having homozygous recessive genotypes. For example, for a Punnett square showing offspring having one *GG*, two *Gg*, and one *gg* genotypes, the genotypic ratio is 1:2:1.

A phenotypic ratio expresses the number of offspring demonstrating the dominant trait and then the number of offspring demonstrating the recessive trait. For the example just given, the one *GG* and two *Gg* genotypes produce three offspring demonstrating the dominant trait, and the one *gg* genotype produces one offspring demonstrating the recessive trait. So the phenotypic ratio is 3:1.

7. Mark an *X* on each Punnett square that represents a cross producing offspring with a genotypic ratio of 0:4:0.

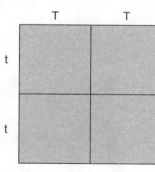
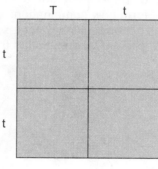
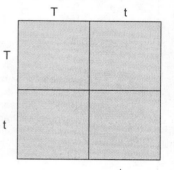

8. Mark an *X* on each Punnett square that represents a cross producing offspring with a phenotypic ratio of 3:1.

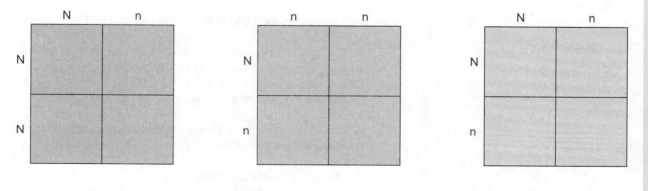

Use Context Clues

Use with *Student Book* pp. 24–25

SCIENCE CONTENT TOPIC: L.e.3
SCIENCE PRACTICES: SP.1.a, SP.1.b, SP.1.c, SP.3.b, SP.7.a

① Review the Skill

If you are struggling to understand a word, a phrase, or an idea, look for **context clues** to help you. When you **use context clues**, you find words and sentences around an unfamiliar part of a text that give hints about its meaning. Sometimes other parts of a text restate or define a particular word or explain how a complex idea relates to a simpler one. Visual elements also can help you understand something unfamiliar.

② Refine the Skill

By refining the skill of using context clues, you will improve your study and test-taking abilities, especially as they relate to the GED® Science Test. Study the information and diagram below. Then answer the questions that follow.

ⓐ Often, words or sentences preceding unfamiliar text provide context for it. This sentence gives clues to the meaning of the term *Prophase I* in the next sentence.

ⓑ A diagram can provide context clues. This diagram shows that chromosomes cross over and exchange material during genetic recombination.

ROLE OF GENETIC RECOMBINATION IN GENETIC VARIATION

A child does not look exactly like either parent because the child inherits genes from both parents. Humans, like other organisms that reproduce sexually, are genetically varied. One reason for this genetic variation is the occurrence of genetic recombination during meiosis. With meiosis, a parent cell divides, and then its daughter cells divide to form gametes. During Prophase I of meiosis, replicated homologous chromosomes come together, and their parts may cross over each other. At this point, the chromosomes may break apart and rejoin to form new combinations of genes, leading to greater genetic variation in the resulting gametes. The diagram depicts the crossing over and genetic recombination that can occur during meiosis.

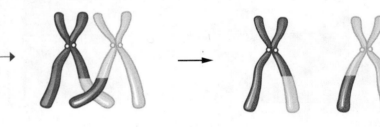

TEST-TAKING TIPS

Context clues take different forms in relation to the relevant word, phrase, or idea. A context clue can be an explanation, an example, a restatement, a synonym, or an antonym.

1. Context clues indicate that the **I** in **Prophase I** relates to

   A. the first cell division in meiosis.
   B. one chromosome in a chromosome pair.
   C. the single parent cell.
   D. the period before meiosis.

2. Which phrase from the passage helps explain the process of **genetic recombination**?

   A. inherits genes from both parents
   B. homologous chromosomes come together
   C. break apart and rejoin to form new combinations
   D. leading to greater genetic variation

DIRECTIONS: Study the information and table, read each question, and choose the **best** answer.

GENETIC MUTATIONS

Errors in DNA replication can result in changes in the sequence of nucleotide bases in the DNA of a sexually reproducing organism. These mutations can be classified in various ways, some of which are shown in the table below. Sometimes these changes are to genes; sometimes they are not. A change to a gene can alter the gene's ability to give correct instructions for protein synthesis. Whether a genetic mutation has a negative impact depends on where the mutation is and whether it significantly affects production of proteins. For example, in some cases, a mutation may lead to production of an incomplete protein. Such a mutation can have devastating effects. In other cases, a genetic mutation can go completely unnoticed.

Mutation Type	Example	
Substitution	CGATGC	CGAGGC
Insertion	CGATGC	CGAGCGTGC
Deletion	CGATGC	CGGC
Frameshift	CGA TGC TAG	C GAT GCT AG

3. What is a **genetic mutation**?

   A. any change to DNA
   B. a change having a negative effect
   C. any change that goes unnoticed
   D. a change to a gene

4. What does the term **protein synthesis** mean?

   A. an understanding of what proteins do
   B. the making of proteins
   C. instruction from a gene
   D. a mutation affecting a protein

5. According to information in the table, which words describe an **insertion mutation**?

   A. the addition of extra nucleotide bases
   B. the subtraction of nucleotide bases
   C. the restructuring of nucleotide bases
   D. the swapping of one nucleotide base for another

DIRECTIONS: Read the passage and question, and choose the **best** answer.

LINKING ENVIRONMENTAL FACTORS AND COMPLEX TRAITS

The advancing field of molecular genetics has given us new tools to use when examining traits in twins. Because they are genetically the same but their environments become more unique as they age, identical twins are an excellent model for studying how environment and genes interact. This has become increasingly important when studying complex behaviors and diseases.

For example, when only one identical twin in a pair gets a disease, researchers look for elements in the twins' environments that are different. Data are collected and compared for large numbers of affected twins and coupled with DNA and gene product analysis. These types of twin studies can help pinpoint the exact molecular mechanism of a disease and determine the extent of environmental influence. Having this information can lead to the prevention and treatment of complex diseases.

To illustrate, for twin pairs where schizophrenia occurs, in 50% of cases both identical twins in a pair develop the disease, while only 10-15% of cases in fraternal twins show this pattern. This is evidence for a strong genetic component in susceptibility to schizophrenia. However, the fact that both identical twins in a pair don't develop the disease 100% of the time indicates that there are other factors involved.

From the learn.genetics.utah.edu article IDENTICAL TWINS: PINPOINTING ENVIRONMENTAL IMPACT ON THE EPIGENOME, accessed 2013

6. The author provides statistics as "evidence for a strong genetic component in susceptibility to schizophrenia." In this context, what does **genetic component** mean?

   A. an influence from the environment
   B. a factor involving an organism's genes
   C. a trait seen only in identical twins
   D. a specific piece of DNA

DIRECTIONS: Read the passage and question, and choose the **best** answer.

MUTATIONS IN GENE SWITCHES

Mutations in DNA can occur in genes or in other places, such as gene switches. Mutations to gene switches do not affect *how* proteins are made because instruction for making proteins comes from genes. However, a mutation to a gene switch can cause changes in where, when, and how much of a protein is produced. A mutation can add, break, or modify a gene switch. When a switch is added, it can make a gene active in a new location. When a switch is broken, a gene may not be expressed. When a switch is modified, it can make a gene more or less active than it normally is, resulting in more or less protein being made. As with certain mutations to genes, mutations to gene switches can lead to dramatic results.

7. What is the role of a gene switch in protein production?

   A. It regulates the location, timing, and extent of protein production.
   B. It gives instruction for how a protein is produced.
   C. It can add, break, or modify a protein during its production.
   D. It has little to no effect on protein production.

DIRECTIONS: Read the passage and question, and choose the **best** answer.

MUTATIONS IN GERM LINE CELLS

Mutations can occur in either somatic cells or germ line cells. When a mutation happens in a somatic cell, it affects only the organism in which it occurs. When a mutation occurs in a germ line cell, it can be passed to offspring.

8. Based on context clues in the passage, what are **germ line cells**?

   A. cells that are diseased
   B. brain cells that control gene expression
   C. cells involved in sexual reproduction
   D. body cells used in growth

DIRECTIONS: Read the passage. Then read each question, and choose the **best** answer.

DEVELOPMENT OF NEW ALLELES

The DNA in a human cell contains about six billion nucleotide base pairs. When a cell divides, it must copy this DNA code. If an error occurs, the cell has the ability to correct the error. An error that goes uncorrected causes a mutation. Most mutations have no effect on an individual. A mutation can have an effect only if it relates to the 3 percent of DNA that makes up genes. The other 97 percent of the DNA in a human cell is noncoding DNA.

Some mutations have an impact beyond an individual. These mutations occur in a germ line cell. After fertilization occurs, the mutation can be copied into every new cell of the growing embryo. If the mutation affects a gene, the result is a new allele, or new version of that gene. The new allele can then be passed on to future generations.

9. Based on context clues in the passage, what is the meaning of **noncoding DNA**?

   A. a strand of DNA that is not involved in replication
   B. a portion of DNA that does not have instructions for proteins
   C. a section of DNA that does not produce mutations
   D. a stretch of DNA that is not able to correct errors

10. The passage states that a mutation can have "an impact beyond an individual." In the context of the passage, this means that the mutation affects

   A. the individual's ancestors.
   B. the individual's siblings.
   C. other members of the population.
   D. future generations.

11. The word *development* has multiple meanings. What is the meaning of **development** in the title of the passage?

   A. growth
   B. formation
   C. progress
   D. improvement

DIRECTIONS: Study the information, read the question, and choose the **best** answer.

ENVIRONMENT AND GENE EXPRESSION

The role the environment plays in expression of genes is becoming clearer and clearer to researchers. There is an entire field—epigenetics—devoted to studying the relationship between an organism's environment and its genes.

The epigenome is comprised of the chemical compounds that are not part of DNA but affect an organism's DNA. Some ways in which the epigenome directly affects organisms are readily seen. For example, Siamese cats have a specific color pattern, as shown in the picture.

Siamese cats are colored this way due to a particular gene for pigment. This gene is affected by temperature, which is an environmental factor, not a genetic factor. The gene is expressed to a greater degree at lower temperatures. When you look at the picture, you can see that the cat has darker fur on its ears, nose, paws, and tail. These areas of dark fur are called color points, and this coloration is caused by the temperature-sensitive gene. The ears, nose, paws, and tail of the cat are cooler than the rest of its body and, therefore, are darker in color.

12. Based on context clues in the passage and photograph, what is **pigment**?

   A. a substance that gives an organism color
   B. a gene that controls body temperature
   C. an allele for a particular fur color
   D. an environmental factor affecting coloration

DIRECTIONS: Read the passage. Then read each question, and choose the **best** answer.

STUDYING THE EPIGENOME

Epigenetics, or the study of the epigenome, offers reasons for both concern and optimism. First, epigenetics has shown that unhealthy lifestyle choices, such as overeating or smoking, can alter the epigenetic tags at the top of one's DNA, thereby affecting related genes. For example, these epigenetic tags can cause genes for obesity to be more strongly expressed or genes for longevity to be less strongly expressed. Thus, in addition to immediate health consequences of negative lifestyle choices, such behaviors can subject one's children to greater risk of illness and shorter life spans.

It is now possible for scientists to manipulate epigenetic marks in the lab. They have learned to fight illnesses by creating drugs that activate good genes and suppress bad ones. The Food and Drug Administration (FDA) approved its first epigenetic drug in 2004.

Since then, the FDA has approved a group of epigenetic drugs believed to work in part by activating tumor-blocking genes made inactive by illness. Turning certain epigenetic tags on and off allows scientists to make dormant genes that play a role in disease. Scientists hope that epigenetics one day will help combat several significant diseases. Early clinical trials of epigenetic therapy have shown encouraging results for patients with certain illnesses of the blood. Such developments suggest that our epigenomes and their impacts on our children can indeed be changed for the better.

13. What is an example that helps explain the idea that scientists are "learning to manipulate epigenetic marks"?

   A. a behavior that can change epigenetic marks
   B. a gene that plays a role in disease
   C. an epigenetic mark that can be inherited
   D. a drug that stimulates tumor-suppressor genes

14. What does the phrase **lie dormant** mean as it is used in the last paragraph in the excerpt?

   A. begin attacking oneself
   B. use greater amounts of energy
   C. remain inactive and unexpressed
   D. activate tumor-suppressor genes

Understand Scientific Evidence

Use with *Student Book* pp. 26–27

SCIENCE CONTENT TOPIC: L.f.1
SCIENCE PRACTICES: SP.1.a, SP.1.b, SP.1.c, SP.3.a, SP.3.b, SP.4.a, SP.6.a, SP.6.c, SP.7.a, SP.8.b

UNIT 1

① Review the Skill

Scientific evidence is required to develop ideas that answer questions in science. For example, when a scientist observes something about an object or a process, that observation either supports or does not support current scientific ideas. New evidence is being collected constantly, continually shedding new light on how the world works. When you **understand scientific evidence**, you broaden your knowledge of science.

② Refine the Skill

By refining the skill of understanding scientific evidence, you will improve your study and test-taking abilities, especially as they relate to the GED® Science Test. Study the information and diagram below. Then answer the questions that follow.

CLADOGRAMS

Scientists use cladograms to organize evidence that has been collected through examining specimens of organisms. A cladogram can show evolutionary relationships among groups of organisms or individual organisms. One trait, the original characteristic, is present in all the organisms included in a cladogram. Other traits, derived characteristics, are present only in some. For example, all the animals shown in the cladogram below have vertebrae, but only salamanders, turtles, and leopards have four legs. Scientists can trace evolutionary history by combining several cladograms to make a family tree.

ⓐ The organism having only the original characteristic is lowest on a cladogram. Moving up, each organism has a greater number of derived characteristics than the previous organism.

ⓑ You need not know what a trait is to follow a cladogram. For example, you may not know what an amniotic egg is, but you know that of the animals shown, only turtles and leopards have this trait.

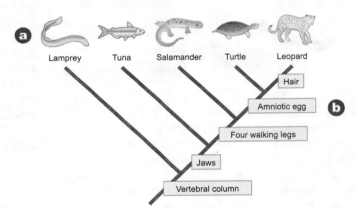

USING LOGIC

When you understand cladogram format, you know that organisms on higher branches have more derived characteristics. Use logic to decide which animal has the most derived characteristics.

1. Based on the evidence represented by the cladogram, which trait do all the animals have?

    A. amniotic egg
    B. four walking legs
    C. jaws
    D. vertebral column

2. Which animal has the greatest number of derived characteristics?

    A. leopard
    B. tuna
    C. turtle
    D. lamprey

DIRECTIONS: Study the illustration and information, read the question, and choose the **best** answer.

WHALE EVOLUTION

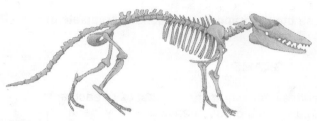

Pakicetus skeleton

Scientists compare animals living today with the fossilized remains of animals that no longer exist. By doing so, they can obtain evidence supporting the idea of common ancestry. Studies of whales provide an example of the idea of common ancestry.

Evidence shows that mammals evolved from reptiles. Today, most mammals are land animals. However, whales are mammals adapted to live entirely in the sea. Consequently, they have always intrigued scientists.

Fossils give clues to the whale's evolutionary story. Scientists have found fossilized remains of a series of animals that are relatives of today's whales. The fossil discoveries include a skull of a land animal, *Pakicetus*, that is similar to both extinct wolf-sized land animals and today's whales. Especially important is that the ear region of the skull represents a transition between the ear of a land mammal and the ear of an aquatic mammal. This structure and other transitional features give scientists evidence of whales' evolutionary trip from the land to the sea.

3. Which statement does the fossil evidence support?

    A. Whales once lived on land.
    B. Whales descended from wolves.
    C. Animals related to whales once lived on land.
    D. The skulls of whales have transitional features.

DIRECTIONS: Read the passage. Then read each question, and choose the **best** answer.

VESTIGIAL STRUCTURES

A vestigial structure is a feature that is inherited from an ancestor but is less functional or no longer functional in the organism that exists today. For example, fish that live in most bodies of water have functional eyes that were modified over time to make better use of light. These fish use their eyes to avoid predators and find food. Fish that live in dark caves have no need for eyes. Even so, they have nonfunctioning vestigial eyes. The vestigial eyes are evidence that these fish evolved from sighted organisms. Other examples of vestigial structures are the tailbone in humans and bones for nonexistent legs in snakes.

4. Which statement describes vestigial structures?

    A. An organism living today has the same vestigial structures as its ancestors.
    B. Vestigial structures are less important to organisms having them today than they were to the organisms' ancestors.
    C. Vestigial structures affect only vision in today's organisms.
    D. Features that have evolved to allow organisms to survive in certain places are vestigial structures.

5. Often, a vestigial structure in one species is homologous to a fully functioning structure in another species. How does this evidence support evolutionary theory?

    A. The species with the vestigial structure probably is no longer living today.
    B. The two species probably share a common ancestor.
    C. The embryos of the two species probably develop in the same way.
    D. In the future, fossils of the two species probably will appear similar.

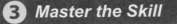
★ Spotlighted Item: **DRAG-AND-DROP**

DIRECTIONS: Read the passage and question. Then use the drag-and-drop options to complete the cladogram.

DEVELOPING CLADOGRAMS

Scientists can use a cladogram to organize various animals based on characteristics of each animal. To develop such a cladogram, scientists observe certain traits in a group of animals. They identify the original characteristic, or the trait common to all the animals, and record that trait lowest on the trunk of the cladogram. Next, they determine which animal has only the original characteristic and not any of the derived characteristics, or other traits. They record the name of that animal on the lowest branch of the cladogram. They continue recording traits and animal names on the cladogram until they have recorded the name of the animal having all the traits at the top of the cladogram.

6. Create a cladogram based on observation of certain traits in a group of animals. Determine the best placement in the cladogram for each drag-and-drop option. Then record each animal name in the appropriate box.

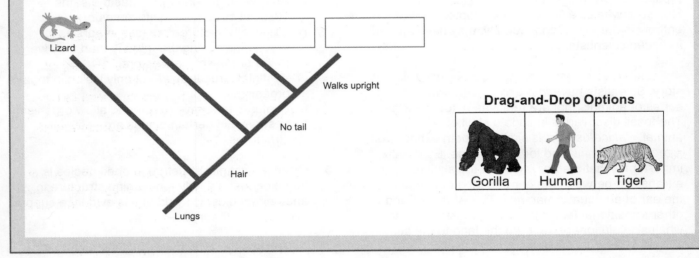

DIRECTIONS: Read the passage and question, and choose the **best** answer.

VALUE OF THE FOSSIL RECORD

Charles Darwin reasoned that living things evolve slowly in form from organisms of the past. However, he had no direct evidence because the fossil record was incomplete. He suggested that if scientists could find fossils that covered every period of time, they would see the gradual evolution in the forms of organisms. Though the fossil record is still far from complete, newly discovered fossils help scientists piece together the story of how the structures of organisms have changed over time.

7. Based on the information, which type of evidence **best** supports Darwin's reasoning?

A. living animals of the same species with different characteristics

B. living animals of the same species with the same characteristics

C. fossils from different time periods with characteristics that become more similar to those of living animals

D. fossils of animals of the same species from the same time period but with different characteristics

DIRECTIONS: Study the diagram and information, read each question, and choose the **best** answer.

COMPARISON OF DNA SEQUENCES

Fly gene
GTATCAAATGGATGTGTGAGCAAAATTCTCGGGAGGTATTATGAAACAGGAAGCATACGA

Mouse gene
GTATCCAACGGTTGTGTGAGTAAAATTCTGGGCAGGTATTACGAGACTGGCTCCATCAGA

DNA contains genes carrying codes that direct the manufacture of proteins. These proteins are building blocks of organisms. For example, DNA contains not only genes that cause a person to have a particular eye color but also genes involved in placing a person's eyes in the right position on the body. Because DNA relates to how organisms are formed, similarities in the DNA of different organisms suggest that those organisms have a common ancestor.

Scientists use DNA to gain evidence of common ancestry by comparing different species' genomes. A genome is the entire set of genes for a species. The more similar the DNA sequences in their genomes, the more closely related different organisms are. One aspect of scientists' research related to genomes of different species has to do with eye development. Scientists have found similarities in DNA sequences on genes related to eye development among various species. Vertebrate animals, such as mice, sharks, and humans, have similarly structured eyes. Logically, similar sequences exist on the genes involved in the development of their eyes. Flies, on the other hand, have compound eyes that differ significantly from vertebrates' eyes. Yet the DNA sequence on a gene involved in developing a fly eye is very similar to that on a gene involved in developing a mouse eye.

The diagram above shows similarities in coding in DNA sequences of the fly gene and the mouse gene. Scientists assert that this finding suggests that insects and mammals, which have evolved separately over millions of years, share homologous versions of a master control gene for eye development. By comparing the DNA sequences of fly and mouse genes, researchers have gathered evidence of common ancestry that may have been impossible to detect otherwise.

8. How many similar sets of DNA sequences exist in the fly and mouse genes represented in the diagram?

   A. 2
   B. 11
   C. 12
   D. 23

9. What evidence is provided by the DNA sequences to support the idea that flies and mice have a common ancestor?

   A. The sequences show that scientists have compared the animals' DNA.
   B. The sequences show that the DNA for all organisms is the same.
   C. The sequences show that the animals have similarly structured eyes.
   D. The sequences have a high percentage of identical coding.

10. When scientists implanted the gene involved in mouse eye development in the leg of a fly, the fly grew eyes on its leg. Based on evidence, how is this possible?

   A. Mice and flies have similar versions of a gene for eye development.
   B. A common ancestor of mice and flies could develop eyes on its legs.
   C. Flies and mice have identical DNA sequences on many of their genes.
   D. Fly genes are more easily manipulated than mouse genes.

SCIENCE CONTENT TOPIC: L.f.2
SCIENCE PRACTICES: SP.1.a, SP.1.b, SP.1.c, SP.3.a, SP.3.b, SP.7.a

UNIT 1

1 Review the Skill

Textual and visual presentations convey the significance of some details but allow meaning to be implied by other details. An **inference** is a logical guess about the implied meaning of some part of a textual or visual presentation. When you **make an inference**, you ensure that your guess is logical by basing it on facts, evidence, experience, observation, or reasoning.

When the significance of a detail is stated, the author is making the inference. To fully understand the material, you must be able to **identify the inference** and recognize the details that support it.

2 Refine the Skill

By refining the skill of making and identifying inferences, you will improve your study and test-taking abilities, especially as they relate to the GED® Science Test. Read the passage below. Then answer the questions that follow.

a The author presents his evidence and then uses logic to form his ideas into a cohesive statement. This cohesive statement is his inference.

b Making an inference can be like trying to solve a mystery without all the clues. For example, scientists cannot go back in time to see how moles evolved to have small eyes, so they collect evidence and make a guess as an explanation.

EYES IN BURROWING ANIMALS

The eyes of moles and of some burrowing rodents are rudimentary in size, and in some cases are quite covered up by skin and fur. This state of the eyes is probably due to gradual reduction from disuse. ... In South America, a burrowing rodent, the tuco-tuco ... is even more subterranean in its habits than the mole; and ... they were frequently blind; one which I kept alive was certainly in this condition, the cause, as appeared on dissection, having been inflammation of the nictitating membrane. As frequent inflammation of the eyes must be injurious to any animal, and as eyes are certainly not indispensable to animals with subterranean habits, a reduction in their size ... might in such case be an advantage....

From ON THE ORIGIN OF SPECIES BY MEANS OF NATURAL SELECTION by Charles Darwin, © 1859

TEST-TAKING TIPS

A test item may ask you to identify an inference. Writers typically state an inference after presenting evidence. Inferences often include the following wording: if...then, as...then, might, could, probably.

1. What inference does Darwin make about the link between eye size and living underground?

   A. Burrowing animals have small eyes but strong eyesight.
   B. Burrowing underground causes an animal to develop large eyes.
   C. Burrowing animals' small eyes are beneficial to their survival.
   D. Moles have smaller eyes than certain burrowing rodents.

2. What key word or phrase helps you understand that Darwin's statement about an advantageous trait is an inference?

   A. if ... then
   B. might
   C. could
   D. probably

DIRECTIONS: Study the information and graph, read each question, and choose the **best** answer.

MODIFICATION OF TRAITS OVER TIME

Natural selection is a process that causes evolutionary change in a population. Certain traits caused by genetic differences can result in organisms that are better able to survive in the environment in which they live. Those individuals that are better able to survive are more likely to reproduce and pass on their genetic information. If a beneficial trait is heritable, such as fast running speed in rabbits, it will be passed on to future generations. Over time, more and more members of the population will have the trait.

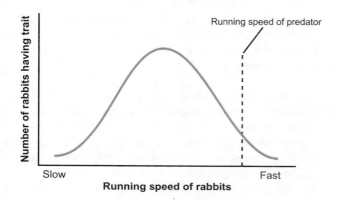

3. The graph represents the running speeds of all the rabbits in a population. What inference can be made based on the data shown on the graph?

   A. The predator is able to capture very few rabbits.
   B. Only one type of predator feeds on the rabbits in the population.
   C. Rabbits represented by the left side of the curve are more likely to be caught than those represented by the right.
   D. Rabbits represented by the left side of the curve are more likely to reproduce than those represented by the right.

4. Running speed is a heritable trait. Assuming that environmental conditions remain the same, what inference can be made?

   A. Eventually all rabbits in the environment will have the same running speed.
   B. In the future, most rabbits in the environment will be able to run faster than their predator.
   C. Slower running speed will become a common trait in the population of the rabbits' predator.
   D. Over time, more members of the rabbit

population will have faster running speed.

DIRECTIONS: Study the information and table, read each question, and choose the **best** answer.

EFFECTS OF ENVIRONMENTAL CHANGE

Two types of moths, one light gray and the other dark gray, live in the same area. At one time, the light gray moths were able to stay hidden from predators while resting on light-colored tree trunks. Those predators could easily see the darker moths, however. When factories were built in the area, soot from smokestacks blackened the tree trunks.

A scientist observed the light-colored moth and dark-colored moth populations over a period of time. She counted the number of individuals in each moth population and compared her numbers to population data from before the factories were built. The table shows the data she compiled.

	Light Moths	Dark Moths
Population numbers before factories	243	104
Population numbers after factories	150	227

5. What inference can be made based on data in the table?

   A. The population of light-colored moths decreased over time.
   B. The population of dark-colored moths decreased over time.
   C. Both populations remained stable.
   D. Both populations increased.

6. What additional inference can be made about the trait of color?

   A. Dark-colored animals can live for a longer time in polluted environments.
   B. Light color was an advantage when tree trunks were light; dark color became an advantage when trunks got darker.
   C. Dark-colored moths always have a better chance of survival than light-colored moths.
   D. Color is unlikely to determine the survival of a population.

DIRECTIONS: Study the information and illustration, read each question, and choose the **best** answer.

GALÁPAGOS ISLAND FINCHES

Charles Darwin left Britain for a three-year voyage around the world in 1831. The trip gave him the chance to observe and collect plants and animals from many different places. In late 1835, Darwin spent several weeks on the Galápagos Islands off the coast of South America. He collected several finches from the islands and brought the specimens back to London. Once home, Darwin studied the birds. He was amazed to find that although they were all finches from the same group of islands, they had beaks of different sizes and shapes. Darwin wrote, "One might really fancy that…one species had been taken and modified for different ends."

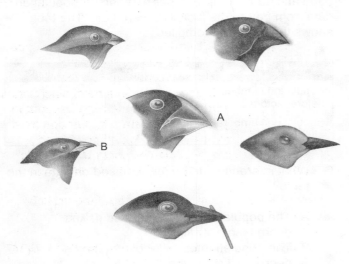

7. According to the passage, Darwin considered the possibility that a species had been modified for different purposes. What inference is Darwin making?

   A. Finches from different islands have different beak shapes.
   B. Birds on the Galápagos Islands are different from birds in London.
   C. Climate variations affect the shapes of bird beaks.
   D. The different finches had come from the same ancestor.

8. Based on the passage and illustration, what inference can be made about Bird A and Bird B?

   A. The birds probably do not compete for food.
   B. Bird B is an ancestor of Bird A.
   C. Bird A is more likely to reproduce than Bird B.
   D. Bird B's beak is smaller than Bird A's beak.

DIRECTIONS: Read the passage and question, and choose the **best** answer.

NATURAL SELECTION AND SKIN COLOR

Today, we protect our skin and obtain the vitamin D we need by using products such as sunscreen and multivitamin supplements. However, as humans evolved, these benefits of technology were not available. Instead, variations in skin color offered advantages and disadvantages that led to the predominance of certain skin colors in certain environments.

The earliest humans lived in a hot and sunny environment and had dark skin. Their dark skin benefited them because darker skin offers more protection from damage caused by the sun than lighter skin. As groups of humans migrated to colder, less sunny environments, lighter skin became more common in some populations. Lighter skin was a beneficial trait in those populations because it produces vitamin D more efficiently than darker skin.

9. Exposure to sunlight can cause vitamin D synthesis in humans. What information from the passage supports the inference that individuals with darker skin living in less sunny environments were unable to obtain adequate amounts of vitamin D from exposure to sunlight?

   A. Lighter skin, which produces vitamin D more efficiently than darker skin, became more common in populations living in less sunny environments.
   B. Regardless of skin color or environment, humans today can obtain adequate amounts of vitamin D by taking multivitamin supplements.
   C. Groups of humans migrated from environments that were hot and sunny to environments that were colder and less sunny.
   D. Darker skin produces vitamin D less efficiently than lighter skin but offers greater protection against damage from the sun.

ARTIFICIAL SELECTION

Artificial selection is the selective propagating or breeding of plants or animals by humans. Through selective breeding, humans affect the development of characteristics in living things. With natural selection, an individual's opportunity to reproduce is the factor that leads to future generations having particular traits. With artificial selection, humans choose which individuals will reproduce to create future generations having desired traits. Both processes lead to the same result: Certain traits become more common in a population over time.

You need look no further than the family pet to observe the results of artificial selection. Dogs still have genomes very similar to their ancestor, the gray wolf. However, they have widely varying body types, sizes, colors, abilities, and other characteristics. Through artificial selection over thousands of years, humans have bred dogs to have particular physical attributes and to have behaviors suitable for hunting, herding, guarding, and serving as companions.

10. What inference can be made about the process of artificial selection?

   A. Parent organisms having certain traits are bred with parent organisms lacking those traits.
   B. Parent organisms lacking certain traits are bred to produce offspring having those traits.
   C. Parent organisms having certain traits are bred to produce offspring lacking those traits.
   D. Parent organisms having certain traits are bred to produce offspring having those traits.

11. Law enforcement agencies use dogs that have been selectively bred to detect drugs. You can infer that the dogs have been bred to have which trait?

   A. a fast running speed
   B. a large, strong body type
   C. a keen sense of smell
   D. a tendency to guard objects, places, or people

CROP-IMPROVEMENT TECHNOLOGIES

Much of the food we eat comes from plants. From the first people to grow plants for food to modern agricultural conglomerates, farmers have always used technology to produce crops with certain traits.

Our agricultural species are derived from naturally occurring plants that changed in form over time. Corn, for example, descended from teosinte, a grass plant that produced small ears of tiny kernels. Thousands of years ago, natives of Mexico gathered teosinte as a food source. Later, ancient farmers began planting its kernels (seeds) to grow their own food. As early farmers noticed that some plants tasted better or grew larger than others, they used selection to grow more plants having these traits.

Today, genetic engineering also is used to produce improved crops. Genetic engineering involves introducing genes from one organism into the genome of another organism. For example, scientists have transferred a gene from insect-killing bacteria to corn to make the corn more resistant to damage from insects. Genetic engineering is sometimes called genetic modification, but scientists note that genetic modification applies to artificial selection as well.

12. What inference can be made about the artificial selection process used by the earliest farmers?

   A. Farmers ate only plants having desirable traits and discarded all other plants.
   B. Farmers saved kernels from plants with desirable traits to plant later.
   C. Farmers improved crops only by accidentally growing plants with desirable traits.
   D. Farmers found a way to transplant genetic material from one plant into another.

13. What inference can be made about why the term *genetic modification* describes both genetic engineering and artificial selection?

   A. Both processes change the genetic makeup of a species over time.
   B. The result of both processes is always plants with genes that make them resistant to insects.
   C. Both processes involve transferring genes from one organism to another organism.
   D. For both processes, humans choose which crops need improved traits.

UNIT 1

Draw Conclusions

Use with *Student Book* pp. 30–31

SCIENCE CONTENT TOPICS: L.c.5, L.f.3
SCIENCE PRACTICES: SP.1.a, SP.1.b, SP.3.a, SP.3.b, SP.6.c, SP.7.a

UNIT 1

1 Review the Skill

When you **draw a conclusion** about a topic, you consider all the information you have about the topic as well as any inferences you have made. A valid conclusion does not contradict available facts, evidence, or observations. Also, it is not an over-generalization of available information.

Because a conclusion is a reasoned understanding of something, it is not irrefutable. After drawing a conclusion, you may encounter information or have experiences that support the conclusion or contradict it.

2 Refine the Skill

By refining the skill of drawing conclusions, you will improve your study and test-taking abilities, especially as they relate to the GED® Science Test. Read the passage below. Then answer the questions that follow.

CLIMATE AND ADAPTATION

a To draw a conclusion, recall what you already know about a topic. What do you know about adaptations?

b Think about what is implied by the text. This sentence implies that migration helps an animal survive.

Different regions of the world have different climates. Temperate deciduous forests receive moderately large amounts of rainfall and are neither extremely hot in summer nor extremely cold in winter. Deserts are very dry and can be very hot. Tundras are relatively dry and cold.

Living things have adaptations related to surviving in the climates in which they live. These adaptations take many forms. Some adaptations are physical characteristics. For example, plants that live in dense forests can be very tall. This physical trait allows these plants to get the sunlight they need by growing above other plants in the forest. Other adaptations involve behaviors. Migration is an example of a behavioral adaptation. Animals that live primarily in regions having cold winters may move to warmer areas before winter and return after winter.

Some adaptations that allow an organism to survive in a particular climate would be harmful traits in organisms living in another climate. Consider desert life forms. Desert plants and animals have adaptations that help them eliminate excess heat and prevent water loss. Such adaptations could cause animals living in a tundra, on the other hand, to have difficulty surviving in their environment.

1. What conclusion can be reached about an animal that migrates from a region during winter?

   A. The animal has an adaptation that allows it to live in cold areas.
   B. The animal cannot survive in the region's winter temperatures.
   C. The animal will move away from the region permanently.
   D. The animal mistakenly moved to a place where it cannot survive.

2. A valid conclusion is that desert plants and animals likely have adaptations related to surviving

   A. with little water.
   B. in moderate temperatures only.
   C. for only short periods of time.
   D. in tundras as well as deserts.

TEST-TAKING TIPS

The GED Test® has varied item types. For multiple choice, decide whether a choice fits the information provided. For short answer, consider how well your response aligns with the information provided.

⭐ Spotlighted Item: **SHORT ANSWER**

DIRECTIONS: Read the passage and question. Then write your response on the lines. This task may take approximately 10 minutes to complete.

SPECIATION

Sometimes, environmental conditions cause speciation to occur. Speciation is the development of a distinct species through evolution. In other words, one species becomes two or more species.

Most commonly, speciation happens when populations of a species are geographically divided so that they can no longer interbreed, or breed with each other. As genetic differences are introduced in individuals of each population, the traits useful in a particular environment accumulate through natural selection. Because each population is in a different location, different adaptations may develop. After a period of time, the two groups may have different mating rituals and different genetic makeups. They no longer are willing to interbreed or able to interbreed successfully and, therefore, have become different species.

3. Suppose that a hurricane causes fruits from a mainland to be transported to a remote island. The fruits contain fruit fly larvae. The larvae mature, and the adult fruit flies breed, producing a new generation of fruit flies on the island. Draw a conclusion about how the fruit flies on the island could develop into a species distinct from the fruit flies on the mainland. Include support from the passage in your response.

_____

_____

_____

_____

_____

_____

_____

_____

_____

_____

_____

_____

_____

UNIT 1

★ Spotlighted Item: **SHORT ANSWER**

DIRECTIONS: Read the passage and question. Then write your response on the lines. This task may take approximately 10 minutes to complete.

ADAPTATION IN MICROBES

Microbes, such as bacteria, viruses, fungi, and protozoans, are minute organisms that multiply often and spread easily from place to place. Some microbes are helpful to the human body; others cause disease.

Because microbes reproduce so frequently, microbe populations have rapid turnover of generations. Therefore, populations of microbes are able to adapt swiftly to changing environments. When a selection pressure in their environment is in the form of a new chemical, such as a new medicine intended to kill them or limit their growth, microbes become resistant to the drug.

The ability of microbes to become resistant to drugs relatively easily makes it more difficult for doctors to treat patients effectively. The more often a drug is used, the more quickly the affected microbes evolve to have resistance. As more of the microbes in a population develop resistance to a drug, the less useful the drug becomes.

4. Draw a conclusion about the significance of natural selection in the development of drug-resistant microbes. Include support from the passage in your response.

_____

_____

_____

_____

_____

_____

_____

_____

_____

_____

_____

_____

_____

_____

UNIT 1

Spotlighted Item: **SHORT ANSWER**

DIRECTIONS: Read the passage and question. Then write your response on the lines. This task may take approximately 10 minutes to complete.

EXTINCTION

Whereas adaptation leads to survival and even speciation, lack of adaptation can lead to extinction. Extinction is the state of no longer existing. When an entire species dies off because its members cannot develop traits needed to survive and reproduce in an altered environment, the species becomes extinct.

Extinction is an ordinary part of the evolutionary process, with one to five species typically becoming extinct each year. However, scientists estimate that the occurrence of extinction currently is 1,000 to 10,000 times this rate. Some estimate that as many as 50 percent of all species could be extinct by the middle of the century.

Concerned groups have studied the link between human endeavors and increasing extinctions. Scientists, world leaders, and others suggest that the rapid increase in the rate of species' extinctions is due to human activities, such as destruction of habitat and alteration of climate through global warming. One organization points out that the increase in extinction rates is closely correlated with population growth and increasing energy use among humans.

5. Draw a conclusion about how humans exert selection pressures that affect the rate of extinction. Include support from the passage in your response.

Understand Scientific Models

Use with **Student Book** pp. 42–43

SCIENCE CONTENT TOPIC: P.c.1
SCIENCE PRACTICES: SP.1.a, SP.1.b, SP.1.c, SP.6.b, SP.7.a

1 Review the Skill

Scientific models are used to represent objects or processes that cannot be observed directly, such as very small or very large objects or processes that occur very slowly or very rapidly. By **understanding scientific models**, you can more clearly comprehend descriptions and explanations of science concepts.

Scientific models usually cannot show objects or processes as they actually are. Instead, models represent things in creative ways. Types of scientific models include two-dimensional or three-dimensional illustrated models, groupings of symbols, and mathematical equations.

2 Refine the Skill

By refining the skill of understanding scientific models, you will improve your study and test-taking abilities, especially as they relate to the GED® Science Test. Study the information and model below. Then answer the questions that follow.

ATOMS AND SUBATOMIC PARTICLES

The matter that makes up the observable universe is composed of atoms. Atoms, in turn, are made up of protons, neutrons, and electrons. Protons, neutrons, and electrons are subatomic particles, or particles that are smaller than an atom. Protons and neutrons move within an atom's nucleus, and electrons are in constant motion around the nucleus. An atom's nucleus and electron cloud are held together by the electrical charges of the atom's subatomic particles. A proton has a positive charge and often is represented in models by a plus sign. An electron has a negative charge and can be represented by a minus sign. A neutron has no charge. An atom has the same number of protons and electrons, so it is electrically balanced.

a Atoms are too small to be observed directly. An illustrated model can help you develop a mental picture of an atom.

b Protons and neutrons cluster in the nucleus, and electrons move rapidly in energy levels surrounding the nucleus. The model represents these subatomic particles in two-dimensional form.

MAKING ASSUMPTIONS

All parts of an object or a process may not be labeled in a model. If an unlabeled part matches a labeled part, you can assume that it is the same thing.

1. How many protons does the atom represented by the model have?

A. 1
B. 7
C. 14
D. 21

2. Which sentence describes the atom represented by the model?

A. It has no net charge.
B. It has more electrons than protons.
C. It is a hydrogen atom.
D. Each of its neutrons has a positive charge.

DIRECTIONS: Study the information and model, read the question, and choose the **best** answer.

ELEMENTS, ATOMS, AND IONS

Scientists have identified over 116 elements, each composed of only one kind of atom. An atom is the smallest unit of matter that has the characteristic traits of a particular element. Hydrogen, carbon, oxygen, aluminum, calcium, uranium, and many other commonly known forms of matter are elements.

Atoms are made up of protons, neutrons, and electrons. All protons are alike, as are all neutrons and all electrons. Yet the atoms that make up an element are unique to that element. The factor that distinguishes atoms—say, a carbon atom from a uranium atom—is the number of protons the atom has. A carbon atom has six protons, whereas a uranium atom has ninety-two.

An atom has equal numbers of positively charged protons and negatively charged electrons. However, an atom can lose or gain electrons. When this occurs, the particle changes from a neutral atom to an ion. An ion is an electrically charged particle produced when electrons are lost or gained by an atom.

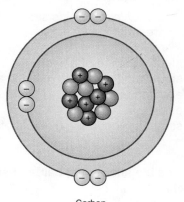

Carbon

3. Why is it clear that the model represents a carbon atom, not a carbon ion?

   A. The nucleus contains equal numbers of protons and neutrons.
   B. The number of electrons equals half the number of particles in the nucleus.
   C. The number of electrons equals the number of protons.
   D. The particle has a charge.

DIRECTIONS: Study the model, read the question, and choose the **best** answer.

EXAMPLE OF WHAT OCCURS WHEN AN ATOM BECOMES AN ION

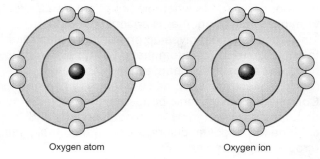

Oxygen atom   Oxygen ion

4. Which statement describes the oxygen ion?

   A. It is negatively charged.
   B. It is positively charged.
   C. It resulted from an atom gaining two protons.
   D. It resulted from an atom losing two neutrons.

DIRECTIONS: Study the information and model, read the question, and choose the **best** answer.

COVALENT BONDING

Atoms can bond through the sharing of electrons or the transfer of electrons. A bond that forms when atoms share electrons is a covalent bond. When atoms join through covalent bonding, they form a molecule. Atoms bond in a fixed ratio to become a particular type of molecule. For example, one atom of carbon and two atoms of oxygen share electrons to form a carbon dioxide molecule, as shown by the model. In scientific models, lines or rods connecting atoms represent covalent bonds. Compounds formed through covalent bonding are covalent compounds. Prefixes such as *di* in compound names tell how many atoms of a certain kind are in each of a compound's molecules.

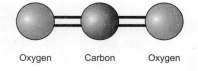

Oxygen   Carbon   Oxygen

5. Based on the passage and model, what does **dioxide** mean?

   A. made up of carbon and oxygen
   B. having three atoms
   C. containing oxygen
   D. having two oxygen atoms

DIRECTIONS: Study the information and model, read each question, and choose the **best** answer.

IONIC BONDING

A bond that forms when electrons are transferred from one atom to another is an ionic bond. In an ionic bond, an atom gives up one or more electrons to another atom. The atom that gives up electrons becomes a positively charged ion. The atom that receives electrons becomes a negatively charged ion. Compounds having ionic bonds are ionic compounds, or salts. As illustrated by the model, sodium and chlorine form sodium chloride, or common table salt, through ionic bonding.

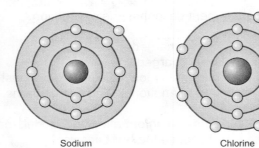

Sodium   Chlorine

Sodium ion   Chloride ion

6. Based on the model, which statement describes the bond between sodium and chlorine in sodium chloride?

   A. Sodium and chlorine share electrons.
   B. One electron is transferred from sodium to chlorine.
   C. One electron is transferred from chlorine to sodium.
   D. Electrons move back and forth between sodium and chlorine.

7. Why does the model include a plus sign label for the sodium ion?

   A. An electron has been added to the sodium ion.
   B. The sodium ion has more protons than the chlorine ion.
   C. The sodium ion is positively charged.
   D. Any compound containing sodium has an electrical charge.

DIRECTIONS: Study the models, read each question, and choose the **best** answer.

TWO MODELS OF A HYDROGEN MOLECULE

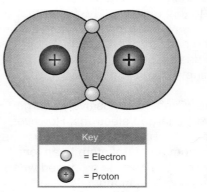

Hydrogen atom

Key	
◯	= Electron
⊕	= Proton

8. What does each circled plus sign in the model on the left represent?

   A. the electron cloud of a hydrogen atom
   B. the single electron in a hydrogen atom
   C. the addition of one atom to another to form a molecule
   D. the single proton in the nucleus of a hydrogen atom

9. What does the stick in the ball-and-stick model on the right represent?

   A. rod-like structures in the molecule
   B. movement of the atoms
   C. atomic nuclei
   D. a covalent bond between the atoms

10. Both models indicate that a hydrogen molecule is formed when

   A. two hydrogen atoms share electrons.
   B. one hydrogen atom loses an electron.
   C. one hydrogen atom gains an electron.
   D. two hydrogen atoms are connected by a rod.

UNIT 2

DIRECTIONS: Read the passage and question. Then use the drag-and-drop options to respond.

REPRESENTING ELEMENTS AND COMPOUNDS

Each element is represented by a symbol, such as H for hydrogen, C for carbon, and O for oxygen. A chemical formula tells the number of atoms of each type in a molecule of an element. For example, the chemical formula for hydrogen is H_2 because a hydrogen molecule consists of two hydrogen atoms. Chemical formulas can be represented visually by structural formulas.

11. The structural formulas for three compounds containing oxygen are shown. Examine the chemical formulas listed as drag-and-drop options, and determine which drag-and-drop option each structural formula represents. Then record the appropriate chemical formula under each structural formula.

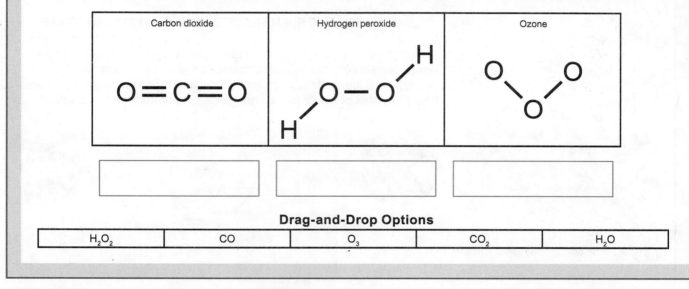

Drag-and-Drop Options

H_2O_2	CO	O_3	CO_2	H_2O

DIRECTIONS: Study the information and model, read the question, and choose the **best** answer.

WATER MOLECULES

Ancient people believed that water was a basic element. Then, in the late 1700s, a French chemist discovered that water was actually made up of hydrogen (H) and oxygen (O). Because of the way the hydrogen and oxygen atoms are bonded together, one side of the molecule has a slight positive charge, and the other side has a slight negative charge. In a sample of water, which contains many water molecules, the positive end of each molecule attracts the negative end of another molecule. This attraction is not as strong as the bonds between the hydrogen and oxygen atoms. However, it is strong enough to produce many important traits of water, including its ability to absorb heat.

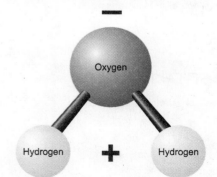

12. What inference about water can be made?

A. A water molecule is magnetic.
B. H atoms in one molecule attract the O atom in another.
C. Water is an element.
D. The atoms in a water molecule form a line.

Interpret Complex Visuals

Use with **Student Book** pp. 44–45

SCIENCE CONTENT TOPIC: P.c.2
SCIENCE PRACTICES: SP.1.a, SP.1.b, SP.1.c, SP.3.b, SP.7.a

1 Review the Skill

A **complex visual** is a detailed or complicated illustration, graph, diagram, or other graphic element. In fact, a complex visual can have aspects of more than one kind of visual aid, such as aspects of a diagram and a graph.

Like other graphic elements, complex visuals help you make connections between pieces of data, ideas, objects, or events. They may show sequences, similarities and differences, or other types of relationships. When you **interpret complex visuals**, identify each relationship being represented, and then focus on the details of the relationship.

2 Refine the Skill

By refining the skill of interpreting complex visuals, you will improve your study and test-taking abilities, especially as they relate to the GED® Science Test. Study the information and complex diagram below. Then answer the questions that follow.

TEMPERATURE, PRESSURE, AND CHANGES IN STATE

The three basic states, or phases, of matter are solid, liquid, and gas. Under certain conditions, matter changes states. For example, when heated, solid ice melts to become liquid water. A phase diagram indicates how the states of a substance change as temperature and pressure change.

a This phase diagram has labels for states of matter, such as solid, and for events, such as melting. Also, it has pictures showing the space between particles in the three states of matter.

b A phase diagram has aspects of a graph. Follow the information up to understand what happens as pressure increases and right to understand what happens as temperature increases.

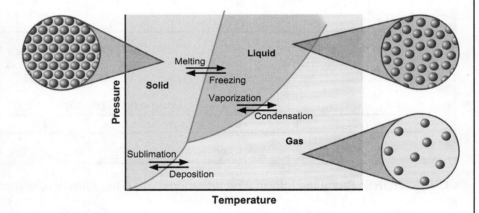

TEST-TAKING TIPS

Study a complex visual and any related text to understand the main ideas before looking at a test question. Then review the visual before answering a question to find information specific to that question.

1. Under the conditions of low pressure and high temperature, the substance represented by the diagram is

   A. a gas.
   B. a liquid.
   C. a solid.
   D. boiling.

2. Based on the diagram, what happens to a substance during sublimation?

   A. It changes from a solid to a liquid.
   B. It changes from a liquid to a gas.
   C. It changes from a solid to a gas.
   D. It changes from a gas to a solid.

UNIT 2

DIRECTIONS: Study the diagram and information, read each question, and choose the **best** answer.

PROPERTIES OF SOLIDS, LIQUIDS, AND GASES

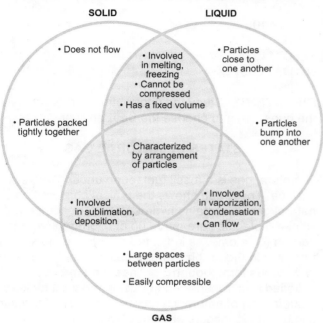

In our everyday lives, we encounter matter in three basic states—solid, liquid, and gas. Regardless of what substance it is, matter in each state has certain characteristics, or properties, as indicated by the diagram. For example, the amount of space between particles in a substance changes as the substance's state changes. In the solid state, particles are packed tightly in an orderly fashion and do not move relative to one another. In the liquid state, particles are spaced close together, but not as closely as particles in a solid. Also, particles in liquids move around and constantly bump into one another. Particles in gases are spaced far apart and move around freely.

3. The diagram indicates that only matter in the solid state

   A. is not involved in vaporization and condensation.
   B. is involved in the melting and freezing processes.
   C. has particles that bump into each other.
   D. contains individual particles.

4. According to the diagram, what characteristic do solids, liquids, and gases share?

   A. They cannot be compressed.
   B. They are identifiable by how their particles are arranged.
   C. They go through sublimation and then condensation.
   D. They can flow.

5. Which inference can be made based on the information in the diagram?

   A. During melting, the spacing between particles decreases.
   B. The spacing between particles is unrelated to a substance's state.
   C. Increases in the spacing between particles lead to decreases in compressibility.
   D. The spacing between particles changes more during sublimation than during melting.

DIRECTIONS: Study the information and illustration, read each question, and choose the **best** answer.

MATTER AND SHAPE

One property of matter in certain states is the ability or inability of the matter to hold its shape. The illustration provides information about the relationship of this characteristic to the three primary states of matter. It depicts substances having different states of matter in the same type of closed container.

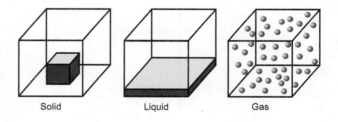

Solid   Liquid   Gas

6. Which statement is an accurate comparison of states of matter represented in the illustration?

   A. Liquids and gases hold their shape regardless of the shapes of their containers.
   B. Solids and liquids tend to fill their containers.
   C. Solids and liquids are always box-shaped.
   D. Liquids and gases assume the shapes of their containers.

7. What conclusion can be drawn, based on the illustration?

   A. A liquid in any container cannot change to another state.
   B. Gas will escape from an open container.
   C. A sample of liquid will fit in any container.
   D. Any two samples of matter in the solid state will fit into the same size container.

UNIT 2

DIRECTIONS: Study the information and diagram, read each question, and choose the **best** answer.

PROPERTIES OF COMPOUNDS

Compounds are produced when atoms form covalent or ionic bonds. Because of the nature of the two different kinds of bonds, covalent compounds and ionic compounds tend to have very different properties. For example, covalent compounds typically have much lower boiling points than ionic compounds. Although covalent bonds between atoms are strong, the attraction of covalently bonded molecules to one another is relatively weak. On the other hand, the ions that make up an ionic compound show a strong attraction to one another. In other words, it takes a more significant change in energy to cause the particles in an ionic compound to move apart from one another; therefore, more heat is required to cause ionic compounds to boil. The diagram gives the boiling points in degrees Celsius (°C) of a sampling of compounds.

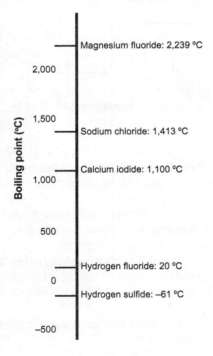

8. Which statement does the diagram support?

   A. No compound boils at a temperature of less than 0°C.
   B. Sodium chloride, or table salt, has a boiling point of greater than 2,000°C.
   C. Boiling point is a property that varies greatly among compounds.
   D. Covalent compounds tend to have higher boiling points.

9. A scientist studies an unknown compound and concludes that the compound is ionic. Based on the information, which temperature is the **most likely** boiling point for the compound?

   A. −100 °C
   B. 15 °C
   C. 110 °C
   D. 1,300 °C

DIRECTIONS: Study the information and graph, read the question, and choose the **best** answer.

STATES OF NATURAL GAS

Natural gas is a fossil fuel found under Earth's surface. The graph shows the typical composition of natural gas. It contains hydrocarbons, or compounds whose molecules are made up of hydrogen (H) and carbon (C) atoms, as indicated by the chemical formulas in the graph. Natural gas may be transferred in gaseous form though pipelines, or it may be liquefied and transported in trucks or ocean tankers. Liquefaction of natural gas, or the process of turning it into a liquid, occurs at a temperature of −161 °C and causes it to be 600 times more compressed. Therefore, liquefied natural gas is more economical to transport than natural gas in its gaseous form.

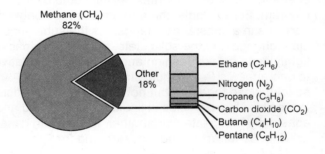

10. What does the graph suggest about the composition of natural gas?

    A. C_3H_8 is the main ingredient of natural gas.
    B. Natural gas is not composed entirely of hydrocarbons.
    C. Not all ingredients of natural gas are able to be liquefied.
    D. CH_4 is not found in natural gas.

DIRECTIONS: Study the diagram, read each question, and choose the **best** answer.

TEMPERATURES OF STATE CHANGES FOR WATER AND TERT-BUTYL ALCOHOL

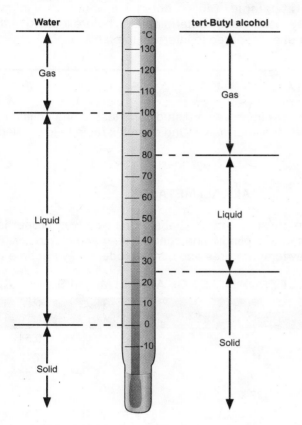

11. How do the freezing points and boiling points of tert-butyl alcohol and water compare?

    A. The freezing point and boiling point of tert-butyl alcohol are higher than those of water.
    B. Water has a boiling point, but tert-butyl alcohol does not.
    C. The substances have the same freezing point and boiling point.
    D. The freezing point of tert-butyl alcohol is higher than that of water, and the boiling point is lower than that of water.

12. Within the range of temperatures at which water is a liquid, in which state or states can tert-butyl alcohol exist?

    A. gas, liquid, or solid
    B. gas or liquid only
    C. liquid or solid only
    D. liquid only

DIRECTIONS: Study the information and diagrams, read each question, and choose the **best** answer.

SUBLIMATION

Under certain conditions, substances can change from solid to gas without first going through a liquid state. This process is called sublimation. Frozen carbon dioxide, or dry ice, is a good example of a solid that undergoes sublimation at ordinary air pressure. Carbon dioxide can exist as a liquid only under high pressure. The diagrams show temperatures for state changes for water and carbon dioxide.

Water	Carbon dioxide
Gas	Gas
100 °C	
Liquid	−78.5 °C
0 °C	
Solid	Solid

13. According to the diagrams, if samples of water and carbon dioxide are heated from −100 °C to −50 °C, what happens?

    A. Both the water and the carbon dioxide sublimate.
    B. The water evaporates, and the carbon dioxide boils.
    C. Both the water and the carbon dioxide melt.
    D. The water remains unchanged, and the carbon dioxide sublimates.

14. Which idea does the information suggest?

    A. Sublimation is the process of a gas becoming a solid.
    B. The carbon dioxide represented by the diagram is not under high pressure.
    C. Sublimation is the process of a liquid becoming a gas.
    D. Sublimation of carbon dioxide occurs at all temperatures.

Interpret Complex Tables

SCIENCE CONTENT TOPIC: P.c.2
SCIENCE PRACTICES: SP.1.a, SP.1.b, SP.1.c, SP.3.b, SP.3.d, SP.7.a, SP.7.b, SP.8.b

1 Review the Skill

All tables have columns and rows. A **complex table** may have several columns and rows. It may even have combined cells within a column or a row. As you **interpret complex tables**, determine what kind of information each column contains and what each row represents. By making such determinations before looking at the information in each cell of a complex table, you will be better prepared to interpret the table.

2 Refine the Skill

By refining the skill of interpreting complex tables, you will improve your study and test-taking abilities, especially as they relate to the GED® Science Test. Study the information and complex table below. Then answer the questions that follow.

ALKALI METALS

The alkali metals are six elements that share a variety of properties. These metals are soft and pliable and conduct heat and electricity. They melt at relatively low temperatures and can explode if they become wet.

a When interpreting a complex table, scan the table before studying it more closely. Note how the information in the table is arranged, and look for any patterns that the arrangement suggests.

b Important details may not fit in a particular part of a table. Additional symbols may refer you to another place to find information. Look at the key below the table to find additional information

SELECT PROPERTIES OF ALKALI METALS

Element	Atomic Number[1]	Atomic Weight[2]	Melting Point[3]
Lithium	3	6.94	180.54
Sodium	11	22.99	97.72
Potassium	19	39.10	63.65
Rubidium	37	85.47	38.89
Cesium	55	132.91	28.5
Francium	87	223	27.0

[1]Atomic number—the number of protons in a single atom of an element
[2]Atomic weight—the average mass of atoms of an element, in atomic mass units (AMU)
[3]Melting point—the temperature at which an element melts, in degrees Celsius

MAKING ASSUMPTIONS

For numerical data, units often are stated in a key or column heading. All values in a column are expressed in the stated unit. Also, numerical data may be provided in a particular order.

1. Which alkali metal melts at the lowest temperature?

   A. lithium
   B. potassium
   C. rubidium
   D. francium

2. What pattern does the information in the table suggest?

   A. the greater the atomic weight, the lower the melting point
   B. the smaller the atomic weight, the lower the melting point
   C. the greater the atomic number, the higher the melting point
   D. the greater the atomic number, the smaller the atomic weight

UNIT 2

DIRECTIONS: Study the table on this page and information on the next page. Then read each question, and choose the **best** answer.

PERIODIC TABLE OF ELEMENTS

Main-Group Elements

Main-Group Elements

Transition Metals

Inner-Transition Metals

6
C
Carbon
12.01

Atomic number
Symbol
Element name
Atomic weight

Metal	Metalloid
Nonmetal	

*Lanthanides

**Actinides

Period 1
1A — 1 **H** Hydrogen 1.01
8A — 2 **He** Helium 4.00

Period 2
2A — 4 **Be** Beryllium 9.01
3 **Li** Lithium 6.94
3A — 5 **B** Boron 10.81
4A — 6 **C** Carbon 12.01
5A — 7 **N** Nitrogen 14.01
6A — 8 **O** Oxygen 16.00
7A — 9 **F** Fluorine 19.00
10 **Ne** Neon 20.18

Period 3
11 **Na** Sodium 22.99
12 **Mg** Magnesium 24.31
13 **Al** Aluminum 26.98
14 **Si** Silicon 28.09
15 **P** Phosphorus 30.97
16 **S** Sulfur 32.07
17 **Cl** Chlorine 35.45
18 **Ar** Argon 39.95

Period 4
19 **K** Potassium 39.10
20 **Ca** Calcium 40.08
21 **Sc** Scandium 44.96
22 **Ti** Titanium 47.87
23 **V** Vanadium 50.94
24 **Cr** Chromium 52.00
25 **Mn** Manganese 54.94
26 **Fe** Iron 55.85
27 **Co** Cobalt 58.93
28 **Ni** Nickel 58.69
29 **Cu** Copper 63.55
30 **Zn** Zinc 65.41
31 **Ga** Gallium 69.72
32 **Ge** Germanium 72.64
33 **As** Arsenic 74.92
34 **Se** Selenium 78.96
35 **Br** Bromine 79.90
36 **Kr** Krypton 83.80

Period 5
37 **Rb** Rubidium 85.47
38 **Sr** Strontium 87.62
39 **Y** Yttrium 88.91
40 **Zr** Zirconium 91.22
41 **Nb** Niobium 92.91
42 **Mo** Molybdenum 95.94
43 **Tc** Technetium (98)
44 **Ru** Ruthenium 101.07
45 **Rh** Rhodium 102.91
46 **Pd** Palladium 106.42
47 **Ag** Silver 107.87
48 **Cd** Cadmium 112.41
49 **In** Indium 114.82
50 **Sn** Tin 118.71
51 **Sb** Antimony 121.76
52 **Te** Tellurium 127.60
53 **I** Iodine 126.90
54 **Xe** Xenon 131.29

Period 6
55 **Cs** Cesium 132.91
56 **Ba** Barium 137.33
57–71*
72 **Hf** Hafnium 178.49
73 **Ta** Tantalum 180.95
74 **W** Tungsten 183.84
75 **Re** Rhenium 186.21
76 **Os** Osmium 190.23
77 **Ir** Iridium 192.22
78 **Pt** Platinum 195.08
79 **Au** Gold 196.97
80 **Hg** Mercury 200.59
81 **Tl** Thallium 204.38
82 **Pb** Lead 207.2
83 **Bi** Bismuth 208.98
84 **Po** Polonium (209)
85 **At** Astatine (210)
86 **Rn** Radon (222)

Period 7
87 **Fr** Francium (223)
88 **Ra** Radium (226)
89–103**
104 **Rf** Rutherfordium (261)
105 **Db** Dubnium (262)
106 **Sg**
107 **Bh** Bohrium (264)
108 **Hs** Hassium (277)
109 **Mt** Meitnerium (268)
110 **Ds** Darmstadtium (269)
111 **Rg** Roentgenium (272)
112 **Uub** Ununbium (285)
114 **Uuq** Ununquadium (289)
116 **Uuh** Ununhexium (292)

Lanthanides:
57 **La** Lanthanum 138.91
58 **Ce** Cerium 140.17
59 **Pr** Praseodymium 140.91
60 **Nd** Neodymium 144.24
61 **Pm** Promethium (145)
62 **Sm** Samarium 150.36
63 **Eu** Europium 151.96
64 **Gd** Gadolinium 157.25
65 **Tb** Terbium 158.93
66 **Dy** Dysprosium 162.50
67 **Ho** Holmium 164.93
68 **Er** Erbium 167.26
69 **Tm** Thulium 168.93
70 **Yb** Ytterbium 173.04
71 **Lu** Lutetium 174.97

Actinides:
89 **Ac** Actinium (227)
90 **Th** Thorium 232.04
91 **Pa** Protactinium 231.04
92 **U** Uranium 238.03
93 **Np** Neptunium (237)
94 **Pu** Plutonium (244)
95 **Am** Americium (243)
96 **Cm** Curium (251)
97 **Bk** Berkelium (247)
98 **Cf** Californium (251)
99 **Es** Einsteinium (252)
100 **Fm** Fermium (257)
101 **Md** Mendelevium (258)
102 **No** Nobelium (259)
103 **Lr** Lawrencium (262)

UNIT 2

UNDERSTANDING THE PERIODIC TABLE

After the first scientific discovery of an element in 1649 and as more elements became known, chemists studied their properties rigorously. They began to recognize patterns in properties and to classify elements according to those patterns. By 1869, Russian chemist Dmitri Mendeleev had published a periodic table of the 63 known elements—the basis for today's periodic table.

The periodic table arranges the elements in a way that shows the periodicity, or regular recurrence, of their physical and chemical properties. The columns in the periodic table are called groups. Elements in the same group have a number of common traits, including similar physical and chemical properties. Atomic mass, or atomic weight, increases from top to bottom in each column. The rows in the periodic table are called periods. Across a period from left to right, atomic number increases. Atomic radius tends to decrease across a period and increase down a group.

3. On the periodic table, where are the elements having the largest masses shown?

    A. upper left corner
    B. upper right corner
    C. lower left corner
    D. lower right corner

4. Which statement is supported by information in the periodic table?

    A. Neon is a metal.
    B. Carbon and silicon have similar properties.
    C. Potassium and krypton have similar properties.
    D. Calcium is not a metal.

5. Which statement describes a way to use the periodic table?

    A. To determine the melting point of titanium, look at its atomic number.
    B. To find elements with higher atomic numbers than cadmium, look left in the row in which cadmium is shown.
    C. To find elements with properties similar to helium, look in the column in which helium is shown.
    D. To determine which properties fluorine and chlorine share, look at the column in which those elements are shown.

CALCULATING MASS, VOLUME, AND DENSITY

Mass, volume, and density are physical properties of matter. Mass is the amount of matter an object has. Volume is the amount of space a quantity of matter takes up. Density is the amount of matter in a certain volume. The table shows the densities of some common substances. Because mass, volume, and density are related, one value can be calculated if the other two are known by using the following formula:

$$density = \frac{mass}{volume}$$

DENSITIES OF SELECT SUBSTANCES

Material	Density (g/cm³)*
Solids	
Aluminum	2.7
Lead	11.3
Ice (at 0 °C)	0.92
Liquids	
Water (at 4 °C)	1.0000
Gasoline	0.70
Mercury	13.6
Gases	
Carbon monoxide	0.00125
Hydrogen	0.00009
Nitrogen	0.001251

*g/cm³—grams per cubic centimeter
Note: Density in kilograms per cubic meter (kg/m³) can be obtained by multiplying a value by 1,000.

6. An unknown substance has a mass of 5.4 g and a volume of 2 cm³. Based on information from the table, the substance **most likely** is

    A. aluminum.
    B. gasoline.
    C. mercury.
    D. carbon monoxide.

7. Based on information from the table, which value is another representation of the density of nitrogen?

    A. 0.00001251 kg/m³
    B. 1.25 kg/m³
    C. 1,000 kg/m³
    D. 1.251 kg/m³

PHYSICAL AND CHEMICAL CHANGES

Matter can undergo physical changes or chemical changes. In a physical change, the chemical makeup of a substance is not affected. The substance is different in some way, but it is still the same substance. In a chemical change, or chemical reaction, the chemical makeup of a substance changes to form a different substance altogether.

SELECT PHYSICAL AND CHEMICAL PROPERTIES AND CHANGES

	Physical	Chemical
Properties	Texture	Reactivity to air
	Color	Reactivity to water
	Shape	Flammability
	State	Corrosiveness
Indicators of change	Change in texture	Change in color
	Change in color	Change in temperature
	Change in shape	Noticeable odor
	Change in state	Formation of bubbles
Actions that result in change	Sanding of rough wood	Rusting of metal lawn furniture
	Painting of a metal mailbox	Tarnishing of silverware
	Freezing of water to make ice cubes	Rotting of food

8. After pouring two fluids together, a scientist smells a new odor and sees foam forming. Based on the information in the table, what is the **most likely** explanation?

   A. A physical change has occurred.
   B. The textures of the substances have changed.
   C. A chemical reaction has occurred.
   D. The substances have changed from liquids to solids.

9. While conducting an investigation, a scientist observes the effects of her actions on various substances. Which effect does not suggest with certainty whether a physical change or a chemical change has occurred?

   A. changing color
   B. bursting into flames
   C. changing from a liquid to a gas
   D. decreasing in temperature

DIRECTIONS: Study the table and information, read each question, and choose the **best** answer.

pH SCALE

Description	pH	[H+]	[OH-]
Basic	14	1×10^{-14}	1×10^{0}
	13	1×10^{-13}	1×10^{-1}
	12	1×10^{-12}	1×10^{-2}
	11	1×10^{-11}	1×10^{-3}
	10	1×10^{-10}	1×10^{-4}
	9	1×10^{-9}	1×10^{-5}
	8	1×10^{-8}	1×10^{-6}
Neutral	7	1×10^{-7}	1×10^{-7}
Acidic	6	1×10^{-6}	1×10^{-8}
	5	1×10^{-5}	1×10^{-9}
	4	1×10^{-4}	1×10^{-10}
	3	1×10^{-3}	1×10^{-11}
	2	1×10^{-2}	1×10^{-12}
	1	1×10^{-1}	1×10^{-13}
	0	1×10^{0}	1×10^{-14}

H+ = hydrogen ion
OH− = hydroxide ion

Acidity and basicity (alkalinity) are important properties of some substances. The acidity or basicity of a substance is determined by the concentration of hydrogen ions (H^+) in the substance. Because H^+ concentration can vary over an extremely wide range, the pH scale was developed to address this range of values. The table shows the pH scale, which runs from 0 to 14. The values used in the pH scale correspond to the exponent that defines the H^+ concentration. For example, pH 3 corresponds to an H^+ concentration of 1×10^{-3}.

10. Based on the table, what pH change would be expected for a substance if its H^+ concentration were changed from 1×10^{-7} to 1×10^{-6}?

    A. It would increase from 6 to 7.
    B. It would decrease from 7 to 6.
    C. It would increase from 5 to 6.
    D. It would decrease from 6 to 5.

11. Battery acid is an example of a concentrated acid. Based on the information, what **most likely** is the pH of battery acid?

    A. pH 14
    B. pH 12
    C. pH 8
    D. pH 0

Understand Chemical Equations

Use with **Student Book** pp. 48–49

SCIENCE CONTENT TOPICS: P.c.2, P.c.3
SCIENCE PRACTICES: SP.1.a, SP.1.b, SP.1.c, SP.3.b, SP.6.b, SP.7.a, SP.8.b

1 Review the Skill

Chemical equations are among science's content-based tools. They represent chemical reactions. They indicate the ways in which particles are rearranged during chemical reactions and the relative amounts of the substances involved. **Understanding chemical equations** is vital for knowing how chemical reactions form the basis for events that occur in all areas of science.

2 Refine the Skill

By refining the skill of understanding chemical equations, you will improve your study and test-taking abilities, especially as they relate to the GED® Science Test. Read the passage below. Then answer the questions that follow.

CHEMICAL REACTIONS AND CONSERVATION OF MASS

Chemical reactions occur when the particles that make up particular substances rearrange to form different substances. The substances involved initially are reactants. The new substances formed are products.

Matter cannot be created or destroyed when a chemical reaction occurs. This concept is known as the law of conservation of mass. Because of conservation of mass, a chemical equation must be balanced. That is, it must have equal amounts of each type of atom on both sides of its directional arrow. For example, the chemical equation below represents the reaction that produces water (H_2O).

a Use information from the passage to make inferences about chemical equations. They have two equal sides separated by a directional arrow. The directional arrow is like an equals sign.

$$2H_2 + O_2 \rightarrow 2H_2O$$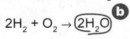

b A typical chemical equation uses chemical formulas to identify substances. Coefficients, or numbers in front of formulas, indicate the proportions of the substances involved.

The equation is balanced because the number of hydrogen (H) atoms on one side equals the number of hydrogen atoms on the other side and the number of oxygen (O) atoms on one side equals the number of oxygen atoms on the other side.

USING LOGIC

A subscript tells the number of atoms in one molecule of a substance. A coefficient tells the number of molecules of a substance represented in an equation. Interpret these numbers to understand equations.

1. What does the equation indicate about the chemical reaction that forms water?

    A. Hydrogen and oxygen are the reactants.
    B. Hydrogen is one of the products.
    C. Particles are not rearranged during the reaction.
    D. The number of oxygen atoms doubles during the reaction.

2. Which part of the equation indicates that the reactants produce two molecules of water?

    A. the coefficient 2 in $2H_2$
    B. the coefficient 2 in $2H_2O$
    C. the subscript 2 in O_2
    D. the subscript 2 in $2H_2O$

DIRECTIONS: Read the passage. Then read each question, and choose the **best** answer.

TYPES OF CHEMICAL REACTIONS

Various events can take place during chemical reactions. For example, in the chemical reaction that produces water, two substances combine to form one different substance. Chemical reactions can be classified by type, depending on what happens when they occur.

- In a synthesis reaction (A + B → AB), two or more reactants combine to form a single product.

- In a decomposition reaction (AB → A + B), a single reactant forms two or more products.

- In a single displacement reaction (AB + C → AC + B), one element takes the place of another element in a compound.

- In a double displacement reaction (AB + CD → AD + CB), two reactants form two new products.

3. Based on the general form equations for types of chemical reactions, which observation indicates that a decomposition reaction **most likely** has occurred?

   A. Two gases are formed from a liquid.
   B. A solid and a liquid form a different solid and a different liquid.
   C. A liquid is formed from two gases.
   D. A solid is formed from two liquids.

4. A scientist observes a chemical reaction in which iron powder reacts with copper sulfate to form iron sulfate and copper, as shown in the following equation:

$$Fe + CuSO_4 \rightarrow FeSO_4 + Cu$$

   Based on the equation, which type of reaction did the scientist observe?

   A. a synthesis reaction
   B. a decomposition reaction
   C. a single displacement reaction
   D. a double displacement reaction

DIRECTIONS: Read the passage and question, and choose the **best** answer.

OXIDATION INVESTIGATION

Moistened steel wool is placed in a test tube. Then the test tube with the moistened steel wool and an empty test tube are placed upside-down in a pan of water about $\frac{1}{2}$ inch deep and set aside undisturbed for 24 hours. During this time, the iron (Fe) in the steel wool reacts with oxygen (O_2) in the air inside the test tube to form iron oxide (Fe_2O_3), or rust.

5. What is the correct balanced equation for the reaction that occurs during the investigation?

   A. $Fe + O_2 \rightarrow Fe_2O_3$
   B. $4Fe + 3O_2 \rightarrow 2Fe_2O_3$
   C. $2Fe_2O_3 \rightarrow 4Fe + 3O_2$
   D. $Fe_2O_3 \rightarrow Fe + O_2$

DIRECTIONS: Study the models, read the question, and choose the **best** answer.

CHEMICAL EQUATION MODELS

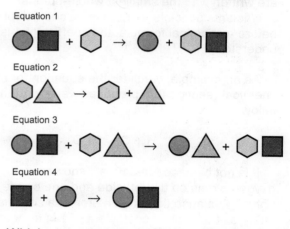

6. Which statement correctly describes a reaction represented by the models?

   A. Equation 1 represents a decomposition reaction.
   B. Equation 2 represents a synthesis reaction.
   C. Equation 3 represents a double displacement reaction.
   D. Equation 4 represents a single displacement reaction.

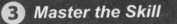

★ Spotlighted Item: **FILL-IN-THE-BLANK**

DIRECTIONS: Read the passage. Then read the question, and fill in your answers in the boxes.

BALANCING CHEMICAL EQUATIONS

Because the law of conservation of mass indicates that the quantity of each element does not change in a chemical reaction, a chemical equation must be balanced. That is, each side of a chemical equation must represent the same quantity of any particular element. The process of balancing a chemical equation involves determining the coefficients that represent the proportions of whole molecules in the chemical reaction.

A scientist balances a simple chemical equation by inspecting the equation and, as needed, changing the coefficient for each chemical formula, beginning with the most complex formula. Ordinarily, balanced equations are written with the smallest whole-number coefficients possible. If there is no coefficient before a chemical formula, the coefficient 1 is understood.

As an example, consider the equation for the chemical reaction that produces water written as follows:

$$H_2 + O_2 \rightarrow H_2O$$

It is not balanced because it shows two oxygen atoms on the left side and one on the right. To balance the oxygen atoms, a scientist changes the implied coefficient of 1 in front of H_2O to the coefficient 2. Then the number of hydrogen atoms on the left side of the equation is two, and the number on the right side is four. So the scientist changes the coefficient in front of H_2 to 2 to balance the hydrogen atoms, making the balanced equation for water:

$$2H_2 + O_2 \rightarrow 2H_2O$$

7. Examine this equation for the burning of methane:

$$CH_4 + O_2 \rightarrow CO_2 + H_2O$$

It is not balanced. Use the steps to balance the equation.

Step 1: Remember that if no coefficient is in front of a chemical formula, the coefficient is assumed to be 1. Determine whether the one carbon (C) atom in the CH_4 molecule is balanced on the other side of the equation, and change a coefficient as needed. How does the equation look after completing this step?

Step 2: Determine whether the four hydrogen atoms in the CH_4 molecule are balanced on the other side of the equation, and change a coefficient as needed. How does the equation look after completing this step?

Step 3: Determine whether the two oxygen atoms in the O_2 molecule are balanced on the other side of the equation, and change a coefficient as needed. How does the equation look after completing this step?

Step 4: Count each type of atom on both sides to check your work, and make corrections as needed. What is the balanced equation?

DIRECTIONS: Study the information and table, read the question, and choose the **best** answer.

CHANGES IN MATTER

Matter can undergo a physical change or a chemical change. When matter undergoes a physical change, the molecules involved stay the same. When matter undergoes a chemical change, the molecules change by breaking apart or recombining in different ways. The table identifies molecules of substances before and after changes in matter.

Before	After
$3H_2$ and N_2	$2NH_3$
$2Mg$ and O_2	$2MgO$
$AgNO_3$ and NaI	AgI and $NaNO_3$
H_2O (water)	H_2O (ice)
HCl and $NaOH$	$NaCl$ and H_2O

8. Which equation represents a chemical reaction identified in the table?

   A. H_2O (water) $\rightarrow$ H_2O (ice)
   B. $2Mg + O_2$
   C. $2NH_3 \rightarrow 3H_2 + N_2$
   D. $AgNO_3 + NaI \rightarrow AgI + NaNO_3$

DIRECTIONS: Read the passage and question, and choose the **best** answer.

METALS INVESTIGATION

Small pieces of three different metals are placed in separate test tubes. Acid is added to each test tube, and chemical reactions occur. The products of each chemical reaction are a salt and hydrogen gas.

9. Based on the information, what is the general word equation describing what happens when a metal reacts with an acid?

   A. Metal $\rightarrow$ acid + salt + hydrogen
   B. Metal + acid $\rightarrow$ salt + hydrogen
   C. Metal + acid $\rightarrow$ hydrogen
   D. Salt + hydrogen $\rightarrow$ metal + acid

DIRECTIONS: Study the information and structural formulas, read the question, and choose the **best** answer.

ALKANES

Alkanes are a group of hydrocarbons. Highly combustible, they are clean-burning fuels with a wide variety of practical uses. The structural formulas below represent molecules of three common alkanes. Methane is the main component of natural gas. Butane is a fuel used in camp stoves and other products. Octane is an ingredient in gasoline. In the presence of oxygen (O_2) and a spark, alkanes burn to produce carbon dioxide (CO_2) and water (H_2O).

Methane

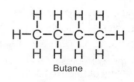

Butane

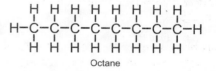

Octane

10. Based on the information, what is the balanced chemical equation representing the burning of butane?

   A. $2C_4H_{10} + 13O_2 \rightarrow 8CO_2 + 10H_2O$
   B. $CH_4 + 2O_2 \rightarrow CO_2 + 2H_2O$
   C. $2C_8H_{18} + 25O_2 \rightarrow 16CO_2 + 18H_2O$
   D. $C_4H_{10} + O_2 \rightarrow CO_2 + H_2O$

Predict Outcomes

Use with *Student Book* pp. 50–51

SCIENCE CONTENT TOPIC: P.c.4
SCIENCE PRACTICES: SP.1.a, SP.1.b, SP.1.c, SP.3.c, SP.3.d, SP.6.c, SP.7.a

1 Review the Skill

Scientists follow the general sequence of observing, analyzing, and making predictions as they carry out investigations to discover new knowledge about the universe. By looking for patterns in data and observations, they are able to develop hypotheses, or guesses, that can be tested through further experimentation. As you study science, you can implement the same practices scientists use, including **predicting outcomes**.

2 Refine the Skill

By refining the skill of predicting outcomes, you will improve your study and test-taking abilities, especially as they relate to the GED® Science Test. Study the information and table below. Then answer the questions that follow.

ACIDS, BASES, AND SALTS

A solution is a homogeneous mixture of at least one substance (solute) dissolved in another substance (solvent). The properties are the same throughout a homogeneous mixture because the molecules of the substances that make it up are distributed in the same proportions throughout it. Some common solutions are formed when an acid, a base, or a salt is dissolved in water. All three of these types of substances ionize, or break apart into ions, when dissolved in water. The table provides examples of these ionization reactions.

a Use similarities you see among the examples in each group of compounds to learn defining characteristics of the compound type. For example, notice that all the acids ionize to produce H^+ ions.

b Remember that chemical equations represent what occurs during chemical reactions. You can use them to increase your knowledge of expected outcomes in scientific investigations.

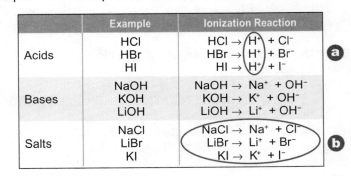

	Example	Ionization Reaction	
Acids	HCl	$HCl \rightarrow H^+ + Cl^-$	
	HBr	$HBr \rightarrow H^+ + Br^-$	**a**
	HI	$HI \rightarrow H^+ + I^-$	
Bases	NaOH	$NaOH \rightarrow Na^+ + OH^-$	
	KOH	$KOH \rightarrow K^+ + OH^-$	
	LiOH	$LiOH \rightarrow Li^+ + OH^-$	
Salts	NaCl	$NaCl \rightarrow Na^+ + Cl^-$	
	LiBr	$LiBr \rightarrow Li^+ + Br^-$	**b**
	KI	$KI \rightarrow K^+ + I^-$	

USING LOGIC

Looking for patterns and trends in groups of data or observations can help you make generalizations. The ability to generalize can make it easier to predict future outcomes.

1. An investigation of the compounds listed in the table **most likely** would lead to the observation that which compound has the most properties in common with HBr?

   A. NaOH
   B. LiBr
   C. HCl
   D. Br

2. Which equation shows the outcome of a salt dissolved in water?

   A. $Na^+ + Cl^- \rightarrow NaCl$
   B. $NaOH \rightarrow Na^+ + OH^-$
   C. $HCl \rightarrow H^+ + Cl^-$
   D. $NaCl \rightarrow Na^+ + Cl^-$

★ Spotlighted Item: **SHORT ANSWER**

DIRECTIONS: Read the passage, and study the diagram. Then read the question, and write your response on the lines. This task may take approximately 10 minutes to complete.

UNSATURATED AND SATURATED SOLUTIONS

Solubility is the amount of a solute that can be dissolved in a given amount of solvent at a specific temperature. A solution is unsaturated as long as more solute can be dissolved. The solution reaches saturation when no more solute can be dissolved. The investigation represented by the diagram illustrates this concept. In the first step, 30.0 grams (g) NaCl are added to 100 milliliters (ml) water. In the next step, another 10.0 g NaCl are added slowly to the mixture. Under the conditions of the investigation, the solution becomes saturated when 36.0 g NaCl have dissolved. At this point, a precipitate will begin to form in the solution.

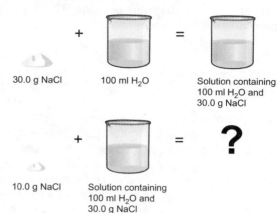

30.0 g NaCl   100 ml H₂O   Solution containing 100 ml H₂O and 30.0 g NaCl

10.0 g NaCl   Solution containing 100 ml H₂O and 30.0 g NaCl   ?

3. Based on the information, describe what occurs during the investigation, and predict the outcome.

_____

_____

_____

_____

_____

_____

_____

DIRECTIONS: Read the passage and question, and choose the **best** answer.

STRONG AND WEAK ACIDS

Acids can be strong or weak. Strong acids ionize completely in solution so that all hydrogen is in the H^+ (hydrogen ion) form. An example is HCl ($HCl \rightarrow H^+ + Cl^-$). Weak acids do not ionize completely in solution. When weak acids dissociate, some of the hydrogen remains bonded to the parent molecule. An example is HNO_2 ($HNO_2 \Leftrightarrow H^+ + NO_2^-$). In the equation, the double arrow indicates that not all the HNO_2 ionizes.

4. Acetic acid is a weak acid. It would be expected

   A. to have more H^+ ions in solution than HCl.
   B to ionize completely in solution.
   C. to have fewer H^+ ions in solution than HCl.
   D. not to undergo ionization in solution.

DIRECTIONS: Read the passage. Then read each question, and choose the **best** answer.

NEUTRALIZATION OF ACIDIC SOLUTIONS

Acids are compounds that ionize to form H⁺ (hydrogen ions). The concentration of H⁺ in solution is used to measure the acidity of a solution. The greater the H⁺ concentration, the more acidic the solution is. HCl and H_2SO_4 are examples of acids. Their ionization reactions are shown below.

$$HCl \rightarrow H^+ + Cl^-$$

$$H_2SO_4 \rightarrow 2H^+ + SO_4^{2-}$$

Bases are compounds that can react with H⁺ ions to reduce their concentration in solution. Bases can, therefore, neutralize acidic solutions. An example of a base is NaOH. When NaOH is mixed with an acid, OH⁻ (hydroxide ion) combines with H⁺ from the acid to form water. The overall equation showing the reaction of NaOH with HCl and a general reaction scheme are shown below.

$$HCl + NaOH \rightarrow H_2O + NaCl$$

$$Acid + Base \rightarrow Water + Salt$$

Notice that water is one product of the reaction, and salt is another product. These reactions are called neutralization reactions because both H⁺ and OH⁻ ion concentrations are lowered as a result of the reaction.

5. A student mixes the following pairs of compounds in solution. What is predicted to occur in each case?

$$KOH + NaOH$$
$$HI + KBr$$
$$H_2SO_4 + KOH$$

A. no neutralization reaction, no neutralization neutralization reaction, neutralization reaction
B. neutralization reaction, neutralization reaction, neutralization reaction
C. no neutralization reaction, no neutralization reaction, no neutralization reaction
D. neutralization reaction, neutralization reaction, no neutralization reaction

6. A scientist prepares two solutions using equal numbers of molecules of HCl and H_2SO_4. She can predict that the HCl solution will be

A. half as acidic as the H_2SO_4 solution.
B. exactly as acidic as the H_2SO_4 solution.
C. twice as acidic as the H_2SO_4 solution.
D. three times as acidic as the H_2SO_4 solution.

DIRECTIONS: Study the information and diagram, read the question, and choose the **best** answer.

PRESSURE AND SOLUBILITY

Solutes and solvents can be gases, liquids, or solids. A carbonated beverage is an example of a solution in which a gas is dissolved in a liquid. When you open a can of soda, you hear a pop and observe gas escaping. Soda is under pressure when it is bottled so that the carbon dioxide (CO_2) will stay in solution. When you open the can, the pressure that exists above the liquid in the can is decreased. The decrease in pressure causes the CO_2 to become less soluble, and it releases from solution. The diagram shows how solubility of a gas increases as pressure increases.

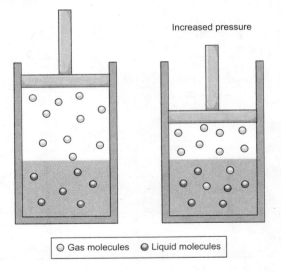

Increased pressure

○ Gas molecules ● Liquid molecules

7. Based on the diagram, what outcome can be predicted when the pressure of a gas above the surface of a solution is increased?

A. Less gas will dissolve in solution.
B. More gas will dissolve in solution.
C. The gas will become a liquid.
D. No change in solubility will occur.

RULES OF SOLUBILITY

The rules of solubility are generalizations that provide information about the solubility of certain substances. They can be used to determine which compounds are soluble and not soluble in water, based on specific criteria. The table lists basic rules of solubility.

Rule	Exceptions
1. All compounds of the alkali metals are soluble.	
2. All ammonium (NH_4^+) salts are soluble.	
3. All nitrate (NO_3^-), chlorate (ClO_3^-), perchlorate (ClO_4^-), and acetate (CH_3COO^- or $C_2H_3O_2^-$) salts are soluble.	
4. Most chloride (Cl^-), bromide (Br^-), and iodide (I^-) salts are soluble.	Compounds of Ag^+, Pb^{2+}, and Hg_2^{2+}
5. Most sulfate (SO_4^{2-}) salts are soluble.*	Compounds of Ba^{2+}, Sr^{2+}, Ca^{2+}, Pb^{2+}, Hg_2^{2+}
6. Most hydroxide (OH^-) salts are insoluble.	Compounds of the alkali metals and Ba^{2+}, Ca^{2+}, and Sr^{2+}
7. Most sulfide (S^{2-}) salts are insoluble.	Compounds of the alkali metals and alkali earths
8. Most sulfite (SO_3^{2-}), carbonate (CO_3^{2-}), chromate (CrO_4^{2-}), and phosphate (PO_4^{3-}) salts are insoluble.	Compounds of NH_4^+ and alkali metals

*Compounds of Hg^{2+}, Ca^{2+}, and Ag^+ are only moderately soluble.

8. Which equation represents an outcome that occurs based on Rule 2?

A. $AgCl \rightarrow Ag^+ + Cl^-$
B. $KCl \rightarrow K^+ + Cl^-$
C. $NH_4OH \rightarrow NH_4^+ + OH^-$
D. $KNO_3 \rightarrow K^+ + NO^{3-}$

9. A sample of the hydroxide $Mg(OH)_2$ is mixed with a sample of water. Based on the rules of solubility, what outcome can be expected?

A. The $Mg(OH)_2$ will completely dissociate into Mg^+ and OH^- ions.
B. The $Mg(OH)_2$ will moderately dissociate in solution.
C. The $Mg(OH)_2$ will not be soluble in water.
D. The $Mg(OH)_2$ and water will react to form a new compound.

DIRECTIONS: Study the information and table, read each question, and choose the **best** answer.

AMALGAMS

An alloy is a solid solution made up of two metals or a metal and a nonmetal. Amalgams are alloys that contain mercury as the solvent and various other metals, such as silver, tin, copper, and zinc, as solutes. An example of an amalgam is the solution used to fill cavities caused by tooth decay: dental amalgam. Dental amalgam consists of liquid mercury and a powdered alloy typically made up of silver, tin, and copper. The table shows advantages and disadvantages of the uses of various solutes in dental amalgam.

Property	Ingredient			
	Silver	Tin	Copper	Zinc
Strength	Increases			
Durability	Increases			
Hardness			Increases	
Expansion	Increases	Decreases	Increases	
Flow	Decreases	Increases	Decreases	
Color	Imparts			
Setting time	Decreases	Increases	Decreases	
Workability		Increases		Increases
Cleanliness				Increases

10. What outcome can be predicted if copper is added to a dental amalgam?

A. The amalgam will expand more.
B. The setting time will increase.
C. The filling will not be as hard.
D. A change in color will occur.

11. What outcome can be predicted based on the information in the table?

A. The dissolution of any metal in mercury increases the durability of the amalgam.
B. The properties of an amalgam of silver dissolved in mercury and an amalgam of tin dissolved in mercury will differ.
C. Using silver, tin, or copper as a solute in an amalgam decreases the amount of time required for a filling to set.
D. Tin and copper used as solutes have the same effect on an amalgam.

Calculate to Interpret Outcomes

Use with **Student Book** pp. 52–53

SCIENCE CONTENT TOPICS: P.b.1, P.b.2
SCIENCE PRACTICES: SP.1.a, SP.1.b, SP.1.c, SP.6.b, SP.7.b, SP.8.b

1 Review the Skill

When scientific texts include diagrams containing numerical values, it is often possible to use those values to **calculate to interpret outcomes**. You can calculate values such as time, speed, velocity, or acceleration from the information provided in diagrams.

2 Refine the Skill

By refining the skill of calculating to interpret outcomes, you will improve your study and test-taking abilities, especially as they relate to the GED® Science Test. Study the information and diagram below. Then answer the questions that follow.

a Understanding the variables in an equation helps you determine the values needed to make calculations.

DISTANCE, SPEED, AND TIME

Distance traveled, speed of travel, and time taken to travel are values that can be calculated by using the equation $d = st$. In "distance, speed, and time" equations, <u>d represents distance, s represents speed, and t represents the amount of time needed to travel the distance</u>. The only requirement to calculate one of these values is that the other two must be known. The equation also can have the form $s = \frac{d}{t}$ or $t = \frac{d}{s}$.

The diagram shows the average speed in miles per hour (mi/hr) at which a cyclist, Raul, rode a 100-mile race.

b Identify the numbers in the diagram represented by each variable in the equation. In this case, d is 100 miles, and s is 15 mi/hr.

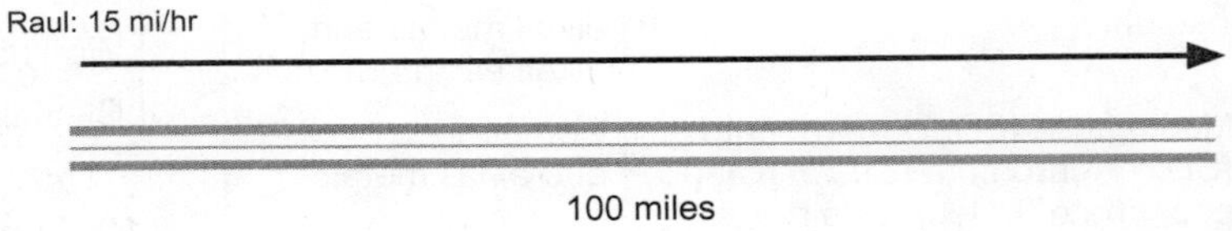

Raul: 15 mi/hr

100 miles

TEST-TAKING TIPS

If the same operation is performed on both sides of an equation, the equation will still be true. Therefore, to solve for t, divide both sides of $d = st$ by s, resulting in $\frac{d}{s} = t$.

1. How long did it take Raul to finish the race?

   A. 0.15 hour
   B. 6.7 hours
   C. 10 hours
   D. 15 hours

2. Raul rides in another 100-mile race, but his average speed is half of what it was in the first. How long does the second race take him?

   A. half as long as the first race
   B. twice as long as the first race
   C. three times longer than the first race
   D. four times longer than the first race

UNIT 2

DIRECTIONS: Study the information and diagrams, read each question, and choose the **best** answer.

DISTANCE AND DISPLACEMENT

Distance is the amount of space between two positions. Displacement measures distance and direction, that is, a measurement of how far out of place and in which direction an object is in relation to its original position.

In the diagrams below, Person 1 and Person 2 each walk from Point A to Point B. Person 1 walks a straight line between the two points. Person B walks the long way around the block.

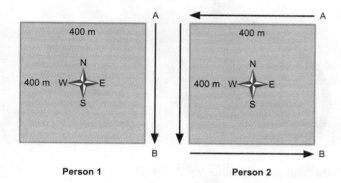

Person 1   Person 2

3. What distances in meters (m) do the people walk?

   A. Person 1 walks 400 m, and Person 2 walks 800 m.
   B. Person 1 and Person 2 both walk 400 m.
   C. Person 1 walks 400 m, and Person 2 walks 1,200 m.
   D. Person 1 and Person 2 both walk 800 m.

4. What is each person's displacement?

   A. Person 1 and Person 2 both have displacements of 0 m.
   B. Person 1 has a displacement of 400 m south, and Person 2 has a displacement of 1,200 m south.
   C. Person 1 and Person 2 both have displacements of 400 m south.
   D. Person 1 has a displacement of 400 m south, and Person 2 has a displacement of 400 m west.

DIRECTIONS: Study the information and diagram, read each question, and choose the **best** answer.

AVERAGE SPEED AND VELOCITY

Average speed is the rate at which an object changes position and is calculated by dividing distance by time—for example, meters per minute (m/min). Average velocity is a measurement of the rate at which an object changes position in a given direction.

The diagram below shows the time, distance, and direction of a car traveling from a home to a shopping mall.

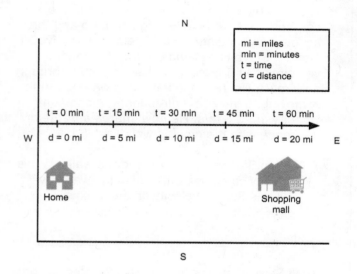

5. What is the car's average speed between home and the shopping mall?

   A. 20 mi/hr east
   B. 30 mi/hr east
   C. 20 mi/hr
   D. 40 mi/hr

6. What is the car's average velocity between home and the shopping mall?

   A. 20 mi/hr east
   B. 30 mi/hr east
   C. 20 mi/hr
   D. 40 mi/hr

DIRECTIONS: Read the information, and study the diagram. Then read each question, and fill in your answer in the box.

CALCULATING RELATIVE MOTION

Relative motion describes how moving objects appear to one another when they are in different frames of reference. In a car, you share a frame of reference with the car. You do not appear to be moving when observed by someone else in the car, but someone standing by the road sees both you and the car move past. The following scenario and the accompanying diagram also relate to relative motion. Steve is walking briskly at a constant velocity of +1.5 meters per second (m/s) through an airport. He steps on a moving walkway that is moving in the same direction at a constant velocity of +0.5 m/s. He now shares a frame of reference with the moving walkway.

Direction of motion

7. When Steve steps on the moving walkway, his velocity combines with that of the walkway. What is Steve's velocity on the walkway?

8. If Steve maintains his velocity after stepping on the moving walkway, what is his velocity relative to someone standing still on the same walkway?

9. Still maintaining his +1.5 m/s velocity on the moving walkway, Steve passes a woman sitting near the walkway. What is his velocity relative to that woman?

DIRECTIONS: Study the information, read the question, and choose the **best** answer.

SPEED OF SOUND

Speed is a measure of how fast something moves. Average speed is calculated by dividing the distance traveled by the time required for the movement. The equation that represents this calculation is $s = \frac{d}{t}$. When a person talks, sound waves are produced. Sound waves move away from their source and, therefore, have a speed.

10. Delaney shouts and hears an echo. The sound has reflected from a building that is 680 m away. If the speed of sound is 340 m/s, how much time elapsed between Delaney's shout and when she heard the echo?

A. 1 seconds
B. 2 seconds
C. 4 seconds
D. 8 seconds

FREE FALL

Acceleration is a change in velocity. It tells whether something is speeding up or slowing down. The diagram below shows an object in free fall. As time increases, the distance the object travels per second increases. Due to the force of gravity, when an object is dropped, its acceleration is constant at 9.8 meters per second squared (m/s^2). The velocity of a dropped object increases at a rate proportional to the amount of time it falls. An equation to express this is **v = gt,** where **v** represents velocity, **g** is a constant equal to 9.8 m/s^2, and **t** represents time.

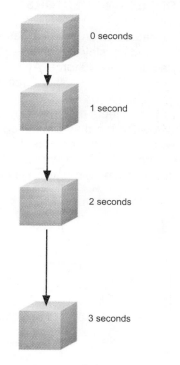

0 seconds

1 second

2 seconds

3 seconds

11. What is the velocity of the block at 3 seconds?

    A. 3 m/s downward
    B. 3.26 m/s downward
    C. 9.8 m/s downward
    D. 29.4 m/s downward

12. What will be the velocity of the block at 4 seconds compared to its velocity at 3 seconds if it continues to free fall?

    A. It will be the same.
    B. It will have increased to 39.2 m/s downward.
    C. It will have increased by 2.5 m/s downward.
    D. It will have increased by 29.4 m/s downward.

CHANGE IN VELOCITY

Velocity is a measurement of the rate at which an object changes position in a given direction. Acceleration is the change in velocity over time. The formula that is used to calculate acceleration is $\frac{(v2 - v1)}{t}$; that is, the difference between the final velocity and the initial velocity divided by time. When an object is slowing down, acceleration is negative. Negative acceleration is known as deceleration.

A camera is set up so that a photograph is automatically taken once every second. The camera is used to photograph an object moving in a straight line. The resulting individual photographs are combined to form the dot diagram shown below. In this dot diagram, the distances between the dots represent the object's change in position over time from second to second. Each "tick" in the diagram represents a distance of 1 meter. Thus, the greater the distance between the dots in each one-second interval, the greater the velocity of the object.

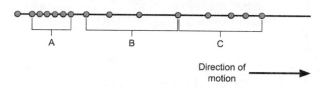

13. Which statement describes the object's motion during Interval A?

    A. It is moving at a constant velocity of 1 m/s to the right.
    B. It is accelerating at a rate of 1 m/s^2 to the right.
    C. It is accelerating at a rate of 1 m/s^2 from a stopped position.
    D. Its velocity and its acceleration are both 1 m/s to the right.

14. Which statement describes the object's motion during Interval B?

    A. It is traveling at a constant velocity of 11 m/s.
    B. It is accelerating at a rate of 1 m/s^2 to the right.
    C. It is accelerating at a rate of 3 m/s^2 to the right.
    D. It is decelerating at a rate of 1 m/s^2 to the left.

Understand Vector Diagrams

Use with *Student Book* pp. 54–55

SCIENCE CONTENT TOPIC: P.b.2
SCIENCE PRACTICES: SP.1.a, SP.1.b, SP.1.c, SP.3.a, SP.7.a, SP.7.b, SP.8.a

1 Review the Skill

Vector diagrams use arrows to represent forces. The size—usually the length—of the arrow is reflective of the strength of the force. The direction of the arrow indicates the direction in which the force is acting. **Understanding vector diagrams** enables you to determine the magnitude and direction of the net force acting on an object.

2 Refine the Skill

By refining the skill of understanding vector diagrams, you will improve your study and test-taking abilities, especially as they relate to the GED® Science Test. Study the information and diagram below. Then answer the questions that follow.

NET FORCES AND VECTORS

Newton's first law of motion states that an object at rest tends to stay at rest, and an object in motion tends to stay in motion—with a constant velocity—unless acted on by an unbalanced force. An unbalanced force is one that is not balanced—or canceled—by another force or forces.

a The passage explains that objects can be subjected to more than one force at a time. These individual forces are each represented by a separate arrow in a vector diagram.

The diagram below shows two objects that are subjected to more than one force. The vector arrows in the diagram indicate the directions and magnitudes of the forces acting on the objects. Each arrow is also labeled to indicate the force's magnitude in newtons (N). If the forces do not cancel one another, then the resulting net force is an unbalanced force that will move the object.

b The questions ask you to find net force. Net force is the sum of all forces acting on an object. To find net forces, find differences between forces that act in opposite directions.

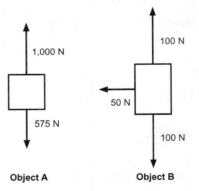

UNIT 2

MAKING ASSUMPTIONS

You can assume that processes and forces described in one situation apply to other similar situations. Making this assumption allows you to apply known concepts to new situations.

1. What is the net force on Object A?

   A. 1,000 N upward
   B. 1,575 N downward
   C. 425 N upward
   D. 575 N downward

2. What is the net force on Object B?

   A. 250 N to the left
   B. 50 N to the left
   C. 150 N downward
   D. 150 N upward

★ Spotlighted Item: DROP-DOWN

DIRECTIONS: Study the diagram. Then read the incomplete passage that follows. Use information from the diagram to complete the passage. For each drop-down item, choose the option that **best** completes the sentence.

UNBALANCED FORCES AND VECTORS

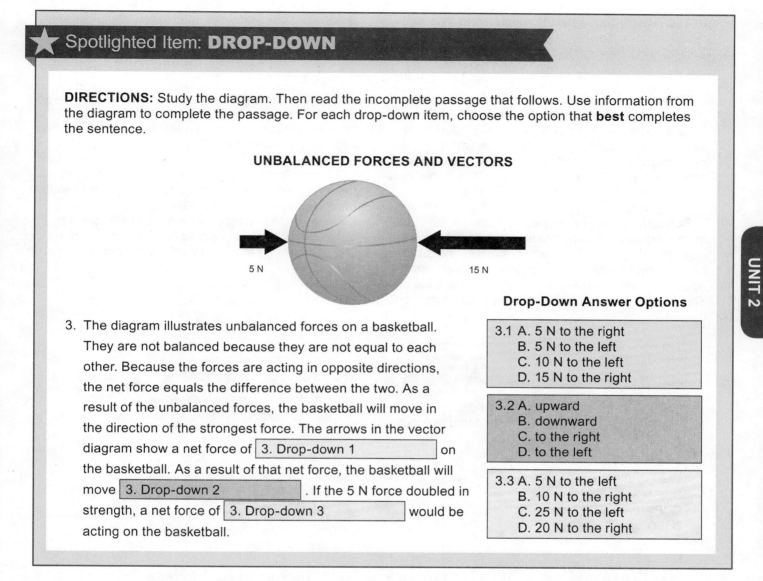

5 N   15 N

3. The diagram illustrates unbalanced forces on a basketball. They are not balanced because they are not equal to each other. Because the forces are acting in opposite directions, the net force equals the difference between the two. As a result of the unbalanced forces, the basketball will move in the direction of the strongest force. The arrows in the vector diagram show a net force of | 3. Drop-down 1 | on the basketball. As a result of that net force, the basketball will move | 3. Drop-down 2 | . If the 5 N force doubled in strength, a net force of | 3. Drop-down 3 | would be acting on the basketball.

Drop-Down Answer Options

3.1 A. 5 N to the right
B. 5 N to the left
C. 10 N to the left
D. 15 N to the right

3.2 A. upward
B. downward
C. to the right
D. to the left

3.3 A. 5 N to the left
B. 10 N to the right
C. 25 N to the left
D. 20 N to the right

DIRECTIONS: Study the diagram and information, read the question, and choose the **best** answer.

MAGNETISM: FORCE AT A DISTANCE

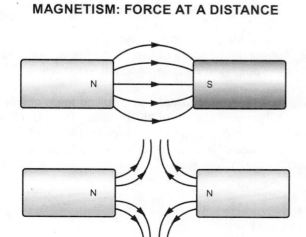

Magnetism is an example of a force that can act over a distance. Magnets have two poles where lines of force are concentrated. These poles are designated "north" and "south." The arrows in the vector diagram show the directions and magnitudes of the magnetic forces that interact when the poles of two magnets are brought together.

4. What does the vector diagram demonstrate?

A. Like magnetic poles attract each other.
B. Like magnetic poles repel each other.
C. Magnets always repel each other.
D. Magnets always attract each other.

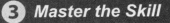

DIRECTIONS: Study the information and diagram, read each question, and choose the **best** answer.

FRICTION AND VECTORS

Friction is the resistance that results from two pieces of matter rubbing against each other. The force of friction between an object and a surface can be calculated by the equation $F = \mu m$, where F is the force caused by friction (expressed in newtons), μ is a constant that varies by substance, and m is the mass of the object.

Before an object will move, the force on the object must be greater than the frictional force between the object and the surface on which it rests. The diagram below shows a wooden box sitting on a concrete floor. The mass of the box is 50 kg and μ is 0.62. This frictional force is shown by the vector arrow on the left.

Frictional force of 31 N ← | → Force needed to push the box

5. Which equation explains why the force of friction shown in the diagram is 31 N?

A. $F = \dfrac{50 \text{ kg}}{0.62 \, \mu}$

B. $F = 31 \text{ kg} \cdot \mu$

C. $F = 0.62 \, \mu \cdot 50 \text{ kg}$

D. $50 \text{ kg} = F \cdot 0.62 \, \mu$

6. Which is the least force that would allow the box to begin moving across the floor to the right?

A. 0 N
B. 10 N
C. 30 N
D. 32 N

7. If the floor became wet and caused the value of μ to decrease to 0.2, what would be the result?

A. More force would be needed to move the box.
B. Less force would be needed to move the box.
C. The mass of the box would increase.
D. The mass of the box would decrease.

DIRECTIONS: Study the information and diagram, read each question, and choose the **best** answer.

FORCES AND VECTORS

A force is a push or a pull on an object that results from its interaction with another object. A force can be measured in newtons (N) and is described by both its strength and its direction.

The net force acting on an object is the sum of all the forces acting on it. Balanced forces cancel each other because they are equal and have opposite directions. Unbalanced forces also act in opposite directions but they are not equal. The arrows in the vector diagram below show the forces that act on a wagon.

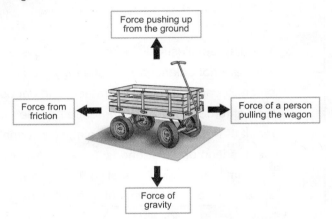

Force pushing up from the ground

Force from friction

Force of a person pulling the wagon

Force of gravity

8. Which statement describes the force pushing on the wagon from the ground and the force of gravity?

A. They are balanced forces.
B. They are unbalanced forces.
C. The upward force is stronger.
D. The downward force is stronger.

9. Suppose the wagon is moving to the right. Which could be the force of friction on the wagon and the pulling force being applied to the wagon?

A. force of friction of 10 N, pulling force of 5 N
B. force of friction of 25 N, pulling force of 15 N
C. force of friction of 25 N, pulling force of 20 N
D. force of friction of 15 N, pulling force of 20 N

DIRECTIONS: Study the information and diagram, read each question, and choose the **best** answer.

THE FORCE OF GRAVITY

Newton's second law of motion states that the force acting on an object is equal to the object's mass times its acceleration, or $F = ma$. This equation can be used to calculate an object's acceleration when acted on by a force: $a = \frac{F}{m}$. Newton also calculated the acceleration of an object due to Earth's gravity as 9.8 meters per second squared (m/s^2).

The diagram below shows two meteors falling toward the surface of the moon. They are both the same size, came under the influence of the moon's gravity at the same time, and are falling in parallel paths, but Meteor A has a mass of 25 kilograms (kg) and Meteor B has a mass of 50 kg. The moon has one-sixth the mass of Earth; therefore, acceleration due to gravity on the moon is 1.6 m/s^2.

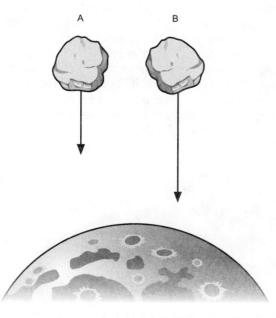

10. What do the arrows in the vector diagram represent?

    A. velocity
    B. force
    C. acceleration
    D. mass

11. What will happen when the meteors strike the moon's surface?

    A. Meteor B will strike first and with the same force as Meteor A.
    B. Meteor B will strike first and with more force than Meteor A.
    C. They will both strike at the same time, but Meteor B with strike with more force.
    D. They will both strike at the same time and with the same force.

DIRECTIONS: Study the information and diagram, read the question, and choose the **best** answer.

EQUAL AND OPPOSITE FORCES

According to Newton's third law of motion, for every action force there is an equal and opposite reaction force. This means that if one object applies a force on a second object, then the second object applies an equal and opposite force on the first object. This also means that forces always occur in pairs, each acting on two different objects.

The diagram shows a person pushing a large box. Arrows A and B represent the vectors of forces that are equal and opposite, as do arrows C and D, where the person's feet are applying a backward force to the floor as the person pushes on the box and the floor is pushing back on the person's feet with a forward force that is equal in magnitude to the backward force.

12. What has to occur to make the box move?

    A. The forces must remain balanced.
    B. The sum of forces C and D must be equal to the sum of forces A and B.
    C. Force A has to be greater than force B.
    D. Force D has to be greater than force C.

Apply Scientific Laws

Use with **Student Book** pp. 56–57

SCIENCE CONTENT TOPICS: P.b.1, P.b.2
SCIENCE PRACTICES: SP.1.a, SP.1.b, SP.1.c, SP.3.a, SP.3.c, SP.7.a, SP.7.b, SP.8.b

UNIT 2

① Review the Skill

Scientific laws are statements that describe natural phenomena. They are based on repeated observations and experimentation and often provide mathematical formulas. When you **apply scientific laws**, you can use these statements or mathematical formulas to predict or analyze the phenomena they describe.

A scientific law implies and assumes a universal cause-and-effect relationship. That is, the laws must always apply under the same set of conditions, regardless of whether those conditions occur here on Earth or somewhere else in the universe.

② Refine the Skill

By refining the skill of applying scientific laws, you will improve your study and test-taking abilities, especially as they relate to the GED® Science Test. Study the information and diagram below. Then answer the questions that follow.

APPLYING NEWTON'S SECOND LAW

ⓐ The passage provides information about how to apply Newton's second law of motion to make determinations about weight and mass.

Mass measures the amount of matter in an object, whereas weight measures the pull of gravity on the object. The relationship between mass and weight can be demonstrated by applying Newton's second law of motion. Since weight is the gravitational force acting on an object, it can be expressed in a variation of the equation $F = ma$ as $w = mg$, where w is weight in newtons (N), m is mass in kilograms (kg), and g is acceleration due to the force of gravity in meters per second squared (m/s²). Using this formula, the weight of a 1 kg mass on Earth can be calculated as shown in the diagram below. Remember, g at Earth's surface is always approximately 9.8 m/s².

ⓑ Think critically about scientific laws. Mass is the amount of matter in an object. The mass of an object remains the same, regardless of any change in the object's temperature, shape, or position in space.

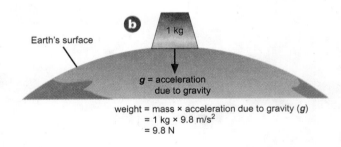

Earth's surface

ⓑ 1 kg

g = acceleration due to gravity

weight = mass × acceleration due to gravity (g)
= 1 kg × 9.8 m/s²
= 9.8 N

TEST-TAKING TECH

While taking the GED® Test, use the calculator function to make calculations before looking at the answer choices. Then look for the same result among the answer choices.

1. What is the mass of a person weighing 637 N?

    A. 65 kg
    B. 6.5 kg
    C. 637 kg
    D. 63.7 kg

2. Acceleration due to gravity on planet Mercury is 3.7 m/s². What would the mass of a person weighing 637 N be on Mercury?

    A. 65 kg
    B. 6.5 kg
    C. 637 kg
    D. 63.7 kg

DIRECTIONS: Study the information and diagram, read each question, and choose the **best** answer.

DIRECTIONS: Study the information and graph, read each question, and choose the **best** answer.

APPLYING THE LAW OF CONSERVATION OF MOMENTUM

Momentum is defined as the mass of an object multiplied by the object's velocity, or $p = mv$, where p is momentum, m is mass in kg, and v is velocity in meters per second (m/s). The law of conservation of momentum states that within a system, momentum remains constant.

Although the total momentum of a system remains constant, the momentum of the individual parts of a system can change. The formula for the change in momentum is $Ft = mv$. This means the momentum imparted on an object by a force is proportional to the force (F) multiplied by the length of time the force is applied (t).

The diagram shows a force being applied to a stationary object.

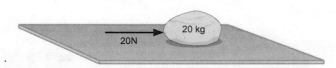

3. Which quantity is not directly related to determining either the momentum or the change in momentum of the object?

   A. the distance the object moves in meters
   B. the magnitude of the force applied to the object in newtons
   C. the amount of time over which the force is applied to the object in seconds
   D. the mass of the object in kilograms

4. What is the object's velocity after the 20 N force is applied for 5 seconds?

   A. 2 m/s to the right
   B. 5 m/s to the right
   C. 10 m/s to the right
   D. 100 m/s to the right

5. What will the momentum of the object be after the force is applied for 5 seconds?

   A. 4 kg • m/s to the right
   B. 20 kg • m/s to the right
   C. 100 kg • m/s to the right
   D. 100 kg • m/s to the left

CHANGING MOMENTUM

Newton's first law can be stated in terms of momentum: an object at rest has a momentum of zero and will maintain that momentum unless acted on by a force. An object in motion has a momentum of $p = mv$ and will maintain that momentum unless acted on by a force. The effect of a force depends on more than simply the magnitude of the force. It also depends on how long the force is applied. Multiplying that length of time by the average magnitude of the applied force yields the change in momentum over time, or impulse.

The graph shows how the momentum of a 2.5 kg object changes over time as a constant force is applied.

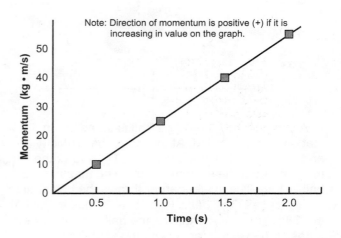

6. What is the momentum of the object at 1 second?

   A. +2.5 kg • m/s
   B. +25 kg • m/s
   C. −2.5 kg • m/s
   D. −25 kg • m/s

7. What is the velocity of the object at 0.5 seconds?

   A. +12.5 m/s
   B. +10.0 m/s
   C. +6.0 m/s
   D. +4.0 m/s

8. What does the line in the graph represent?

   A. impulse
   B. force
   C. momentum
   D. time

DIRECTIONS: Study the information and diagram, read each question, and choose the **best** answer.

MOMENTUM AND THE THIRD LAW OF MOTION

Although conservation of momentum is implied by all three laws of motion, it is perhaps best represented by the third law of motion: any time two objects exert a force on each other, the forces are equal in magnitude and opposite in direction. Does that mean nothing happens? Consider the example below.

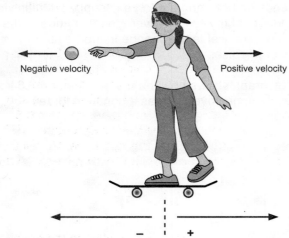

A skateboarder holding a ball is standing on a stationary skateboard. At this point, her velocity and that of the ball are both zero. Therefore, the momentum of the system is zero. The mass of the ball is 1 kg. The skateboarder throws the ball straight out to the left. The ball's velocity is 20 m/s to the left, or −20 m/s. After she throws the ball, the combined mass of the skateboarder and the skateboard is 40 kg. By using the equation for momentum, $p = mv$, and ignoring the effect of friction, you can make determinations about the system.

9. What is the total momentum of this system after the ball has been thrown?

   A. +20 kg • m/s
   B. −20 kg • m/s
   C. 0
   D. −25 kg • m/s

10. What is the momentum of the skateboarder and skateboard as the ball is moving?

    A. 0 kg • m/s
    B. −5 kg • m/s
    C. −10 kg • m/s
    D. +20 kg • m/s

11. What is the velocity of the skateboarder and skateboard as the ball is moving?

    A. +0.5 m/s
    B. −0.5 m/s
    C. +20 m/s
    D. −20 m/s

DIRECTIONS: Study the information and diagram, read each question, and choose the **best** answer.

LAWS OF MOTION AT WORK

The diagram shows a roller conveyer used in a shipping facility. The conveyer is virtually frictionless, making it easier to move heavy packages from place to place. Package A was sitting stationary on the conveyer when someone put Package B on the conveyer and gave it a strong push. Package B soon ran into Package A. After the collision, the packages had a total combined mass of 10 kg. Recall that the equation that determines momentum is $p = mv$, where p is momentum, m is mass, and v is velocity.

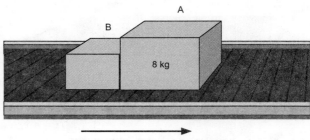

Velocity after collision: +2.5 m/s

12. What is the mass of Package B?

    A. 10 kg
    B. 2 kg
    C. 16 kg
    D. 30 kg

13. What was the velocity of Package B as it moved toward Package A?

    A. +2.5 m/s
    B. +0 m/s
    C. +25 m/s
    D. +12.5 m/s

DIRECTIONS: Study the information and diagram, read each question, and choose the **best** answer.

MOTORCYCLE PHYSICS

Average force can be calculated by multiplying the mass of an object by its change in velocity and dividing that result by the time interval during which the force took place. In the case of collisions, the change in velocity is the difference between an object's velocity when it is in motion and its velocity when it is stopped by the collision ($v - 0$), and the time interval is the amount of time it took the object to stop completely after the collision. Therefore, the following equation can be used to find the average force acting on an object in a collision:

$$F_{average} = \frac{mv}{t}$$

In the diagram of a motorcycle crash test shown below, a 247 kg motorcycle with rider is moving at a velocity of 21 m/s.

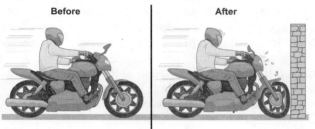

Before | After

v = 21 m/s; m = 247 kg

14. What is the momentum of the moving motorcycle?

   A. +21 kg • m/s
   B. +210 kg • m/s
   C. +51,870 kg • m/s
   D. +5,187 kg • m/s

15. If the motorcycle crashes into a wall and stops over a time interval of 0.05 seconds, what is the average force acting on the motorcycle?

   A. 5,187 N
   B. 10,374 N
   C. 103,740 N
   D. 51,870 N

16. While the 247 kg motorcycle is moving, a motorcycle with a mass of 105 kg is following it, at a velocity of 50 m/s. How does its momentum compare with that of the larger motorcycle?

   A. It is slightly greater.
   B. It is about two times greater.
   C. It is the same.
   D. It is slightly less.

DIRECTIONS: Read the passage. Then read each question, and choose the **best** answer.

SEAT BELTS IN ACTION

The effect of using a seat belt can be calculated from Newton's second law: $F = ma$. When a car traveling at 90 kilometers per hour (km/hr), or 25 m/s, comes to a sudden stop, even though the car has stopped moving forward, the driver is still moving forward at 90 km/hr. Unless restrained by a seat belt, an airbag, or both, the driver is likely to be killed or seriously injured by colliding with the inside of the car—mainly the windshield.

Consider a car that has collided with a barrier and come to a sudden stop. The velocity of the car just before impact was 25 m/s. The mass of the driver is 60 kg. The airbag deploys, and the seat belt and airbag stop the driver's forward momentum in 0.5 seconds. The change in the car's momentum can be expressed as the car's average force. Recall that the average force of an object is determined with this formula:

$$F_{average} = \frac{mv}{t}$$

17. What is the average force applied to the driver by the seat belt and airbag?

   A. 3,000 N
   B. 4,500 N
   C. 5,400 N
   D. 10,800 N

18. If the driver had not been wearing a seat belt and there had not been an airbag, the windshield would have stopped the driver's forward momentum in 0.002 seconds. What average force would the windshield have exerted on the driver?

   A. 75,000 N
   B. 108,000 N
   C. 750,000 N
   D. 2,700,000 N

19. Why would the force of the collision have been so much greater without the seat belt and airbag?

   A. The force would have been applied over a longer period of time.
   B. The force would have been applied over a shorter period of time.
   C. The driver would have traveled less distance before stopping.
   D. The driver would have hit a smaller surface.

Access Prior Knowledge

Use with **Student Book** pp. 58–59

SCIENCE CONTENT TOPIC: P.b.3
SCIENCE PRACTICES: SP.1.a, SP.1.b, SP.1.c, SP.3.b, SP.7.b, SP.8.b

1 *Review the Skill*

Think of all the topics you know something about. For example, you might know about dog breeds or routine car maintenance. You acquire knowledge through formal learning experiences and everyday events. Everything you already know about a topic is called **prior knowledge**.

Prior knowledge is very useful when you are learning something new. When you **access prior knowledge**, learning gets easier because you are adding to what you already know.

2 *Refine the Skill*

By refining the skill of accessing prior knowledge, you will improve your study and test-taking abilities, especially as they relate to the GED® Science Test. Study the information and diagram below. Then answer the questions that follow.

WORK AND LEVERS

Work is done when a force moves an object. The amount of work done is a product of the size (magnitude) of the force multiplied by the distance over which the force is applied. Simple machines make work easier by reducing the size or changing the direction of the force needed to move an object. One type of simple machine is a lever. A lever is a rigid bar that moves about a fulcrum, or pivot point. The object to be moved by a lever is called the load or resistance. With one type of lever, the force is applied to one end, the load is at the other end, and the fulcrum is between the force and the load. The illustration shows how a claw hammer can be used as this type of lever.

a To access prior knowledge, think broadly. If you lack experience with hammers, consider other devices that move about a fulrum to do work. Examples are seesaws, crowbars, and bottle openers.

b Access prior knowledge to grasp terms. Think about using levers with which you are familiar. Visualize where the force is applied and where the load and fulcrum are located for each lever.

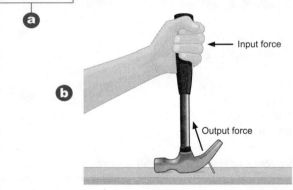

a

b

Input force

Output force

1. When a claw hammer is used to pull a nail from a board, the load is

   A. the hand.
   B. the handle of the hammer.
   C. the claw of the hammer.
   D. the nail.

2. Holding the end of a hammer's handle makes work easier. Why?

   A. The hammer moves more swiftly about the fulcrum.
   B. The distance from the fulcrum to the load is lengthened.
   C. Less force is needed because the force is applied over a greater distance
   D. The direction of the force is not changed.

USING LOGIC

Think about what you know as you read the answer choices for a test question. If prior knowledge tells you that an answer choice does not make sense, you can eliminate it as a possible correct answer.

UNIT 2

DIRECTIONS: Read the passage and question, and choose the **best** answer.

WORK AND POWER

Work and power are values related to the forces required to move objects. Work is done when a force moves an object. Expressed in joules(J), the amount of work done is calculated by multiplying the size of the force by the distance over which the force is applied. Power is the rate at which work is done. Power is expressed in watts(W) and is calculated by dividing the amount of work done by the time used to do the work.

3. Machine A does 8,000(J) of work in 10 seconds, and Machine B does 16,000(J) of work in 5 seconds. Which statement describes the power exerted by the machines?

   A. Each machine exerts less than 800 watts of power.
   B. Machine A exerts less power than Machine B.
   C. Machine A exerts more power than Machine B.
   D. Both machines exert the same amount of power.

DIRECTIONS: Study the information and table, read the question, and choose the **best** answer.

MECHANICAL ADVANTAGE

Machines make work easier. The amount by which a machine makes work easier is the mechanical advantage of that machine. The greater the mechanical advantage, the easier the machine makes doing work. Mechanical advantage is a ratio of the size of the output force to the size of the input force. The table shows input force and output force values in newtons (N) for each of four machines.

Machine	Input Force (N)	Output Force (N)
A	300	900
B	15	150
C	5	10
D	800	1,000

4. Which machine provides the greatest mechanical advantage?

   A. machine A
   B. machine B
   C. machine C
   D. machine D

DIRECTIONS: Study the information and diagram, read each question, and choose the **best** answer.

INCLINED PLANES

An inclined plane is a type of simple machine. It is a flat, sloped surface. A ramp is an example of an inclined plane. Pushing a heavy object up a ramp is easier than picking up the object because less force is needed. However, the force must be applied over a longer distance.

Height = 3 feet

Length = 9 feet

5. Which sentence is an accurate statement about using ramps to move objects?

   A. Pushing objects up shorter ramps is easier than pushing objects up longer ramps.
   B. Ramps should be used to lift lightweight objects.
   C. Ramps can be used to elevate objects that are too heavy to lift.
   D. Pushing an object up a ramp requires less work than lifting the object straight up.

6. What will happen if the length of the ramp shown in the diagram is shortened by two feet?

   A. More force will be needed to move the box up the ramp.
   B. Less force will be needed to move the box up the ramp.
   C. More work will be done when the box is moved.
   D. Less work will be done when the box is moved.

7. Which common household object is **most likely** to be used as an inclined plane?

   A. a claw hammer
   B. a garden spade
   C. a ladder
   D. a rolling pin

DIRECTIONS: Study the information, table, and illustration. Then read each question, and choose the **best** answer.

ADVANTAGES OF USING PULLEYS

A pulley is a simple machine typically used to lift objects. A pulley has two main parts—a rope and a grooved wheel. The rope fits into the groove of the wheel. Using a pulley may change the direction or amount of applied force required to move an object. The table below shows the advantages of the three main types of pulleys. A block-and-tackle pulley contains at least one fixed pulley and one movable pulley, as the illustration shows.

Type of Pulley	Change in Direction of Force	Change in Size of Force
Single, fixed	Yes	No
Movable	No	Yes
Block-and-tackle	Yes	Yes

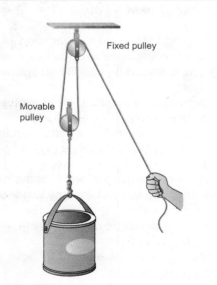

Fixed pulley

Movable pulley

8. Pulleys do not change the amount of work that is done. Which statement explains why?

A. The size of the force needed to move the object is smaller, but the distance is greater.
B. Pulleys fail to cause a change in the size or direction of the force used to move the object.
C. The size of the force required to move an object is always greater when a pulley is used.
D. The time it takes to do the work is longer when a pulley is used to move an object.

9. Which statement describes a benefit of using pulleys?

A. They always decrease the size of the applied force.
B. Block-and-tackle pulleys can be combined to make movable pulleys.
C. They never change the direction of the applied force.
D. Some pulleys allow you to use your own weight to pull an object upward.

DIRECTIONS: Study the information and diagram, read the question, and choose the **best** answer.

SCREWDRIVERS

Screwdrivers make it easier to drive in screws. A screwdriver is a type of simple machine known as a wheel and axle. The axle is a bar that goes through the center of the wheel. Because the wheel has a larger radius than the axle, it moves a greater distance than the axle. A small force applied to the wheel becomes a larger force applied to the axle.

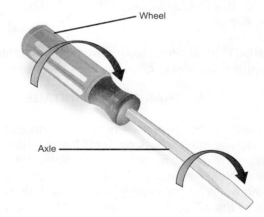

Wheel

Axle

10. Which statement describes how wheels and axles operate as simple machines?

A. They increase the size of the force needed to rotate an object.
B. They change the direction of the force needed to do work.
C. They reduce the distance needed to do the work.
D. They are helpful when a force is required to rotate an object.

DIRECTIONS: Study the diagram, read the question, and choose the **best** answer.

DOING WORK

A ◄——— Length = 5 meters ———► B

11. Suppose the person shown in the diagram uses 5 newtons of force to move the box from Point A to Point B. How much work is done?

   A. 25 joules
   B. 25 meters
   C. 5 newtons
   D. 5 joules

DIRECTIONS: Study the table, read each question, and choose the **best** answer.

MECHANICAL ADVANTAGE OF DIFFERENT MACHINES

Machine	Mechanical Advantage
Wedge A	1.5
Wedge B	5.0
Pulley	3.0
Ramp	2.5

12. What does the information in the table suggest?

   A. All simple machines have a mechanical advantage of at least 1.5.
   B. All the machines listed in the table make doing work easier.
   C. Pulleys always make work easier than wedges.
   D. Machines that are not listed in the table do not have a mechanical advantage.

13. If an input force of 5 and an output force of 12.5 were used to move an object, which machine was used to do the work?

   A. wedge A
   B. wedge B
   C. the pulley
   D. the ramp

DIRECTIONS: Study the information and illustration, read each question, and choose the **best** answer.

COMPOUND MACHINES

Levers, wedges, inclined planes, pulleys, screws, and wheels and axles are the six types of simple machines. However, most machines are not simple machines. Most machines are compound machines. A compound machine contains two or more simple machines. A bicycle is a compound machine. The illustration shows some simple machines that make up a bicycle.

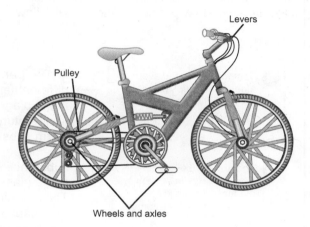

Levers

Pulley

Wheels and axles

14. What are the types of simple machines involved in making a bicycle move forward?

   A. pulleys and wheels and axles
   B. wheels and axles and levers
   C. levers and pulleys
   D. pulleys, levers, and wheels and axles

15. The purpose of the levers shown in the illustration is to make the bicycle

   A. begin moving.
   B. move faster.
   C. move more easily uphill.
   D. stop moving.

16. Based on the information, which object is a compound machine?

   A. a drill bit
   B. a boat ramp
   C. a pair of scissors
   D. a wagon wheel

Link Microscopic and Observable Events

Use with **Student Book** pp. 60–61

SCIENCE CONTENT TOPICS: P.a.1, P.a.3, P.a.5
SCIENCE PRACTICES: SP.1.a, SP.1.b, SP.1.c, SP.3.b, SP.3.c, SP.4.a, SP.7.a

UNIT 2

① Review the Skill

We use our senses to perceive what is happening around us, but many of those events are caused by other events that we cannot observe directly. For example, energy transfer is the observable, or macroscopic, result of movement of the microscopic particles that make up matter. **Linking microscopic and observable events** allows you to understand how events that cannot be perceived directly relate to those that can.

② Refine the Skill

By refining the skill of linking microscopic and observable events, you will improve your study and test-taking abilities, especially as they relate to the GED® Science Test. Study the information and diagram below. Then answer the questions that follow.

HOW A THERMOMETER WORKS

ⓐ Temperature is the average kinetic energy of all the particles that make up a substance.

ⓑ The greater the average kinetic energy in the liquid, the more the liquid rises in the tube of the thermometer.

The transfer of energy by conduction occurs when substances of different temperatures come into contact with each other. As shown in the diagram, a thermometer uses this phenomenon to measure temperature. When a glass thermometer comes into contact with a warm substance, the rapidly moving particles of the substance cause the particles in the glass to vibrate faster. The vibrating glass particles then cause the particles in the thermometer's liquid to move faster. The glass and the liquid expand as the distance between their particles increases to allow more movement. The expanding liquid moves up the glass tube until the substance and the thermometer reach the same temperature, or establish a thermal equilibrium.

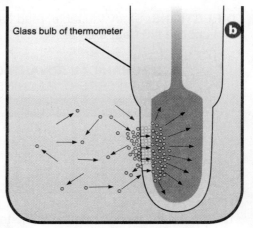

Glass bulb of thermometer

ⓑ

USING LOGIC

Read carefully the process explained in the passage. Understanding it will allow you to make predictions based on the conditions presented in the questions. Then compare your predictions to the answer choices.

1. When a thermometer is placed in a substance that is cooler than it is, the average kinetic energy of the substance

    A. decreases until equilibrium is reached.
    B. decreases and then increases.
    C. increases until equilibrium is reached.
    D. increases and then decreases.

2. When a thermometer is placed in a substance that is cooler than it is, the average kinetic energy of the thermometer

    A. decreases until equilibrium is reached.
    B. decreases and then increases.
    C. increases until equilibrium is reached.
    D. increases and then decreases.

DIRECTIONS: Study the information and diagram, read the question, and choose the **best** answer.

KINETIC ENERGY AT WORK

An increase in thermal energy causes matter to expand. That expansion is a macroscopic effect of a microscopic event. That is, the particles in matter moving faster and farther apart as the matter expands is a microscopic event. The effect of this microscopic event—expansion of matter—is macroscopic because it can be observed.

This expansion is more apparent in a gas than in a solid because particles are not as free to move in a solid. Thermal expansion is one way that kinetic energy can be used to do work. The diagram illustrates this process.

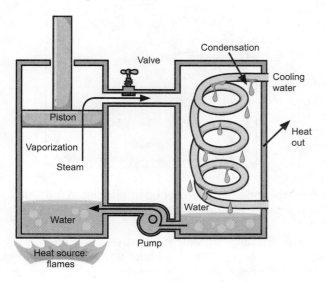

3. Which action is the microscopic event that allows the heat engine in the diagram to do work?

   A. the upward and downward movement of the piston
   B. the expansion of the water as its particles gain kinetic energy
   C. the transfer of thermal energy from the flames to the water
   D. the changing of the steam back into water by the cooling coil

DIRECTIONS: Study the information and illustration, read the question, and choose the **best** answer.

THERMAL ENERGY IN A GAS

Adding energy to a gas enclosed in a cylinder will cause the gas to expand as the gas particles move faster and push one another farther apart. This principle can be used to do work, as when an expanding gas is used to apply force to the piston depicted in the illustration below. When the gas pushes against the piston, moving the piston upward, the gas loses energy, and its temperature decreases.

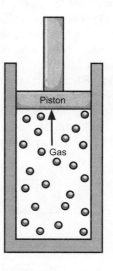

4. What would happen to the gas in the illustration if the piston were suddenly forced downward?

   A. The force of the piston would slow down the movements of the gas particles. As a result, the thermal energy of the gas would decrease and the gas would cool down.
   B. The rapidly moving particles of the gas would resist the piston's downward movement. As a result, the volume of the gas would be less, but its thermal energy would stay the same.
   C. As the piston moved downward, more and more gas particles would collide with it, cooling the piston. Eventually the piston's thermal energy and that of the gas would decrease.
   D. As the piston forced the gas particles into a smaller space, they would collide with one another more often, which would make them move even faster. This would cause a rapid increase in the temperature of the gas.

DIRECTIONS: Study the information and diagram, read the question, and choose the **best** answer.

DIRECTIONS: Study the information and diagram, read the question, and choose the **best** answer.

COMPARING HEAT TRANSFER

The particles that make up matter are always in motion. Although that motion occurs at the microscopic level, its effect can be observed at the macroscopic level as thermal energy. Heat is the transfer of thermal energy from warmer to cooler areas, objects, and systems naturally by three means. Convection occurs in gases and liquids as currents of less dense, warmer particles exchange places with currents of denser, cooler particles until the substance reaches thermal equilibrium. Conduction occurs when objects of different temperatures come into contact with each other and moving particles of one object cause increased movement of particles in the other object. Radiation occurs when energy is carried away from a source and to another object or system by electromagnetic waves. Unlike conduction and convection, radiation can occur across empty space, without having to travel through matter.

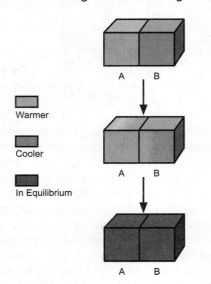

5. How is heat being transferred between the two solid objects in the diagram?

   A. Conduction is transferring thermal energy from the warm object to the cold object.
   B. Radiation between the two objects is moving heat from the warm object to the cold object.
   C. Convection currents are moving heat from warmer areas to colder areas within each object.
   D. The fastest-moving particles are moving from one object to the other.

COOKING ON A GRILL

Most people who use grills never think about how their food is cooked. In a cooking grill, energy is transferred between solids by conduction and within a gas (air) by convection. Radiation, or the transfer of thermal energy by electromagnetic waves, also plays a role. When electromagnetic waves strike an object, they cause the particles in the object to vibrate rapidly. This increases the kinetic energy and, thus, the temperature of the object. Dark, dull, or rough surfaces absorb more radiant energy than light-colored, smooth, or polished surfaces, which tend to reflect the radiation rather than absorb it.

6. How does food wrapped in aluminum foil, such as a potato in the diagram, cook on a grill?

   A. Electromagnetic waves penetrate the surface of the aluminum and cook the potato. Conduction and convection play a minor role.
   B. Electromagnetic waves are mostly reflected by the aluminum. The potato cooks by conduction where the aluminum touches the grill and the potato and convection from the currents that develop around it.
   C. Electromagnetic waves warm the aluminum. The aluminum then cooks the potato by conduction. Convection plays a minor role.
   D. Electromagnetic waves are mostly reflected by the aluminum. Thermal energy is transferred by convection from the potato to the aluminum and from the aluminum to its surroundings.

DIRECTIONS: Study the information and illustration, read the question, and choose the **best** answer.

HEAT TRANSFER IN A MUG

Heat is the transfer of energy from warmer areas to cooler areas by three different means: conduction, convection, and radiation. Energy transfer by conduction occurs in solid matter as rapidly vibrating warmer particles agitate adjacent particles, causing them to vibrate faster, too. Convection is energy transfer through a gas or liquid by currents that carry warmer particles to cooler areas. Radiation transfers energy through air or space by means of electromagnetic waves. The illustration shows how energy from hot coffee can be transferred to the coffee mug and to the air.

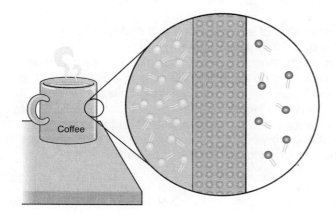

7. Which description explains how thermal energy is being transferred by conduction, convection, and radiation?

   A. by conduction via currents in the coffee; by convection through the solid material in the mug; by radiation from the inside surface of the mug
   B. by conduction via currents in the coffee; by convection from the inside surface of the mug; by radiation from the outside surface of the mug
   C. by conduction through the solid material of the mug; by convection via currents in the coffee; by radiation from the inside surface of the mug
   D. by conduction through the solid material of the mug; by convection via currents in the coffee; by radiation from the outside surface of the mug

DIRECTIONS: Study the information and diagram, read the question, and choose the **best** answer.

ENERGY TRANSFER ON EARTH

Energy flows from warmer to cooler objects and systems by conduction, convection, or radiation. The diagram helps explain how all three means of transferring thermal energy are at work in Earth's atmosphere.

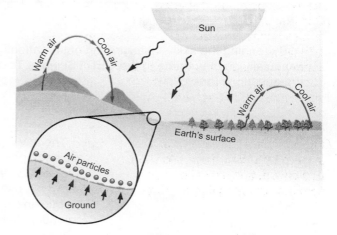

8. Four people have provided explanations for how thermal energy is transferred in Earth's atmosphere. Evaluate the explanations, and choose the correct one.

   A. Explanation 1: Radiation from the sun warms air molecules, which warm Earth's surface by conduction. Energy from Earth's surface then causes convection currents.
   B. Explanation 2: Air molecules conduct radiation from the sun to Earth's surface. Earth's surface then transfers energy to the atmosphere by radiation. This energy causes convection currents.
   C. Explanation 3: The sun transfers thermal energy by conduction to air molecules and by radiation to molecules near Earth's surface. This energy then causes convection currents.
   D. Explanation 4: Radiation from the sun warms Earth's surface, which warms air molecules at the surface by conduction. The warm air rises and causes convection currents.

Interpret Observations

SCIENCE CONTENT TOPICS: P.a.2, P.a.3
SCIENCE PRACTICES: SP.1.a, SP.1.b, SP.1.c, SP.3.a, SP.3.b, SP.7.a

① Review the Skill

An **observation** is something perceived directly with the body's senses. Science is based on careful observations. A scientific observation is a more disciplined perception than a casual observation. A scientific observation may involve taking measurements, and it certainly involves recording and documenting what is observed.

Interpreting an observation is a means of explaining what has been observed. As you learn about science, you have opportunities to interpret observations that you make or read about in presentations of scientific information.

② Refine the Skill

By refining the skill of interpreting observations, you will improve your study and test-taking abilities, especially as they relate to the GED® Science Test. Study the information and graph below. Then answer the questions that follow.

LAW OF CONSERVATION OF ENERGY

a Read the passage before trying to interpret the graph. The text may provide information about data contained in the graph. The text here tells you how the two data sets are related.

The law of conservation of energy states that energy cannot be created or destroyed. It can only change form. Energy changes from potential to kinetic energy and vice versa. Potential energy is stored energy. A ball that is sitting on the edge of a desk has potential energy. Kinetic energy is the energy of motion. As the ball falls off the desk, its potential energy changes to kinetic energy. <u>The total amount of energy is always equal to the sum of the potential energy and the kinetic energy.</u> The graph below shows how energy, measured in joules (J), changes in a model rocket that is launched and then falls to Earth.

b Graphs, which can aid in interpreting observations, do not always contain legends or keys. This graph identifies the data sets next to the lines. Bar graphs may identify the data sets in the bars.

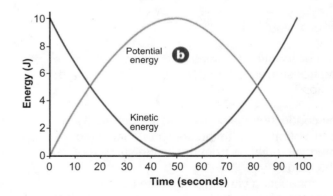

1. Which statement describes the total energy of the rocket?

   A. It always equals twice the kinetic energy.
   B. It decreases and then increases again.
   C. It is equal to 10 J.
   D. It is equal to 0 J.

2. What happens to the rocket's kinetic energy at 50 seconds?

   A. It is at maximum.
   B. It is greater than the total amount of energy.
   C. It is equal to the amount of potential energy.
   D. It has transformed completely into potential energy.

USING LOGIC

Questions based on data in graphs often require you to interpret the trends shown in the graphs. In multi-line graphs, it is helpful to look at the trend of each individual data set before comparing them.

DIRECTIONS: Study the information and graph, read each question, and choose the **best** answer.

TOY CAR INVESTIGATION

A group of students tests the law of conservation of energy by measuring the potential energy and kinetic energy of a toy car rolling down a ramp. The graph shows the results of their investigation. At the top of the ramp, the car has only potential energy. The potential energy transforms to kinetic energy as the car rolls down the ramp. At the bottom of the ramp, all the potential energy should be transformeded into kinetic energy. However, forces such as friction transform some energy into thermal energy.

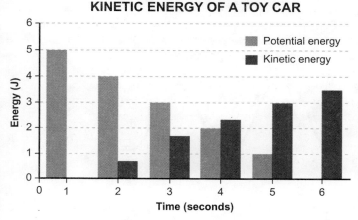

POTENTIAL ENERGY AND
KINETIC ENERGY OF A TOY CAR

3. What interpretation can be made about the potential energy and kinetic energy of the toy car?

   A. The toy car's potential energy at the top of the ramp equals its kinetic energy at the bottom of the ramp.
   B. As the toy car's potential energy decreases, its kinetic energy increases.
   C. The students proved that sometimes a system's energy is not conserved.
   D. The car had more energy at the end of the ramp than it did at the top of the ramp.

4. What conclusion can be drawn about the investigation?

   A. About 1.5 J of energy changed into thermal energy during the investigation.
   B. About 1.5 J of energy were destroyed during the investigation.
   C. The students did not measure the kinetic energy correctly.
   D. The car had a total energy of about 8.5 J.

DIRECTIONS: Study the information and graph, read each question, and choose the **best** answer.

RECHARGEABLE VERSUS NON-RECHARGEABLE BATTERIES

Batteries contain stored chemical energy. The chemical energy in batteries changes to electrical energy when a battery-powered device is turned on. When rechargeable batteries are recharged, electrical energy is changed back into chemical energy. The voltage of a battery is a measure of the potential energy stored in the battery.

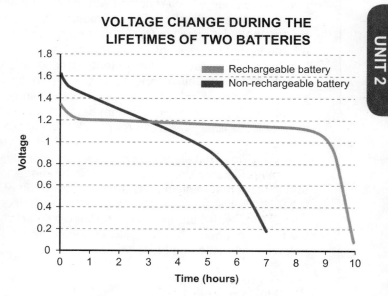

VOLTAGE CHANGE DURING THE
LIFETIMES OF TWO BATTERIES

5. The graph supports the interpretation that the non-rechargeable battery has more potential energy when the batteries are new by showing that its voltage

   A. decreases more rapidly.
   B. reaches 0.2 first.
   C. is greater at zero hours.
   D. is greater after two hours.

6. What interpretation can be made about the rechargeable battery?

   A. Its voltage after five hours is about the same as its voltage after one hour.
   B. It always has more voltage than the non-rechargeable battery.
   C. The change in voltage is relatively constant during the 10-hour period.
   D. It does not last as long as the non-rechargeable battery.

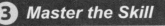

★ Spotlighted Item: HOT SPOT

DIRECTIONS: Read the passage. Then read each question, and answer by marking the appropriate hot spot or hot spots.

PHYSICS OF ROLLER COASTERS

Mechanical energy is the energy a mechanical system or machine has because of its motion or its position. So, it is the sum of the system's potential and kinetic energy. Any machine with mechanical energy is able to do work. That is, mechanical energy makes it possible for the system to apply a force to and move an object or another system. In most mechanical systems, potential and kinetic energy are continually changing from one into the other. In an "ideal" machine, this process would go on forever, but in reality it does not because the system loses energy to friction.

An example that illustrates mechanical energy is a roller coaster. The observation can be made that a chain mechanism pulls the cars to the top of the first hill, and then the only force working on the cars is gravity. As the roller coaster moves over the track, its energy is constantly changing from potential to kinetic and back again.

7. On the diagram below, mark an X on the point or points where potential energy is the greatest on the roller coaster.

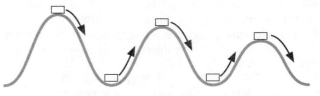

8. On the diagram below, mark an X on the point or points where energy is beginning to change from kinetic to potential.

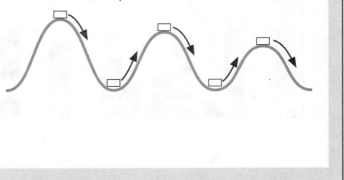

DIRECTIONS: Read the passage. Then read each question, and choose the **best** answer.

CHEMICAL BONDS

Chemical energy is energy stored in the bonds formed between atoms and molecules. It takes energy to form the bonds, but it also takes energy to break them apart; otherwise, no stable molecules would exist.

All chemical reactions need energy to make atoms go from one molecular configuration to another. In some reactions, the products contain more energy than the reactants. This type of reaction is endothermic. The reaction, in effect, absorbs energy from the environment to form the product. Sometimes, however, a chemical reaction results in a product that has less energy than the reactants, indicating that energy was released into the surroundings during the reaction. This type of reaction is exothermic. Combustion is a type of exothermic reaction that produces light and heat.

Hot or cold packs used to reduce swelling exemplify endothermic and exothermic reactions. The pouch of the hot or cold pack contains a dry chemical and an inner pouch of water. A reaction is started when the seal on the pouch of water is broken, mixing the water with the chemical.

9. What kind of reaction makes a cold pack feel cold?

A. energetic
B. endothermic
C. combustion
D. exothermic

10. What kind of reaction makes a hot pack feel hot?

A. energetic
B. endothermic
C. combustion
D. exothermic

DIRECTIONS: Study the information and graph, read each question, and choose the **best** answer.

CHEMICAL REACTIONS

Some chemical reactions produce energy, and others absorb it. An exothermic chemical reaction produces thermal energy. For example, when a match burns, chemical energy changes to thermal energy. An endothermic chemical reaction absorbs thermal energy. Often this thermal energy comes from the surroundings. For example, when citric acid and baking soda react, energy is absorbed from the surroundings to drive the reaction. Thermal energy changes to chemical energy.

ENERGY DURING A CHEMICAL REACTION

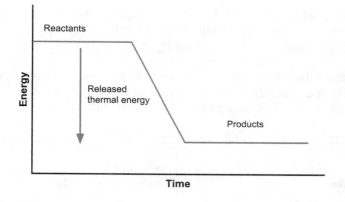

11. The graph shows how the energy of a reaction system changed over time. What interpretation of the data explains why this is an exothermic reaction?

    A. The reactants had more energy than the products have.
    B. The products have more energy than the reactants had.
    C. The reactants and products gained energy during the reaction.
    D. The reactants and products lost energy during the reaction.

12. If a student put his hand around a beaker containing citric acid and baking soda, the solution would feel cold. Why?

    A. Energy is going into his hand.
    B. The solution is generating an electrical charge.
    C. Liquids are always cooler than their surroundings.
    D. Energy is being drawn from his hand.

DIRECTIONS: Read the passage. Then read each question, and choose the **best** answer.

PHOTOSYNTHESIS

Plants make their own food through a process called photosynthesis. This process changes one form of energy—light—to another form of energy—chemical energy. The energy from sunlight is used in the leaves of a plant to combine carbon dioxide and water to produce sugar and oxygen. The plant stores the sugar in its tissues and releases oxygen into the air as a waste product. The reaction can be written as:

$$6CO_2 + 6H_2O \text{ (+ light energy)} \rightarrow C_6H_{12}O_6 + 6O_2$$

When another organism eats the plant, the organism's cells convert chemical energy stored in the plant's sugar to mechanical energy (used for motion) and thermal energy (used for other life processes). The conversion of chemical energy to other usable forms of energy in an organism's cells is called respiration. The reaction can be written as:

$$C_6H_{12}O_6 + 6O_2 \rightarrow 6CO_2 + 6H_2O + \text{mechanical and thermal energy}$$

13. What interpretation can be made about photosynthesis and respiration?

    A. Photosynthesis is exothermic, and respiration is endothermic.
    B. Photosynthesis is endothermic, and respiration is exothermic.
    C. Both photosynthesis and respiration are endothermic.
    D. Both photosynthesis and respiration are exothermic.

14. While changing energy from one form to another, both photosynthesis and respiration reactions yield waste products. A waste product is something that a cell releases instead of using. What are the waste products of respiration?

    A. carbon dioxide and water
    B. carbon dioxide, water, and energy
    C. carbon dioxide, oxygen, and energy
    D. carbon dioxide and oxygen

Link Content from Varied Formats

Use with *Student Book* pp. 64–65

SCIENCE CONTENT TOPIC: P.a.5
SCIENCE PRACTICES: SP.1.a, SP.1.b, SP.1.c, SP.3.b, SP.7.a

UNIT 2

1 Review the Skill

Knowing how to **link content from varied formats** will help you gain a complete understanding of the information presented. When elements such as text, illustrations, graphs, or diagrams are presented together, they may contain different but related information.

2 Refine the Skill

By refining the skill of linking content from varied formats, you will improve your study and test-taking abilities, especially as they relate to the GED® Science Test. Study the information and diagram below. Then answer the questions that follow.

THE ELECTROMAGNETIC SPECTRUM

a Text may give you information that is not in a graphic. In this case, the text tells you what the diagram includes. →

Electromagnetic(EM) waves differ from other types of waves because they can travel through empty space. <u>The diagram shows the electromagnetic spectrum, which is made up of every type of electromagnetic wave.</u> These types of waves have different properties because they have different amounts of energy. Amount of energy in the EM spectrum depends on wavelength. EM waves with longer wavelengths have less energy than EM waves with shorter wavelengths.

b The diagram has information not found in the text: the different types of waves in the electromagnetic spectrum and their wavelengths.

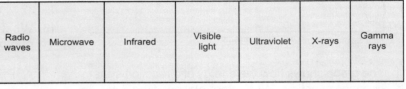

Radio waves	Microwave	Infrared	Visible light	Ultraviolet	X-rays	Gamma rays

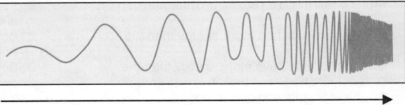

Decreasing wavelength

1. Which electromagnetic waves have the most energy?

   A. gamma rays
   B. radio waves
   C. microwaves
   D. visible waves

2. Which conclusion is supported by the information presented?

   A. Radio waves cannot travel through empty space.
   B. Visible light is not part of the electromagnetic spectrum.
   C. Sound waves are electromagnetic waves.
   D. Microwaves have less energy than infrared waves.

TEST-TAKING TIPS

For a multiple-choice question that involves text and a graphic, check to make sure that your answer choice is supported by both the text and the graphic.

DIRECTIONS: Study the information and diagram, read each question, and choose the **best** answer.

SOUND AND LIGHT WAVES

When waves pass through a substance, they cause the particles in the substance to vibrate. Waves are classified by the direction in which they make the particles vibrate. The diagram shows the two main types of waves.

A longitudinal wave causes particles to vibrate in the direction that the wave moves. A transverse wave causes particles to vibrate perpendicular to the direction of the wave. A longitudinal wave is similar to a spring that is vibrating back and forth. Shaking a rope up and down can make a transverse wave in the rope.

Sound waves are longitudinal, and light waves are transverse. Longitudinal waves are made up of a repeating pattern of areas where the particles are compressed together and areas where they are spread out. Transverse waves are made up of a repeating pattern of high and low points.

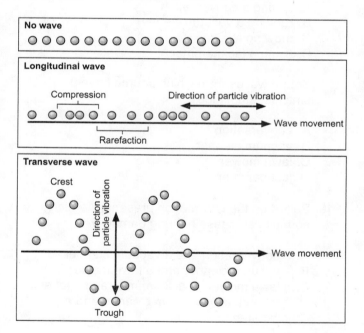

3. Which statement is supported by the information presented?

   A. Rarefactions are found only in transverse waves.
   B. Compressions are the areas in longitudinal waves where particles are farthest apart.
   C. The vibrating particles in light waves form compressions and rarefactions.
   D. Light waves can be characterized by their crests and troughs.

4. When a speaker produces a sound wave, what happens to the particles in air as the sound wave passes through that air?

   A. Crests and compressions are formed in the air.
   B. Where they are pressed together, the particles in the air form troughs.
   C. The particles move back and forth perpendicular to the wave's direction.
   D. The particles move back and forth in the same direction that the wave is moving.

5. The shaking felt during an earthquake is the result of movements within Earth's crust. These movements cause waves known as S and P waves. P waves shake the ground back and forth in a direction that is parallel to the direction of the wave. What type of waves are P waves?

   A. longitudinal waves, because they form compressions and rarefactions
   B. transverse waves, because they form compressions and rarefactions
   C. longitudinal waves, because they form crests and troughs
   D. transverse waves, because they form crests and troughs

DIRECTIONS: Study the information and diagram, read each question, and choose the **best** answer.

SURFACE WAVES

Surface waves move along the boundary between two different substances. Water waves are surface waves that move at the boundary between water and air. Earthquakes also produce surface waves, known as Rayleigh waves, that travel along the boundary between Earth's surface and air. Surface waves have both transverse and longitudinal characteristics. The diagram shows how a Rayleigh wave causes Earth's crust, or outermost layer, to move.

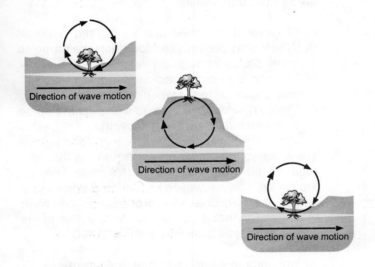

Direction of wave motion

Direction of wave motion

Direction of wave motion

6. Water waves affect objects floating in the water in a way similar to how Rayleigh waves affect objects on Earth's surface. What **most likely** would happen to a leaf floating on a lake if a chain of water waves were to pass it?

   A. It would move away from the shore.
   B. It would move up and down in a circular path.
   C. It would move parallel to the shore.
   D. It would move side to side in straight lines.

7. Why does the Rayleigh wave demonstrated by the diagram affect the tree?

   A. It travels along the boundary between Earth's crust and air.
   B. It moves in two directions at once.
   C. It travels deep beneath Earth's surface.
   D. It moves along the boundary between water and air.

DIRECTIONS: Study the information and table, read each question, and choose the **best** answer.

VOLUME OF SOUND

The volume of sound is related to wave amplitude. The larger the amplitude, the greater the volume. Volume is measured in decibels (dB). A higher decibel level means a louder sound. Hearing damage can result from sounds beginning at a level of about 85 dB. The table lists the decibel levels of some sounds.

Sound	Decibel Level (dB)
Conversation	50–65
Vacuum cleaner	70
Lawn mower	85–90
Jackhammer	110
Jet engine	140

8. Which action makes the loudest noise?

   A. having a conversation
   B. running a vacuum cleaner
   C. mowing a lawn
   D. using a jackhammer

9. Sound waves from which source have the smallest amplitude?

   A. conversation
   B. vacuum cleaner
   C. lawn mower
   D. jackhammer

10. Based on the information presented, which sounds can cause hearing damage?

   A. a conversation and a vacuum cleaner
   B. a vacuum cleaner and a lawn mower
   C. a lawn mower, a jackhammer, and a jet engine
   D. a jet engine, a vacuum cleaner, and a jackhammer

DIRECTIONS: Study the information and diagram, read each question, and choose the **best** answer.

VISIBLE LIGHT

The waves in the electromagnetic spectrum have a large range of frequencies and wavelengths, but humans can see only a small portion of the spectrum. The part of the spectrum that humans can see is visible light. The diagram shows the visible light portion of the electromagnetic spectrum. The main colors in the visible light spectrum are red, orange, yellow, green, blue, and violet.

In a vacuum, all electromagnetic waves travel at the speed of light. However, the waves in the electromagnetic spectrum have different frequencies and wavelengths. Frequency, measured in Hertz (Hz or s^{-1}), and wavelength, measured in nanometers (nm), are related to speed. Because the speed of all light waves is the same, waves with higher frequencies have shorter wavelengths. Wavelength and frequency are also related to energy. Waves with higher frequencies and shorter wavelengths have more energy than waves with lower frequencies and longer wavelengths.

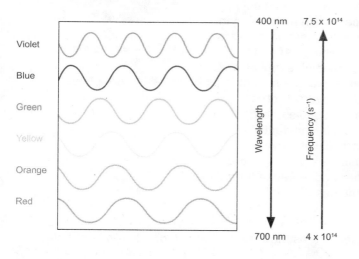

11. A scientist has detected a wave of visible light with a wavelength of approximately 500 nm. What color could this wave be?

    A. violet
    B. green
    C. orange
    D. red

12. Which statement describes blue and orange light?

    A. Blue light has a shorter wavelength and more energy than orange light.
    B. Blue light has a shorter wavelength and less energy than orange light.
    C. Blue light has a shorter wavelength and lower frequency than orange light.
    D. Blue light has a longer wavelength and more energy than orange light.

13. White light, such as the light from the sun, is made up of waves of every color of light. What conclusion about white light is supported by the information presented?

    A. White light travels six times faster than any one color of light.
    B. The wavelengths of the waves that make up white light have a range of 400 nm to 700 nm.
    C. All the waves that make up white light have the same frequency.
    D. White light has a short wavelength and high frequency.

DIRECTIONS: Study the information and table, read the question, and choose the **best** answer.

COMPARING SPEEDS OF SOUNDS

The speed of a wave is equal to its frequency multiplied by its wavelength. The table shows the speed of sound waves in meters per second (m/s) in various substances.

Substance	Speed of Sound Waves (m/s)
Air	330
Water	1,490
Lead	1,320
Rubber	1,600

14. Suppose sound waves traveling in each of the substances listed in the table have the same wavelength. In which substance do the sound waves have the highest frequency?

    A. air
    B. water
    C. lead
    D. rubber

SCIENCE CONTENT TOPIC: P.a.4
SCIENCE PRACTICES: SP.1.a, SP.1.b, SP.1.c, SP.3.a, SP.3.b, SP.5.a, SP.6.c, SP.7.a

1 Review the Skill

When you **draw conclusions from mixed sources**, you interpret the information that you find in graphs, tables, diagrams, and different types of texts. You can use the information to make inferences and to draw conclusions that explain the facts found in all the sources and your interpretations of those facts.

2 Refine the Skill

By refining the skill of drawing conclusions from mixed sources, you will improve your study and test-taking abilities, especially as they relate to the GED® Science Test. Study the information and graph below. Then answer the questions that follow.

a Use details from each source of information when drawing a conclusion. Check to make sure that no fact in either source contradicts the inferences you make to form your conclusion.

ENERGY SOURCE TYPES

There are different types of energy sources. Some energy sources, such as fossil fuels, are nonrenewable. These energy sources take millions of years to form and are limited in supply. There are also renewable energy sources. A renewable energy source takes a fairly short time to restore itself or is in unlimited supply. Biomass sources, such as trees, can be renewed over a timespan of years. Other renewable energy sources are inexhaustible—their supplies are limitless. For example, the moving water that powers hydroelectric plants is an inexhaustible energy source because it is constantly recycled by Earth's water cycle. Other inexhaustible energy sources are the sun and wind because their supplies are endless.

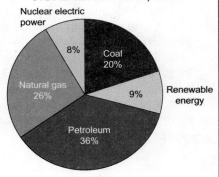

U.S. ENERGY USE, 2011

Nuclear electric power 8%
Coal 20%
Natural gas 26%
Renewable energy 9%
Petroleum 36%

Note: Sum of components may not equal 100 percent due to independent rounding.

Source: U.S. Energy Information Administration

CONTENT PRACTICES

Reasoning to draw conclusions is an important science practice addressed by the GED® Test. Mastering this skill will help you improve your score.

1. In the United States, how much energy comes from hydroelectric plants?

   A. about 5 percent
   B. less than 9 percent
   C. at least 8 percent
   D. more than 10 percent

2. The conclusion can be drawn that the United States

   A. will soon run out of energy resources.
   B. uses more petroleum and natural gas than any other country.
   C. gets half of its energy from renewable sources.
   D. relies mostly on nonrenewable energy sources.

DIRECTIONS: Study the diagrams, read the question, and choose the **best** answer.

HYDROELECTRIC POWER PLANT

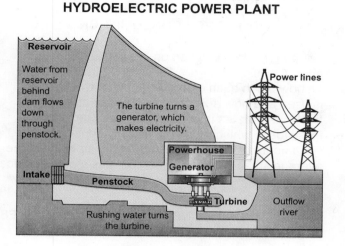

COAL-FIRED POWER PLANT

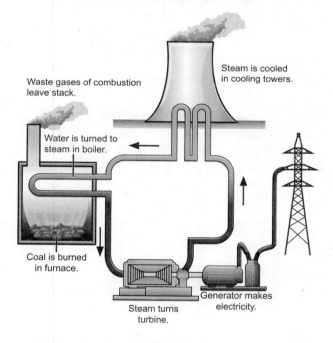

3. What is one advantage of a hydroelectric power plant compared to a coal-fired power plant?

   A. The hydroelectric plant does not use a generator.
   B. The hydroelectric plant is cheaper to maintain.
   C. The hydroelectric plant also runs on wind power.
   D. The hydroelectric plant does not produce air pollution.

DIRECTIONS: Read the passage, and study the diagram. Then read each question, and choose the **best** answer.

ENERGY FROM NUCLEAR FISSION

Nuclear energy is produced by splitting the bonds that hold together the nuclei of atoms. This releases tremendous amounts of energy in a process called nuclear fission. Nuclear power plants use nonrenewable uranium-235 (U-235) as the fuel for fission. The process begins when a neutron splits a U-235 atom. A chain reaction results as an increasing number of neutrons bombard other U-235 atoms. Nuclear plants do not produce the air pollutants that fossil-fuel plants produce. However, they do produce radioactive waste. As of early 2013, there were 65 nuclear power plants in the United States, with 104 nuclear reactors. No new nuclear plants have been built since 1996. However, the first new plant in many years is scheduled to open by 2017.

NUCLEAR FISSION

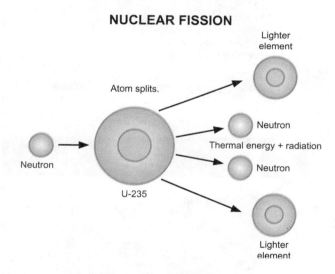

4. What form does energy released by fission take?

   A. thermal energy
   B. neutrons
   C. thermal energy and radiation
   D. neutrons and thermal energy

5. What could prevent nuclear energy from becoming the most important energy source?

   A. The United States will run out of U-235 soon.
   B. Nuclear fission produces neutrons that stop fission reactions eventually.
   C. U-235 is a nonrenewable energy source.
   D. The construction of nuclear power plants in the United States has stopped.

UNIT 2

DIRECTIONS: Read the passage, and study the maps. Then read the question, and choose the **best** answer.

SOLAR POWER

Solar energy systems convert the energy of the sun into forms that we can use. Concentrating solar energy systems harness the sun's energy to produce electricity. Photovoltaic systems use panels of solar cells to convert sunlight directly into electricity.

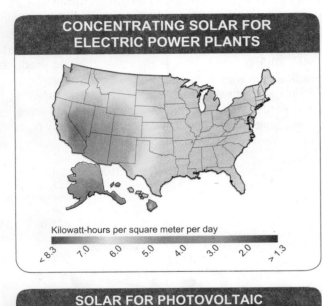

CONCENTRATING SOLAR FOR ELECTRIC POWER PLANTS

Kilowatt-hours per square meter per day

< 8.3   7.0   6.0   5.0   4.0   3.0   2.0   > 1.3

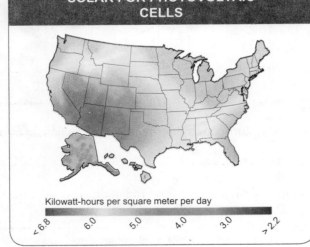

SOLAR FOR PHOTOVOLTAIC CELLS

Kilowatt-hours per square meter per day

< 6.8   6.0   5.0   4.0   3.0   > 2.2

6. Which part of the country is **best** for the use of solar power?

   A. the Northeast
   B. the Southeast
   C. the Northwest
   D. the Southwest

DIRECTIONS: Read the passage, and study the pictograph. Then read the question, and choose the **best** answer.

ENERGY CONSUMPTION

Energy bills are based on the consumption of energy in kilowatt hours. As a result, the bills depend on how much each electrical appliance or system is used and how efficient it is. Most electricity in the United States is produced by the burning of fossil fuels, which produces air pollution. Therefore, the amount of electricity used affects air quality. The average small office or home contains many electrical appliances.

ELECTRICITY CONSUMPTION OF APPLIANCES IN THE UNITED STATES, 2010

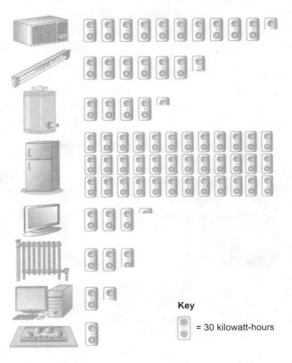

Key

= 30 kilowatt-hours

7. A shop owner is concerned about the environment and wants her business decisions to reflect that concern. Based on the information, what is the **best** decision she can make to help reduce air pollution?

   A. Turn off the computer at night and when it is not in use.
   B. Buy a smaller refrigerator for the break room.
   C. Recycle plastic, glass, and paper at the shop.
   D. Set the air conditioner thermostat in the shop lower in summer so that windows can stay closed.

DIRECTIONS: Read the passage, and study the graph. Then read the question, and write your response on the lines. This task may take approximately 10 minutes to complete.

CARBON DIOXIDE

The graph shows emissions of carbon dioxide. Carbon dioxide is produced when fossil fuels are burned to change their stored chemical energy into energy people can use. Carbon dioxide is also a greenhouse gas, or one of the gases in Earth's atmosphere that trap thermal energy to warm the planet. Data on average temperature have been tracked since 1895. The hottest contiguous 12-month periods on record in the United States have occurred between June 1999 and July 2012.

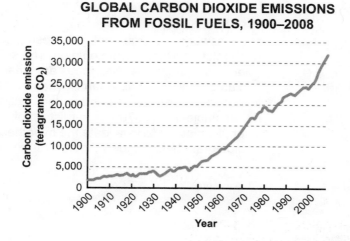

GLOBAL CARBON DIOXIDE EMISSIONS FROM FOSSIL FUELS, 1900–2008

8. What conclusions can be drawn about the possible relationship between carbon dioxide emissions and climate data?

_____

_____

_____

_____

_____

_____

_____

_____

_____

UNIT 2

Understand Investigation Techniques

Use with **Student Book** pp. 68–69

SCIENCE CONTENT TOPICS: P.a.1, P.a.4, P.b.1, P.c.1, P.c.2, P.c.3, P.c.4
SCIENCE PRACTICES: SP.2.b, SP.2.c, SP.2.d, SP.2.e, SP.3.b, SP.3.c, SP.3.d, SP.5.a, SP.6.c, SP.7.a, SP.8.a, SP.8.b

UNIT 2

1 Review the Skill

Once scientists have posed a question and formed a hypothesis, they must design and conduct an investigation. Scientists use **investigation techniques** to gather accurate data and results. By analyzing and interpreting the results of an investigation, they either validate or invalidate the hypothesis. **Understanding investigation techniques** deepens your knowledge of science.

2 Refine the Skill

By refining the skill of understanding investigation techniques, you will improve your study and test-taking abilities, especially as they relate to the GED® Science Test. Study the information and diagram below. Then answer the questions that follow.

SCIENTIFIC METHOD

a A question that leads to a hypothesis usually arises from an observation. Thus, the first step in some definitions of the scientific method is the most basic science skill: observing.

b Someone conducting an investigation considers all the results. If the results do not support the hypothesis, the investigator looks for errors in the analysis and the investigation's design. If no errors exist, he or she can conclude that the hypothesis is incorrect.

Before the scientific method was used, science was largely a matter of guesswork and argument. As a result, scientific knowledge often was indistinguishable from opinion. The scientific method has allowed scientists to show that their ideas are clearly supported by observations and data. Following the scientific method also has enabled scientists to identify incorrect ideas and to demonstrate why they are incorrect. For example, in the 1700s, chemist Antoine Lavoisier used the scientific method to invalidate the hypothesis that water is an element. The diagram below shows the steps in the scientific method.

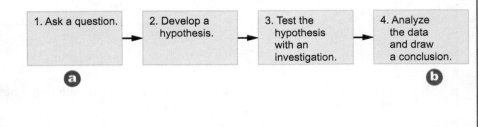

1. Ask a question. → 2. Develop a hypothesis. → 3. Test the hypothesis with an investigation. → 4. Analyze the data and draw a conclusion.

a   **b**

USING LOGIC

A valid hypothesis is a testable answer to a scientific question. A question that can be answered with an opinion or a feeling is not a scientific question. An answer to such a question cannot be a hypothesis.

1. Which aspect of Lavoisier's investigation **best** supported the hypothesis that water is a compound of hydrogen and oxygen?

   A. Members of England's Royal Academy of Sciences witnessed the investigation, in which a combustion reaction produced water.
   B. The amounts of hydrogen and oxygen used were controlled.
   C. Lavoisier used a special tool to hold the hydrogen and oxygen.
   D. The weight of water produced in a chemical reaction roughly equaled the weight of the reactants hydrogen and oxygen.

2. Analysis of data in an investigation indicates unlikely properties of a substance. What should the investigator do?

   A. Change the periodic table.
   B. Analyze the investigation design.
   C. Modify the results to show different properties.
   D. Consult experts in chemistry.

DIRECTIONS: Study the information and table, read each question, and choose the **best** answer.

STATISTICS

Statistical methods can be used to analyze and interpret data. For example, knowing the mean and median of a data set might be important. The mean is the average of the data set. The median is the midpoint in the data set.

An outlier is a data point that is numerically distant from the others in the set. Usually outliers are just erroneous data points. However, before eliminating an outlier, a researcher should try to understand why it exists.

Examining a real-world investigation can clarify how researchers use statistics. Environmental scientists compiled data to determine radiation levels in streams and ponds within a kilometer of a site where nuclear materials were being stored. First they collected water samples and took them back to the laboratory. Then they tested the samples by using equipment to count the number of radioactive particles emitted by each sample. They recorded their data in a table similar to the one shown.

RADIATION LEVELS

Sample Number	Microroentgens Per Hour (µR/h)
1	390.0
2	500.0
3	530.0
4	5.0
5	350.0
6	420.0
7	475.0
8	400.0

3. What is the mean value of this data set, rounded to the nearest whole number?

    A. 475 µR/h
    B. 440 µR/h
    C. 3,070 µR/h
    D. 384 µR/h

4. What is the probable significance of the value for Sample 4?

    A. The pond from which the sample was drawn is not contaminated.
    B. It is statistically important and should be included in the results.
    C. It represents an error in sampling or testing and should be ignored.
    D. It casts doubt on the random sampling process that was used.

DIRECTIONS: Read the passage. Then read each question, and choose the **best** answer.

VARIABLES IN AN INVESTIGATION

Mick notices that soup seems to get cold faster when it is in a bowl than when it is in a cup. He uses this observation to form a hypothesis: Liquid cools faster in wide, shallow containers than it does in tall, narrow containers. To test his hypothesis, he designs an investigation that tests whether the shape of a container affects the rate at which water cools from boiling, 100 degrees Celsius (°C), to room temperature, 25°C. He identifies an independent variable that he will modify and a dependent variable that he will observe.

5. What is the dependent variable in this investigation?

    A. rate of cooling
    B. shape of container
    C. volume of water
    D. temperature of room

6. What is the independent variable in this investigation?

    A. rate of cooling
    B. shape of container
    C. volume of water
    D. temperature of room

7. In the design of this investigation, which factor should be held constant?

    A. volume of water in each container
    B. time of day the test is run
    C. rate of cooling of water
    D. the boiling temperature of water

DIRECTIONS: Read the passage. Then read each question, and choose the **best** answer.

ORGANIZATION IN AN INVESTIGATION

When preparing to conduct an investigation, a researcher must be organized. He or she should plan all testing procedures and gather all necessary equipment and materials before beginning the investigation. Also, the researcher should consider in advance any safety concerns and be prepared.

During the investigation, the researcher should record data in one location, such as in a notebook. Any measurements should be made carefully and accurately. The researcher should record all results, as well as any insights or unexpected events, as soon as they occur. This information will be important when it is time to analyze and interpret the data gathered during the investigation.

8. A researcher plans to test the hypothesis that particular physical properties of a substance change under certain conditions. How should he create a record of testing and results?

A. Pay close attention during the test to changes in the physical properties, and then write down observations after the test is complete.
B. Before the test, read a description of the substance's physical properties, and then write a report the next day about how the substance differed after the test.
C. Record the test with a video camera while narrating descriptions of and insights about the physical properties before, during, and after the test.
D. Take no notes about the physical properties observed before, during, and after the test, but repeat the same procedures the following day.

9. A researcher conducts an investigation of the effect of a new airbag design on forces that occur during collisions. Which step in the scientific process should follow the investigation?

A. formulating the hypothesis that the new airbag design will result in decreased injury
B. developing a theory that airbags always reduce forces in collisions
C. making a prediction that an additional improvement to airbag design will further reduce the chance for injury in a collision
D. analyzing and interpreting measurements taken during the investigation, such as velocities and magnitudes of forces

DIRECTIONS: Study the information and graph, read the question, and choose the **best** answer.

INVESTIGATING CARBON DIOXIDE

Researchers are conducting an investigation on the solubility of carbon dioxide (CO_2) in distilled water. They already know that CO_2 goes into solution more easily under greater air pressure. However, they want to find out how the temperature of the distilled water affects the gas's solubility. Usually warmer water dissolves solutes more readily than colder water. But after several tests, when they analyze their results, the researchers discover that the solubility of CO_2 decreases as the temperature of the water increases. Repeated testing, even by other researchers, yields the same results. The research teams plot data points on graphs like the one shown.

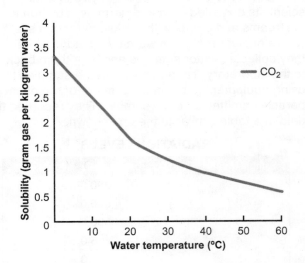

10. One researcher is aware that Earth's oceans are a major CO_2 "sink," dissolving great amounts of CO_2 every day. What prediction might she be likely to make after analyzing the results of the solubility investigation?

A. If salt were added to the distilled water and the investigation run again, more CO_2 would dissolve.
B. As climate change causes the oceans to warm, less CO_2 will be dissolved by the oceans.
C. If researchers used ocean water instead of distilled water, the results most likely would be different.
D. If distilled water were pumped into oceans, more CO_2 would dissolve in them.

DIRECTIONS: Read the passage and question. Then write your response on the lines. This task may take approximately 10 minutes to complete.

SOLUBILITY OF SALT IN WATER

A researcher reads a report about the results of investigations demonstrating that CO_2 is less soluble in warm water than in cold water. She wonders whether salt might be less soluble in warm water, as well. If so, then increasingly warm oceans resulting from climate change would mean that over time the oceans would become less salty as salts precipitated out of solution and fell to the bottom of the ocean. She forms a hypothesis: The solubility of salt in water decreases as water temperature increases.

11. Design a controlled experiment that the researcher could use to test her hypothesis. Identify the dependent and independent variables. Include a description of how the data should be collected and analyzed and how the researcher will determine whether her hypothesis is correct.

_____

_____

_____

_____

_____

_____

_____

_____

_____

_____

UNIT 2

DIRECTIONS: Read the passage and question, and choose the **best** answer.

ATOMIC THEORY

Scientific investigation involves building on existing assumptions and theories. For example, in 1807, chemist John Dalton proposed a theory of matter that formed the basis for modern atomic theory. One incorrect assumption of Dalton's theory, however, was that atoms are solid spheres that cannot be broken down into smaller particles. In the years after Dalton proposed his theory, other scientists made discoveries that advanced understanding of the structure and characteristics of atoms.

12. Which discovery **most likely** caused scientists to reject Dalton's assumption that the atom is a single solid particle?

A. Atoms have electrical charges.
B. Atoms contain electrons.
C. Atoms join in fixed proportions to form various compounds.
D. The electrons that exist within atoms are arranged in energy levels.

Evaluate Scientific Information

Use with *Student Book* pp. 70–71

SCIENCE CONTENT TOPICS: P.a.1, P.a.3, P.a.5, P.b.1, P.b.2, P.c.2, P.c.3
SCIENCE PRACTICES: SP.1.a, SP.1.b, SP.1.c, SP.2.a, SP.2.b, SP.2.c, SP.2.e, SP.3.b, SP.4.a, SP.5.a, SP.7.a

1 Review the Skill

With so much information available today in print and on the Internet, it is important to develop the skill of **evaluating scientific information**. This skill allows you to assess scientific investigations and to discern between reliable and unreliable information. Science information can be evaluated by examining the source of the information. If the information is the result of sound scientific investigation, it is reliable. If not, it is not.

2 Refine the Skill

By refining the skill of evaluating scientific information, you will improve your study and test-taking abilities, especially as they relate to the GED® Science Test. Read the passage below. Then answer the questions that follow.

a Pseudoscience—or false science—usually begins with a conclusion and then tries to force evidence to match the conclusion. Pseudoscience is rarely, if ever, testable using the scientific method.

b Investigations need to be carefully documented so that they can be repeated by other investigators. The more a hypothesis is validated by repeated testing, the more likely that it is true.

EVALUATING AN INVESTIGATION

Scientific information can be evaluated by looking at how it was generated. Were dependent and independent variables clearly identified? Does the evidence uncovered by the investigation support the conclusion? Can the investigation be repeated? What about conflicting results? Can they be reconciled? Or do they indicate that the investigation was poorly designed or that the hypothesis was wrong?

The soundness of an investigation depends partly on how well the hypothesis is stated. For example, it is easily observable that some materials conduct thermal energy better than others. In particular, metals seem to be more conductive than nonmetals. Using that observation, a researcher develops a hypothesis: All metals conduct thermal energy faster than nonmetals do.

To test this hypothesis, the researcher designs and conducts an investigation. He inserts a copper rod and a glass rod into a candle flame. He uses a stopwatch to time how quickly the temperatures of the rods change. Data indicate that the copper rod conducts thermal energy faster than the glass rod does.

CONTENT PRACTICES

Several science practices addressed by the GED® Test relate to evaluating scientific information. Mastering this skill will help you improve your score.

1. What hypothesis is supported by the results of this investigation?

   A. All metals conduct thermal energy faster than nonmetals do.
   B. Copper is the best conductor of thermal energy.
   C. Copper is a better conductor of thermal energy than glass is.
   D. Glass is the poorest conductor of thermal energy.

2. How was this investigation flawed?

   A. The hypothesis was too vague to be investigated validly.
   B. It did not show that metals are good thermal energy conductors.
   C. It did not include dependent and independent variables.
   D. The procedure and results were not recorded.

UNIT 2

DIRECTIONS: Study the information and diagram, read each question, and choose the **best** answer.

SUBLIMATION INVESTIGATION

Jackson knows that dry ice is frozen carbon dioxide (CO_2). He also knows that instead of melting, dry ice usually changes to a gas. This kind of change of state is called sublimation. He does some research and finds the phase diagram for CO_2 shown below in his chemistry textbook. It shows how CO_2 changes state as pressure, measured in atmospheres (atm), and temperature, indicated in degrees Celsius (°C), increase.

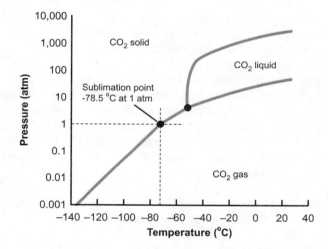

In studying the diagram, Jackson realizes that if dry ice were subjected to a pressure considerably higher than standard atmospheric pressure of 1 atm, it would melt, rather than sublimate as the temperature increased. He wonders whether the same principle might apply to water. He forms a hypothesis: Under decreased pressure, as temperature rises, water in its solid state (ice) will sublimate instead of melt.

3. Is Jackson's hypothesis testable? Why or why not?

    A. No; water is a different substance and probably would not change states.
    B. No; the phase diagram on which it is based is unreliable because it is from a less-than-credible source.
    C. Yes; water vapor could be subjected to lower pressure to see if it changes state directly to ice.
    D. Yes; ice could be put in a vacuum chamber, where pressure can be controlled, and observed as temperature in the chamber is increased.

4. After one test, Jackson finds that his hypothesis has not been validated. What should he do?

    A. Revise his hypothesis to match the investigation results.
    B. Run more tests so that he can get a statistical average of the results.
    C. Assume that he was wrong, and redesign the investigation to prove that he was wrong.
    D. Ask other researchers to repeat the investigation to see what results they get.

DIRECTIONS: Read the passage and question, and choose the **best** answer.

TESTING THE EFFECTS OF FIRING A GUN

A physicist wants to prove that a bullet fired straight up into the air is as dangerous as one fired into a crowd. He explains that as the bullet rises into the air and is slowed to a stop by the force of gravity, it exchanges all its kinetic energy for potential energy. As it comes back down, it regains its kinetic energy. The result is that its velocity is the same when it reaches the ground as when it was fired from the gun.

He sets up an investigation that uses a speed detection device to measure the velocity of the bullet at approximately five feet off the ground, both when the bullet is fired and as it returns to the ground. He records the results, which consistently show the final velocity of the bullet to be 50 to 200 meters per second (m/s) downward, which is lower than the initial velocity of 300 to 1,000 m/s upward. Even though his results are not what he expects, his point stands. The final velocity of the bullet is high enough to cause significant injury or death.

5. The physicist failed to take into account an important variable when formulating the initial hypothesis. This omission explains why the results did not support the hypothesis. Which variable is this?

    A. the mass of the bullet
    B. the force of air resistance
    C. the angle of the bullet's path
    D. the type of bullet

DIRECTIONS: Read the passage. Then read each question, and choose the **best** answer.

INVESTIGATING THE SECOND LAW OF MOTION

Iona wants to investigate how the force of gravity affects different masses. She knows that acceleration due to gravity at Earth's surface is 9.8 meters per second squared (m/s^2). By applying the second law of motion, which states that force equals mass multiplied by acceleration, she knows that acceleration is a constant (9.8 m/s^2) and that only force and mass can change.

With that knowledge, Iona writes a hypothesis in her notebook: Objects with more mass hit the ground with more force. To test her hypothesis, she designs an investigation. She obtains a yardstick to use as a measure of height. She selects eight ball bearings having different masses. Iona measures and records the mass of each ball bearing. She drops each ball bearing into a bar of modeling clay positioned at the base of the yardstick—making certain to use the same kind of clay and controlling for its thickness. She plans to measure the depth of the hole that each ball bearing makes when it hits the clay, reasoning that ball bearings with greater masses will hit with greater force and make deeper holes. She expects to find a direct relationship between hole depth and ball-bearing mass.

6. What is the dependent variable in this investigation?

   A. the initial height of the ball bearing
   B. the mass of the ball bearing
   C. the size of the ball bearing
   D. the depth of the hole in the clay

7. What is the independent variable in this investigation?

   A. the initial height of the ball bearing
   B. the mass of the ball bearing
   C. the size of the ball bearing
   D. the depth of the hole in the clay

8. Iona failed to control an important factor in her investigation. As a result, the data she obtained did not support her hypothesis. Which factor might she have failed to take into account?

   A. the initial height of the ball bearing
   B. the mass of the ball bearing
   C. the size of the ball bearing
   D. the depth of the hole in the clay

DIRECTIONS: Read the passage. Then read each question, and choose the **best** answer.

HYPOTHESES AND THEORIES

A hypothesis is a tentative prediction based on a question. It gives a researcher a starting point from which to begin testing and analysis. When analysis of test results does not produce facts that confirm a hypothesis, the hypothesis may be modified or even abandoned. In other words, a hypothesis is a possible explanation for a specific observation. For example, the hypothesis "if a metal tool is left submerged in water, it will rust faster than if it is left outdoors" can help explain a specific observation. In contrast, a scientific theory is an explanation for a large number of related observations. A valid scientific theory is supported by all available data, explains all available observations, and can be used to make predictions about future investigations. For example, the theory of conservation of mass, which states that mass can be neither created nor destroyed, explains all available relevant observations. A theory remains valid as long as no new evidence is found to dispute it. This means that scientific theories are not dogma; they are always subject to change or rejection.

9. What situation might call into question the validity of the theory of conservation of mass?

   A. Repeated controlled investigations indicate that the quantity of matter in certain reactants is unequal to the quantity of matter in their products.
   B. A prominent scientist believes that matter is destroyed in certain chemical reactions.
   C. Nonscientists do not understand that matter cannot be created or destroyed.
   D. It is possible that sometime in the future scientists will discover evidence suggesting that matter may be created or destroyed.

10. Consider the hypothesis and the theory identified in the passage. Which statement describes the difference between a hypothesis and a theory?

   A. A hypothesis explains observations, but a theory does not.
   B. A theory is always true and cannot be challenged, but a hypothesis is not always true.
   C. A theory explains a wider range of observations than a hypothesis does.
   D. A hypothesis relies on more accurate data than a theory does.

UNIT 2

DIRECTIONS: Read the passage and question, and choose the **best** answer.

EVALUATING A HYPOTHESIS

A researcher wonders whether the colors of light that make up the visible light spectrum have different temperatures. So he places a thermometer in each color. From violet light to red light, the temperatures increase. Curious, he decides to measure the temperature beyond the red light in an area outside the spectrum. He finds that this area has an even higher temperature than the red light.

11. Which hypothesis **most likely** would be formed from this observation?

    A. Darker areas are always warmer than lighter areas.
    B. Special equipment is most likely needed to measure the temperature of light.
    C. All parts of the visible light spectrum have a measurable temperature.
    D. An invisible, warmer area of energy lies next to the red area.

DIRECTIONS: Read the passage and question, and choose the **best** answer.

NULL HYPOTHESES

A null hypothesis is one that is commonly accepted but has not been validated by repeated controlled testing. For example, long ago many people thought that the sun revolved around Earth. The null hypothesis at that time was, "Earth is the center of the universe." A null hypothesis is usually dubious in nature; therefore, researchers work to nullify it. They most often do this by validating an alternate hypothesis. An alternate hypothesis that can be demonstrated through scientific means is the best evidence for refuting a null hypothesis.

12. Which alternate hypothesis would have been used to nullify the null hypothesis identified in the passage?

    A. Earth is a planet that revolves around the sun.
    B. Gravity pulls objects toward Earth's center.
    C. Earth is a sphere.
    D. Earth rotates on an axis.

DIRECTIONS: Read the passage and question, and choose the **best** answer.

THEORY OF PHLOGISTON

In the 1700s, scientists developed the theory of phlogiston to explain fire. It had popular support among scientists because it appeared to explain every related observation. The theory stated that substances that are flammable contain an element called phlogiston. Scientists even developed what seemed to be balanced chemical equations that included phlogiston. One such equation suggested that iron decomposes to yield calx (a powdery substance formed in chemical reactions) and phlogiston.

For a while, when a flaw in the theory was identified, the theory was revised to cover the flaw. Eventually, scientist Antoine Lavoisier designed and conducted an investigation that disproved the theory of phlogiston.

Lavoisier heated mercury and air in a closed container. A substance called red mercury calx—or mercury oxide—formed, and the volume of air decreased by 8 cubic inches, from 50 cubic inches to 42 cubic inches. The air was considered to be "phlogistocated" air, meaning that it contained phlogiston. Lavoisier then heated the calx and produced 8 cubic inches of dephlogisticated air (oxygen). Lavoisier had demonstrated the principle of conservation of mass in a chemical reaction. Combustion reactions, or reactions in which a reactant burns in the presence of oxygen, caused the formation of a calx, a process that had previously been explained as the release of phlogiston. Thus, Lavoisier proved the theory of phlogiston wrong and proposed a new theory, the theory of conservation of mass, which has taken its place.

13. Why was the theory of phlogiston rejected?

    A. It did not have popular support because it did not explain every combustion reaction.
    B. It could not be represented by the use of chemical equations.
    C. Conflicting evidence was discovered by controlled, repeatable scientific investigation.
    D. Scientists who opposed the theory were more influential than those who supported it.

Understand Scientific Theories

Use with *Student Book* pp. 82–83

SCIENCE CONTENT TOPICS: ES.b.4, ES.c.1
SCIENCE PRACTICES: SP.1.a, SP.1.b, SP.1.c, SP.3.a, SP.3.b, SP.4.a, SP.5.a, SP.7.a

1 Review the Skill

Scientists are continuously making observations about the natural world. Based on these observations, they ask questions and carry out investigations to explain what they observe. Each question they ask can be turned into a hypothesis—a proposed response to the question. A **scientific theory** restates one or more hypotheses that have been validated by testing. When you **understand scientific theories**, you comprehend both a statement about the natural world and an explanation of how and why.

A scientific theory is not the same as a scientific law. A scientific law states an observation about something in the natural world, but it does not give an explanation.

2 Refine the Skill

By refining the skill of understanding scientific theories, you will improve your study and test-taking abilities, especially as they relate to the GED® Science Test. Read the passage below. Then answer the questions that follow.

THEORY OF CONTINENTAL DRIFT

a Scientific theories begin with a question. Here, Wegener thought the continents looked like they were once joined. He asked: If that were so, how did the continents get to the places where they are today?

Almost one century ago, scientist Alfred Wegener wondered why some continents looked like they were once joined. He then developed the hypothesis that 250 million years ago, the continents of today were one landmass. He called it Pangaea. Wegener hypothesized that Pangaea broke apart long ago. Over millions of years, the new continents slowly drifted to where they are now.

b Experimentation helps a scientist support or refute a hypothesis. A correct hypothesis can become part of a scientific theory.

Many other scientists disagreed with Wegener. Yet Wegener persisted. He gathered evidence to support his hypothesis that the continents move slowly over time. That evidence became part of his theory of continental drift.

TEST-TAKING TIPS

When answering multiple-choice questions, read the question and pause before reading the answer choices. Predict the correct answer, and then look for the answer closest to your prediction.

1. What was Wegener's hypothesis?

   A. Continents have many different shapes.
   B. Continents broke apart and moved to their present positions.
   C. Today's continents will one day form another Pangaea.
   D. The continents of today are larger than continents of the past.

2. What did Wegener need to add to his hypothesis for it to become a theory?

   A. an explanation for how the continents move
   B. evidence supporting his hypothesis
   C. support from many other scientists
   D. an outdated theory from which to build his new theory

UNIT 3

⭐ Spotlighted Item: **DROP-DOWN**

DIRECTIONS: Study the diagram. Then read the incomplete passage that follows. Use information from the diagram to complete the passage. For each drop-down item, choose the option that **best** completes the sentence.

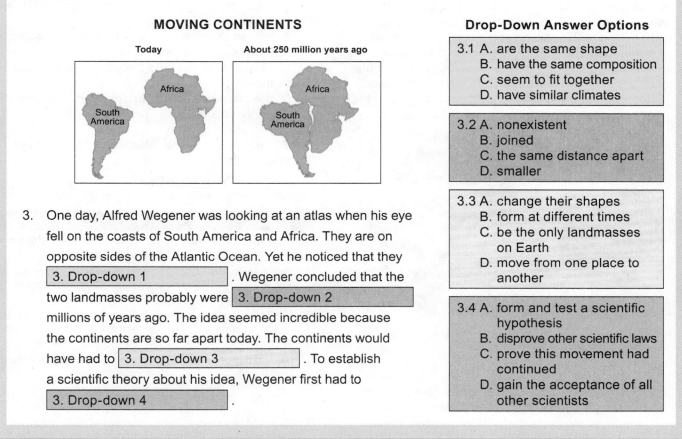

MOVING CONTINENTS

Today

About 250 million years ago

Drop-Down Answer Options

3.1 A. are the same shape
B. have the same composition
C. seem to fit together
D. have similar climates

3.2 A. nonexistent
B. joined
C. the same distance apart
D. smaller

3.3 A. change their shapes
B. form at different times
C. be the only landmasses on Earth
D. move from one place to another

3.4 A. form and test a scientific hypothesis
B. disprove other scientific laws
C. prove this movement had continued
D. gain the acceptance of all other scientists

3. One day, Alfred Wegener was looking at an atlas when his eye fell on the coasts of South America and Africa. They are on opposite sides of the Atlantic Ocean. Yet he noticed that they | 3. Drop-down 1 | . Wegener concluded that the two landmasses probably were | 3. Drop-down 2 | millions of years ago. The idea seemed incredible because the continents are so far apart today. The continents would have had to | 3. Drop-down 3 | . To establish a scientific theory about his idea, Wegener first had to | 3. Drop-down 4 | .

DIRECTIONS: Read the passage and question, and choose the **best** answer.

COSMIC BACKGROUND RADIATION

The Big Bang theory, which proposes an explanation of the universe's origin, is supported by various evidence, including the presence of cosmic background radiation. In the 1940s, a scientist noted that the Big Bang should have left hot, high-energy radiation throughout the universe. As the universe aged, this energy would have cooled. Scientists predicted that by present day, this background radiation would exist in the form of microwaves. In the 1960s, two other scientists detected this radiation. Later, satellites confirmed that cosmic background radiation is fairly uniform throughout the universe—a remnant of the Big Bang.

4. Why is cosmic background radiation evidence for the Big Bang theory?

A. Radiation left over from the Big Bang could be detected only from Earth.
B. The Big Bang would have spread this type of radiation throughout the universe.
C. The existence of cosmic background radiation confirms the age of the universe.
D. Microwave radiation is the only type that would have been created by the Big Bang.

DIRECTIONS: Study the information and diagram, read each question, and choose the **best** answer.

MESOSAURUS FOSSIL LOCATIONS

Geologists have discovered fossils of an ancient reptile called *Mesosaurus* in just two places on Earth: eastern South America and southwestern Africa. Evidence from fossil-dating techniques indicates that *Mesosaurus* lived during the Permian Period, about 300 million to 270 million years ago. It was about 1 meter long and lived in freshwater habitats. A valid hypothesis is that the fossils were found only where they were because those places were once joined. Scientists use the fossils as evidence to support the theory of continental drift.

5. Scientists continue to look for evidence to support existing theories. Which finding would strengthen the fossil evidence support for the continental drift theory?

A. *Mesosaurus* fossils are equally common all over the world.
B. *Mesosaurus* was a poor long-distance swimmer.
C. A species today exists that descended from *Mesosaurus*.
D. The *Mesosaurus* fossils on the two continents actually came from different species.

6. Fossils of an ancient fern also have been cited as evidence for the continental drift theory. Based on the locations of Earth's continents, where have these fossils **most likely** been found?

A. southern Africa and Antarctica
B. South America and North America
C. Asia and Europe
D. Canada and Mexico

7. Some scientists did not accept *Mesosaurus* fossils as evidence that South America and Africa once were joined. They hypothesized that the animals might have moved between the continents on a land bridge. What evidence would have supported the land bridge hypothesis and helped refute the continental drift theory?

A. maps showing how the land bridge would have looked
B. signed statements from other scientists expressing the same idea
C. remnants of the land bridge on the seafloor today
D. the presence of land bridges between some continents today

DIRECTIONS: Study the table, read the question, and choose the **best** answer.

SOME MAJOR EVIDENCE FOR PLATE TECTONIC THEORY

General Evidence	Examples
A. Shapes of coastlines	"Fit" of southwestern Africa and eastern South America
B. Fossil evidence	Fossils of an animal found only in eastern South America and southwestern Africa
C. Similarities in rock layers on separate continents	Appalachian Mountains in North America and mountains in Europe with same layers of rock
D. Geologic processes (earthquakes, volcanic eruptions)	Occurrence most common around the Pacific Ocean

8. The theory that tectonic plates—huge slabs of rock covering Earth's surface—push together and pull apart to cause landforms developed from many lines of evidence. Which pieces of evidence for plate tectonic theory also relate to the theory of continental drift?

A. A and B
B. A and C
C. A, B, and C
D. B, C, and D

DIRECTIONS: Study the information and illustration, read each question, and choose the **best** answer.

SEAFLOOR SPREADING

In the 1950s and 1960s, scientists developed the seafloor-spreading hypothesis. New discoveries showed that seafloor forms from magma that pushes up through cracks in the crust at mid-ocean ridges. The magma cools and hardens to become new seafloor. As this process continues over time, seafloor spreads outward from the ridges.

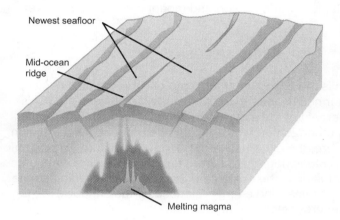

Newest seafloor

Mid-ocean ridge

Melting magma

9. Which piece of evidence would support the hypothesis that the seafloor spreads?

A. Continents on either side of a mid-ocean ridge are moving closer together over time.
B. Rocks on one side of a mid-ocean ridge are older than the rocks on the other side.
C. Rocks in seafloor farther away from a mid-ocean ridge are older than those closer to the ridge.
D. Fossils are absent near a mid-ocean ridge.

10. How does evidence for seafloor spreading support Wegener's older continental drift theory?

A. It shows that continents can be pushed apart.
B. It shows that continents float on the oceans.
C. It shows that there was once a landmass called Pangaea.
D. It shows that oceans move but continents do not.

DIRECTIONS: Study the information and map, read each question, and choose the **best** answer.

PLATE TECTONIC THEORY AND EARTHQUAKES

The theory of plate tectonics not only explains how many of Earth's features formed but also sheds light on many geologic processes, such as volcanic eruptions and earthquakes. The map below shows the locations of earthquakes around the world.

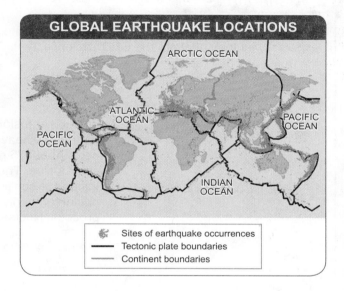

GLOBAL EARTHQUAKE LOCATIONS

ARCTIC OCEAN

ATLANTIC OCEAN

PACIFIC OCEAN

PACIFIC OCEAN

INDIAN OCEAN

Sites of earthquake occurrences
Tectonic plate boundaries
Continent boundaries

11. Which hypothesis is **best** supported by the information on the map?

A. Earthquakes happen only at the edges of continents, not the interiors.
B. The boundaries of continents represent plate boundaries.
C. Earthquakes are most dangerous in the Pacific Ocean.
D. Earthquakes are most common at plate boundaries.

12. What part of the plate tectonic theory do the locations of earthquakes **most clearly** support?

A. Effects of plate movement are significant at plate boundaries.
B. Earth's surface is composed of plates.
C. Plates contain continents but not oceans.
D. Plates are composed of solid rock.

Summarize Complex Material

SCIENCE CONTENT TOPIC: ES.c.1
SCIENCE PRACTICES: SP.1.a, SP.1.b, SP.1.c, SP.6.c, SP.7.a

❶ Review the Skill

Summarizing complex material can help you better understand the important ideas presented in text and in visual elements, such as illustrations, tables, graphs, maps, and diagrams. In many cases, a visual adds key information to a written passage. When this happens, you should include information from both the text and the visual in your summary.

❷ Refine the Skill

By refining the skill of summarizing complex material, you will improve your study and test-taking abilities, especially as they relate to the GED® Science Test. Study the information and model below. Then answer the questions that follow.

a When summarizing, first determine the main idea of the passage. Then identify the most important details. Usually these are broad, not specific, details.

b The title, labels, and caption on a visual can help you summarize it. As you study the model, look for ways that the information in it relates to the main idea of the passage.

NUCLEAR FUSION

Nuclear fusion is the fusing, or combining, of lighter atomic nuclei to produce heavier nuclei and energy. Fusion takes place in the sun's core. About 75 percent of the mass of the sun is hydrogen, the fuel for solar fusion. The other 25 percent is helium, the product of solar fusion. Inside the sun's core, the extremely high heat and pressure slam atomic nuclei (primarily protons) together so hard that they fuse in a multi-step process. Nuclear fusion is the opposite of nuclear fission, which creates energy by splitting atoms. The energy released by fusion, however, is greater than the energy released through fission.

NUCLEAR FUSION IN THE SUN

^3_1H + ^2_1H → ^4_2He + n + E

Protons

Neutrons

Two forms of hydrogen (H) fuse to create one helium (He) atom. The reaction releases a neutron and energy.

TEST-TAKING TIPS

Summarizing is not the same as identifying the main idea. The main idea of a paragraph belongs in a summary. However, a good summary includes both the main idea and the most important details.

1. A summary of the passage might state that nuclear fusion occurs

   A. in all parts of the sun.
   B. in primarily the neutrons of hydrogen atoms.
   C. within the atoms of most gases.
   D. in the core of the sun.

2. Which statement identifies the main idea to include in a summary of the passage and model?

   A. The sun contains mostly hydrogen and helium.
   B. In fusion, the nuclei of atoms fuse to produce energy.
   C. Nuclear fusion produces heavier elements.
   D. Fusion produces more energy than fission.

UNIT 3

DIRECTIONS: Study the diagram and information, read each question, and choose the **best** answer.

HOW STARS DIE

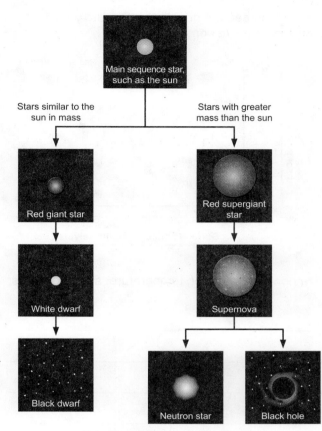

Note: Sizes of stars are not to scale.

All stars are born in much the same way. However, as the diagram indicates, the way a star dies depends on its mass. Main sequence stars, such as the sun, convert hydrogen to helium through fusion. An average-sized star like the sun undergoes fusion for billions of years before its hydrogen fuel runs out. Some of the hottest and largest stars remain main sequence stars for only several million years before their supply of hydrogen is used up. Regardless of a star's temperature or mass, it eventually will run out of hydrogen fuel. At that stage, fusion of heavier elements such as helium and carbon begins. Stars with a mass similar to that of the sun expand and shrink before burning out. They become tiny, but white-hot, white dwarfs before becoming cold black dwarfs. Stars far more massive than the sun explode before collapsing into small, dark, extremely dense bodies.

3. Which detail would **best** fit in a summary of the information?

   A. Stars can fuse atoms of carbon.
   B. Black dwarfs are cold.
   C. Stars more massive than the sun explode.
   D. The sun is an average-sized star.

4. Which statement **best** summarizes the diagram and passage?

   A. Stars of the sun's mass eventually shrink and end as black dwarfs, while more massive stars explode and end as small, dark, dense bodies.
   B. When nuclear fusion begins in a star's core, the star becomes a main sequence star.
   C. The last stage of a massive star's existence is a very dense body.
   D. All stars, regardless of mass, are born in the same way.

DIRECTIONS: Read the passage and question, and choose the **best** answer.

ELEMENTS PRODUCED BY STARS

The Milky Way is a huge galaxy 120,000 light-years wide. Our sun is just one of the Milky Way's billions of stars. The galaxy's stars create helium in the fusion chambers of their cores. However, stars create other elements as well, especially at the end of their life cycles. These elements include iron, magnesium, silicon, and oxygen. When a massive star explodes, the elements produced deep within the star are shot into space, where they become the building materials for new stars and planets. Such elements were part of the cloud of gas and dust from which our solar system formed billions of years ago. These elements are still abundant in the crust of Earth and other rocky planets in our solar system and are important for living things.

5. A student wrote the following summary of this passage: "The Milky Way is a huge galaxy 120,000 light-years wide. Our sun is just one of the Milky Way's billions of stars. The galaxy's stars create helium in the fusion chambers of their cores—but they create other elements as well, especially at the end of their life cycles." What is the **main** problem with this summary?

   A. It does not give details about the Milky Way.
   B. It is shorter than the passage.
   C. It uses the same wording as the passage.
   D. It does not define *galaxy*.

UNIT 3

Spotlighted Item: **SHORT ANSWER**

DIRECTIONS: Read the passage, and study the diagram. Then read the question, and write your response on the lines. This task may take approximately 10 minutes to complete.

TRAITS OF STARS

The universe contains stars of different colors, temperatures, and magnitudes (brightnesses). The graph shown here is known as the Hertzsprung-Russell (H-R) diagram. It shows how color, temperature, and brightness are related in stars.

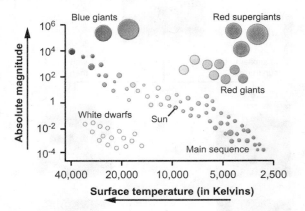

6. Examine the H-R diagram. Then use it to summarize how a star's color, temperature, and brightness are related.

_____

_____

_____

_____

_____

_____

_____

_____

_____

_____

_____

_____

_____

_____

_____

DEATH OF LARGE STARS

The sun is a medium-sized star. When a star far more massive than the sun reaches the end of its life cycle, it explodes in a supernova. The explosion blasts most of the star's mass into space, but the central part of the star is left behind. Without the outward pressure from fusion in the star's core, the inward pull of gravity collapses the star into an extremely dense mass that becomes either a neutron star or a black hole, depending on the star's size.

When large stars die in a supernova, in many cases a neutron star forms. Neutron stars are formed primarily of neutrons. They are extremely tiny, dense bodies—only about 20 kilometers in diameter but with a mass almost 1.5 times that of the sun. Just one teaspoonful of material from a neutron star would weigh one billion tons.

When the most massive stars collapse after a supernova, they leave behind an object with more than three times the mass of the sun. When this object collapses in on itself, it becomes a black hole—an object so tiny and with such immense density that its gravity pulls in anything around it, including its own light. Astronomers can locate black holes by detecting energy emitted by nearby objects being pulled into them. As matter is drawn into a black hole, it forms a hot disk that gives off X-rays and gamma rays that astronomers can detect.

7. Based on the passage, which statement **best** summarizes how neutron stars and black holes are similar?

   A. Neutron stars and black holes can form only before a supernova.
   B. Neutron stars and black holes are so dense that light cannot escape them.
   C. Neutron stars and black holes are made of only neutrons.
   D. Neutron stars and black holes form at the end of the life cycles of large stars.

LIFE CYCLE OF THE SUN

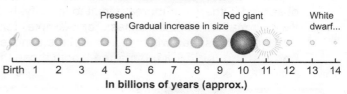

In billions of years (approx.)

THE SUN'S END

The sun is nearly 5 billion years old and is expected to exist for several billion years more. When the sun has used up its hydrogen fuel, fusion will cease in the core, and the core will collapse due to gravity. Pressure from the collapsing core will cause the sun to heat up while its outer layers expand, forming a giant red ball called a red giant. At this point, the sun's diameter will reach to about the orbit of Venus. Earth will be so close to the sun that life as we know it will not exist. Some scientists think that the sun will swell so much that it will engulf Earth. The sun's outer layers will gradually separate and leave the white-hot core as a white dwarf. At the very end of the sun's life, the white dwarf will cool to form a solid, dense structure called a black dwarf.

8. Which statement **best** summarizes the information in the timeline and the passage?

   A. When the sun has used all its hydrogen fuel in about 5 billion years, it will become a red giant and then end several billion years later as a black dwarf.
   B. The sun formed almost 5 billion years ago and will gradually swell during the next 5 billion to 6 billion years.
   C. Several billion years from now, there will be no life on Earth as we know it.
   D. When the sun's hydrogen has been used up, nuclear fusion in its core will stop.

Understand Patterns in Science

SCIENCE CONTENT TOPICS: ES.c.1, ES.c.2
SCIENCE PRACTICES: SP.1.a, SP.1.b, SP.1.c, SP.3.b, SP.3.c, SP.6.c, SP.7.a

① Review the Skill

Some **patterns in science**, such as the passage of day and night or the changing seasons, are easily observed. Others are more difficult to identify. In fact, some patterns can be examined and explained only through mathematical formulas. For example, scientists have devised formulas for the shape of planetary orbits and the speed with which the planets move around the sun. To fully grasp science topics, you must **understand patterns in science**—both those that are easily observed and those that are more complex.

② Refine the Skill

By refining the skill of understanding patterns in science, you will improve your study and test-taking abilities, especially as they relate to the GED® Science Test. Study the information and diagram below. Then answer the questions that follow.

SEASONS

The seasons make up a pattern that repeats year after year. The seasons result from Earth's tilt and revolution around the sun. Although Earth's tilt on its axis stays the same, its tilt, or orientation, toward or away from the sun changes during the year. During winter in the northern hemisphere, for example, Earth is tilted its farthest away from the sun. The sun's energy is less direct, and temperatures are colder. The diagram shows the seasonal effect of Earth's tilt on the northern hemisphere.

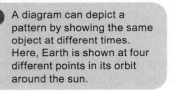

a A diagram can depict a pattern by showing the same object at different times. Here, Earth is shown at four different points in its orbit around the sun.

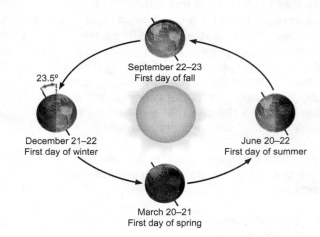

23.5°

September 22–23
First day of fall

December 21–22
First day of winter

June 20–22
First day of summer

March 20–21
First day of spring

b Consider the ways in which changing a variable might affect a pattern.

USING LOGIC

Think about the effect of Earth's tilt on the pattern of seasons. Then predict how the pattern would be changed without this factor.

1. The northern hemisphere gets the most solar energy during

   A. fall.
   B. winter.
   C. spring.
   D. summer.

2. Which statement would describe the pattern of seasons if Earth did not tilt on its axis?

   A. Seasons would be the same because of Earth's revolution.
   B. The seasons would be much shorter than they are now.
   C. It would be either summer or winter all year.
   D. There would be no seasons without Earth's tilt.

DIRECTIONS: Study the illustration and information, read each question, and choose the **best** answer.

DIRECTIONS: Study the diagram and information, read each question, and choose the **best** answer.

CONSTELLATIONS

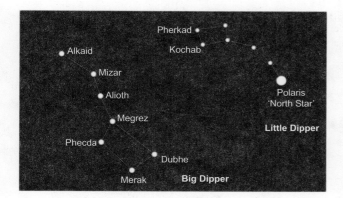

Constellations, such as the Big Dipper and Little Dipper, are patterns that people on Earth saw among the stars in the night sky in ancient times. Some were named for animals or common objects; others were named for mythological people or creatures. Although stars in constellations appear motionless, they are actually streaking around the galaxy, just like our sun. They are just too far away for us to detect their movement. Still, over tens of thousands of years, constellations do change position. The pattern of constellations that is visible to us also changes throughout the year as Earth revolves around the sun.

3. Based on the information, why do constellations appear to be in different parts of the sky at different times of the year?

   A. The constellations change shape throughout the year.
   B. Constellations exist only for a short period, and then completely new ones form.
   C. As Earth circles the sun, we see different areas of the sky.
   D. It is difficult to see constellations during summer when Earth is tilted toward the sun.

4. How will the Big Dipper **most likely** look in 100,000 years?

   A. It will no longer be recognizable as the Big Dipper.
   B. It will look very much the same as it does now.
   C. It will have the same shape but will be much larger.
   D. It will be much dimmer than it is today but will retain the same shape.

THE CORIOLIS EFFECT

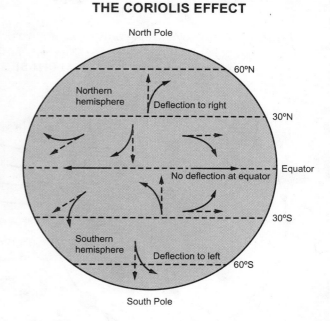

The Coriolis effect is the deflection of fluids (air and water) to the left or to the right due to Earth's rotation. Consider its effect on wind. If the Earth did not rotate, winds would blow straight from areas of high pressure to areas of low pressure. Because of the Coriolis effect, air is deflected to the right in the northern hemisphere and to the left in the southern hemisphere, as shown in the diagram.

5. What do the dotted arrows in the diagram represent?

   A. wind direction with the Coriolis effect
   B. the rotation of Earth
   C. wind direction without the Coriolis effect
   D. winds at the equator and the poles

6. Which statement describes the pattern produced by the Coriolis effect?

   A. It causes straight-line winds.
   B. It creates high air pressure at Earth's poles.
   C. It deflects winds and ocean currents.
   D. It makes Earth rotate.

UNIT 3

⭐ Spotlighted Item: **FILL-IN-THE-BLANK**

DIRECTIONS: Study the diagram and information. Then complete each statement by filling in the box or boxes.

PHASES OF THE MOON

First quarter

Waxing gibbous

Waxing crescent

Full moon

New moon

Sun's rays

Waning gibbous

Waning crescent

Last quarter

Earth and the moon spin and orbit together around the sun.

The moon does not look the same in the sky from night to night. Sometimes, it is a bright, round disk. Other times, it is a half circle or a crescent. These are phases of the moon, the different shapes the moon appears to take throughout the 29.5-day lunar month. The moon does not make its own light but reflects the light of the sun. As it revolves around Earth, half of the moon is always lit. Yet because the moon is always moving around Earth, we see different parts of its lighted side at different times of the month. During a full moon, we see its whole disk, and during a first-quarter moon, we see only half of it.

7. People on Earth see lunar phases because of the moon's ☐ around Earth.

8. A ☐ is the phase of the moon that occurs when the moon is between Earth and the sun.

9. During half of the lunar month, the phases are "waxing." During the other half, the phases are "waning."

When the phases are waxing, the moon appears to be growing ☐. It appears to be

growing ☐ during waning phases.

DIRECTIONS: Read the passage and question, and choose the **best** answer.

COMETS

Comets are balls of frozen gases and dust orbiting the sun in elongated elliptical orbits. A comet's orbit approaches the sun at one end and swings to the outer parts of the solar system at the other end. When a comet nears the sun, it heats up and forms a glowing atmosphere that streams out behind it in a "tail." The famous Halley's Comet has an orbit period of 76 years and last came into Earth's vicinity in 1986.

10. Which statement describes a pattern followed by Halley's Comet?

A. It follows an elliptical orbit around Earth.
B. It forms a tail when it is very far from the sun.
C. It completes an orbit every 76 years.
D. It follows the path of all other comets in the solar system.

SOLAR AND LUNAR ECLIPSES

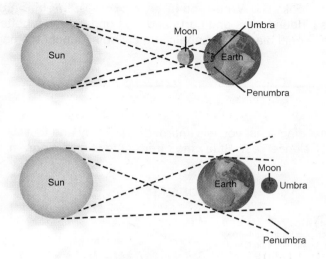

An eclipse happens when one body in space blocks the light of another by passing in front of it. The shadow cast on the surface of an object when an eclipse occurs has different parts. The central part of the shadow is the umbra, and the outer part is the penumbra. There are solar eclipses and lunar eclipses. When a solar eclipse occurs, the moon moves between the sun and Earth. The moon looks like a large, dark ball, with the halo of the sun's corona around it. Only people in the part of Earth that is in the umbra see a total eclipse. People in the larger penumbra see a partial eclipse, in which the moon covers just a portion of the sun. During a lunar eclipse, Earth is between the sun and the moon, and people on Earth see the moon in a dim reddish light. People in one whole hemisphere of Earth can view a total lunar eclipse because they—and the whole moon disk—are within Earth's umbra.

11. Which pattern of movement is responsible for solar eclipses?

    A. Earth's rotation on its axis
    B. the moon's revolution around Earth
    C. the moon's rotation on its axis
    D. the production of energy in the core of the sun

KEPLER'S LAWS OF PLANETARY MOTION

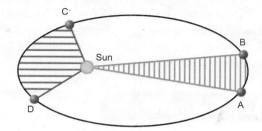

Johannes Kepler was a German mathematician who lived during the 1500s and 1600s. He used observation and mathematics to identify laws that govern the movement of objects in our solar system. These laws are known as Kepler's laws of planetary motion, and the diagram depicts his second law. We now know that objects throughout the universe obey these patterns. The following list explains Kepler's Laws:

1) Planets move around the sun in an ellipse, with the sun at the focus.
   Explanation: Every planet in our solar system has an orbit shaped like an ellipse, or oval.
2) The line connecting the sun to a planet sweeps out equal areas in equal times.
   Explanation: Planets move faster in their orbits when they are nearest to the sun.
3) The square of the orbital period of a planet is proportional to the cube of the mean distance from the sun.
   Explanation: The farther away from the sun a planet is, the slower it moves in orbit around the sun.

12. Kepler discovered universal patterns related to

    A. the distances of planets from stars.
    B. the ways in which planets form.
    C. the movement of orbiting bodies.
    D. the relationship of mass to motion.

UNIT 3

Interpret Three-Dimensional Diagrams

Use with *Student Book* pp. 88–89

SCIENCE CONTENT TOPICS: ES.b.4, ES.c.3
SCIENCE PRACTICES: SP.1.a, SP.1.b, SP.1.c, SP.3.b, SP.3.d, SP.7.a

1 Review the Skill

A **three-dimensional diagram** shows the structure of something. Such diagrams may have sections cut away so that you can see what the inside of the object looks like. When you **interpret three-dimensional diagrams**, you can get information about an object's hidden layers and parts and thus understand it better. Familiar structures might look different in three-dimensional diagrams. Labels and callouts identify the parts of the diagram and explain how they are related.

2 Refine the Skill

By refining the skill of interpreting three-dimensional diagrams, you will improve your study and test-taking abilities, especially as they relate to the GED® Science Test. Study the three-dimensional diagram below. Then answer the questions that follow.

LAYERS OF EARTH

a Labels identify and describe the parts of the object in the diagram. They are generally only a few words long and give the name or a brief description of a structure.

b Callouts are blocks of text that describe part of a figure in detail. They may describe how parts of an object work. Leader lines point from labels and callouts to parts of the diagram they identify or describe.

Crust
The crust is Earth's outermost layer. Living things on Earth live on or in the crust.

Mantle
The mantle is a thick layer of hot, solid rock. The rock in this layer is constantly flowing, even though it is solid.

Core
The core is the inner most layer of Earth. It is made up of iron and nickel. Part of it is liquid, and part of it is solid.

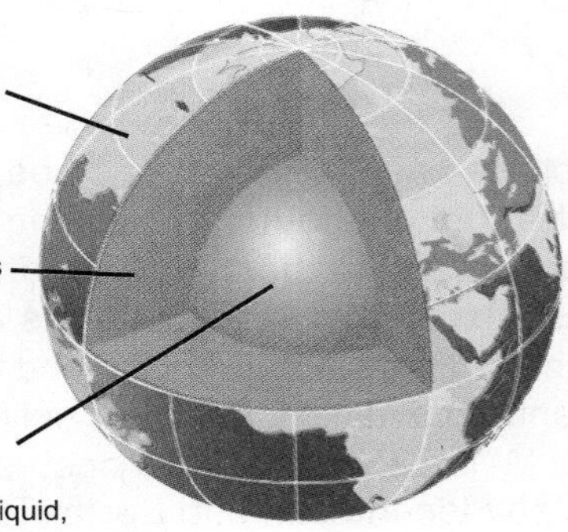

UNIT 3

MAKING ASSUMPTIONS

A scale diagram is one in which the relative sizes of the parts of the diagram are the same as in real life. Unless a diagram states that it is to scale, assume that it is not.

1. Which interpretation can be made based on the diagram?

   A. The mantle layer can be seen from Earth's surface.
   B. The core is less dense than the mantle.
   C. Temperature inside Earth decreases with depth.
   D. The crust makes up only a minute portion of Earth.

2. The conclusion can be drawn that Earth's landforms are

   A. found only in Earth's mantle.
   B. located in the liquid part of Earth's core.
   C. part of Earth's crust.
   D. located in the solid part of Earth's core.

DIRECTIONS: Study the information and diagram, read each question, and choose the **best** answer.

EARTHQUAKES

An earthquake happens when rock beneath Earth's surface shifts suddenly. This movement produces waves of energy that travel away from the break. The shaking we think of as an earthquake occurs when the waves reach Earth's surface. The diagram below shows how an earthquake occurs along a fault.

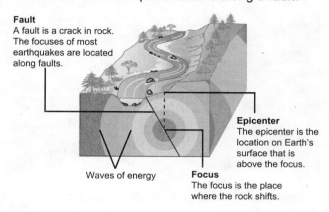

Fault
A fault is a crack in rock. The focuses of most earthquakes are located along faults.

Epicenter
The epicenter is the location on Earth's surface that is above the focus.

Waves of energy

Focus
The focus is the place where the rock shifts.

3. Which statement describes the locations of the epicenter and the focus of an earthquake?

   A. Both are on Earth's surface.
   B. The epicenter lies below the fault, and the focus lies above the fault.
   C. Both lie directly on the fault.
   D. The focus is directly below the epicenter.

4. Based on the passage and diagram, how do waves produced by a shift in rock travel?

   A. They travel outward from the focus.
   B. They travel along the fault until they reach the surface.
   C. They travel from the epicenter to the fault.
   D. They travel inward from the surface.

DIRECTIONS: Study the information and diagram, read each question, and choose the **best** answer.

VOLCANOES

A volcano is a vent in Earth's surface that allows melted rock, or magma, from beneath the surface to escape. Most volcanoes also release gases and ash and eject rock fragments, or pyroclastics.

The material that erupts from the volcano builds up over time, forming layers.

Lava
Lava is melted rock on Earth's surface. It cools and hardens after it erupts.

Main vent
Side vent

Magma chamber
Magma is melted rock below Earth's surface. It is stored in a chamber below the volcano. When the chamber fills, the volcano erupts.

5. Based on the passage and diagram, what materials make up the layers of a volcano?

   A. ash, rock fragments, and cooled lava
   B. various gases
   C. rock fragments
   D. magma and cooled gas

6. Which description of volcanoes is supported by the passage and diagram?

   A. Lava always erupts from the center of a volcano.
   B. Most volcanoes erupt continuously.
   C. Most volcanoes are small when they first form.
   D. Volcanoes cannot erupt ash and lava at the same time.

UNIT 3

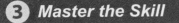

DIRECTIONS: Study the information and diagram, read each question, and choose the **best** answer.

MOUNT ST. HELENS

Mount St. Helens is a large volcano in the state of Washington. Mount St. Helens was inactive for many years. Then in 1980, it erupted. The diagram shows the structure of Mount St. Helens before and after it erupted. Although there have been no major eruptions at Mount St. Helens since the 1980s, there have been periods of activity, when the volcano has emitted smoke and ash.

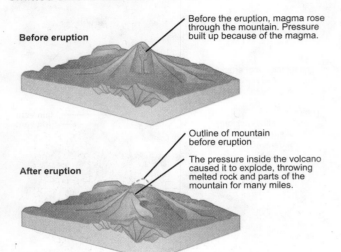

Before eruption

Before the eruption, magma rose through the mountain. Pressure built up because of the magma.

Outline of mountain before eruption

After eruption

The pressure inside the volcano caused it to explode, throwing melted rock and parts of the mountain for many miles.

7. Based on the diagram, how did the eruption in 1980 change Mount St. Helens?

    A. It made the volcano narrower.
    B. It made the volcano shorter.
    C. It completely destroyed the volcano.
    D. It made the volcano larger.

8. What was flung into the air when Mount St. Helens erupted?

    A. only rock from below the surface
    B. a mixture of rock from below the surface and rock from the mountain
    C. only gas from near the surface
    D. mostly crushed rock from inside the magma chamber

DIRECTIONS: Study the information and diagram, read each question, and choose the **best** answer.

MOVEMENT OF TECTONIC PLATES

Earth's crust is broken into several large pieces called tectonic plates. There are about 8 large plates and many smaller plates. These plates are constantly moving in different directions, as indicated by the diagram.

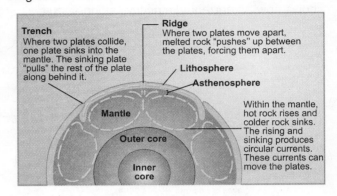

Trench
Where two plates collide, one plate sinks into the mantle. The sinking plate "pulls" the rest of the plate along behind it.

Ridge
Where two plates move apart, melted rock "pushes" up between the plates, forcing them apart.

Lithosphere
Asthenosphere

Mantle

Outer core

Inner core

Within the mantle, hot rock rises and colder rock sinks. The rising and sinking produces circular currents. These currents can move the plates.

9. Based on the diagram, what causes tectonic plates to move?

    A. earthquakes that occur where plates collide
    B. friction between plates
    C. melted rock rising from the core
    D. motions of rock in the mantle

10. Based on the passage and diagram, tectonic plates are located in which of Earth's layers?

    A. lithosphere
    B. lower mantle
    C. asthenosphere
    D. outer core

11. What is a trench?

    A. It is the edge of a tectonic plate.
    B. It is the surface of a tectonic plate.
    C. It is the area where one plate moves under another.
    D. It is the area where two plates move apart.

UNIT 3

DIRECTIONS: Read the passage and question. Then answer by marking the appropriate hot spot or hot spots.

USING ROCK LAYERS TO FIND RELATIVE AGE

Before radiometric dating allowed scientists to determine the exact age of rocks, relative dating was their only tool. To tell the relative ages of rocks, they relied on the following principles:

- In a sequence of undisturbed rock layers, each layer is older than the one above it.

- Layers of rock are deposited horizontally.

- Rock is deposited in continuing layers. If a layer is cut by a canyon or fault, the canyon or fault is younger than the rock it cuts across.

- Where one feature in rock cuts across another, the feature that is cut across is older.

12. The diagram shows a simple representation of layers of rock in a landform. Apply the principles for determining relative rock age to make an interpretation about the layers of rock represented. Mark an *X* on the letter of any feature of the rock that is younger than Feature D.

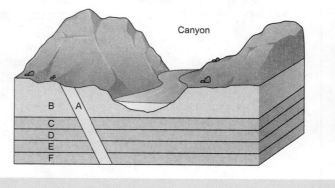

DIRECTIONS: Study the diagram, read each question, and choose the **best** answer.

CRUST FORMATION AT MID-OCEAN RIDGE

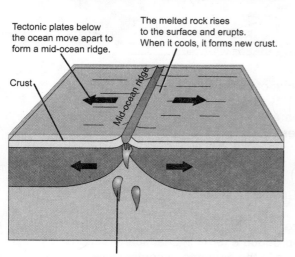

Tectonic plates below the ocean move apart to form a mid-ocean ridge.

The melted rock rises to the surface and erupts. When it cools, it forms new crust.

Crust

Mid-ocean ridge

Rock in the mantle rises toward the surface. As it rises, the pressure on it decreases, causing the rock to melt.

13. Based on the diagram, where does the rock that becomes new crust originate?

A. deep within the core
B. in the crust
C. in sediment far from the ridge
D. in the mantle

14. How is convection—heat transfer that occurs in liquids as particles from warmer areas move to cooler areas—involved in the crust-formation process represented in the diagram?

A. Heat is transferred from particles within the crust to particles within the mantle.
B. Melted rock from Earth's hot mantle rises to Earth's cooler surface.
C. Heat from a warmer tectonic plate is transferred to a cooler tectonic plate.
D. Particles in air above the surface of the ocean are heated by warmer particles in the ocean waters.

Apply Science Concepts

Use with *Student Book* pp. 90–91

SCIENCE CONTENT TOPICS: ES.a.1, ES.b.1, ES.b.2
SCIENCE PRACTICES: SP.1.a, SP.1.b, SP.1.c, SP.3.a, SP.3.b, SP.3.c, SP.7.a

1 Review the Skill

A **concept** is a body of information related to a particular subject. It can be expressed as a topic, such as "sources of energy" or "heat transfer in matter." A concept also can be a statement about one aspect of a topic. When you **apply science concepts**, you interpret new content by relating it to ideas you already understand.

2 Refine the Skill

By refining the skill of applying concepts, you will improve your study and test-taking abilities, especially as they relate to the GED® Science Test. Study the information and map below. Then answer the questions that follow.

EFFECTS OF THE GULF STREAM

a Consider what you know about the concept of sources of energy to determine how the Gulf Stream waters are warmed.

b You know that when a warmer substance is in contact with a cooler substance, a transfer of energy occurs. Apply the concept of energy transfer to deepen your understanding of this statement.

Ireland and Newfoundland are both located at about 50 degrees north latitude. Yet they do not have similar climates. The average winter temperature in Ireland is about 20 degrees Celsius warmer than the average winter temperature in Newfoundland. Most scientists think this difference is caused primarily by the Gulf Stream, which is shown in the map. The Gulf Stream is a warm ocean current that originates in the Gulf of Mexico and then crosses the North Atlantic to graze the northern edge of Western Europe, where Ireland is located. The current warms the atmosphere above it. Then the prevailing westerly winds bring that warm air with them as they travel across Western Europe, making the climate milder.

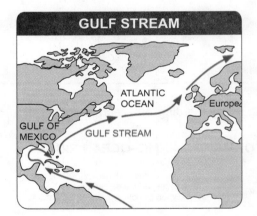

GULF STREAM

ATLANTIC OCEAN

Europe

GULF OF MEXICO

GULF STREAM

UNIT 3

USING LOGIC

When applying concepts, look for logical connections between new facts and what you already know. Keep in mind that many Earth and space science concepts relate to physical science concepts.

1. What is the source of energy that warms the Gulf Stream?

    A. the atmosphere
    B. nearby shores
    C. the sun
    D. precipitation

2. Why does the Gulf Stream warm the atmosphere above it?

    A. Its waters are warmer than the air with which they have contact.
    B. Its particles produce energy in chemical reactions.
    C. When particles in the air come in contact with its waters, their movement slows.
    D. It has internal kinetic energy, and the atmosphere does not.

Spotlighted Item: **DROP-DOWN**

DIRECTIONS: Study the diagram. Then read the incomplete passage that follows. Use information from the diagram and your understanding of related concepts to complete the passage. For each drop-down item, choose the option that **best** completes the sentence.

WATER CYCLE

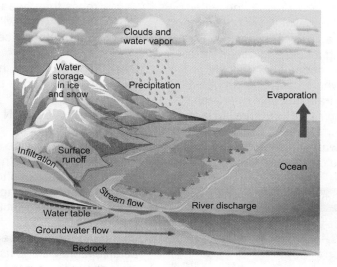

3. Earth's waters constantly change from one state to another in the water cycle. The energy that drives the water cycle originates from the ⬚ 3. Drop-down 1 ⬚ , which strikes Earth's surface, including its oceans. This action causes liquid water to become a gas called water vapor through the process of ⬚ 3. Drop-down 2 ⬚ . The gaseous water vapor in the air cools as it rises. Through condensation, water vapor in the atmosphere changes from a gas into a ⬚ 3. Drop-down 3 ⬚ and forms droplets that become clouds. When these cloud droplets become large and heavy enough, they fall to Earth as precipitation. As the precipitation in clouds gets cold enough, it ⬚ 3. Drop-down 4 ⬚ and falls from the clouds as snow and ice. Snow and ice on Earth's surface eventually warm, change from the ⬚ 3. Drop-down 5 ⬚ to the liquid state, and flow as part of rivers down to oceans to start the cycle again.

Drop-Down Answer Options

3.1 A. clouds
   B. wind
   C. ozone
   D. sun

3.2 A. condensation
   B. deposition
   C. sublimation
   D. evaporation

3.3 A. solid
   B. gas
   C. liquid
   D. plasma

3.4 A. freezes
   B. condenses
   C. melts
   D. evaporates

3.5 A. plasma
   B. solid
   C. gaseous
   D. slushy

DIRECTIONS: Study the information and map, read each question, and choose the **best** answer.

EFFECTS OF THE GLOBAL CONVEYER BELT

The global conveyer belt, shown in the map, is a worldwide underwater current. It is driven by differences in water density and temperature. Near the poles, extremely cold temperatures cause ocean water to freeze. The frozen sea ice that forms is virtually salt free because when water molecules in the saltwater solution freeze, salt remains. As a result, the water near the sea ice has a higher salinity, or concentration of salt, making it denser than normal seawater. This denser water sinks, forming a cold and dense water current that flows along the ocean floor. It flows south toward Antarctica, where it turns north again and splits. As the two separate currents approach the equator, they warm and rise toward the surface, continuing to loop around the oceans until they return to the Atlantic again as a warm surface current that cools, sinks, and starts the cycle once more.

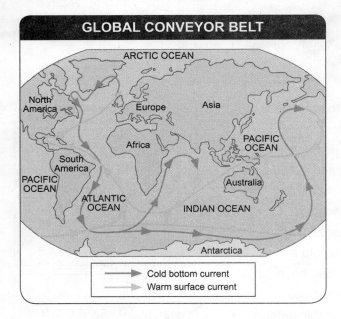

4. Based on the information and concepts related to solutions, why does salt remain when ocean water near the poles freezes?

   A. Salt is not evenly distributed in the water before the water freezes.
   B. As the temperature of the ocean water decreases, its solubility increases.
   C. As the temperature of the ocean water decreases, its solubility decreases.
   D. Ocean water becomes saturated at a temperature above its freezing point.

5. Based on concepts related to the properties of matter, why is ocean water with higher salinity denser than ocean water with lower salinity?

   A. Ocean water with higher salinity has a greater ratio of mass to volume than ocean water with lower salinity.
   B. Ocean water with higher salinity has a greater ratio of volume to mass than ocean water with lower salinity.
   C. Ocean water with higher salinity has more mass than ocean water with lower salinity.
   D. Ocean water with higher salinity has more volume than ocean water with lower salinity.

DIRECTIONS: Read the passage. Then read each question, and choose the **best** answer.

OCEAN ACIDIFICATION

The carbon dioxide released by the burning of fossil fuels enters both the atmosphere and the ocean. In the atmosphere, carbon dioxide has been linked to climate change. In the ocean, elevated levels of carbon dioxide react with seawater to produce carbonic acid. This reaction is causing a gradual change in the pH of seawater, leading to ocean acidification. Scientists have discovered a 30 percent increase in the overall acidity of the ocean since the beginning of the Industrial Revolution.

The natural pH of the ocean is slightly basic. Ocean waters contain calcium carbonate, which many marine organisms use to make their shells and skeletons. The increased acidity of today's ocean destroys calcium carbonate. This destruction of calcium carbonate could cause animals such as oysters, clams, and corals difficulty in making the shells and skeletons they need to survive.

6. Based on the information and the concept of pH, which change would fit the overall pH trend in the oceans?

   A. from 7.0 to 9.0
   B. from 8.0 to 6.0
   C. from 10.0 to 12.0
   D. from 12.0 to 10.0

7. Based on the information, which phrase might describe pH in the ocean 100 years from now?

   A. more acidic
   B. neutral or slightly basic
   C. strongly basic
   D. strictly neutral

DIRECTIONS: Study the information and diagram, read each question, and choose the **best** answer.

FORMATION OF A HURRICANE

Hurricanes form over warm tropical ocean waters where surface temperature is at least 82 degrees Fahrenheit. The thermal energy of the ocean is transferred to the atmosphere, providing the energy that builds up huge banks of clouds around a low pressure area, or a low. As the low intensifies and the system begins to spin, a hurricane can develop. Hurricanes can maintain their strength and even grow as long as they remain over warm ocean waters. But as they travel away from the tropics, they move over cooler waters and often land. As they do, they lose their source of energy and break up.

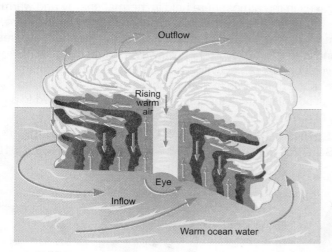

8. Based on the concept of energy transfer and the information, how is energy transferred between the ocean surface and the air right above it?

   A. by radiation
   B. by convection
   C. by saturation
   D. by conduction

9. In hurricanes, the warm air rises, cools, and then sinks to be warmed again. What is this type of energy transfer called?

   A. convection
   B. condensation
   C. radiation
   D. conduction

10. Which concept does the formation of hurricanes demonstrate?

    A. The prevailing winds in the middle latitudes blow from the west in the northern hemisphere.
    B. The density of ocean water increases with salinity.
    C. As air warms, it becomes less dense than the cooler air around it and rises.
    D. Energy can be neither created nor destroyed.

DIRECTIONS: Study the information and map, read the question, and choose the **best** answer.

SURFACE OCEAN CURRENTS

An ocean current is a distinct ribbon of water that moves within the larger ocean. There are two major types of currents. Deep ocean currents move along the ocean floor. Surface currents move through a thin layer of water at the surface. The flow of ocean currents is caused by a combination of factors. These include surface winds, the shape of nearby landforms, and the Coriolis effect. The map below shows Earth's surface ocean currents.

11. What concept **most likely** explains how the Coriolis effect determines the path of ocean currents?

    A. Earth's revolution causes fluids to move in circles.
    B. The sun's gravitational attraction causes currents to curve on Earth.
    C. Earth's rotation causes currents to be deflected from a straight path.
    D. Ocean currents shift direction of movement with weather changes.

Express Scientific Information

SCIENCE CONTENT TOPICS: ES.b.1, ES.b.3
SCIENCE PRACTICES: SP.1.a, SP.1.b, SP.1.c, SP.5.a, SP.6.a, SP.6.c, SP.7.a

① Review the Skill

Scientific information can be communicated in numerous ways. Certain types of information might be best communicated in one particular way. For instance, scientific data often are best expressed numerically. The ability to **express scientific information** in a variety of ways will help you choose the most effective way to communicate your knowledge and understanding of science concepts.

② Refine the Skill

By refining the skill of expressing scientific information, you will improve your study and test-taking abilities, especially as they relate to the GED® Science Test. Study the information and graphs below. Then answer the questions that follow.

GREENHOUSE GAS EMISSIONS

Greenhouse gases in the atmosphere hold in thermal energy and warm the planet. Some of the release of greenhouse gases into the atmosphere is natural. For example, the burning of forests due to lightning strikes releases carbon dioxide and is a natural occurrence. However, since the start of the Industrial Revolution, human activities have released huge additional amounts of greenhouse gases into the atmosphere through the burning of fossil fuels. Most scientists think that this increase has contributed to a gradual warming of Earth.

a After interpreting the first graph, you can express scientific information about how individual gases relate to total U.S. greenhouse gas emissions.

b The second graph seems simple but can be interpreted to express a great deal of scientific information.

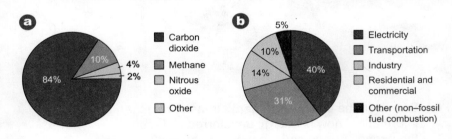

U.S. GREENHOUSE GAS EMISSIONS, 2010

- Carbon dioxide
- Methane
- Nitrous oxide
- Other

84%, 10%, 4%, 2%

U.S. CARBON DIOXIDE EMISSIONS BY SOURCE, 2010

- Electricity
- Transportation
- Industry
- Residential and commercial
- Other (non–fossil fuel combustion)

40%, 31%, 14%, 10%, 5%

Source: Inventory of U.S. Greenhouse Gas Emissions and Sinks 1990-2010

USING LOGIC

When using content from a visual to express scientific information, consider how its parts relate to its main idea or theme. Also, look for ways to compare or connect the individual parts of the visual.

1. Expressed numerically, what proportion of greenhouse gases is carbon dioxide, according to 2010 data?

   A. 10 percent
   B. 16 percent
   C. 84 percent
   D. 100 percent

2. Expressed numerically, which proportion of carbon dioxide emissions in 2010 resulted from electricity production, transportation, or industry?

   A. 14 percent
   B. 31 percent
   C. 40 percent
   D. 85 percent

UNIT 3

DIRECTIONS: Study the information and diagram, read each question, and choose the **best** answer.

LAYERS OF THE ATMOSPHERE

The atmosphere might look like one uniform substance, but it is not. It changes in relation to distance from Earth's surface. In general, particles of air are fairly close together near Earth's surface but can be kilometers apart at the atmosphere's upper edge. The atmosphere is also warmer near Earth's surface than at its upper edge, where it merges into outer space. Scientists use the way the atmosphere changes with altitude to organize it into the layers shown in the diagram.

UPPER ATMOSPHERE

Exosphere
Air particles are miles apart; outer edge blends into space; orbits of satellites and space station are here.

Thermosphere
Air is thin, but temperatures increase because atoms absorb high-energy solar radiation; auroras and ionosphere are here.

MIDDLE ATMOSPHERE

Mesosphere
Space debris and meteoroids start to burn up here; coldest part of atmosphere, with temperatures as low as −130°F (−90°C) at top, are here.

Stratosphere
Most ozone is here; temperatures rise with altitude; highest commercial airplanes fly here.

LOWER ATMOSPHERE

Troposphere
Most weather, along with clouds and water vapor, is here; temperature decreases with altitude.

EARTH

3. To express information about layers of the atmosphere in which people **most likely** are found, you would discuss

   A. the exosphere and the thermosphere.
   B. the thermosphere and the mesosphere.
   C. the mesosphere and the stratosphere.
   D. the stratosphere and the troposphere.

4. Which statement expresses a difference between the troposphere and the other layers?

   A. It is the coldest part of the atmosphere.
   B. It contains most clouds, rain, and wind.
   C. It is the only layer in which airplanes fly.
   D. It contains particles that are miles apart.

DIRECTIONS: Study the information and diagram, read each question, and choose the **best** answer.

IONOSPHERE

The ionosphere is a layer of electrically charged particles in the lower part of the thermosphere. As they absorb high-energy radiation from the sun, nitrogen molecules and oxygen atoms are stripped of electrons, becoming ions or other charged particles. The freed electrons form electrical currents in the upper atmosphere. The ionosphere has three layers. From the closest to Earth outward, they are D, E, and F. During daylight hours, the D layer absorbs radio signals, so AM radio signals stay within a limited number of kilometers from the radio transmitter. Without solar energy to ionize particles, the D and E layers disappear at night, leaving only the highest F layer. The diagram shows why this means that late at night you can pick up radio signals from unusually distant locations.

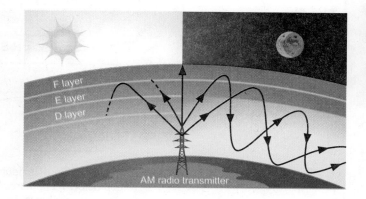

F layer
E layer
D layer
AM radio transmitter

5. What do the black arrows in the diagram express?

   A. charged particles
   B. radio signals
   C. nitrogen molecules and oxygen atoms
   D. radiation from the sun

6. Which statement expresses the reason why AM radio signals from faraway stations can be heard only at night?

   A. Transmitters send out more powerful signals at night.
   B. The ionosphere gives radio signals more energy at night.
   C. Radio waves bouncing off the ionosphere travel longer distances at night.
   D. Sunlight during the daylight hours blocks radio signals.

⭐ Spotlighted Item: **DRAG-AND-DROP**

DIRECTIONS: Read the passage and question. Then use the drag-and-drop options to complete the diagram.

ACID PRECIPITATION

When factories, electric power plants, and vehicles burn fossil fuels, millions of tons of pollutants pour into the atmosphere. Some of these substances, such as sulfur dioxide and nitrogen oxide, can combine with the water in the air to form acids. This acidic water then falls from the sky as acid rain or snow. Rain is slightly acidic naturally, with a pH of about 5.6. But acid rain is more acidic. Most acid rain has a pH of between 5.0 and 5.5. Even levels of 3.0 have been recorded. Acid precipitation kills trees. It also can cause the death of all aquatic life in lakes that become too acidic. Freshwater habitats usually have a pH that ranges between 6.5 and 9. The pH of ocean water is typically around 8.0. Today, regulations require electric power plants and other facilities that burn fossil fuels to decrease emissions of pollutants such as sulfur dioxide that contribute to acid precipitation.

7. Express scientific information visually. Determine where the drag-and-drop options belong in the pH scale. Then record the name of each substance in the appropriate diagram label box.

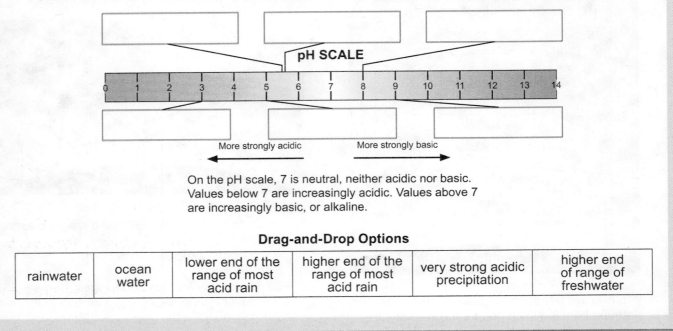

On the pH scale, 7 is neutral, neither acidic nor basic. Values below 7 are increasingly acidic. Values above 7 are increasingly basic, or alkaline.

Drag-and-Drop Options

rainwater	ocean water	lower end of the range of most acid rain	higher end of the range of most acid rain	very strong acidic precipitation	higher end of range of freshwater

DIRECTIONS: Read the passage and question, and choose the **best** answer.

WIND POWER

Wind produced only about 3 percent of the energy in the United States in 2011. But it was still the second-largest source of renewable energy after hydropower. The disadvantage of wind energy is that power is generated only when the wind blows. The greatest advantages are that it is free and produces no pollution. The amount of wind energy generated in the United States increased from 20 terawatt hours in 2006 to 120 terawatt hours in 2011.

8. Which statement **best** expresses the state of wind power in the United States?

A. The country is using wind power less and less.
B. Use of wind power is too controversial to be effective.
C. Use of wind power is increasing.
D. Wind is not an important source of renewable energy.

DIRECTIONS: Study the information and graph, read the question, and choose the **best** answer.

AIR PRESSURE

Air pressure is the force of the atmosphere pressing down on Earth's surface. Gravity's downward force compresses air molecules the most at sea level. As a result, the density of the air—and, therefore, the air pressure—is greater closer to sea level. As altitude increases, such as on a high mountain, the force of gravity decreases, and the pressure decreases as well. Air pressure is not usually felt, because it is exerted in all directions at once. The graph below shows the relationship between air pressure and altitude.

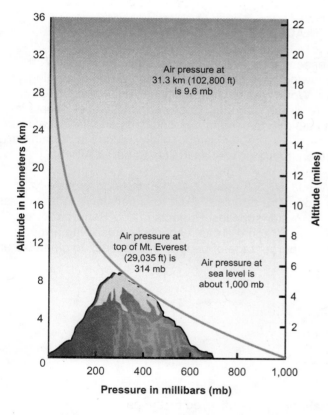

9. Which statement expresses the relationship between air pressure and altitude?

   A. Air pressure is lowest at sea level.
   B. Air pressure decreases as distance from mountains increases.
   C. Air pressure increases as altitude increases.
   D. Air pressure increases as altitude decreases.

DIRECTIONS: Study the information and model, read the question, and choose the **best** answer.

OZONE LAYER

The atmosphere contains oxygen molecules (O_2), oxygen atoms (O), and ozone molecules (O_3). Ozone is a form of oxygen that is produced when oxygen molecules and oxygen atoms bond. Ozone production in the atmosphere is a continually occurring process.

Atmospheric ozone is important because it blocks most of the sun's harmful ultraviolet radiation. That is why scientists were alarmed to discover during the mid-1970s that Earth's layer of ozone was thinning in places. The source of the problem was chlorine atoms (Cl) from chemicals called chlorofluorocarbons (CFCs). To protect atmospheric ozone, more than 180 countries agreed to phase out products that used or contained substances such as CFCs in the late 1980s.

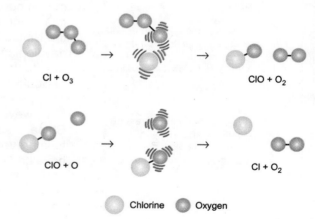

10. What information about ozone is expressed by the model?

    A. Ozone is produced when oxygen molecules and oxygen atoms bond.
    B. Chlorine combines with ozone in the atmosphere to break down the ozone.
    C. Ozone production in the atmosphere is a continually occurring process.
    D. Ozone is a form of oxygen found in the atmosphere.

Identify Problem and Solution

SCIENCE CONTENT TOPICS: ES.a.1, ES.a.2, ES.a.3, ES.b.1
SCIENCE PRACTICES: SP.1.a, SP.1.b, SP.1.c, SP.3.a, SP.3.b

1 Review the Skill

Many scientific texts present **problems** and explore related **solutions**. Learning to **identify problem and solution** in texts can help you evaluate an author's arguments and ideas and think of alternate solutions that the author may not have presented.

2 Refine the Skill

By refining the skill of identifying problem and solution, you will improve your study and test-taking abilities, especially as they relate to the GED® Science Test. Read the passage below. Then answer the questions that follow.

ACCESS TO CLEAN WATER

a One problem is clearly identified in the passage's first two sentences. However, there are other problems mentioned in the paragraph. It is important to decide which is the main problem.

Clean water is essential for every person. Today, more than 780 million people worldwide have no access to clean water, according to a report from the World Health Organization (WHO) and UNICEF, the United Nations children's agency. Each year, millions of people in developing nations die due to unsanitary conditions and lack of access to safe drinking water. The problem is especially serious in certain parts of South and Southeast Asia as well as in sub-Saharan Africa.

b Typically, an author presents solutions after naming problems. Look in this paragraph for solutions.

However, the WHO/UNICEF report called East Asia, especially China, a success story. The people of East Asia now have more access to improved, piped-in water supplies. Projects in sub-Saharan Africa have had less success. In some areas, especially those with armed conflicts, only a small percentage of people have access to clean water.

TEST-TAKING TIPS

If you identify a problem, write it down. Read on to find out whether a solution is revealed. You might see several, or none. Look at solutions critically to determine whether they could cause larger problems.

1. What is the **main** problem conveyed by the passage?

A. armed conflicts in Africa
B. lack of clean water
C. reporting by WHO/UNICEF
D. unsuccessful projects in sub-Saharan Africa

2. What solution to this widespread problem is identified in the passage?

A. conserving water supplies
B. improving WHO/UNICEF projects
C. reducing armed conflicts
D. expanding access to piped-in water

DIRECTIONS: Study the information and images, read each question, and choose the **best** answer.

HURRICANE SANDY

When Hurricane Sandy hit the Atlantic coast in October 2012, it struck as a Category 1 storm, the weakest type of hurricane. But because it hit a densely populated area, it caused devastating damage, as shown by the airborne lidar images below. Sandy flooded communities and wrecked thousands of homes and businesses, some of which were swept out to sea. After Sandy, many people started to rebuild homes or businesses. But some people question the wisdom of this tactic. With climate change, storms like Sandy are expected to become more frequent. So homes built in the same low lying, vulnerable areas run the risk of being destroyed again.

Before Sandy	After Sandy

Credit: U.S. Geological Survey

3. What solution might make it more likely for homes, offices, and factories to withstand future storms on the coast?

   A. Build barrier walls, and raise structures above flood-line levels.
   B. Construct much larger buildings so that winds cannot knock them down.
   C. Construct more bridges so that people can escape in time to avoid danger.
   D. Build structures farther apart from one another so that the area is less densely populated.

4. Some people think low-lying areas along the shore should be abandoned. Based on the information presented, why do they believe the solution is to avoid rebuilding in such areas?

   A. Houses are very expensive in shore areas.
   B. In the future, most hurricanes will hit the Atlantic coast of the United States.
   C. Storms likely will hit the areas struck by Sandy and destroy the homes again.
   D. No home can ever withstand a hurricane at the shore.

DIRECTIONS: Study the information and list, read each question, and choose the **best** answer.

EMERGENCY KITS

A hurricane emergency kit solves one big problem. It provides hurricane victims with supplies that will be needed if they have no water and electricity after a storm. The Federal Emergency Management Agency suggests that all people in hurricane-prone areas have emergency kits. Such a kit should include the items listed below.

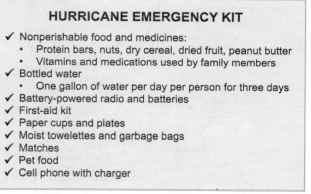

HURRICANE EMERGENCY KIT

✓ Nonperishable food and medicines:
   • Protein bars, nuts, dry cereal, dried fruit, peanut butter
   • Vitamins and medications used by family members
✓ Bottled water
   • One gallon of water per day per person for three days
✓ Battery-powered radio and batteries
✓ First-aid kit
✓ Paper cups and plates
✓ Moist towelettes and garbage bags
✓ Matches
✓ Pet food
✓ Cell phone with charger

5. What is the purpose of a hurricane emergency kit?

   A. to help people exit an area when a hurricane occurs
   B. to provide information about what to do when a hurricane is approaching
   C. to provide supplies that may be needed in the aftermath of a hurricane
   D. to ensure that people have food and water when a hurricane occurs

6. Which item missing from the list of kit supplies would be **most** useful?

   A. fresh milk
   B. pots and pans
   C. electric blankets
   D. a flashlight

UNIT 3

DIRECTIONS: Study the information and diagram, read each question, and choose the **best** answer.

NITROGEN CYCLE

All plants and animals need nitrogen. Essential proteins in living cells cannot form without it. Given that most of Earth's atmosphere is composed of nitrogen, it might seem that living things have no problem getting it. But plants and animals cannot use nitrogen from the air in its elemental form. The flowchart below shows the way the nitrogen cycle solves this problem as it rotates nitrogen through Earth's living and nonliving environment.

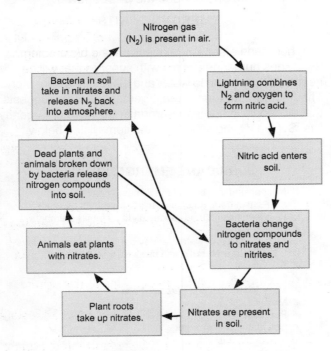

7. What is the basic problem related to the use of nitrogen by plants and animals?

   A. They cannot use nitrogen in any form.
   B. The atmosphere has only limited amounts of nitrogen.
   C. They cannot use nitrogen in the elemental form found in the atmosphere.
   D. The use of nitrogen breaks down needed proteins in plants and animals.

8. What problem would lack of nitrogen cause for plants and animals?

   A. Their systems would have too much protein.
   B. They would be infected by harmful bacteria.
   C. There would be no beneficial bacteria in soil.
   D. Their systems would have no protein.

9. Based on the diagram, how does the nitrogen cycle provide nitrogen for plants?

   A. Plants' roots take up nitrogen from the air.
   B. Bacteria turn into nitrogen inside plants.
   C. Bacteria break down a nitrogen compound into forms of nitrogen plants can use.
   D. Plant-eating animals break down nitrogen compounds into forms of nitrogen plants can use.

DIRECTIONS: Read the passage and question, and choose the **best** answer.

VOLCANO MONITORING

Volcanoes can erupt violently, with flows of red-hot lava, clouds of scorching steam, showers of rock and ash, and debris flows that can sweep away anything in front of them. Volcanic eruptions also kill many people.

To save lives, volcanologists have developed tools to identify volcanic activity that could mean an eruption will occur soon. Instruments are placed on volcanoes to detect changes in their slopes because magma moving inside a volcano can cause it to swell before an eruption. In addition, seismographs record more earthquake activity as the magma inside a volcano moves. Scientists also monitor gases escaping from volcanoes, looking for those that are most likely to signal a coming eruption.

10. What is the **main** problem that volcano monitoring helps solve?

    A. the need to stop volcanoes from erupting
    B. the need to have early warnings of eruptions
    C. the need to reduce the number of volcanic eruptions
    D. the need to understand how volcanic eruptions happen

EARTHQUAKE-RESISTANT BUILDINGS

Many deaths and injuries caused by earthquakes result from buildings and other structures collapsing. For this reason, engineers have tried to design structures that can resist the forces that cause structures to collapse. The most damaging waves traveling from an earthquake's focus are those that cause buildings to shake from side to side. This motion creates stress on connections that link walls, floors, and beams. Earthquake-resistant design strengthens those connections. Floors and roofs are connected to diaphragms for horizontal strength. Sheer walls and cross-bracing strengthen vertical elements. Some design features allow structures to bend and sway instead of breaking. Movement-resisting frames have connections between beams that allow beams to bend, not snap. Base isolation places buildings on materials that deflect a quake's energy rather than transmit it through the structure.

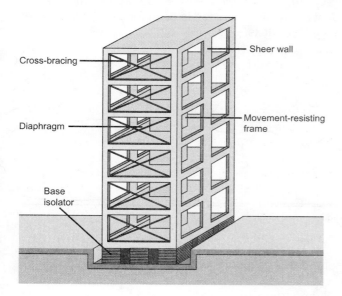

Cross-bracing

Diaphragm

Base isolator

Sheer wall

Movement-resisting frame

11. How does earthquake-resistant design solve a problem?

    A. It keeps earthquakes from happening in an area.
    B. It lowers construction costs.
    C. It reduces the likelihood of the destruction of buildings.
    D. It ensures that buildings constructed after earthquakes occur are more attractive.

TORNADO ALERTS

A tornado is a rotating column of air that extends from the clouds of a severe thunderstorm to the ground. Tornadoes have some of the most violent winds of any storm—up to 300 miles per hour. The powerful winds of a tornado can spread destruction over an area many miles wide. Also, twisters are responsible for dozens of deaths in the United States each year. For these reasons, knowing where and when tornadoes are about to form is important.

The National Weather Service has devised a system of watches and warnings to alert people when several types of severe weather are approaching or occurring in an area. Information for tornadoes is presented in the table.

Tornado Watch	Tornado Warning
The conditions are right for tornadoes in your area. Keep alert for an approaching storm.	A tornado is in your area. It has been sighted or spotted on weather radar. Take cover where you can.

12. What problem caused the National Weather Service to create tornado watches and warnings?

    A. Scientists needed a better understanding of how tornadoes form.
    B. People wanted help getting services after tornadoes.
    C. People needed to find out when tornadoes are nearby.
    D. Scientists wanted to help weather forecasters track tornadoes more easily.

13. What should a store owner do before tornado season to prepare?

    A. Buy a book on tornadoes to loan to employees.
    B. Make sure employees know where to go if a tornado warning is issued.
    C. Plan to close the shop whenever there is a severe thunderstorm.
    D. Get the number of the National Weather Service to call for details when a watch or warning is issued.

Analyze and Present Arguments

Use with *Student Book* pp. 96–97

SCIENCE CONTENT TOPICS: ES.a.1, ES.a.3
SCIENCE PRACTICES: SP.1.a, SP.1.c, SP.3.a, SP.3.b, SP.4.a

1 Review the Skill

An **argument**, or point of view about a topic, is only as good as the data that support it. When you **analyze an argument**, you determine whether it is supported by facts from a reputable source. When you **present an argument**, you state and defend a particular point of view. This requires knowledge of both your viewpoint and the one that you will argue against. Therefore, when you present arguments, you must have a comprehensive understanding of the subject in question.

2 Refine the Skill

By refining the skill of analyzing and presenting arguments, you will improve your study and test-taking abilities, especially as they relate to the GED® Science Test. Study the information and graph below. Then answer the questions that follow.

ENERGY PRODUCTION AND CONSUMPTION

a References within a passage to other material often direct you to a visual element that adds more detailed information. All available information is important when analyzing or presenting an argument.

For most of the last few decades, U.S. energy consumption has trended upward <u>as shown in the graph below</u>. So has energy production, although its upward trend has not kept pace with that of consumption. For the time being, the United States has adequate supplies of coal and natural gas but largely must import oil, the fossil fuel we use most. An overwhelming amount of the oil consumed is used for transportation—in cars, airplanes, trains, and trucks.

b Graphs often show trends that support arguments. This graph not only shows a contrast between the energy produced and consumed but also shows that comparison as a trend over several decades.

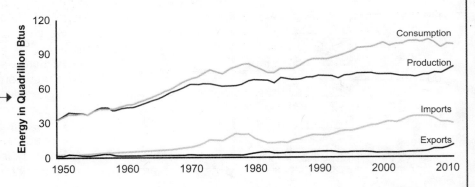

USING LOGIC

You sometimes will find that all answer options are true statements. Look for the one that is most useful in supporting the argument in question, and eliminate the others.

1. The data presented **best** supports which of the following policies?

   A. Increase U.S. imports of oil.
   B. Strengthen air pollution regulations.
   C. Decrease prices of imported oil.
   D. Design vehicles with better gas mileage.

2. Which statement **best** supports an argument in favor of the use of renewable energy sources?

   A. The United States has adequate supplies of coal and natural gas.
   B. Most oil consumed is used in transportation.
   C. Energy consumption continues to trend upward.
   D. Energy production continues to trend upward.

DIRECTIONS: Read the passage. Then read each question, and choose the **best** answer.

MOVING TAR SANDS

The United States uses about 20 million barrels of oil each day. Much of this oil is supplied by countries overseas. However, an enormous supply of oil exists in Canada, in the form of tar sands. Tar sands are sandy goo that is part petroleum and part gritty sediment.

Plans are in place to build a new 1,700-mile-long pipeline to bring the tar sands from Alberta, Canada, to Texas. Some people view the presence of a massive oil supply in a friendly neighboring country as good news. Others worry about the proposed path of the pipeline across the Ogallala Aquifer, a huge groundwater source that provides water to millions of people for drinking and farming. They worry that a leak in the pipeline would pollute the aquifer. However, pipeline supporters state that there are safeguards that make such leaks unlikely.

3. What would be an appropriate source to use to obtain unbiased information for presenting an argument about the tar sands pipeline?

   A. American Tar Sands Association
   B. Citizens Against the Keystone Pipeline
   C. Students to Support a Clean Ogallala
   D. U.S. Department of Energy

4. Which detail from the passage would **best** support an argument in favor of building this particular pipeline?

   A. Petroleum can be obtained from the sands.
   B. Safeguards likely will prevent leaks in the pipeline.
   C. The oil supply is in a friendly neighboring country.
   D. The United States uses about 20 million barrels of oil each day.

5. Which detail from the passage would **best** support an argument against the pipeline?

   A. A leak in the pipeline could pollute the aquifer.
   B. Tar sands are part petroleum and part gritty sediment.
   C. The aquifer supplies water to many people.
   D. The United States imports a great deal of oil.

DIRECTIONS: Study the information and photos, read each question, and choose the **best** answer.

CLIMATE CHANGE

For the last few decades, climate scientists have gathered data that support the idea that Earth is warming, largely as a result of human activities such as the burning of fossil fuels. In late 2012, scientists at the National Oceanic and Atmospheric Administration reported that temperatures in the United States that year were the hottest on record. Above-normal temperatures also were recorded each month for a 16-month period from June 2011 to September 2012—another record. Additionally, scientists stated in 2010 that nine of the ten hottest years on record occurred between 2000 and 2010.

Clear signs of climate change also exist in the environment. An example is visible to visitors at Glacier National Park in Montana, as seen in the photographs of a glacier below. The photo on the left was taken in 1913; the photo on the right was taken in 2005.

Photographs by W. C. Alden (left), courtesy of U.S. Geological Survey (USGS) Photographic Library, and Blase Reardon (right), courtesy of USGS

6. What do the photographs show to provide useful evidence in making the argument that Earth is warming?

   A. The glacier was very small in 1913.
   B. The glacier has shrunk over the years.
   C. The glacier is in a rocky area.
   D. The glacier is moving downhill.

7. Which situation would provide additional evidence for an argument supporting the idea that climate change is occurring?

   A. the crumbling of mountains around the glacier
   B. the presence of sand dunes in front of the mountain
   C. the absence of the glacier in 2020
   D. a lack of change in the glacier's size by 2015

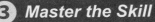

DIRECTIONS: Study the information and table, read each question, and choose the **best** answer.

TO DRILL OR NOT TO DRILL

The United States uses a tremendous amount of imported oil. As a result, oil companies are always on the lookout for new domestic supplies. An untapped domestic oil supply sits on the Arctic Slope of Alaska, beneath the Arctic National Wildlife Refuge (ANWR). Many people think this supply of oil should be used to help meet the growing energy needs of the United States. Others believe that drilling in ANWR is an environmental risk. The table presents some of the main arguments on both sides of the issue.

For Drilling in the Arctic National Wildlife Refuge
• It would decrease dependence on foreign oil.
• It would create some new jobs.
• Only a small part of the refuge would be affected.
• It would create revenues for state and federal governments.
• It would provide oil to meet the increasing energy needs of the United States.

Against Drilling in the Arctic National Wildlife Refuge
• It would disturb a sensitive environment.
• It would not produce enough oil to be worth the risk.
• It is unlikely to lower oil prices.
• It does not address the real problem, which is excessively high consumption levels.
• A majority of Americans oppose it.

8. Based on the information, what do some people argue is the basic underlying issue related to energy use in the United States?

   A. U.S. oil use is too high.
   B. Few uses for oil exist in the United States today.
   C. The United States depends on foreign oil.
   D. Any extraction of fossil fuels disturbs the environment.

9. Based on the information, which group is **most likely** to support drilling in ANWR?

   A. foreign oil producers
   B. people who prioritize job creation over protection of the environment
   C. environmentalists
   D. people concerned about oil prices

DIRECTIONS: Read the passage. Then read each question, and choose the **best** answer.

HYDROELECTRIC POWER

Hydroelectric dams provide most of the renewable energy used in the United States today. As with any energy source, debate exists over the use of hydropower.

An advantage of hydropower is that it makes use of a free energy source—flowing water—to produce electricity. In addition, hydropower does not directly release pollutants into air or water.

However, hydropower requires the construction of large dams that create huge reservoirs behind them. These reservoirs may submerge wide areas that were once farmland, forest, canyon land, or even small towns. The dams affect wildlife, too. On some rivers, they block salmon runs. They also change the environmental conditions of rivers downstream, creating a situation that in turn can negatively affect the aquatic ecosystems that depend on these rivers.

10. Which statement is a valid argument against the construction of a hydroelectric dam?

    A. The dam could threaten the survival of some species of fish.
    B. The dam could produce too much air and water pollution.
    C. The fuel to run a hydroelectric dam is much too expensive.
    D. Hydroelectric dams can be built only where there are no rivers or lakes nearby.

11. Which statement is a valid argument in favor of the construction of a hydroelectric dam?

    A. Hydroelectric dams can be built anywhere.
    B. Maintenance of hydroelectric dams is costly.
    C. Hydroelectric dams produce no pollution.
    D. The use of hydroelectric dams has little impact on wildlife.

DIRECTIONS: Study the information and graph, read each question, and choose the **best** answer.

DWINDLING ENERGY RESOURCES

Although some energy experts urge the United States to shift to renewable energy sources, such as wind and solar power, the United States remains one of the world's top five consumers of coal. The country has huge coal reserves, but a drawback of depending on nonrenewable resources is that they are in limited supply and eventually will run out. According to some estimates, at the current consumption rates, U.S. coal could last another 112 years. That is a long time compared to expectations for world petroleum reserves, which could be used up in less than 50 years. Of course, these are just estimates. As countries with large populations, such as China and India, continue to develop and use more energy, reserves of fossil fuels could dwindle even faster.

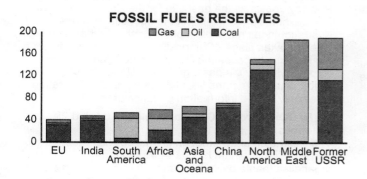

FOSSIL FUELS RESERVES

12. Which argument is supported by the size of North American fossil fuel reserves?

   A. North America should continue to rely on coal as a major energy source.
   B. Increasing the use of oil will make North America more energy independent.
   C. Continued use of coal will make North America more dependent on China.
   D. Increasing the use of natural gas rather than coal is more sustainable for North America.

13. In which area of the world would data on current fossil fuel reserves **best** support an argument to switch to renewable energy sources?

   A. North America
   B. European Union (EU)
   C. Middle East
   D. China

14. Which idea **best** supports the argument that fossil fuel reserves will dwindle at a faster rate in the future?

   A. Current estimates are probably wrong.
   B. Fossil fuels will be the only energy sources in the future.
   C. Developed countries will decrease their use of fossil fuels.
   D. Developing countries with large populations will use increasing amounts of fossil fuels.

DIRECTIONS: Study the information and graphs, read the question, and choose the **best** answer.

WATER RESOURCES

The graphs below show the percentages of freshwater and salt water on Earth and the uses of freshwater. People use freshwater for certain household (domestic) activities, such as drinking, cooking, and washing. However, most freshwater is used for irrigation. Irrigation is the practice of bringing water to a field through artificial means to grow crops in a place that is otherwise too dry for them. Much of the world's food is grown on irrigated land. Salt can be removed from ocean water through desalination to produce more freshwater. However, this process is expensive.

TOTAL WORLD WATER

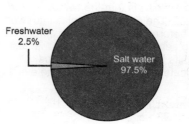

BREAKDOWN OF FRESHWATER USE

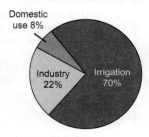

15. Which argument is **best** supported by the information presented?

   A. Raising crops where they can grow with rainfall alone will conserve water significantly.
   B. Using desalination to produce drinking water will make the biggest impact in water conservation.
   C. To save the most water, restrictions should be placed on factory water usage.
   D. Expanding irrigated land will force people and businesses to conserve water.

Answer Key

UNIT 1 LIFE SCIENCE

LESSON 1, pp. 2–5
1. B; DOK Level: 1; **Content Topic:** L.d.1; **Practices:** SP.1.b, SP.1.c, SP.7.a
The illustration label for a lysosome indicates that lysosomes contain digestive enzymes. The illustration shows that the cell membrane and vacuoles are parts of the cell, not substances contained in lysosomes. The illustration shows that food particles enter the cell, not that lysosomes contain food particles.

2. C; DOK Level: 2; **Content Topic:** L.d.1; **Practices:** SP.1.b, SP.1.c, SP.7.a
Based on the illustration, the food vacuole forms when food enters the cell and then moves through the cell and fuses with the lysosome, so its purpose is to transport food to lysosomes. Its purpose is not to digest food particles because this is the job of the lysosome. It also does not make digestive enzymes; the illustration shows that lysosomes contain digestive enzymes but does not explain how digestive enzymes are made. The food vacuole carries food that enters through the cell membrane, but the vacuole itself does not enter through the cell membrane.

3. A; DOK Level: 2; **Content Topics:** L.d.2, L.d.3; **Practices:** SP.1.a, SP.1.b, SP.1.c, SP.7.a
The illustration shows that in meiosis, the gametes have half the number of chromosomes as the original parent cell. The parent cell in the illustration has four chromosomes. Each gamete has two chromosomes. A gamete that comes from a cell with four chromosomes, should not have four, six, or eight chromosomes.

4. C; DOK Level: 2; **Content Topics:** L.d.2, L.d.3; **Practices:** SP.1.a, SP.1.b, SP.1.c, SP.7.a
The illustration shows that of the events listed, the last event that occurs during meiosis is that the two daughter cells split to form gametes. The parent cell splits into two identical daughter cells before the two daughter cells split. The chromosomes swap sections of genetic material just before the parent cell splits to form two daughter cells. The chromosomes replicate at the beginning of the events shown.

5. D; DOK Level: 2; **Content Topics:** L.d.2, L.d.3; **Practices:** SP.1.a, SP.1.b, SP.1.c, SP.7.a
The chromosomes in the gametes in the illustration are all different, indicating that exchanging sections of genetic material leads to gametes having different genetic material. The illustration does not indicate that exchanging genetic material makes gametes unable to be damaged. The illustration shows that the gametes all have the same number of chromosomes. The illustration shows the production of gametes as the end of the process; the gametes do not divide to form new cells.

6. D; DOK Level: 2; **Content Topic:** L.d.1; **Practices:** SP.1.a, SP.1.b, SP.1.c, SP.7.a
The title and labels of the illustration indicate that the illustration shows the structures of a cell membrane, not the way cells reproduce, the nucleus of a cell, or all the contents of a typical cell.

7. B; DOK Level: 2; **Content Topics:** L.b.1, L.d.1; **Practices:** SP.1.a, SP.1.b, SP.1.c. SP.7.a
The illustration shows that the upper epidermis, mesophyll, and lower epidermis are parts of the leaf that are stacked, indicating that they are layers in the leaf structure. The label for chloroplasts indicates that photosynthesis occurs in structures located in the mesophyll, not in the other layers, and that individual cells make up the three layers. The illustration shows that gases (carbon dioxide and oxygen) are exchanged in the lower epidermis, not in all three layers.

8. D; DOK Level: 2; **Content Topics:** L.b.1, L.d.1; **Practices:** SP.1.a, SP.1.b, SP.1.c, SP.7.a
The passage states that photosynthesis happens in the chloroplasts, and the illustration shows that the chloroplasts are located in the mesophyll, so photosynthesis happens in the mesophyll. There are no chloroplasts in the xylem, the stoma, or the cuticle, so photosynthesis does not happen in those places.

9. A; DOK Level: 3; **Content Topics:** L.b.1, L.d.1; **Practices:** SP.1.a, SP.1.b, SP.1.c, SP.7.a
The illustration shows the structure of a leaf and identifies parts related to photosynthesis, so "Leaf Structure and Photosynthesis" is the best title for the illustration. "How Photosynthesis Works" is not the best title because the illustration does not explain photosynthesis; it only shows where it takes place. "Composition of Chlorophyll" is not the best title because the illustration does not mention chlorophyll; only the passage does. "Understanding Chloroplasts" is not the best title because the illustration gives only limited information about chloroplasts.

10. B; DOK Level: 2; **Content Topics:** L.d.1, L.d.2; **Practices:** SP.1.b, SP.1.c
The illustration shows that an animal cell has most parts that a bacterium has as well as four more types of organelles than a bacterium, so the structure of an animal cell is more complex than the structure of a bacterium. A bacterium does not have a nucleus, but an animal cell does. The illustration does not indicate whether a bacterium has more cytoplasm than an animal cell. An animal cell cannot move more easily than a bacterium; the opposite is true because a bacterium has a flagellum and an animal cell does not.

11. A; DOK Level: 2; **Content Topics:** L.d.1, L.d.2; **Practices:** SP.1.b, SP.1.c, SP.7.a
The illustration shows and explains that a pore is an opening in the nuclear envelope, so its most likely function is to let materials into and out of the nucleus. The pore is an opening, so it does not enclose or seal anything. Also, it does not form proteins; that is the job of the nucleolus.

12. C; DOK Level: 2; **Content Topics:** L.b.1, L.d.1; **Practices:** SP.1.a, SP.1.b, SP.1.c, SP.7.a
According to the illustration, the citric acid cycle and glycolysis produce ATP; however, the illustration shows three arrows for ATP from the citric acid cycle and only one arrow for ATP from glycolysis, indicating that the citric acid cycle produces more ATP than glycolysis. Replenishment is a process that occurs between fermentation and glycolysis and does not produce ATP. Fermentation produces lactate, not ATP.

13. A; DOK Level: 2; Content Topics: L.b.1, L.d.1; **Practices:** SP.1.b, SP.1.c, SP.7.a

The illustration shows that the products of fermentation include lactate (as well as NAD⁺). Water and carbon dioxide are products of the citric acid cycle. Pyruvate is a product of glycolysis.

14. D; DOK Level: 3; Content Topics: L.b.1, L.d.1; **Practices:** SP.1.a, SP.1.b, SP.1.c, SP.7.a

According to the illustration, fermentation produces NAD⁺ from NADH. NAD⁺ is used during glycolysis to make ATP. Fermentation uses NADH; it does not provide NADH for use in the citric acid cycle. Fermentation is not involved in glucose entering the cell. Fermentation does not provide pyruvate; it uses pyruvate.

15. B; DOK Level: 2; Content Topics: L.b.1, L.d.1; **Practices:** SP.1.b, SP.1.c, SP.7.a

The illustration shows a cutaway of a mitochondrion, revealing what it looks like inside. Therefore, the purpose of the illustration is to show the parts of a whole mitochondrion. The illustration shows one mitochondrion at one point in time, so its purpose is not to show how a mitochondrion changes over time. The illustration shows only one organelle of a cell, a mitochondrion, so its purpose is not to show how materials move through cells. Mitochondria do make energy, but the illustration does not show this process.

16. B; DOK Level: 2; Content Topics: L.b.1, L.d.1; **Practices:** SP.1.b, SP.1.c, SP.7.a

The illustration and labels indicate that a mitochondrion has an outer membrane and an inner membrane. The illustration shows only a mitochondrion, so its size cannot be compared to the sizes of other structures in a cell. The mitochondrion and the nucleolus are two separate structures within a cell. The illustration does not address the movement of a mitochondrion.

17. D; DOK Level: 2; Content Topics: L.b.1, L.d.1; **Practices:** SP.1.b, SP.1.c, SP.7.a

The caption tells that a function of a mitochondrion is to release energy. The illustration, not the caption, shows the location of the matrix. The caption does not discuss the specific parts of a mitochondrion.

LESSON 2, *pp. 6–9*

1. A; DOK Level: 2; Content Topic: L.d.2; **Practices:** SP.1.b, SP.1.c

The graphic uses descriptions of functions to identify the levels at which cells are organized in a multicellular organism, so the main idea is that in a multicellular organism, cells are organized by function. The graphic indicates nothing about cell size. Although multicellular organisms have many organs with differing functions, the graphic shows all levels of organization, not just organs. The groupings on the graphic do not imply that a multicellular organism has more systems than organs. In fact, the opposite is true.

2. C; DOK Level: 2; Content Topic: L.d.2; **Practices:** SP.1.b, SP.1.c

The statement that groups of similar cells form tissues expresses a detail provided in the "Tissue" section of the graphic. The ideas that skin is made up of three layers, cells are different shapes and sizes, and muscles can be smooth, cardiac, or skeletal are facts, but they are not expressed by the information provided in the graphic.

3. A; DOK Level: 2; Content Topic: L.a.1; **Practices:** SP.1.a, SP.1.b, SP.7.a

The passage explains the involvement of the heart, lungs, and blood vessels in moving oxygen through the body, so the main idea of the passage is that the circulatory system and the respiratory system work together to get oxygen to the body's cells. The ideas that blood moves from the cells to the heart with very little oxygen, the heart provides power to pump blood through the body, and oxygen is taken in by the lungs and moved to the blood are details that support the main idea.

4. D; DOK Level: 2; Content Topic: L.a.1; **Practices:** SP.1.a, SP.1.b, SP.7.a

The main idea of the passage is that some body systems work in tandem. The example that the large intestine is part of the digestive tract but also helps eliminate waste supports this main idea. The ideas that water is absorbed in the large intestine, compact waste materials are called feces, and nutrients are absorbed through the wall of the small intestine are details that help explain the example of how the large intestine is part of two body systems; they are not details that provide direct support for the statement that some body systems work in tandem.

5. C; DOK Level: 2; Content Topic: L.a.1; **Practices:** SP.1.a, SP.1.b

The statement that the three types of muscle play different roles in the muscular system expresses the main idea because it relates to the breadth of information provided in the passage. Each of the other answer choices is a reference to a specific type of muscle, which is too specific to be the main idea of the passage.

6. D; DOK Level: 2; Content Topic: L.a.1; **Practices:** SP.1.a, SP.1.b

The details of the passage support the main idea that the three types of muscle play different roles in the muscular system by describing each type of muscle and the role it plays. Although supporting details can identify data from an investigation, the details of this passage do not do so. The details of the passage describe how skeletal muscles move the body, but they do not list all the ways in which skeletal muscles move the body. The fact that smooth muscles push food through the digestive tract is a detail in the passage, but this question asks about the way in which the details of the passage support the main idea, not about identifying a specific detail.

UNIT 1 (continued)

7. A; DOK Level: 3; **Content Topics:** L.a.1, L.d.2; **Practices:** SP.1.a, SP.1.b, SP.1.c, SP.7.a
The main idea of the illustration and passage is that nerve impulses follow a specific path through different neurons that determine meaning and make the body react. The illustration shows this sequence, and the passage discusses it. The statements that effector neurons carry out instructions from the brain, the brain and spinal cord are responsible for making sense of signals, and motor neurons and sensory neurons deliver messages are details that support the main idea.

8. C; DOK Level: 3; **Content Topics:** L.a.1, L.d.2; **Practices:** SP.1.a, SP.1.b, SP.1.c, SP.7.a
The illustration describes the specific functions of three types of neurons (receptor, association, and effector neurons) to support the main idea that nerve impulses follow a specific path through different neurons that determine meaning and make the body react. The shapes of the different types of neurons show that they are different but tell nothing about their functions. The location of neurons in the brain and spinal cord is described, but the role of the brain and spinal cord is not fully explained. The passage, not the illustration, provides an example of something the body senses.

9. B; DOK Level: 2; **Content Topics:** L.a.1, L.d.2; **Practices:** SP.1.a, SP.1.b, SP.1.c, SP.7.a
The main idea of the passage and illustration is that nerve impulses follow a specific path through different neurons that determine meaning and make the body react. The detail that there are three classes of neurons each with hundreds of different types of neurons best supports this main idea because it provides more information about the neurons through which nerve impulses flow. The passage and illustration do not discuss the cellular structure of neurons, so the detail about the nucleus and genetic material does not support the main idea. The detail that neurons are the longest cells in the body does not support the main idea that there are different types of neurons. The illustration and passage do not discuss death of neurons, so the detail that some brain diseases are caused by unnatural death of neurons does not support the main idea.

10. B; DOK Level: 2; **Content Topic:** L.a.1; **Practices:** SP.1.a, SP.1.b
The passage explains that hormone-secreting glands make up the endocrine system and gives examples of the regulating roles the hormones play. So the main idea of the passage is that the endocrine system is made up of glands that make hormones to regulate body systems. The location of the endocrine system is not discussed in the passage, and the statement that the endocrine system is centrally located in the body is untrue. The endocrine system does keep the body in a state of balance, but you cannot know this from the passage. The endocrine system does control sexual maturation, but the passage talks about more than just the parts of the endocrine system involved in sexual maturation.

11. A; DOK Level: 2; **Content Topic:** L.a.1; **Practices:** SP.1.a, SP.1.b
The passage describes the endocrine system as being made up of glands that secrete hormones, so the statement explaining why the pituitary gland is a major part of the endocrine system would be the best supporting detail to add. The statements about the structure, location, and size of the pituitary gland are too specific to support the main idea that the endocrine system is made up of a variety of hormone-secreting glands.

12. D; DOK Level: 2; **Content Topic:** L.a.1; **Practices:** SP.1.a, SP.1.b, SP.1.c
The illustration shows endocrine glands and their locations, so the statement that glands throughout the body are part of the endocrine system best expresses the main idea of the illustration. The statement that the pancreas is the largest endocrine gland, the information about the location of the thyroid gland, and the description of glands being involved in sexual development are supporting details.

13. C; DOK Level: 3; **Content Topic:** L.a.1; **Practices:** SP.1.a, SP.1.b, SP.1.c, SP.7.a
The illustration shows and tells about feedback mechanisms involved in stimulating and inhibiting the release of growth hormone, so "Growth Hormone Regulation in the Body" best describes the main idea and, therefore, is the best title. The illustration shows how growth hormone release is both stimulated and inhibited to keep balance in the body, not just how growth hormone is inhibited, so the title "How Growth Hormone Is Inhibited" is too specific. The title "Endocrine Feedback Loop" is not specific enough because the illustration is about growth hormone specifically. The title "Monitoring of Growth in the Human Body" is not accurate because the illustration is about growth hormone, not growth in the body.

LESSON 3, pp. 10–13

1. A; DOK Level: 2; **Content Topic:** L.a.3; **Practices:** SP.1.a, SP.1.b, SP.1.c
The title, column headings, and key provide information indicating that the table shows the number of Calories needed by males and females at different ages based on their levels of activity. The title indicates that the table shows the number of Calories that should be taken in daily, not after periods of light or heavy activity. Although the table shows ages, activity level, and caloric intake, the caloric intake is based on age and activity level; the ages are not based on caloric intake. The description "differences in Calories males and females need at various ages" is not a detailed enough description of the information in the table.

2. C; DOK Level: 2; **Content Topic:** L.a.3; **Practices:** SP.1.a, SP.1.b, SP.1.c
The information in the column for an active male indicates that the number of Calories recommended increases and then stabilizes early in life. The table shows that the number of Calories recommended at age 30 is 3,000 and that the number of Calories recommended at age 40 is 2,800. So the number of Calories needed begins to decrease at age 40, not at age 20, 30, or 50.

3. **B**; **DOK Level:** 2; **Content Topic:** L.a.3; **Practices:** SP.1.a, SP.1.b, SP.1.c, SP.3.b

Someone who has a calcium deficiency should eat more foods rich in calcium. According to the table, milk, cheese, and yogurt are rich in calcium. These foods are dairy products. Meat and beans are helpful for an iron deficiency; nuts are helpful for a folic acid deficiency; and salt is helpful for a sodium deficiency.

4. **A**; **DOK Level:** 3; **Content Topic:** L.a.3; **Practices:** SP.1.a, SP.1.b, SP.1.c, SP.3.b

Someone who feels weak and tired lacks energy and, therefore, is most likely lacking an adequate amount of iron because iron carries oxygen through the blood to cells and organs to maintain energy. Calcium, sodium, and folic acid deficiencies do not lead to feeling weak and tired, as an iron deficiency does.

5. **B**; **DOK Level:** 2; **Content Topic:** L.a.3; **Practices:** SP.1.a, SP.1.b, SP.1.c

According to the table, the recommended daily values of these nutrients are 300 g carbohydrates, 80 µg vitamin K, and 1,000 mg phosphorus, so the person who is getting 300 g carbohydrates, 100 µg vitamin K, and 1,200 mg phosphorus is getting at least the recommended daily values. The others are all getting too little of at least one nutrient.

6. **B**; **DOK Level:** 1; **Content Topic:** L.a.3; **Practices:** SP.1.a, SP.1.b, SP.1.c

The table shows that the number of Calories in a slice of colby cheese is 112. The table also shows that 1 cup of broccoli has 30 Calories, an oatmeal cookie has 60 Calories, and 1 cup of low-fat milk has 102 Calories.

7. **C**; **DOK Level:** 2; **Content Topic:** L.a.3; **Practices:** SP.1.a, SP.1.b, SP.1.c, SP.8.b

The two items that have a total of more than 200 Calories combined are a slice of colby cheese and an ear of corn, with one slice of colby cheese having 112 Calories and one ear of corn having 96 Calories, for a total of 208 Calories. The other combinations of items have Calorie totals that are less than 200.

8. **D**; **DOK Level:** 2; **Content Topic:** L.a.3; **Practices:** SP.1.a, SP.1.b, SP.1.c, SP.3.b

The column headings indicate that the purpose of the table is to identify the number of Calories in servings of certain foods. The table does not try to encourage people to choose foods with fewer Calories; it just gives information. Although this table could provide information useful in preparing a weekly menu, there are not enough options in the table to plan a complete menu. Different serving sizes of the same foods are not given, so comparing them is not a purpose for the table.

9. **B**; **DOK Level:** 2; **Content Topic:** L.a.3; **Practices:** SP.1.a, SP.1.b, SP.1.c, SP.8.b

According to the table, this person should have 3 cups of vegetables and 2 cups of fruits each day. Because 3 minus 2 equals 1, the person should have 1 more cup of vegetables than fruits. The incorrect answer choices might be reached through incorrect calculations or misunderstanding of concepts.

10. **C**; **DOK Level:** 2; **Content Topic:** L.a.3; **Practices:** SP.1.a, SP.1.b, SP.1.c, SP.3.b

The table provides information about how much of certain foods a person should eat each day, so the most likely use of the information would be to plan a diet based on taking in the specified amounts each day. A person could use the information to plan what to eat for breakfast; however, the information is better suited for a more general use. The table does not provide appropriate information for calculating Calorie intake or finding out how much protein is in a food.

11. **A**; **DOK Level:** 2; **Content Topic:** L.a.3; **Practices:** SP.1.a, SP.1.b, SP.1.c

The passage states that sodium can be beneficial in small amounts, and the table shows sodium as a macronutrient that supports muscle functioning, so combined information from the passage and the table indicates that in the proper amount, sodium supports good muscle functioning. According to the passage, an unlimited sodium intake can be harmful, not beneficial. Neither the passage nor the table indicates that sodium serves a greater number of functions in the body than iodine does. Neither the passage nor the table prioritizes macronutrients needed by the body.

12. **D**; **DOK Level:** 2; **Content Topic:** L.a.3; **Practices:** SP.1.a, SP.1.b, SP.1.c

The information in the table shows that both calcium and sodium are involved in muscle function. Sodium is not an answer choice, so calcium is the correct answer. Zinc, iodine, and potassium are not involved directly in muscle function.

13. **B**; **DOK Level:** 2; **Content Topic:** L.a.3; **Practices:** SP.1.a, SP.1.b, SP.1.c, SP.3.b

The table shows that various body systems are affected by the elements, supporting the idea that deficiencies in macronutrients or micronutrients can affect many different body systems. Not all macronutrients and micronutrients support immune system function; of those listed in the tables, only zinc does. The nervous system depends on copper, which is a micronutrient. The table does not address whether the body needs greater quantities of macronutrients or micronutrients; however, according to the passage, the body needs macronutrients in larger, not smaller, quantities than micronutrients.

14. **D**; **DOK Level:** 2; **Content Topic:** L.a.3; **Practices:** SP.1.a, SP.1.b, SP.1.c

Protein is provided by only two meal items, the banana nut bread and the tuna salad sandwich. The tuna salad sandwich provides more protein and has fewer Calories than the banana nut bread. The vegetable lasagna and tomato soup do not provide protein.

Answer Key

UNIT 1 (continued)

LESSON 4, pp. 14–17
1. **B**; **DOK Level:** 1; **Content Topic:** L.a.2; **Practices:** SP.1.a, SP.1.b, SP.7.a
The passage states that signals from temperature receptors cause the hypothalamus to regulate body temperature. Sweat glands secrete perspiration as a result of the body being too hot. The feedback loop does not start working at a certain point; it is always working. Although the passage does not discuss evaporation of sweat, perspiration does evaporate from the skin, but this evaporation occurs as a result of temperature regulation efforts by the hypothalamus.

2. **A**; **DOK Level:** 2; **Content Topic:** L.a.2; **Practices:** SP.1.a, SP.1.b, SP.3.b, SP.7.a
The passage makes the general statement that the body maintains balance by reacting constantly to feedback, indicating that there are many feedback loops in the body and that the main purpose of these feedback loops is to maintain balance. The temperature feedback loop does involve the hypothalamus, but feedback loops do not control the hypothalamus. Feedback loops both send and receive signals; they do not just receive signals. The temperature feedback loop regulates temperature, but it is just one example of the body's feedback loops.

3.1 **B**; 3.2 **A**; 3.3 **D**; 3.4 **C**; **DOK Level:** 2; **Content Topic:** L.a.2; **Practices:** SP.1.a, SP.1.b, SP.1.c, SP.7.a
3.1 The illustration indicates that an external change that causes a fluctuation in blood pressure is a higher temperature. Irregular heartbeat is an internal, not external, condition and is not related to this process. Lowered blood pressure, an internal change, is the result of the process illustrated. An imbalance of activities is not related to this process.
3.2 According to the illustration, one result of the change in temperature is that receptors send signals to the integrator. The signals elicit a response from the effector after they have been interpreted by the integrator. The signals come from the receptors when they sense the stimulus.
3.3 The job of an integrator is to cause an effector to act in some way. In this case, the integrator is the brain, and it stimulates the heart, which is an effector. The brain does not shut down the heart, or the body would stop functioning. It also does not bypass or inhibit the effector because it needs the effector to produce a response.
3.4 The illustration indicates that the response caused by the effector in this example is that the blood pressure lowers. It does not remain the same, drop to nothing, or increase.

4.1 **B**; 4.2 **A**; 4.3 **B**; 4.4 **D**; **DOK Level:** 2; **Content Topic:** L.a.2; **Practices:** SP.1.a, SP.1.b, SP.1.c, SP.7.a
4.1 A foreign substance is an antigen. The passage indicates that when an antigen enters the body, the immune system sends antibodies to it. The immune system itself does not bind with the antigen; the antibodies do. The immune system does not send antigens; they are the foreign particles. The antibodies do not yet cluster together at this point in the sequence of events.
4.2 The passage explains that the antibodies bind with the antigens. They do not collect, attack, or destroy the antigens.
4.3 The illustration shows that each antibody has binding sites at two ends of its Y-shape that help bring about the result of binding with antigens.
4.4 The passage and illustration indicate that because the antibodies have two binding sites and can, therefore, each attach to two antigens, the antibodies and antigens form large clusters. They do not speed up in the blood. They also do not each increase in size; they just cluster together. They connect to form clusters, not long chains.

5.1 **A**; 5.2 **C**; 5.3 **A**; 5.4 **D**; **DOK Level:** 2; **Content Topic:** L.a.2; **Practices:** SP.1.a, SP.1.b, SP.1.c
5.1 According to the passage, a typical cause of an asthma attack could be dust or pollen. Muscle contractions can happen during an asthma attack, but they do not cause it. Sneezing and a runny nose are associated with a cold, not asthma. Antibodies in the blood fight off antigens; they do not cause asthma attacks.
5.2 Exposure to certain substances can cause air passages to narrow as the muscles tighten, as shown in the illustration. There is less air, not more air, moving into the air passages because the air passages narrow. The air passages constrict, but they do not close and cut off all air. The air passages do not fill completely with fluid during an asthma attack.
5.3 According to the illustration, another result of exposure to certain substances is an increase in mucus. This makes the air passages smaller, not larger. Muscle cramps are not associated with this allergic response. A person whose air passages are smaller than normal will not have relaxed breathing.
5.4 The passage and illustration provide information supporting the idea that the main symptom of an asthma attack is shortness of breath, resulting from the narrowing of the air passages. Headache, joint pain, and upset stomach are not associated with asthma attacks.

LESSON 5, pp. 18–21
1. **C**; **DOK Level:** 1; **Content Topic:** L.a.4; **Practices:** SP.1.a, SP.1.b, SP.1.c
The data point for children for 2010–2011 lies closest to the "50" mark on the *y*-axis, so about 50 percent of children were vaccinated during that flu season. The figures *30 percent* and *40 percent* are too low to be good approximations of the data point for children. The figure *60 percent* is too high to be a good approximation of the data point for children.

2. A; DOK Level: 2; **Content Topic:** L.a.4; **Practices:** SP.1.a, SP.1.b, SP.1.c

The line for adults on the graph is almost straight, indicating that about the same percentage of adults were vaccinated during each year represented by the graph. The line for children goes up, indicating that more children were vaccinated in 2010–2011 and 2011–2012 than in 2009–2010. The line for adults is always lower than the line for children, indicating that for all years represented by the graph, the percentage of adults getting flu shots was lower than the percentage of children getting flu shots. The percentage of children vaccinated in 2011–2012 was below 60 percent because the data point is below the "60" mark on the y-axis.

3. B; DOK Level: 1; **Content Topic:** L.a.4; **Practices:** SP.1.a, SP.1.b, SP.1.c

The blue bars represent males, and the blue bar for the "26–35 years" age group is the tallest bar in the graph, so the majority of adults killed were males 26 to 35 years old, not males 18 to 25 years old. The number of males killed was greater than the number of females killed in every age group.

4. A; DOK Level: 1; **Content Topic:** L.a.4; **Practices:** SP.1.a, SP.1.b, SP.1.c

The last green bar on the graph represents females over 46 years old, and the top of the bar is below the number 20 on the *y*-axis, so the graph shows that in the community represented, fewer than 20 females over 46 years old died from the Black Death. The bar would be higher if the number of females over 46 years old who died from the Black Death had been between 20 and 40, 40 and 60, or 60 and 80.

5. D; DOK Level: 2; **Content Topic:** L.a.4; **Practices:** SP.1.a, SP.1.b, SP.1.c

The data indicate that Sub-Saharan Africa needs a 33 percent increase from 2008 to 2015 in the percentage of the population using improved sanitation (64 percent minus 31 percent) to meet its 2015 goal; this is the highest increase needed among the areas to meet the 2015 goals. The graph shows that many of the areas are close to meeting their 2015 goals, indicating that progress is being made in many areas. According to the graph, Northern Africa had exceeded its 2015 goal by 2008 and Western Asia was very close to meeting its 2015 goal by 2008.

6. C; DOK Level: 3; **Content Topic:** L.a.4; **Practices:** SP.1.a, SP.1.b, SP.1.c, SP.3.c

According to the graph, Northern Africa has met its 2015 goal and three other areas—South-Eastern Asia, Latin America and the Caribbean, and Western Asia—are within 5 percent of their 2015 goals. The other areas are more than 15 percent from their goals, so it is much less likely that they will reach them.

7. B; DOK Level: 2; **Content Topic:** L.a.4; **Practices:** SP.1.a, SP.1.b, SP.1.c

The highest data point on the graph corresponds with 1916, indicating that the incidence of polio peaked around 1916. 1912 is the first year shown on the graph, not the year that the incidence of polio peaked. The data point corresponding with 1952 is high, but not as high as the data point corresponding with 1916, indicating that the incidence of polio was high around 1952 but not at its peak. The lowest data point on the graph corresponds with 1963 and indicates that the incidence of polio was at or near zero around 1963.

8. D; DOK Level: 2; **Content Topic:** L.a.4; **Practices:** SP.1.a, SP.1.b, SP.1.c, SP.3.a

The graph supports the statement from the passage by showing decreased rates of new cases after approval of the vaccine, indicating that more children were getting vaccinated. Vaccinated children were not getting polio, so there was not an increase in the number of polio cases in vaccinated children. In the early 1950s, there was an increase, not a decrease, in the number of polio cases. The graph does not give data about the number of young children in the United States at the time.

9. A; DOK Level: 2; **Content Topic:** L.a.4; **Practices:** SP.1.a, SP.1.b, SP.1.c

Hemodialysis as a source of hepatitis C infection falls into the "Other" category on the graph, which in total accounts for only 5 percent of hepatitis C cases. According to the graph, 15 percent of hepatitis C cases are linked to sexual transmission, whereas only 10 percent of cases result from transfusion occurring before blood was routinely screened for the virus. The graph shows that the cause is unknown for only 10 percent of hepatitis C cases and that the greatest, not the fewest, number of hepatitis C cases are caused by injected-drug use.

10. C; DOK Level: 3; **Content Topic:** L.a.4; **Practices:** SP.1.a, SP.1.b, SP.1.c

According to the graph, the majority of people who contracted hepatitis C did so through injected-drug use, which involves the use of needles. So the group most likely at highest risk is people who share needles while using drugs. Those who work in the healthcare industry are not at the highest risk because they are part of the small group "Other." Those who engage in unprotected sex may contract it through sexual contact, but this cause accounts for only 15 percent of the people who have hepatitis C. Those who donate blood are not included in the data; those who received blood through transfusions before blood was routinely screened for the virus had a small chance of contracting hepatitis C.

Answer Key

UNIT 1 (continued)

11.1 **D**; 11.2 **C**; 11.3 **A**; 11.4 **B**; **DOK Level:** 3; **Content Topic:** L.a.4; **Practices:** SP.1.a, SP.1.b, SP.1.c, SP.3.b
11.1 According to the map key, the states that are colored lighter green have the highest numbers of diagnoses as of 2010. The South, from Florida to Texas, has the largest number of states that are this color. The other areas do not have as many states that are this color and, therefore, do not have as many diagnoses.
11.2 According to the key, the lowest range of diagnoses rates shown on the map is 0.0 to 5.7, so states that have a diagnoses rate at or lower than 5.7 are the states with the lowest diagnoses rates. A figure is provided, so the rates are not unavailable. The highest rate is 23.4 to 50.4. The graph does not address rate of change of diagnoses rates.
11.3 According to the map, the rate of diagnoses in Texas for 2010 was 23.4 to 50.4. This is a higher rate than the 2007 rate of 17.7 to 22.6. This means that the rate of diagnoses increased from 2007 to 2010 in Texas. It did not decrease or stay the same, and the information provided is not specific enough to determine whether it doubled.
11.4 The map shows a range of how many people were diagnosed with HIV in the different states in 2010. To avoid getting HIV and, therefore, a diagnosis of HIV, people need to know how it is transmitted. Greater education on how it is transmitted should help the rates of transmission and, therefore, diagnoses, decline. The graph shows only information for diagnoses rates, not information relevant to access to medications, availability of medical care, or insurance coverage.

LESSON 6, pp. 22–25
1. **C**; **DOK Level:** 2; **Content Topic:** L.c.2; **Practices:** SP.1.a, SP.1.b, SP.1.c, SP.7.a
There are arrows from the "Grasshopper," "Caterpillar," "Beetle," and "Spider" boxes to the "Sparrow" box. Therefore, the diagram indicates that sparrows eat grasshoppers, caterpillars, beetles, and spiders. There is no arrow from the "Grass," box to the "Sparrow" box, so the diagram does not show that sparrows eat grass. There is an arrow from the "Grasshopper" box to the "Sparrow" box but no arrow from the "Dandelion" box to the "Sparrow" box, so the diagram shows that sparrows eat grasshoppers but not dandelions. The arrows from the "Sparrow" box to the "Hawk" box and the "Snake" box indicate that hawks and snakes eat sparrows, not vice versa.

2. **A**; **DOK Level:** 2; **Content Topic:** L.c.2; **Practices:** SP.1.a, SP.1.b, SP.1.c, SP.7.a
The two arrows to the "Snake" box and three arrows to the "Spider" box indicate that snakes have two food sources and spiders have three food sources. The multiple arrows leading to each animal in the food web indicate that each animal has more than one kind of food source. Only the arrows from the "Toad," "Sparrow," and "Snake" boxes lead to the "Hawk" box. Toads, sparrows, and snakes are all animals; therefore, the diagram indicates that hawks eat only animals. Of all the living things identified in the diagram, only three—toads, sparrows, and spiders—eat insects.

3. **A**; **DOK Level:** 2; **Content Topics:** L.c.1, L.c.2; **Practices:** SP.1.a, SP.1.b, SP.1.c
Lizards and snakes are listed in the "Secondary consumers" box of the diagram. Ants and beetles are listed in the "Second trophic level" section of the diagram. Hawks and foxes are listed in the "Fourth trophic level" section of the diagram. Flowers and shrubs are listed in the "Producers" box of the diagram.

4. **B**; **DOK Level:** 2; **Content Topic:** L.c.2; **Practices:** SP.1.a, SP.1.b, SP.1.c
The diagram shows that scorpions are in the third trophic level. The arrow between the "Second trophic level" and "Third trophic level" sections shows that scorpions get energy by eating organisms in the second trophic level; this group includes the animals mice, ants, and beetles. The diagram shows that plants are producers; they make their own food. The diagram shows that ants are in the second trophic level. The arrow between the "First trophic level" and "Second trophic level" sections shows that ants get energy by eating organisms in the first trophic level; this group includes only plants. The diagram shows that snakes are secondary consumers; the arrow from the "Secondary consumers" box to the "Tertiary consumers" box shows that tertiary consumers eat secondary consumers, not vice versa.

5. **D**; **DOK Level:** 2; **Content Topic:** L.c.1; **Practices:** SP.1.a, SP.1.b, SP.1.c, SP.7.a
To answer the question, you must subtract the amount of energy contained by secondary consumers from the amount of energy contained by primary consumers. The diagram indicates that primary consumers contain 100,000 units of energy and that secondary consumers contain 10,000 units of energy. Therefore, the amount of energy lost during the energy transfer from primary consumers to secondary consumers is 90,000 units, or 100,000 units minus 10,000 units. Although the diagram indicates that primary consumers contain 100,000 units of energy and secondary consumers contain 10,000 units of energy, the question asks for the amount of energy lost during the energy transfer from primary consumers to secondary consumers, not the amount of energy contained by primary consumers or secondary consumers. The amount of energy lost during the energy transfer from primary consumers to secondary consumers is 100,000 units minus 10,000 units, or 90,000 units, not 900,000 units.

6. C; DOK Level: 3; Content Topic: L.c.1; **Practices:** SP.1.a, SP.1.b, SP.1.c, SP.3.b, SP.7.a

The diagram shows that less energy is available to support living things at the fourth trophic level than at the first trophic level. Because organisms require energy to live, this information supports the idea that an ecosystem has fewer living things at the fourth trophic level than at the first trophic level. Although the diagram shows that tertiary consumers are at the fourth trophic level and producers are at the first trophic level, this information does not support the idea that an ecosystem has fewer organisms at the fourth trophic level than at the first trophic level. The sizes of the boxes in the diagram are the same at each level; therefore, box size does not support the idea that an ecosystem has fewer organisms at the fourth trophic level than at the first trophic level. A diagram that is narrower at the top than at the bottom, such as a pyramid, can indicate that fewer organisms live at the fourth trophic level than at the first trophic level. However, this diagram is not narrower at the top than at the bottom. Therefore, its shape does not support the idea that an ecosystem has fewer organisms at the fourth trophic level than at the first trophic level.

7.1 B; 7.2 B; 7.3 D; 7.4 A; DOK Level: 2; Content Topics: L.c.1, L.c.2; **Practices:** SP.1.a, SP.1.b, SP.1.c, SP.7.a

7.1 The lowest level of an energy pyramid shows producers; the diagram indicates that dandelions and grasses are producers. Caterpillars and beetles are in the primary consumers level of the pyramid. Toads and spiders are in the secondary consumers level of the pyramid. Sparrows and snakes are in the tertiary consumers level of the pyramid.

7.2 The position of beetles, caterpillars, and grasshoppers directly below spiders and toads in the pyramid means that they pass on energy to spiders and toads. The position of beetles, caterpillars, and grasshoppers above dandelions and grasses in the energy pyramid means that they get energy by eating dandelions and grasses. Beetles, caterpillars, and grasshoppers are not directly below snakes and sparrows or hawks in the pyramid; therefore, they do not pass on energy to these animals.

7.3 The position of hawks directly above sparrows and snakes in the pyramid means that their food consists of sparrows and snakes. Hawks are not directly above beetles and grasshoppers, dandelions and grasses, or spiders and toads in the pyramid; therefore, they do not feed on these organisms.

7.4 The sentence needs to provide an example of the idea that organisms at higher trophic levels have less energy available to them than organisms at lower trophic levels. The pyramid shows that spiders are at the third trophic level and beetles are at the second trophic level of the ecosystem; therefore, more energy is available for use by beetles than by spiders. The pyramid shows that spiders are at the third trophic level of the ecosystem whereas hawks are at the top trophic level and snakes are at the fourth trophic level; therefore, less energy is available for use by hawks or snakes than by spiders. The pyramid shows that spiders and toads are at the same trophic level of the ecosystem; organisms at the same trophic level of an ecosystem have the same amount of available energy.

8. C; DOK Level: 2; Content Topic: L.c.2; **Practices:** SP.1.a, SP.1.b, SP.1.c

The section of the diagram in which the "White-tailed deer" and "Gray squirrel" ovals overlap shows that white-tailed deer and gray squirrels both eat nuts and corn. The diagram compares and contrasts the diets of three animals; it does not address trophic levels. Red foxes eat all organisms listed in the "Red fox" oval of the diagram; the diagram shows that red foxes eat grasses, fruit, insects, eggs, and frogs as well as mice, rabbits, and birds. The only foods for which gray squirrels and red foxes compete are listed in the section of the diagram in which the "Gray squirrel" and "Red fox" ovals overlap. They are fruit, insects, eggs, and frogs. Gray squirrels also eat seeds, pinecones, and mushrooms. Red foxes also eat grasses, mice, rabbits, and birds.

9. C; DOK Level: 2; Content Topics: L.c.1, L.c.2; **Practices:** SP.1.a, SP.1.b, SP.1.c, SP.7.a

The diagram is a type of food web, with the bottom of the diagram showing the source of energy for the ecosystem. Chemicals inside Earth are shown at the bottom of the diagram; therefore, they are the ultimate source of energy for the ecosystem. Octopuses are at the top of the food web; they are consumers, not the source of energy for the ecosystem. Bacteria are near the bottom of the food web but not at the very bottom; they are producers that use energy from chemicals inside Earth to make food. Although sunlight is the ultimate source of energy for land-based ecosystems, this diagram does not address a land-based ecosystem. This food web shows an ocean floor ecosystem for which chemicals inside Earth are the ultimate source of energy.

10. D; DOK Level: 2; Content Topics: L.c.1, L.c.2; **Practices:** SP.1.a, SP.1.b, SP.1.c, SP.3.b, SP.3.d, SP.7.a

The diagram shows that, like the fish, octopuses eat clams, mussels, tube worms, and crabs. The fish would have a position similar to that of the octopus. The fish eats crabs, mussels, and tube worms, so it would not occupy any of the positions of those animals in the food web.

11. B; DOK Level: 2; Content Topics: L.c.1, L.c.2; **Practices:** SP.1.a, SP.1.b, SP.1.c, SP.7.a

Decomposers and detritivores return nutrients to the soil. Producers get nutrients from soil, air, and water. Consumers get nutrients from producers. Therefore, both producers and consumers rely indirectly on decomposers and detritivores in a nutrients cycle. The arrows in the diagram indicate the flow of nutrients through the ecosystem. Nutrients flow from decomposers and detritivores to soil, not to plants. Therefore, plants do not use decomposers and detritivores as food. When animals die, dead animal matter exists. The diagram does not indicate that decomposers and detritivores cause animals to die or produce dead animal matter. The arrows in the diagram show that animals that eat plants get nutrients only by eating plants, not by eating decomposers and detritivores.

UNIT 1 *(continued)*

LESSON 7, pp. 26–29

1. **C**; **DOK Level:** 2; **Content Topic:** L.c.4; **Practices:** SP.1.a, SP.1.b, SP.1.c

In a mutualistic relationship, according to the table, both organisms benefit. A bee benefits by getting nectar from a flower, and the flower benefits because the bee transfers its pollen, allowing the flower to reproduce. A flea living on a dog and a mosquito biting a human are both examples of parasitism. The flea and the mosquito benefit and have negative effects on the dog and the human. A bat capturing a moth in flight is an example of a predator-prey relationship. The bat is the predator, and the moth is the prey.

2. **A**; **DOK Level:** 2; **Content Topic:** L.c.4; **Practices:** SP.1.a, SP.1.b, SP.1.c

An animal transferring burdock seeds is an example of commensalism because the burdock benefits by having its seeds scattered, but the animal is unaffected. The animal does not benefit, so it is not mutualism. The animal does not eat the burdock, so it is not a predator-prey relationship. The burdock does not harm the animal, so it is not parasitism.

3. **DOK Level:** 2; **Content Topic:** L.c.4; **Practices:** SP.1.a, SP.1.b, SP.1.c, SP.6.c

The table shows examples of a predator-prey relationship. The sea otter, salamander, great horned owl, and cheetah are listed first in the examples given and are capable of killing and eating the other organisms listed, indicating that they all can be classified as **predators**.

4. **DOK Level:** 2; **Content Topic:** L.c.4; **Practices:** SP.1.a, SP.1.b, SP.1.c, SP.6.c

Worms and mites are parasites, so the hosts in the example parasitic relationships listed in the table are **humans, sheep, fish,** and **pigeons**.

5. **DOK Level:** 2; **Content Topic:** L.c.4; **Practices:** SP.1.a, SP.1.b, SP.1.c, SP.6.c

In all three relationships, each organism benefits. Mutualism is a type of symbiotic relationship in which each organism benefits. So the scientist will place all three relationships in the **mutualism** category.

6. **DOK Level:** 2; **Content Topic:** L.c.4; **Practices:** SP.1.a, SP.1.b, SP.1.c, SP.6.c

Mutualism is a type of symbiotic relationship in which both organisms benefit. The scientist recorded the effects of three relationships. In the first relationship, white-winged doves get food, and saguaro cacti get their seeds deposited. In the second relationship, spider crabs get protection from predators in the form of camouflage, and algae get a place to live. In the third relationship, bacteria have a place to live and get food, and humans get help digesting food. These examples all fit into the category of mutualism because **both organisms benefit in each relationship**.

7. **DOK Level:** 2; **Content Topic:** L.c.4; **Practices:** SP.1.a, SP.1.b, SP.1.c, SP.6.c

If the oxpeckers harmed the rhinoceroses, the relationship would be classified as **parasitism**. In a parasitic relationship, one organism benefits, and the other organism is harmed.

8. **DOK Level:** 2; **Content Topic:** L.c.4; **Practices:** SP.1.a, SP.1.b, SP.1.c, SP.6.c

The relationship between the oxpeckers and the insects fits into the **predator-prey** category. The birds eat the insects. They are predators, and the insects are prey.

9. **DOK Level:** 2; **Content Topic:** L.c.4; **Practices:** SP.1.a, SP.1.b, SP.1.c, SP.6.c

The relationship between the barracuda and the cleaning fish is **mutualistic**. Both the barracuda and the cleaning fish benefit. The barracuda gets rid of parasites, and the cleaning fish gets food.

10. **DOK Level:** 3; **Content Topic:** L.c.4; **Practices:** SP.1.a, SP.1.b, SP.1.c, SP.6.c

The relationship between the organisms living on the barracuda and the barracuda itself is **parasitic**. The tiny organisms are parasites, and the barracuda is a host. You can tell that the tiny organisms are parasites because the barracuda needs to get rid of them.

11. **DOK Level:** 3; **Content Topic:** L.c.4; **Practices:** SP.1.a, SP.1.b, SP.1.c, SP.6.c

When the barracuda is not in a heads-up position, the relationship between the barracuda and the cleaning fish is **predator-prey**, or **predation**. The barracuda is a predator that normally eats other fish as prey.

12. **DOK Level:** 2; **Content Topic:** L.c.4; **Practices:** SP.1.a, SP.1.b, SP.1.c, SP.6.c

According to the criteria for classifying symbiotic relationships into categories, the characteristic a relationship must have to be classified as commensalism is that **one species benefits and the other is not affected**.

13. **DOK Level:** 2; **Content Topic:** L.c.4; **Practices:** SP.1.a, SP.1.b, SP.1.c, SP.6.c

The category that fits the scenario in which barnacles living on a whale harm the whale by causing an infection is **parasitism**. A parasitic relationship is one in which one organism benefits and the other is harmed.

14. **DOK Level:** 2; **Content Topic:** L.c.4; **Practices:** SP.1.a, SP.1.b, SP.1.c, SP.6.c

The category needed to classify the eagle-fish relationship is **predator-prey**, or **predation**. Eagles are predators, and fish are their prey.

15. **DOK Level:** 2; **Content Topic:** L.c.4; **Practices:** SP.1.a, SP.1.b, SP.6.c

The relationship between animals that come to an alligator hole seeking food and those that come seeking water is **predator-prey**, or **predation**. Those that are coming to the hole for water become prey for predators searching for food.

16. **DOK Level:** 3; **Content Topic:** L.c.4; **Practices:** SP.1.a, SP.1.b, SP.3.a, SP.3.b, SP.6.c

Possible answers:
Scientists might classify the relationship between alligators and animals that use their holes as commensalism. The animals coming to the holes benefit but the alligator does not benefit because the alligator has left.
Scientists might classify the relationship between alligators and animals that use their holes as predation because the alligators may return to the hole seeking food and eat the animals that come to the hole to drink.

LESSON 8, pp. 30–33

1. **B**; **DOK Level:** 2; **Content Topic:** L.c.3; **Practices:** SP.1.a, SP.1.b, SP.1.c, SP.3.b, SP.3.d
A valid generalization about populations in an ecosystem supported by the data in the graph is that population size can change notably in a relatively short period. The passage and graph do not provide enough information to make the statement that changes in population size are most affected by predation. The reindeer population remained stable for a while, but the data in the graph refute the statement that all populations remain stable for at least a hundred years. The passage and graph do not provide enough information to make the statement that population size continues to increase if resources are abundant.

2. **D**; **DOK Level:** 2; **Content Topic:** L.c.3; **Practices:** SP.1.a, SP.1.b, SP.1.c, SP.3.b
Neither the passage nor the graph provides support for the invalid generalization that the reindeer population decreased due to a new predator. The statements that the reindeer population increased and then decreased and that the reindeer population never exceeded 6,000 are facts supported by the data in the graph; they are not generalizations. The generalization that the population remained stable until 1958 is valid because it is supported by data from the graph.

3. **C**; **DOK Level:** 3; **Content Topic:** L.c.3; **Practices:** SP.1.a, SP.1.b, SP.1.c, SP.3.b
An invalid generalization based on the information is that the number of muskrats an area can support is most influenced by disease. According to the illustration, many factors influence the carrying capacity, not just disease. The other three generalizations are valid because they are supported with facts from the passage and illustration.

4. **B**; **DOK Level:** 3; **Content Topic:** L.c.4; **Practices:** SP.1.a, SP.1.b, SP.3.a
The generalization that human activity can negatively affect a population of organisms is supported by the idea that the killing of gray wolves by settlers drastically reduced their numbers. The other statements are facts from the passage, but they are not ideas that can be used to support the generalization.

5. **A**; **DOK Level:** 3; **Content Topic:** L.c.4; **Practices:** SP.1.a, SP.1.b, SP.3.b, SP.3.d
The passage provides an example about the decimation and revitalization of the gray wolf population that supports the generalization that populations of endangered species can be rebuilt if appropriate actions occur. The passage is not about carrying capacity or a predator-prey relationship. The passage does not provide enough support to justify the statement that competition for resources always leads to the steep decline of a population.

6. **A**; **DOK Level:** 2; **Content Topic:** L.c.4; **Practices:** SP.1.a, SP.1.b, SP.1.c, SP.3.b, SP.3.d
The graph shows that the population changes happened to both the hare and the lynx populations most of the time, so a valid generalization is that populations of predators and prey generally follow the same trends. As the population of prey increases, the population of predators will increase, not decrease. A large number of predators generally will lead to a decrease, not an increase, in the number of prey because there will be more predators to eat the prey. The graph shows that the number of prey is often greater than the number of predators, but not always.

7. **C**; **DOK Level:** 2; **Content Topic:** L.c.4; **Practices:** SP.1.a, SP.1.b, SP.1.c, SP.3.b
The graph does not give enough information to make the generalization that changes in the population of prey are due solely to changes in the population of its predator. The other statements are generalizations that are supported by the graph.

8. **D**; **DOK Level:** 2; **Content Topic:** L.c.3; **Practices:** SP.1.a, SP.1.b, SP.3.b
The statement that most organisms need specific environmental conditions to survive is the generalization. The word *most* is a clue. The statement that living things depend on nonliving things to survive is a fact implied by the passage. The statement that all organisms can live in all types of conditions is inaccurate; in general, certain organisms can live in certain types of conditions. The statement that amount of sunlight affects organisms is a fact implied by the passage.

9. **D**; **DOK Level:** 3; **Content Topic:** L.c.3; **Practices:** SP.1.a, SP.1.b, SP.3.b
A valid generalization is that nonliving features have a significant impact on an ecosystem. The passage explains that nonliving features such as water, amount of sunlight, and temperature limit the organisms that can live in an ecosystem, thereby having the significant impact of affecting the carrying capacities of the ecosystem. The other statements are facts that support the generalization.

10. **B**; **DOK Level:** 2; **Content Topic:** L.c.3; **Practices:** SP.1.a, SP.1.b, SP.3.b
Although the passage discusses the effects of rainfall and sunlight in an ecosystem, it is too broad an assumption to generalize that those are the only nonliving features in an ecosystem. The examples given in the passage provide support for the other answer choices meaning that they are facts or valid generalizations.

11. **A**; **DOK Level:** 2; **Content Topic:** L.c.4; **Practices:** SP.1.a, SP.1.b, SP.1.c, SP.3.b, SP.3.d
A valid generalization is that over time, people generally have become more concerned about their effects on other populations. This generalization is supported by several conservation events shown on the timelines. Data on the timelines show that population size can be changed by human interaction. Conservation events shown on the timelines refute the statement that people perceive all relationships with other populations as a matter of competition for resources. From the information provided, no generalization can be made comparing the importance of physical changes to an ecosystem to human impacts.

Answer Key

UNIT 1 (continued)

12. D; DOK Level: 3; **Content Topic:** L.c.3; **Practices:** SP.1.a, SP.1.b, SP.1.c, SP.3.b
A valid generalization about exponential growth based on the graph is that in populations that are growing exponentially, reproduction usually is occurring constantly because reproduction is necessary for population growth. Exponential growth will not continue beyond carrying capacity because carrying capacity is a maximum number. There is not enough information to support the generalization that rapid exponential growth of populations is always due to a decrease in predation. Population growth eventually is inhibited by factors, but while a population is growing exponentially, it is not inhibited.

13. A; DOK Level: 3; **Content Topic:** L.c.3; **Practices:** SP.1.a, SP.1.b, SP.1.c, SP.3.b
The passage and graph present a hypothetical scenario that cannot continue forever because ecosystems have limited resources that must be shared among all populations. Exponential population growth cannot continue indefinitely because the population itself or its competitors will limit the resources eventually. The other reasons listed are invalid generalizations because they are not based in fact.

LESSON 9, pp. 34–37

1. A; DOK Level: 1; **Content Topic:** L.c.5; **Practices:** SP.1.a, SP.1.b, SP.1.c
The passage states that the populations of certain species of cheetahs, leopards, lions, and lynxes have reached alarmingly low levels, indicating that their populations have all decreased over time. The cheetah is used as an example, and the characteristics of having a population of 12,000 or less, having a population that peaked in 1900, and being African are data and details related to the cheetah, not necessarily to all the animals mentioned.

2. C; DOK Level: 2; **Content Topic:** L.c.5; **Practices:** SP.1.a, SP.1.b, SP.1.c
The highest bar on the graph indicates that the greatest number of cheetahs lived in 1900. The population of cheetahs did not increase between 1900 and 1980; rather, it decreased. There were fewer, not more, cheetahs in 2007 than in 1980 and more, not fewer, cheetahs in 1900 than in 2007.

3. DOK Level: 2; **Content Topic:** L.c.5; **Practices:** SP.1.a, SP.1.b, SP.3.a, SP.6.a, SP.6.c
The characteristics of an area before desertification include **is forested**, **has greater biodiversity**, and **is able to recover from drought**. These characteristics all support a normal healthy balance of activities and vegetation for an area to remain productive. The characteristics of an area after desertification include **is used to grow crops**, **is at greater risk of soil erosion**, and **has less biodiversity**. The clearing of forested land for agricultural crops is a cause of desertification. This action leads to a higher risk for soil erosion and a reduction in plant cover. These factors all lead to lower biodiversity because there is less habitat for the animals and plants living in the ecosystem.

4. DOK Level: 2; **Content Topics:** L.c.2, L.c.5; **Practices:** SP.1.a, SP.1.b, SP.1.c, SP.3.a, SP.6.a
If the population of sea otters drops drastically, the populations of sea urchins, mussels, and clams will **increase** because there will be fewer otters to eat those animals. If the population of sea urchins increases, the kelp population will **decrease** because there will be more sea urchins to eat the kelps. If the populations of mussels and clams increase, the algae population will **decrease** because there will be more mussels and clams to eat the algae. The population of sea lions likely will have **no change** because it is part of the food web that includes the sea otter but not part of the sea otter food chain. Also, the passage explains that the sea lion population has already decreased, resulting in the orca whale's consumption of more sea otters, indicating that the sea lion population is already too low to support the current orca whale population.

5. DOK Level: 2; **Content Topic:** L.c.5; **Practices:** SP.1.a, SP.1.b, SP.3.a, SP.6.a, SP.6.c
The characteristics that apply only to native plants include **historically are part of the ecosystem** and **contribute positively to habitat**. Native plants occur naturally in the ecosystem in which they are growing, and they provide habitat, protective cover, and food for other living things in the ecosystem. The characteristics that apply only to invasive species are **grow uncontrollably**, **spread quickly**, and **choke out other plants**. The kudzu plant is an example of an invasive plant. It grows uncontrollably because there are no other organisms that feed on it to keep it in check. It also spreads quickly because of this. Since it grows uncontrollably and quickly, it can choke out native plants by growing right over them. The characteristic that applies to both native plants and invasive plants is **prevent erosion**. Any plant that is rooted in soil helps prevent erosion because it holds the soil in place so that it is less likely to be carried away by wind or water.

LESSON 10, pp. 38–41

1. C; DOK Level: 2; **Content Topics:** L.d.3, L.e.1; **Practices:** SP.1.a, SP.1.b, SP.1.c, SP.7.a
The text explains that chromosomes replicate just before a cell begins cell division. The illustration shows a cell with chromosomes that have replicated, so the cell is beginning mitosis. There is not enough information to conclude that it is a human cell. A chromosome contains DNA, so the DNA has already been packaged. If the cell were completing cell division, it would be depicted as almost two separate cells.

2. A; DOK Level: 2; **Content Topics:** L.d.3, L.e.1; **Practices:** SP.1.a, SP.1.b, SP.1.c, SP.7.a
The text explains that replication of a chromosome creates two identical units called chromatids, and the illustration shows the two chromatids joined by a centromere. The telomeres are the arms of chromatids; they do not join two chromatids together. A chromosome is two chromatids joined together, not the point where they join. Histones are the proteins that, with DNA, form chromatin.

3. **A**; **DOK Level:** 2; **Content Topics:** L.d.3, L.e.1; **Practices:** SP.1.a, SP.1.b, SP.1.c, SP.7.a
The text describes genes being expressed (activated) and repressed (left inactive) to tell cells what type of cell they should become. This concept is also shown in the diagram with the expression of neuron-specific and epithelial-specific genes, so the correct genes must be activated in a cell for it to become a neuron. It does not matter what genes are present in existing neurons; the correct genes must be activated in a cell that will become a neuron. The genes must code for proteins involved in building nervous system tissue, not bone. The neuron-specific genes in the cells must be expressed rather than repressed.

4. **B**; **DOK Level:** 2; **Content Topics:** L.d.3, L.e.1; **Practices:** SP.1.a, SP.1.b, SP.1.c, SP.7.a
The text states that early embryonic cells are alike but that differentiation begins as a human develops, so an embryonic cell may differentiate as shown in the diagram to form other types of cells, such as liver cells. None of the other types of cells—stomach, muscle, or white blood cells—can differentiate; they can only divide to form more cells of the same type.

5. **D**; **DOK Level:** 2; **Content Topics:** L.d.3, L.e.1; **Practices:** SP.1.a, SP.1.b, SP.1.c, SP.7.a
The text explains that genetic material (DNA) is contained mostly in cell nuclei in eukaryotes and that the cells of prokaryotes do not have nuclei. The table shows that bacteria are prokaryotes, so their cells do not have nuclei in which to contain DNA. The other organisms are eukaryotes, so DNA is contained in their cell nuclei.

6. **DOK Level:** 3; **Content Topics:** L.d.3, L.e.1; **Practices:** SP.1.a, SP.1.b, SP.1.c, SP.6.a, SP.6.c, SP.7.a
The passage and completed parts of the diagram provide information for correctly labeling the diagram. The passage explains that interphase is the period before mitosis and that chromosomes replicate before mitosis, so **DNA replicates** during interphase. The passage states that replicated chromosomes are visible during the first phase of mitosis, which is prophase, so **chromosomes are visible** during prophase. The illustrated parts of the diagram indicate that **chromatids separate** during anaphase. The passage explains that the cell division process is completed during cytokinesis, so **two individual daughter cells form** at the completion of cytokinesis.

7. **B**; **DOK Level:** 2; **Content Topics:** L.d.3, L.e.1; **Practices:** SP.1.a, SP.1.b, SP.1.c, SP.7.a, SP.8.b
According to the passage, each daughter cell receives only one chromosome from each chromosome pair in the parent cell. The diagram shows that the parent cells in the father and mother each have 46 chromosomes, so each daughter cell will receive half of the chromosomes of the parent cell, or 23 chromosomes, not 46, 92, or 12.

8. **C**; **DOK Level:** 2; **Content Topics:** L.d.3, L.e.1; **Practices:** SP.1.a, SP.1.b, SP.1.c, SP.7.a
According to the passage, chromatids are involved in crossing over and swapping genetic material, and the diagram shows that the two chromatids that cross over are nonsister chromatids. The text states that the two chromosomes involved in crossing over are homologous, not nonhomologous. The diagram shows that crossing over happens before the parent cell has divided to form gametes, not after, and that after crossing over, all four of the resulting chromosomes are different from one another.

LESSON 11, *pp. 42–45*

1. **D**; **DOK Level:** 2; **Content Topic:** L.e.2; **Practices:** SP.1.a, SP.1.b, SP.1.c
The Punnett square shows two alleles (*Y* and *y*) for the gene for seed color, indicating that the trait of seed color is controlled by a gene with alleles that can differ. Seed color appears in all plants as either yellow or green, not as yellow-green. The Punnett square indicates that the seed color trait is controlled by two forms of a gene, not by multiple genes. Seed color is a trait that is passed on to offspring, as indicated by the Punnett square.

2. **C**; **DOK Level:** 3; **Content Topic:** L.e.2; **Practices:** SP.1.a, SP.1.b, SP.1.c, SP.3.d, SP.8.b, SP.8.c
Presence of the dominant allele, represented by *Y*, causes a pea plant to have yellow seeds. According to the genotypes shown, the dominant allele will be present in three out of four offspring, so the trait of having yellow seeds will occur in three-fourths, or 75 percent, of offspring. One-fourth, or 25 percent, of offspring will have green seeds. The other percentages listed in the answer choices do not apply.

3. **DOK Level:** 2; **Content Topic:** L.e.2; **Practices:** SP.1.a, SP.1.b, SP.1.c, SP.8.b, SP.8.c
If the Punnett square were complete, the boxes in the left column would show offspring with the genotype *FF*, and the boxes in the right column would show offspring with the genotype *Ff*. A homozygous gene has two identical alleles, so the **offspring in the left column** have homozygous genes for freckles.

4. **DOK Level:** 2; **Content Topic:** L.e.2; **Practices:** SP.1.a, SP.1.b, SP.1.c
In Investigation 2, two plants having the genotype *rr* were crossed. The genotypes of the parent plants form the row headings and column headings of a Punnett square, so the **green Punnett square** represents Investigation 2.

5. **DOK Level:** 3; **Content Topic:** L.e.2; **Practices:** SP.1.a, SP.1.b, SP.1.c, SP.8.b
Someone who has a homozygous genotype for a trait has identical alleles for the trait. Because the trait shown in the pedigree chart is controlled by a dominant allele, all individuals demonstrating the trait have either one or two dominant alleles. The chart shows all individuals who demonstrate the trait but not whether they have heterozygous or homozygous dominant genotypes for the trait. On the other hand, any individual who does not demonstrate the trait has two identical recessive alleles. So all **individuals represented by white shapes** have a homozygous recessive genotype for the trait.

6. **DOK Level:** 2; **Content Topic:** L.e.2; **Practices:** SP.1.a, SP.1.b, SP.1.c, SP.8.b
For an individual to have the trait caused by a recessive gene, the individual must be homozygous for the trait, meaning his or her genotype for the trait must contain two recessive genes. In the chart, **all individuals with the genotype *rr*** have the disease.

7. **DOK Level:** 3; **Content Topic:** L.e.2; **Practices:** SP.1.a, SP.1.b, SP.1.c, SP.8.b, SP.8.c
The **blue Punnett square** represents the genotypic ratio 0:4:0. If the Punnett square were complete, it would show zero *TT* genotypes, four *Tt* genotypes, and zero *tt* genotypes.

Answer Key

UNIT 1 (continued)

8. DOK Level: 3; **Content Topic:** L.e.2; **Practices:** SP.1.a, SP.1.b, SP.1.c, SP.8.b, SP.8.c
The **green Punnett square** represents the phenotypic ratio 3:1. If the Punnett square were complete, it would show that the results of the cross are *NN*, *Nn*, *Nn*, and *nn*. Three of these genotypes—*NN*, *Nn*, and *Nn*—include the dominant allele and, therefore, produce the phenotype of demonstrating the trait. One genotype, *nn*, includes only recessive alleles and, therefore, produces the phenotype of not demonstrating the trait.

LESSON 12, pp. 46–49

1. A; DOK Level: 2; **Content Topic:** L.e.3; **Practices:** SP.1.a, SP.1.b, SP.1.c, SP.3.b, SP.7.a
The passage explains that meiosis consists of two rounds of cell divisions and indicates that Prophase I is a part of meiosis; therefore, it is logical to assume that Prophase I is a stage related to the first round of cell division. Because Prophase I is an action that occurs during meiosis, it is logical to assume that the *I* relates to an event happening during meiosis, not to a thing, such as a chromosome or a cell, and not to an event that occurs before meiosis.

2. C; DOK Level: 2; **Content Topic:** L.e.3; **Practices:** SP.1.a, SP.1.b, SP.1.c, SP.3.b, SP.7.a
The details "break apart" and "rejoin to form new combinations" explain how genetic recombination occurs. The other phrases are related to the topic of genetic recombination but do not explain what it is.

3. D; DOK Level: 2; **Content Topic:** L.e.3; **Practices:** SP.1.a, SP.1.b, SP.1.c, SP.3.b, SP.7.a
The passage explains that mutations are sometimes to genes, so a genetic mutation would be a mutation, or change, to a gene. Changes to DNA are mutations, but they can be mutations that do not affect genes and, therefore, are not necessarily genetic mutations. A genetic mutation can have a negative effect or go unnoticed, but these descriptions do not explain what a genetic mutation is.

4. B; DOK Level: 2; **Content Topic:** L.e.3; **Practices:** SP.1.a, SP.1.b, SP.1.c, SP.3.b, SP.7.a
The passage states that a change to a gene can alter the gene's ability to give correct instructions for protein synthesis and then provides details to further explain that statement. In those details, "protein synthesis" is restated as "production of proteins," so protein synthesis is the production, or making, of proteins. Sometimes the word *synthesis* is used to mean a combining of information to form an understanding; in this context, however, that definition of *synthesis* does not apply. Instruction from a gene brings about protein synthesis; it is not the same thing as protein synthesis. Mutations affect genes, not proteins directly.

5. A; DOK Level: 2; **Content Topic:** L.e.3; **Practices:** SP.1.a, SP.1.b, SP.1.c, SP.3.b, SP.7.a
The example in the "Insertion" row of the table shows that the resulting DNA has more nucleotide bases than the original. This clue tells you that an insertion is the addition of extra nucleotide bases. The subtraction of nucleotide bases describes a deletion. The restructuring of nucleotide bases describes a frameshift, and the swapping of one nucleotide base for another describes a substitution.

6. B; DOK Level: 3; **Content Topic:** L.e.3; **Practices:** SP.1.a, SP.1.b, SP.3.b, SP.7.a
The statistics the author provides have to do with twins showing a similar trait, schizophrenia, much of the time, indicating that the trait of schizophrenia must be related to genetics. From this clue, you can understand that a genetic component is a factor involving an organism's genes. The information discusses both genetic factors and environmental factors, which are elements in the environment, not something involving an organism's genes. Twin studies do help pinpoint molecular mechanisms, but the purpose of this study is to look at environmental factors, which affect everyone, not just twins. So the author would not be discussing evidence that proves something about only twins. Although a gene is a component (part) of DNA, a genetic component in this context is a factor related to genes.

7. A; DOK Level: 3; **Content Topic:** L.e.3; **Practices:** SP.1.a, SP.1.b, SP.3.b, SP.7.a
The passage states that a mutation to a gene switch can cause changes in where, when, and how much of a protein is produced. From that clue, you can determine that a gene switch regulates the location, timing, and extent of production of a protein. A gene, not a gene switch, gives instruction for how a protein is produced. A gene switch does not affect protein as it is being made. A gene switch does affect protein production—by regulating the location, timing, and extent of protein production.

8. C; DOK Level: 2; **Content Topic:** L.e.3; **Practices:** SP.1.a, SP.1.b, SP.3.b, SP.7.a
The passage states that a mutation occurring in a germ line cell can be passed to offspring, indicating that germ line cells are involved in sexual reproduction. Although germs are associated with illness, germ line cells have nothing to do with disease; in this context, the word *germ* has a different meaning. Brain cells are somatic, or body, cells, not cells involved in sexual reproduction. Body cells used in growth is a description of somatic cells.

9. B; DOK Level: 3; **Content Topic:** L.e.3; **Practices:** SP.1.a, SP.1.b, SP.3.b, SP.7.a
The passage contrasts DNA that makes up genes and noncoding DNA. You know that genes code for the production of proteins, so you can determine that noncoding DNA is DNA that does not have instructions for proteins. All DNA, not just noncoding DNA, is involved in replication, mutations, and correction of errors.

ANSWER KEY

10. **D**; **DOK Level:** 2; **Content Topic:** L.e.3; **Practices:** SP.1.a, SP.1.b, SP.3.b, SP.7.a

The statement that mutations can have an impact beyond an individual is the topic sentence of the second paragraph. The rest of the paragraph gives context clues explaining that this statement means that future generations can be affected as well. A mutation that occurs in an individual does not affect the individual's ancestors or siblings or other members of the individual's population.

11. **B**; **DOK Level:** 2; **Content Topic:** L.e.3; **Practices:** SP.1.a, SP.1.b, SP.3.b, SP.7.a

The concluding sentences of the passage explain how a mutation can result in the formation of a new allele, so in this context, the word *development* means "formation." The other words are synonyms for *development* but not as it is used in this context.

12. **A**; **DOK Level:** 2; **Content Topic:** L.e.3; **Practices:** SP.1.a, SP.1.b, SP.1.c, SP.3.b, SP.7.a

The passage explains that a temperature-sensitive gene for pigment leads to the cat being darker colored in the cooler parts of its body. From this clue, you can determine that pigment is a substance that gives an animal, or a plant, color. Pigment is not a gene or an allele; it is a substance whose production is controlled by genes and alleles. Pigment is controlled by an environmental factor in this case, but pigment is itself part of an organism, not an environmental factor.

13. **D**; **DOK Level:** 3; **Content Topic:** L.e.3; **Practices:** SP.1.a, SP.1.b, SP.3.b, SP.7.a

The passage relates scientists' manipulation of epigenetic marks in labs to the development of drugs and then gives as an example drugs that stimulate tumor-suppressing genes. A behavior is an example of ways in which actions and environment can affect one's genome. Genes that play a role in disease and epigenetic marks that can be inherited are topics related to studying the epigenome but are not examples that help explain scientists' manipulation of epigenetic marks in labs.

14. **C**; **DOK Level:** 3; **Content Topic:** L.e.3; **Practices:** SP.1.a, SP.1.b, SP.3.b, SP.7.a

The passage uses the phrase *lie dormant* when describing how scientists hope to control disease-causing genes. You can reason that scientists would want such genes to be inactive, so you can determine that *lie dormant* means "remain inactive and unexpressed." A dormant gene is inactive, or not able to express anything, so it would not be attacking itself, using greater amounts of energy, or activating tumor-suppressor genes.

LESSON 13, *pp. 50–53*

1. **D**; **DOK Level:** 1; **Content Topic:** L.f.1; **Practices:** SP.1.a, SP.1.b, SP.1.c, SP.7.a

The trait at the bottom of a cladogram is the original trait, which all the organisms have. So the cladogram shows that all the animals have a vertebral column. Moving up a cladogram, each organism has a new derived characteristic that the previous organisms do not have. So the cladogram indicates that only certain animals have amniotic eggs, four walking legs, and jaws.

2. **A**; **DOK Level:** 2; **Content Topic:** L.f.1; **Practices:** SP.1.a, SP.1.b, SP.1.c, SP.3.b, SP.7.a

Moving up a cladogram, each organism has a greater number of derived characteristics than the previous organism. So the organism at the top, the leopard in this case, has the greatest number of derived characteristics. All the other animals are lower on the cladogram, so they have fewer derived characteristics than the leopard.

3. **C**; **DOK Level:** 1; **Content Topic:** L.f.1; **Practices:** SP.1.a, SP.1.b, SP.1.c, SP.4.a, SP.7.a

The passage states that the extinct land animal *Pakicetus* is a relative of today's whales. A relative of whales, not whales themselves, once lived on land. Whales did not descend from wolves; instead, whales are related to an animal that is similar to wolves. The skulls of the ancient animal, not the skulls of whales, have transitional features.

4. **B**; **DOK Level:** 1; **Content Topic:** L.f.1; **Practices:** SP.1.a, SP.1.b, SP.7.a

The passage states that a vestigial structure is less functional or no longer functional—and thereby less important—in the organism that exists today. By the definition of a vestigial structure, an organism living today cannot have the same vestigial structures as its ancestor. The passage gives an example of vestigial structures that relate to vision and living in a certain habitat, but vestigial structures are not limited to such functions.

5. **B**; **DOK Level:** 3; **Content Topic:** L.f.1; **Practices:** SP.1.a, SP.1.b, SP.3.b, SP.4.a, SP.7.a

Homologous structures are evidence of common ancestry. Even though the structure in one species is nonfunctioning and the structure in the other species is fully functioning, the structures are still homologous and, therefore, evidence of a common ancestor. There is no evidence that relates having a vestigial structure with extinction. Although the embryos of the two species may have similar development, the presence of homologous structures does not indicate that the embryos develop in exactly the same way. Although the species have homologous structures, the organisms themselves may be very different. Accordingly, their fossils would be different.

6. **DOK Level:** 2; **Content Topic:** L.f.1; **Practices:** SP.1.a, SP.1.b, SP.1.c, SP.3.b, SP.6.a, SP.6.c, SP.7.a

Humans, gorillas, and tigers all have hair, but humans and gorillas do not have tails, and gorillas do not move by using only two feet. So the order of animals on the cladogram's branches, from lowest to highest, is **tiger**, **gorilla**, **human**.

7. **C**; **DOK Level:** 2; **Content Topic:** L.f.1; **Practices:** SP.1.a, SP.1.b, SP.3.a, SP.4.a, SP.7.a

Darwin reasoned that organisms evolve slowly in form from organisms of the past, so fossil evidence from different time periods of organisms with characteristics that become more similar to those of living animals supports his reasoning. Characteristics of living animals or fossils of animals from the same time period provide no evidence to support his reasoning because the evidence must show change over time.

Answer Key

UNIT 1 *(continued)*

8. C; DOK Level: 2; **Content Topic:** L.f.1; **Practices:**
SP.1.a, SP.1.b, SP.1.c, SP.7.a, SP.8.b
The 12 regions colored blue in the diagram show similar
sets of DNA sequences. The numbers *2, 11,* and *23* relate
to other aspects of the diagram. There are 2 genes shown,
11 regions in which the DNA sequences are not identical,
and 23 regions in all.

9. D; DOK Level: 3; **Content Topic:** L.f.1; **Practices:**
SP.1.a, SP.1.b, SP.1.c, SP.3.a, SP.4.a, SP.7.a
The passage states that the more similar the DNA
sequences in the genomes of two species, the more closely
related the species are. The diagram provides evidence of
a common ancestor because it shows a high percentage
of identical coding in a fly gene and a mouse gene even
though insects and mammals have evolved separately for
millions of years. The diagram does show that scientists
have compared the two species' DNA, but that fact alone
does not provide evidence of common ancestry. The
diagram shows that two animals have some similar DNA
sequences, not that the DNA for all organisms is the same
nor that the two animals have similarly structured eyes.

10. A; DOK Level: 3; **Content Topic:** L.f.1; **Practices:**
SP.1.a, SP.1.b, SP.1.c, SP.3.b, SP.7.a
The passage, supported by the diagram, identifies evidence
scientists have found showing that the DNA sequences of
a gene for mouse eye development and a gene for fly eye
development are very similar. Evidence scientists have
found supports the idea that mice and flies have a common
ancestor, but the reason the fly grew eyes is due to DNA
in the current forms of the animals. The passage and
diagram provide information about evidence of similar DNA
sequences on only one particular gene in each animal. The
passage and diagram provide no support for the idea that
fly genes are easier to manipulate than any other animal's
genes.

LESSON 14, *pp. 54–57*

1. C; DOK Level: 1; **Content Topic:** L.f.2; **Practices:**
SP.1.a, SP.1.b, SP.7.a
Darwin infers that small eyes are beneficial to burrowing
animals because the smaller the animal's eyes, the less
chance there is for inflammation to occur. The passage
indicates that burrowing animals are frequently blind and
certainly do not have strong eyesight and that their eyes are
small, not large. The passage gives no information about
whether moles have smaller eyes than certain burrowing
rodents.

2. B; DOK Level: 1; **Content Topic:** L.f.2; **Practices:**
SP.1.a, SP.1.b, SP.7.a
Darwin states that a reduction in eye size *might* be an
advantage. This wording helps you understand that he is
making an inference about the relationship of a trait to an
environment, not stating a fact. The signal wording options
if...then, could, and *probably* are not used.

3. C; DOK Level: 2; **Content Topic:** L.f.2; **Practices:**
SP.1.a, SP.1.b, SP.1.c, SP.3.b, SP.7.a
The rabbits represented by the left side of the graph have
a slower running speed, so they are more easily caught.
According to the graph, very few rabbits have a faster
running speed than the predator, so it is likely that the
predator is able to capture many rabbits. Although the data
on the graph represent one type of predator, it is inaccurate
to infer that only one type of predator feeds on the rabbits.
The rabbits represented by the left side of the graph have a
slower running speed, so they are more likely to be caught
and, therefore, less likely to reproduce.

4. D; DOK Level: 2; **Content Topic:** L.f.2; **Practices:**
SP.1.a, SP.1.b, SP.1.c, SP.3.b, SP.7.a
Due to natural selection, the trait of faster running speed will
become more common in the rabbit population. Running
speed is a trait that is variable within the species; therefore,
all the rabbits will never have the same running speed.
Although faster running speed will become a more common
trait among the rabbits, the curve shows that running
speed would have to change dramatically throughout the
population for most rabbits to be faster than the predator. It
is unlikely that slower running speed will become a common
trait in the predator population because that trait would not
help the predator survive in its environment.

5. A; DOK Level: 2; **Content Topic:** L.f.2; **Practices:**
SP.1.a, SP.1.b, SP.1.c, SP.3.b, SP.7.a.
The data for the period during which the scientist made her
observations and the previously collected data indicate that
there were more light-colored moths before the factories
were built and fewer later, after the factories were built, and
that the opposite was true of dark-colored moths. So the
inference can be made that the population of light-colored
moths decreased over time and the population of dark-
colored moths increased. It is inaccurate to infer that the
populations remained stable or both increased.

6. B; DOK Level: 2; **Content Topic:** L.f.2; **Practices:**
SP.1.a, SP.1.b, SP.1.c, SP.3.b, SP.7.a
The facts that light-colored moths hid on light tree trunks,
the factory smoke blackened the tree trunks, and the
population of light-colored moths decreased support the
inference that because of providing the ability to hide more
easily, light color was an advantage when the tree trunks
were light. On the other hand, dark color was an advantage
when the tree trunks turned dark. There is no evidence that
dark color affects the ability to live in polluted environments
or the chance of survival overall. The information in the
passage and data in the table indicate that color can affect
survival.

7. D; DOK Level: 2; **Content Topic:** L.f.2; **Practices:**
SP.1.a, SP.1.b, SP.1.c, SP.7.a
If a species has been modified for different purposes,
future generations would differ from their ancestors. So
Darwin is inferring that the finches with the varying beaks
have a common ancestor. The passage does not indicate
that the finches with the different beak shapes came from
different islands. Darwin does not discuss a comparison of
birds from the Galápagos Islands with birds from London.
A connection between climate and beak shape is not
related to Darwin's inference.

8. A; DOK Level: 2; **Content Topic:** L.f.2; **Practices:** SP.1.a, SP.1.b, SP.1.c, SP.3.b, SP.7.a
Because the beaks are different sizes and shapes and the beak is used for collecting food, the birds probably eat different types of food. The specimens were collected at the same time, so one bird is not the ancestor of another. From the information provided, it is not possible to infer whether one bird is more likely to reproduce than another. That one beak is smaller than another is an observation, not an inference.

9. A; DOK Level: 2; **Content Topic:** L.f.2; **Practices:** SP.1.a, SP.1.b, SP.3.a, SP.7.a
Along with the fact that sunlight can trigger vitamin D production in humans, the explanation that lighter skin, which produces vitamin D more efficiently, became more common in populations living in less sunny environments supports the inference. The other statements are true, but they are not ideas that support the particular inference stated in the question.

10. D; DOK Level: 3; **Content Topic:** L.f.2; **Practices:** SP.1.a, SP.1.b, SP.3.b, SP.7.a
An understanding of genetics and information in the passage can be used to infer that to obtain offspring having certain traits, parents with those traits are bred. None of the other statements is an accurate explanation of how traits are passed from one generation to the next to produce individuals with or without certain traits.

11. C; DOK Level: 2; **Content Topic:** L.f.2; **Practices:** SP.1.a, SP.1.b, SP.3.b, SP.7.a
Dogs use their sense of smell to locate things, so the trait that would help a dog detect drugs is a keen sense of smell. The other traits are not related to finding something.

12. B; DOK Level: 3; **Content Topic:** L.f.2; **Practices:** SP.1.a, SP.1.b, SP.3.b, SP.7.a
An understanding that artificial selection of plants involves selectively planting the seeds of plants with certain traits leads to the inference that the farmers would have used seeds from plants with desirable traits in future planting seasons. Artificial selection involves propagating or breeding organisms, not discarding organisms having less desirable traits. The passage states that farmers used artificial selection based on an observation, not by accident. It is logical to assume that the earliest farmers did not have the knowledge or technology to transfer genetic material.

13. A; DOK Level: 3; **Content Topic:** L.f.2; **Practices:** SP.1.a, SP.1.b, SP.3.b, SP.7.a
Genetic engineering involves changing the genetic makeup of a species over time by the actual transfer of DNA, but artificial selection also changes the genetic makeup of a species over time by controlling the genetic material that gets passed on to future generations. Both processes can result in insect-resistant plants, but they do not always have this effect. Only genetic engineering involves transferring genes from one organism to another. It is true that humans choose which crops need improving with both processes, but this statement is not an inference about how the term *genetic modification* relates to both processes.

LESSON 15, *pp. 58–61*

1. B; DOK Level: 2; **Content Topic:** L.f.3; **Practices:** SP.1.a, SP.1.b, SP.3.b, SP.7.a
The passage states that living things have adaptations related to surviving in the climates in which they live and that migration is an example of a behavioral adaptation. This information supports the inference that migration helps the animal survive and, therefore, the conclusion that the animal migrates because it cannot survive in the region's winter temperatures. The animal may or may not have adaptations that help it live in cold temperatures, but it does not have adaptations to help it live in weather as cold as the winter temperatures of the region from which it migrates. The animal does not need to move from the region permanently because it uses the adaptation of migration to leave the area as needed. The animal has not moved to a place in which it cannot survive; it survives in the region during other seasons and has adapted by leaving the region during winter.

2. A; DOK Level: 2; **Content Topic:** L.f.3; **Practices:** SP.1.a, SP.1.b, SP.3.b, SP.7.a
The passage states that deserts are very dry and that living things have adaptations related to surviving in the climates in which they live and that desert organisms, specifically, have adaptations related to conserving water. This information supports the conclusion that desert plants and animals likely have adaptations related to surviving with little water. Deserts have hot temperatures, so the plants and animals likely have adaptations for surviving in high temperatures, not moderate temperatures. There is no evidence supporting the idea that desert plants and animals live for only short periods of time. Tundras and deserts have different temperature ranges, so animals adapted for living in the desert are not necessarily likely to be adapted for living in the tundra as well.

3. DOK Level: 3; **Content Topic:** L.f.3; **Practices:** SP.1.a, SP.1.b, SP.3.a, SP.3.b, SP.6.c, SP.7.a
Possible answer:
Ⓐ The fruit flies on the island could develop into a distinct species if the factors required for speciation to occur were present. Ⓑ The island would have to be far enough from the mainland that the two populations could not reach each other to interbreed. The environmental conditions of the island and mainland would have to be different enough that the two populations would experience different selection pressures. The processes of natural selection and adaptation would have to cause the population of fruit flies on the island to develop unique traits that would make them unwilling or unable to breed with the mainland fruit flies if individuals were returned to the mainland.
Ⓐ The first sentence states a conclusion explaining how the fruit flies on the island could develop into a distinct species.
Ⓑ The rest of the paragraph lists specific ways in which the factors required for speciation could cause the population of fruit flies on the island to develop into a distinct species. The conclusion is supported by information from the passage and inferences made using that information.

Answer Key

UNIT 1 *(continued)*

4. DOK Level: 3; **Content Topic:** L.f.3; **Practices:** SP.1.a, SP.1.b, SP.3.a, SP.3.b, SP.6.c, SP.7.a
Possible answer:
Ⓐ Natural selection is critical in the development of drug-resistant microbes. Ⓑ Natural selection results from selection pressures. A selection pressure is a feature of an environment that changes an organism's ability to survive and reproduce in the environment over time. Ⓒ When introduced into a population of microbes, a drug intended to kill or limit the growth of the microbes exerts a selection pressure. Through natural selection, organisms having the trait of resistance to the drug pass that trait on to future generations until the trait becomes common in the population.
Ⓐ The first sentence states a conclusion about the significance of natural selection in the development of drug-resistant microbes.
Ⓑ The second and third sentences state background knowledge about natural selection and selection pressures.
Ⓒ The rest of the paragraph uses inferences and information from the passage to describe the critical role of natural selection in the development of drug-resistant microbes.

5. DOK Level: 3; **Content Topics:** L.c.5, L.f.3; **Practices:** SP.1.a, SP.1.b, SP.3.a, SP.3.b, SP.6.c, SP.7.a
Possible answer:
Ⓐ By changing the environment, humans exert selection pressures that affect the rate of extinction. Ⓑ The environmental changes humans bring about include habitat destruction and alteration of the climate through global warming. When the environment in which a population lives is changed, the selection pressures on the population change. If members of the population are unable to develop traits needed to survive and reproduce in the changed habitat, the population may die off. When all populations of a species die off, the species becomes extinct.
Ⓐ The first sentence states a conclusion about how humans exert selection pressures that affect the rate of extinction.
Ⓑ The rest of the paragraph uses inferences, information from the passage, and background knowledge about selection pressures to explain the ways in which humans affect environments and the potential impacts of those events.

UNIT 2 PHYSICAL SCIENCE

LESSON 1, *pp. 62–65*
1. B; DOK Level: 2; **Content Topic:** P.c.1; **Practices:** SP.1.a, SP.1.b, SP.1.c, SP.7.a
The labels indicate that protons are blue in the model. Also, the passage states that a proton can be represented by a plus sign, and the blue particles have plus signs. So the atom has seven protons. Although only one proton is labeled, other particles look the same, meaning that they also are protons. The atom has fourteen protons and neutrons and twenty-one protons, neutrons, and electrons combined.

2. A; DOK Level: 2; **Content Topic:** P.c.1; **Practices:** SP.1.a, SP.1.b, SP.1.c, SP.7.a
Based on the information in the passage, you know that an atom is electrically balanced, or has no charge, and the model shows an atom. All atoms have the same number of protons as electrons. A hydrogen atom has only one proton, whereas the atom in the model has seven protons. Neutrons in any atom have no charge.

3. C; DOK Level: 3; **Content Topic:** P.c.1; **Practices:** SP.1.a, SP.1.b, SP.1.c, SP.7.a
According to the passage, an atom has equal numbers of protons and electrons, whereas an ion has more or fewer electrons than protons. The model shows six protons and six electrons, so it represents an atom. An atom can have differing numbers of protons and neutrons. The number of electrons in the model does equal half the number of particles in the nucleus; however, the number of electrons in an ion could equal half the number of particles in the nucleus, depending on how many neutrons are in the nucleus. The particle represented by the model does not have a charge because it has equal numbers of protons and electrons.

4. A; DOK Level: 3; **Content Topic:** P.c.1; **Practices:** SP.1.b, SP.1.c, SP.7.a
The particle in the model gains two electrons to change from an atom to an ion. The result is that the ion has a negative charge because it has two more negatively charged electrons than positively charged protons. The ion would have to have more protons than electrons to be positively charged. To become an ion, an atom gains or loses electrons, not protons or neutrons.

5. D; DOK Level: 2; **Content Topic:** P.c.1; **Practices:** SP.1.a, SP.1.b, SP.1.c, SP.7.a
The passage states that prefixes in compound names tell how many atoms of a certain kind are in a molecule of a compound. The model shows that a molecule of carbon dioxide has two oxygen atoms, so it can be inferred that *dioxide* means "having two oxygen atoms." Various compounds are made up of carbon and oxygen; *dioxide* refers to the fact that the number of oxygen atoms in a molecule of the compound carbon dioxide is two. A molecule of carbon dioxide has three atoms, but *dioxide* refers to the two oxygen atoms in the molecule. Various substances contain oxygen; *dioxide* refers specifically to the fact that the number of oxygen atoms in a molecule of carbon dioxide is two.

6. B; DOK Level: 2; **Content Topic:** P.c.1; **Practices:** SP.1.a, SP.1.b, SP.1.c, SP.7.a
The lower part of the model shows that one electron is transferred from sodium to chlorine in the ionic bonding of sodium and chlorine. Atoms share electrons in covalent bonding, not ionic bonding. The electron transferred in the ionic bonding of sodium and chlorine is transferred from the sodium atom to the chlorine atom, not vice versa. In ionic bonding, ions do not move back and forth between particles.

7. C; DOK Level: 3; **Content Topic:** P.c.1; **Practices:** SP.1.a, SP.1.b, SP.1.c, SP.7.a

The sodium atom loses an electron to form the ionic bond represented by the model. The result is that the sodium ion has a positive charge because it has one more positively charged proton than it has negatively charged electrons. The model shows that sodium loses an electron, not that sodium gains an electron. The model shows that the sodium atom has fewer electrons than the chlorine atom, so the sodium atom also would have fewer protons than the chlorine atom. Number of protons does not change when an atom becomes an ion, so the sodium ion has fewer protons than the chlorine ion. The plus sign in the model relates to the sodium ion, not to the charge of a compound as a whole.

8. D; DOK Level: 2; **Content Topic:** P.c.1; **Practices:** SP.1.b, SP.1.c, SP.7.a

According to the key for the model on the left, a circled plus sign represents a proton, so each circled plus sign represents the single proton in the nucleus of one of the two hydrogen atoms that bond to form a hydrogen molecule. The electron cloud for each hydrogen atom is represented by a ring. The single electron in each hydrogen atom is represented by a yellow circle. Molecules are not formed by atoms being added together; they are formed by atoms sharing electrons.

9. D; DOK Level: 3; **Content Topic:** P.c.1; **Practices:** SP.1.b, SP.1.c, SP.7.a

You have learned that in scientific models, lines or rods connecting atoms represent covalent bonds. The stick in the model is a rod connecting the two hydrogen atoms, so it represents a covalent bond between the atoms. The stick in the model is a rod-shaped representation of a bond; it is not a literal representation of a structure in a molecule. The purpose of the model is to show the bond between atoms, not movement of the atoms or the nuclei of the atoms.

10. A; DOK Level: 3; **Content Topic:** P.c.1; **Practices:** SP.1.b, SP.1.c, SP.7.a

The shapes and structures of the models indicate that they represent the covalent bonding of two hydrogen atoms to form a hydrogen molecule. In covalent bonding, atoms share electrons; they do not lose or gain electrons. The rod shape in the model on the right is representative of a covalent bond; it is not a literal representation of the structure of a molecule.

11. DOK Level: 2; **Content Topic:** P.c.1; **Practices:** SP.1.a, SP.1.b, SP.1.c, SP.6.b, SP.7.a

The structural formula for carbon dioxide shows one carbon atom and two oxygen atoms, so the chemical formula for carbon dioxide is CO_2. The structural formula for hydrogen peroxide shows two hydrogen atoms and two oxygen atoms, so the chemical formula for hydrogen peroxide is H_2O_2. The structural formula for ozone shows three oxygen atoms, so the chemical formula for ozone is O_3.

12. B; DOK Level: 3; **Content Topic:** P.c.1; **Practices:** SP.1.a, SP.1.b, SP.1.c, SP.7.a

The passage explains that the positive end of each water molecule attracts the negative end of another molecule, and the model shows that that the hydrogen atoms form the positive end of the molecule and the oxygen atom forms the negative end. So it can be inferred that hydrogen atoms in one molecule attract the oxygen atom in another. Neither the passage nor the model indicates whether water is magnetic. Both the passage and the model indicate that water molecules are made of hydrogen and oxygen and, therefore, that water is not an element. The illustrated model shows that the atoms in a water molecule are not in a line.

LESSON 2, pp. 66–69

1. A; DOK Level: 3; **Content Topic:** P.c.2; **Practices:** SP.1.a, SP.1.b, SP.1.c, SP.7.a

By examining the diagram in the area that is near the bottom of the y-axis but to the far right on the x-axis, you can determine that the substance would be a gas under the conditions of low pressure and high temperature. The substance is a liquid under the conditions of relatively moderate pressure and temperature and a solid under the conditions of relatively high pressure and low temperature. The point at which the substance boils (vaporizes) is at the mid-range of pressure and temperature.

2. C; DOK Level: 3; **Content Topic:** P.c.2; **Practices:** SP.1.a, SP.1.b, SP.1.c, SP.7.a

Under the label "Sublimation" on the diagram, the arrow points from solid to gas, indicating that a substance changes from a solid to a gas during sublimation. The other answer choices result from an incorrect interpretation of the diagram.

3. A; DOK Level: 2; **Content Topic:** P.c.2; **Practices:** SP.1.a, SP.1.b, SP.1.c, SP.7.a

Involvement in vaporization and condensation is shown for liquids and gases, but not for solids. The overlapping area for solids and liquids shows that both solids and liquids are involved in the melting and freezing processes. The area for liquids, not solids, shows the property of having particles that bump into each other. The overlapping area for solids, liquids, and gases indicates that matter in all three states is made up of individual particles.

4. B; DOK Level: 2; **Content Topic:** P.c.2; **Practices:** SP.1.a, SP.1.b, SP.1.c, SP.7.a

The overlapping area for solids, liquids, and gases shows the property of being characterized by arrangement of particles, so the three states of matter share this characteristic. The area for gases shows that gases can be compressed. The diagram shows that only solids and gases are involved in sublimation and only gases and liquids are involved in condensation. The area for solids shows that solids cannot flow.

UNIT 2 (continued)

5. D; DOK Level: 3; **Content Topic:** P.c.2; **Practices:** SP.1.a, SP.1.b, SP.1.c, SP.3.b, SP.7.a
The diagram shows that sublimation involves a change between a solid and a gas and that melting involves a change between a solid and a liquid; the difference in particle spacing between solids and gases is much larger than that between solids and liquids. Melting involves a change from a solid to a liquid, meaning that the spacing between particles increases; it does not decrease. The spacing between particles is related to state of matter in that it differs in different states. Gases have large spaces between particles and are easily compressible, suggesting that increases in spacing between particles leads to increases, not decreases, in compressibility.

6. D; DOK Level: 2; **Content Topic:** P.c.2; **Practices:** SP.1.a, SP.1.b, SP.1.c, SP.7.a
In the illustration, the liquid is taking on the shape of the container in the part of the container it is filling, and the gas is filling the container and, therefore, taking on the shape of the entire container. It is clear from the illustration that liquids and gases do not hold their shapes. The illustration indicates that gases tend to fill their containers, whereas solids retain their shape and size, and liquids fill only a certain amount of a container. The example solid in the illustration is box-shaped, but not all solids are box-shaped. The liquid in the illustration is box-shaped only because liquid takes on the shape of its container.

7. B; DOK Level: 3; **Content Topic:** P.c.2; **Practices:** SP.1.a, SP.1.b, SP.1.c, SP.3.b, SP.7.a
Because gas takes the shape of its container, it will escape from an open container to fill the larger closed area in which it is contained. The other conclusions are not supported by the illustration. Depending on other conditions, liquid can evaporate to become a gas or freeze to become a solid even if it is in a container. The amount of liquid in a sample does not change when the liquid is put into a container, so the container must be big enough to hold the amount of liquid in the sample. As with the other substances, the solid represented in the illustration is an example. Samples of matter in the solid state can be widely varied in shape and size and so do not necessarily fit in the same size container.

8. C; DOK Level: 2; **Content Topic:** P.c.2; **Practices:** SP.1.a, SP.1.b, SP.1.c, SP.7.a
The boiling points shown on the diagram range from −61 °C to 2,239 °C, indicating that boiling point varies widely among compounds. According to the diagram, hydrogen sulfide boils at −61 °C, which is less than 0 °C, and sodium chloride has a boiling point of 1,413 °C, which is less than 2,000 °C. The diagram itself does not indicate whether each compound listed is covalent or ionic; however, the passage states that covalent compounds tend to have relatively lower, not higher, boiling points.

9. D; DOK Level: 3; **Content Topic:** P.c.2; **Practices:** SP.1.a, SP.1.b, SP.1.c, SP.3.b, SP.7.a
The passage states that ionic compounds have much higher boiling points than covalent compounds. From this idea, you can infer that the compounds shown on the diagram with boiling points above 1,000 °C are ionic compounds. Therefore, it is reasonable to assume that other ionic compounds will boil near or above 1,000 °C. The other temperatures align more closely with the boiling points of what you can assume are covalent compounds listed in the diagram.

10. B; DOK Level: 3; **Content Topic:** P.c.2; **Practices:** SP.1.a, SP.1.b, SP.1.c, SP.7.a
The passage explains that hydrocarbons are compounds having molecules made up of hydrogen and carbon. However, the graph indicates that in addition to several hydrocarbons, natural gas typically also contains nitrogen, an element, and carbon dioxide, a compound made up of carbon and oxygen. Propane, or C_3H_8, is included in the "Other" section of the graph, indicating that it is a minor ingredient because it is in a group of ingredients that makes up only 18 percent of natural gas. The graph does not give information about whether all the ingredients identified are able to be liquefied. The graph shows that methane, or CH_4, is the main ingredient in natural gas.

11. D; DOK Level: 3; **Content Topic:** P.c.2; **Practices:** SP.1.b, SP.1.c, SP.7.a
According to the diagram, the freezing points of tert-butyl alcohol and water are about 25 °C and 0 °C, and the boiling points of tert-butyl alcohol and water are 80 °C and 100 °C. So the freezing point of tert-butyl alcohol is higher than that of water, and the boiling point is lower. The other answer choices result from an inaccurate interpretation of the diagram.

12. A; DOK Level: 3; **Content Topic:** P.c.2; **Practices:** SP.1.b, SP.1.c, SP.7.a
The diagram shows that water is a liquid at temperatures of 0 °C to 100 °C. Within this range, tert-butyl alcohol can be a solid (from less than 0 °C to about 25 °C), a liquid (from about 25 °C to 80 °C), and a gas (from 80 °C to greater than 100 °C). The other answer choices result from an inaccurate interpretation of the diagram.

13. D; DOK Level: 3; **Content Topic:** P.c.2; **Practices:** SP.1.a, SP.1.b, SP.1.c, SP.7.a
The diagrams show that water does not melt from solid to liquid until 0 °C is reached, so at −50 °C, it will remain unchanged. The diagrams also show that carbon dioxide changes from solid to gas, or sublimates, at −78.5 °C, so as the temperature is raised from −100 °C to −50 °C, it will sublimate. Each of the other answer choices suggests at least one result that is not possible when the temperature is raised as suggested.

14. B; DOK Level: 3; **Content Topic:** P.c.2; **Practices:** SP.1.a, SP.1.b, SP.1.c, SP.3.b, SP.7.a
The passage states that carbon dioxide under high pressure is a liquid. Because the diagram for carbon dioxide does not show a liquid state for the carbon dioxide, the carbon dioxide must not be under high pressure. The passage states that sublimation is the process of a substance changing directly from a solid to a gas, not the process of a gas becoming a solid or a liquid becoming a gas. The diagram shows that sublimation of carbon dioxide occurs at the temperature of −78.5 °C.

LESSON 3, pp. 70–73

1. D; DOK Level: 1; **Content Topic:** P.c.2; **Practices:** SP.1.a, SP.1.b, SP.1.c, SP.7.a

The entries in the "Melting Point" column indicate that francium melts at the lowest temperature, 27.0 °C. Lithium has the highest, not lowest, melting point, at 180.54 °C. Potassium melts at 63.65 °C, and rubidium melts at 38.89 °C, both temperatures that are higher than the melting point for francium.

2. A; DOK Level: 2; **Content Topic:** P.c.2; **Practices:** SP.1.a, SP.1.b, SP.1.c, SP.3.b, SP.3.d, SP.7.a

As the entries in the column showing atomic weights increase, the corresponding entries in the column showing melting points decrease. Therefore, the greater (not smaller) the atomic weight, the lower the melting point. As the entries in the column showing atomic number increase, the corresponding entries in the column showing melting points decrease and the corresponding entries in the column showing atomic weights increase.

3. D; DOK Level: 1; **Content Topic:** P.c.2; **Practices:** SP.1.a, SP.1.b, SP.1.c

The passage states that atomic mass is the same as atomic weight, and the elements having the highest atomic weights—therefore, the greatest masses—are shown in the lower right corner of the table. The elements shown in the upper left and upper right corners have relatively low atomic weights. The elements shown in the lower left corner have atomic weights that are not as high as those shown in the lower right corner.

4. B; DOK Level: 1; **Content Topic:** P.c.2; **Practices:** SP.1.a, SP.1.b, SP.1.c

The passage explains that elements in the same column, or group, have similar properties. Carbon and silicon are in the same group, so they have similar properties. According to the table key, neon is a nonmetal. Potassium and krypton are in different groups, so they likely do not have similar properties. According to the key, calcium is a metal.

5. C; DOK Level: 2; **Content Topic:** P.c.2; **Practices:** SP.1.a, SP.1.b, SP.1.c

The passage explains that elements in the same column, or group, have similar properties, so to find elements with properties similar to helium, you would look in the column in which helium is shown. A relationship exists between atomic number and melting point, but you cannot determine the melting point of an element just by looking at its atomic number. Atomic numbers increase from left to right in a row, so elements with higher atomic numbers than a particular element are to the right, not left, of that element in the row in which the element is shown. You can use the periodic table to identify elements that share properties but not the properties that those elements share.

6. A; DOK Level: 2; **Content Topic:** P.c.2; **Practices:** SP.1.a, SP.1.b, SP.1.c, SP.7.a

By using the formula provided, you can divide mass (5.4 g) by volume (2 cm³) to identify the density of the unknown substance as 2.7 g/cm³, which the table shows is the density of aluminum. The table shows that the densities of gasoline, mercury, and carbon monoxide are 0.70, 13.6, and 0.00125 g/cm³, respectively.

7. D; DOK Level: 2; **Content Topic:** P.c.2; **Practices:** SP.1.a, SP.1.b, SP.1.c, SP.7.a

The "Note" section of the table explains that density in kg/m³ can be found by multiplying a value in the table by 1,000. The table shows that the density of nitrogen is 0.001251 g/cm³. When you multiply that figure by 1,000, you get 1.251 kg/m³. The incorrect answer choices may result from incorrect calculations or misunderstanding of the information provided.

8. C; DOK Level: 3; **Content Topic:** P.c.2; **Practices:** SP.1.a, SP.1.b, SP.1.c, SP.3.b, SP.3.d, SP.7.a

The table indicates that a change in odor and the formation of bubbles (or foam) are indicators of a chemical change, so most likely a chemical reaction, not a physical change, has occurred. Changes in texture and state are physical changes, not chemical reactions.

9. A; DOK Level: 1; **Content Topic:** P.c.2; **Practices:** SP.1.a, SP.1.b, SP.1.c, SP.7.a

In the "Indicators of change" row of the table, the indicator "change in color" is in both the column for physical changes and the column for chemical changes, suggesting that a change in color can occur during a physical change or a chemical change. In the "Properties" row, the property "flammability" is in the column for chemical changes, indicating that the action of burning is a chemical change. In the "Indicators of change" row, the indicator "change in state" is in the column for physical changes, indicating that the action of changing from a liquid to a gas is a physical change. In the "Indicators of change" row, the indicator "change in temperature" is in the column for chemical changes, indicating that having a decrease in temperature without changing state relates to a chemical change.

10. B; DOK Level: 2; **Content Topic:** P.c.2; **Practices:** SP.1.a, SP.1.b, SP.1.c

The table shows that the pH value for a substance whose H^+ concentration is 1×10^{-7} is 7 and that the pH value for a substance whose H^+ concentration is 1×10^{-6} is 6, so the pH would decrease from 7 to 6. Incorrect answer choices may result from a misinterpretation of the table.

11. D; DOK Level: 2; **Content Topic:** P.c.2; **Practices:** SP.1.a, SP.1.b, SP.1.c

The table shows that acids have pH values ranging from 0 to 6, so of the options listed, the most likely pH of battery acid is 0. The pH values 8, 12, and 14 are for bases, not acids.

LESSON 4, pp. 74–77

1. A; DOK Level: 1; **Content Topic:** P.c.3; **Practices:** SP.1.a, SP.1.b, SP.1.c, SP.7.a

Hydrogen and oxygen are represented on the left side of the equation, so they are reactants. Neither is a product. Particles of hydrogen and oxygen rearrange, forming bonds in new ways to produce water. Mass is always conserved in a chemical reaction, so the number of oxygen atoms cannot change during the reaction.

2. B; DOK Level: 1; **Content Topic:** P.c.3; **Practices:** SP.1.a, SP.1.b, SP.1.c, SP.7.a, SP.8.b

A coefficient indicates the number of molecules of a substance represented in a chemical equation, so the coefficient 2 in $2H_2O$ indicates that the reactants produce two molecules of water. The coefficient 2 in $2H_2$ indicates two hydrogen molecules. Subscripts in a chemical reaction indicate numbers of atoms, not molecules.

Answer Key

UNIT 2 (continued)

3. **A**; **DOK Level:** 3; **Content Topic:** P.c.3; **Practices:** SP.1.a, SP.1.b, SP.1.c, SP.3.b, SP.7.a
In a decomposition reaction, a single reactant forms two or more products. If two gases are formed from a liquid, a decomposition reaction likely has occurred. If a solid and a liquid form a different solid and a different liquid, two reactants have formed two new products in a double displacement reaction. If a liquid is formed from two gases or a solid from two liquids, reactants have combined in a synthesis reaction.

4. **C**; **DOK Level:** 1; **Content Topic:** P.c.3; **Practices:** SP.1.a, SP.1.b, SP.1.c, SP.7.a
In the reaction represented by the equation, iron takes the place of copper to form iron sulfate instead of copper sulfate. So the reaction is a single displacement reaction, not another kind of reaction.

5. **B**; **DOK Level:** 1; **Content Topic:** P.c.3; **Practices:** SP.1.a, SP.1.b, SP.1.c, SP.7.a, SP.8.b
The correct equation shows that iron and oxygen are reactants and iron oxide is the product and has an equal number of each type of atom on both sides. Each of the equations in the incorrect answer choices fails to meet these criteria in some way.

6. **C**; **DOK Level:** 2; **Content Topic:** P.c.3; **Practices:** SP.1.a, SP.1.b, SP.1.c, SP.7.a
Equation 3 shows that two reactants have formed two new products, so it represents a double displacement reaction. Equation 1 shows that one element takes the place of another element, so it represents a single displacement reaction. Equation 2 shows that a single reactant forms two products, so it represents a decomposition reaction. Equation 4 shows that two reactants combine to form a single product, so it represents a synthesis reaction.

7. **DOK Level:** 2; **Content Topic:** P.c.3; **Practices:** SP.1.a, SP.1.b, SP.1.c, SP.6.b, SP.7.a, SP.8.b
The carbon atoms are already the same in the original equation, so after step 1, the equation is still $CH_4 + O_2 \rightarrow CO_2 + H_2O$. The four hydrogen atoms on the left side of the equation are not balanced by the two hydrogen atoms on the right side, so a coefficient must be added to the right side. After step 2, the equation is $CH_4 + O_2 \rightarrow CO_2 + 2H_2O$. Following step 2, the two oxygen atoms on the left side of the equation are not balanced by the four oxygen atoms on the right side, so a coefficient must be added to the left side. After step 3, the equation is $CH_4 + 2O_2 \rightarrow CO_2 + 2H_2O$. After step 3, the number of all atoms is equal, so the balanced equation is $CH_4 + 2O_2 \rightarrow CO_2 + 2H_2O$.

8. **D**; **DOK Level:** 2; **Content Topics:** P.c.2, P.c.3; **Practices:** SP.1.a, SP.1.b, SP.1.c, SP.7.a
$AgNO_3 + NaI \rightarrow AgI + NaNO_3$ represents a chemical reaction identified in the third row of data in the table. The changing of water to ice is a physical change, not a chemical reaction. $2Mg + O_2$ represents only reactants, not an entire chemical reaction. The chemical equation $2NH_3 \rightarrow 3H_2 + N_2$ includes the substances identified in the first row of the table but does not correctly identify the chemical reaction represented in the first row of the table.

9. **B**; **DOK Level:** 2; **Content Topic:** P.c.3; **Practices:** SP.1.a, SP.1.b, SP.1.c, SP.7.a
The passage explains that metal and acid in test tubes reacts to form salt and hydrogen gas in trials using three different metals. So in general, when metal and acid are the reactants in a chemical reaction, salt and hydrogen are the products. The incorrect answer choices misidentify the reactants, the products, or both.

10. **A**; **DOK Level:** 3; **Content Topic:** P.c.3; **Practices:** SP.1.a, SP.1.b, SP.1.c, SP.7.a, SP.8.b
The equations $2C_4H_{10} + 13O_2 \rightarrow 8CO_2 + 10H_2O$ and $C_4H_{10} + O_2 \rightarrow CO_2 + H_2O$ both represent the burning of butane, but only $2C_4H_{10} + 13O_2 \rightarrow 8CO_2 + 10H_2O$ is balanced because it has equal numbers of each type of atom on both sides. The other incorrect answer choices are equations representing the burning of methane and octane.

LESSON 5, pp. 78–81

1. **C**; **DOK Level:** 3; **Content Topic:** P.c.4; **Practices:** SP.1.a, SP.1.b, SP.1.c, SP.3.c, SP.7.a
It is more likely that HCl—not Br, LiBr, or NaOH—will have properties in common with HBr because HCl and HBr are both acids. NaOH is a base. LiBr is a salt. Br is an element, not a compound.

2. **D**; **DOK Level:** 3; **Content Topic:** P.c.4; **Practices:** SP.1.a, SP.1.b, SP.1.c, SP.3.c, SP.7.a
The table indicates that NaCl is a salt, so the equation representing the dissociation of NaCl shows the outcome of a salt dissolved in water. The equation representing the bonding of Na^+ and Cl^- shows how the compound NaCl is formed. The other equations represent the outcomes of a base dissolved in water and an acid dissolved in water.

3. **DOK Level:** 3; **Content Topic:** P.c.4; **Practices:** SP.1.a, SP.1.b, SP.1.c, SP.3.c, SP.6.c, SP.7.a
Possible answer:
Ⓐ When 30 g NaCl are added to the water, an unsaturated solution forms. Ⓑ As the additional 10 g NaCl are added, the solution becomes more concentrated. When 36 g NaCl have been added, the solution reaches saturation. The additional 4 g NaCl cannot dissolve in the solution.
Ⓐ The first sentence explains what happens as a result of the first step of the investigation, based on information from the passage and diagram.
Ⓑ The rest of the paragraph predicts the outcome of the next step of the investigation, based on information provided in the passage and an understanding of solutions.

4. **C**; **DOK Level:** 3; **Content Topic:** P.c.4; **Practices:** SP.1.a, SP.1.b, SP.1.c, SP.3.c, SP.3.d, SP.7.a
The concentration of H^+ ions in a solution of a weak acid is lower, not higher, than that in a solution of a strong acid, such as HCl. The passage explains that a weak acid does not completely ionize in solution; however, it does undergo ionization to some extent.

5. **A**; **DOK Level:** 3; **Content Topic:** P.c.4; **Practices:** SP.1.a, SP.1.b, SP.1.c, SP.3.c, SP.7.a
The first equation represents the mixing of two bases, which probably will produce no reaction. The second equation represents the mixing of an acid and a salt, which probably will produce no reaction. The third equation represents the mixing of an acid and a base, which will result in a reaction.

6. **A**; **DOK Level:** 3; **Content Topic:** P.c.4; **Practices:** SP.1.a, SP.1.b, SP.1.c, SP.3.c, SP.7.a
One molecule of HCl produces one hydrogen ion; one molecule of H_2SO_4 produces two hydrogen ions. Acidity correlates to the ratio of hydrogen ions in solution, so the HCl solution will be half as acidic as the H_2SO_4 solution.

7. **B**; **DOK Level:** 3; **Content Topic:** P.c.4; **Practices:** SP.1.a, SP.1.b, SP.1.c, SP.3.c, SP.7.a
The diagram shows that as the pressure of a gas above the surface of a solution is increased, more molecules of the gas are forced into solution, so more gas, not less gas, dissolves in solution. The diagram indicates that the gas dissolves in solution, not that the gas becomes a liquid. A change in solubility does occur because a change in pressure occurs; solubility of a gas is dependent on pressure.

8. **C**; **DOK Level:** 3; **Content Topic:** P.c.4; **Practices:** SP.1.a, SP.1.b, SP.1.c, SP.3.c, SP.7.a
Rule 2 states that all ammonium salts, or salts formed from NH_4^+, are soluble. So the equation showing the dissociation of a compound formed from NH_4^+ represents an outcome based on Rule 2. The other equations represent outcomes based on other rules of solubility or their exceptions.

9. **C**; **DOK Level:** 3; **Content Topic:** P.c.4; **Practices:** SP.1.a, SP.1.b, SP.1.c, SP.3.c, SP.3.d, SP.7.a
Rule 6 states that most hydroxide salts are insoluble and does not indicate that $Mg(OH)_2$ would be an exception to the rule. So based on Rule 6, $Mg(OH)_2$ will not be soluble in water. If $Mg(OH)_2$ is not soluble in water, it will not dissociate completely or moderately when mixed with water. The prediction that the two substances will form a new compound is not supported by the information provided.

10. **A**; **DOK Level:** 3; **Content Topic:** P.c.4; **Practices:** SP.1.a, SP.1.b, SP.1.c, SP.3.c, SP.7.a
The data in the "Copper" column of the table indicate that when copper is added to a dental amalgam, expansion will increase, setting time will decrease, hardness will increase, and color will not be imparted.

11. **B**; **DOK Level:** 3; **Content Topic:** P.c.4; **Practices:** SP.1.a, SP.1.b, SP.1.c, SP.3.c, SP.7.a
The data in the "Silver" and "Tin" columns of the table indicate that the properties of an amalgam in which silver is the solute are opposite in several categories from the properties of an amalgam in which tin is the solute. The data in the table indicate that silver dissolved in mercury will increase the durability of the amalgam, but not that the dissolution of other metals will do the same. Using silver or copper as a solute in an amalgam decreases the amount of time required for a filling to set; however, using tin increases the setting time required. Tin and copper used as solutes have differing effects on an amalgam in the categories of expansion, flow, and setting time.

LESSON 6, pp. 82–85
1. **B**; **DOK Level:** 1; **Content Topic:** P.b.1; **Practices:** SP.1.a, SP.1.b, SP.1.c, SP.7.b, SP.8.b
Average speed can be calculated by using the formula $s = \frac{d}{t}$. It takes approximately 6.7 hours to travel 100 miles if the average speed is 15 mi/hr (100 divided by 15 equals 6.7). The incorrect answer choices might be reached through incorrect calculations or formula application.

2. **B**; **DOK Level:** 2; **Content Topic:** P.b.1; **Practices:** SP.1.a, SP.1.b, SP.1.c, SP.7.b, SP.8.b
Average speed can be calculated by using the formula $s = \frac{d}{t}$. If speed decreases by half and distance remains the same, then the time must double. The incorrect answer choices might be reached through incorrect calculations or formula application.

3. **C**; **DOK Level:** 1; **Content Topic:** P.b.1; **Practices:** SP.1.a, SP.1.b, SP.1.c, SP.7.b, SP.8.b
Each side of the block is 400 m. Person 1 walks one side (400 m); Person 2 walks three sides (3 multiplied by 400 m equals 1,200 m). The incorrect answer choices might be reached through incorrect calculations.

4. **C**; **DOK Level:** 2; **Content Topic:** P.b.1; **Practices:** SP.1.a, SP.1.b, SP.1.c, SP.7.b, SP.8.b
Displacement is the straight-line distance between the starting and ending point, regardless of the path taken between those points. Person 1 and Person 2 both travel from Point A to Point B. Those points are 400 m apart. Since Point B is south of Point A, displacement is 400 m south. The incorrect answer choices might be reached through incorrect calculations.

5. **C**; **DOK Level:** 1; **Content Topic:** P.b.1; **Practices:** SP.1.a, SP.1.b, SP.1.c, SP.7.b, SP.8.b
The car's average speed is equal to distance divided by time. In this case, that is 20 miles divided by 60 minutes, or one hour, which is 20 mi/hr. Speed does not need to include direction. The incorrect answer choices might be reached through incorrect calculations or formula application.

6. **A**; **DOK Level:** 2; **Content Topic:** P.b.1; **Practices:** SP.1.a, SP.1.b, SP.1.c, SP.7.b, SP.8.b
The car's rate of velocity is equal to displacement divided by time. In this case that is 20 miles (east) divided by 60 minutes, or one hour, which is 20 mi/hr east. Velocity must include direction. The incorrect answer choices might be reached through incorrect calculations or formula application.

7. **DOK Level:** 2; **Content Topic:** P.b.1; **Practices:** SP.1.a, SP.1.b, SP.1.c, SP.6.b, SP.7.b, SP.8.b
Steve's velocity (+1.5 m/s) and that of the walkway (+0.5 m/s) combine for a total velocity of **+2.0 m/s**.

8. **DOK Level:** 2; **Content Topic:** P.b.1; **Practices:** SP.1.a, SP.1.b, SP.1.c, SP.6.b, SP.7.b, SP.8.b
Steve and the person on the walkway share a frame of reference because they are both on the moving walkway. To Steve, the person who is standing still on the walkway seems not to be moving. To that person, Steve is moving forward at **+1.5 m/s**.

9. **DOK Level:** 2; **Content Topic:** P.b.1; **Practices:** SP.1.a, SP.1.b, SP.1.c, SP.6.b, SP.7.b, SP.8.b
Steve and the woman sitting beside the walkway do not share a frame of reference because he is on the moving walkway and she is not. The woman will see Steve pass her at the combined velocities of Steve and the walkway: +1.5 m/s plus +0.5 m/s, or **+2.0 m/s**.

Answer Key

10. C; DOK Level: 2; Content Topic: P.b.1; **Practices:** SP.1.a, SP.1.b, SP.7.b, SP.8.b
The sound must travel 680 m to get to the wall and another 680 m to get back to Delaney. The total distance, 1,360 m, divided by the velocity of sound, 340 m/s, yields an elapsed time of 4 seconds. The incorrect answer choices might be reached through incorrect calculations or formula application.

11. D; DOK Level: 2; Content Topic: P.b.2; **Practices:** SP.1.a, SP.1.b, SP.1.c, SP.7.b, SP.8.b
Velocity is equal to the product of acceleration and time (9.8 m/s² downward multiplied by 3 s equals 29.4 m/s downward). The incorrect answer choices might be reached through incorrect calculations or formula application.

12. B; DOK Level: 2; Content Topic: P.b.2; **Practices:** SP.1.a, SP.1.b, SP.1.c, SP.7.b, SP.8.b
Gravity will continue accelerating the object, increasing its velocity to 39.2 m/s at 4 seconds. This value is obtained by using the formula $v = gt$. The incorrect answer choices might be reached through incorrect calculations or formula application.

13. A; DOK Level: 3; Content Topic: P.b.1; **Practices:** SP.1.a, SP.1.b, SP.1.c, SP.7.b, SP.8.b
Each dot represents the object's change of position per second. Each "tick" is 1 m. Therefore, the object's motion is 5 m/5 sec, or 1 m/s, to the right. The dots are evenly spaced, indicating that the velocity of the object is not changing, but is constant. The incorrect answer choices might be reached through incorrect calculations or formula application.

14. B; DOK Level: 3; Content Topic: P.b.1; **Practices:** SP.1.a, SP.1.b, SP.1.c, SP.7.b, SP.8.b
Each dot represents the object's change of position per second. Each "tick" is 1 m. The first two dots are separated by a distance of 3 meters, the second and third dots by 4 meters, and the third and fourth dots by 5 meters. Because the object's velocity is increasing between dots at the rate of 1 m/s to the right, the object is accelerating at a rate of 1 m/s/s, or 1 m/s², to the right. The incorrect answer choices might be reached through incorrect calculations or formula application.

LESSON 7, pp. 86–89
1. C; DOK Level: 1; Content Topic: P.b.2; **Practices:** SP.1.a, SP.1.b, SP.1.c, SP.7.a, SP.7.b, SP.8.b
The net force is the total force acting on an object. To find out the net force, you add all the forces and take into account the net effect of their directions. In this case, the forces are opposing each other; therefore, the net force is 1,000 N minus 575 N, or 425 N upward. The incorrect answer choices might be reached through incorrect calculations.

2. B; DOK Level: 1; Content Topic: P.b.2; **Practices:** SP.1.a, SP.1.b, SP.1.c, SP.7.a, SP.7.b, SP.8.b
The upward and downward forces are equal; therefore, when you add the three forces together, the upward and downward forces cancel each other, leaving a net force of 50 N to the left. The incorrect answer choices might be reached through incorrect calculations.

3.1 C; 3.2 D; 3.3 A; DOK Level: 1; **Content Topic:** P.b.2; **Practices:** SP.1.a, SP.1.b, SP.1.c, SP.7.a, SP.7.b, SP.8.b
3.1 The net force is equal to the difference between the forces because they oppose each other. That is, 15 N minus 5 N equals 10 N. The direction of the force is to the left. The other answer choices might be reached through incorrect calculations.
3.2 The arrow on the right side of the diagram is longer than the one on the left side of the diagram. Although the forces are opposing each other, the basketball will move in the direction of the stronger force, that is, to the left. The incorrect answer choices might be reached through misinterpretation of the vector diagram.
3.3 The net force is equal to the difference between the forces: 15 N minus 10 N equals 5 N. The direction of the force is to the left. The incorrect answer choices might be reached through incorrect calculations.

4. B; DOK Level: 2; Content Topic: P.b.2; **Practices:** SP.1.a, SP.1.b, SP.1.c, SP.7.a
The arrows in the diagram show forces, so the diagram indicates that like magnetic poles repel each other and opposite magnetic poles attract each other. The diagram shows magnets both repelling and attracting each other, making it clear that magnets do not always either repel or attract each other.

5. C; DOK Level: 1; Content Topic: P.b.2; **Practices:** SP.1.a, SP.1.b, SP.1.c, SP.3.a, SP.7.a, SP.7.b, SP.8.b
The passage explains that the force of friction (F) between an object and a surface can be calculated by using the equation $F = \mu m$, where μ is a constant that varies by substance and m is the mass of the object. The passage also states that for the example shown in the diagram, μ is 0.62 and mass is 50 kg. By plugging these figures into the equation $F = \mu m$, you get the equation $F = 0.62 \, \mu \cdot 50$ kg. The incorrect answer choices may result from an incorrect understanding of the information provided or the equation $F = \mu m$.

6. D; DOK Level: 1; Content Topic: P.b.2; **Practices:** SP.1.a, SP.1.b, SP.1.c, SP.7.a, SP.7.b, SP.8.b
For the box to move, the pushing force needs to be greater than the frictional force, which is 31 N. The only answer choice greater than 31 N is 32 N.

7. B; DOK Level: 2; Content Topic: P.b.2; **Practices:** SP.1.a, SP.1.b, SP.1.c, SP.7.a, SP.7.b
If μ decreases, frictional force decreases, and less pushing is required to overcome the frictional force. Therefore, less force, not more force, would be needed. Changing the value of μ would have no effect on the mass of the box.

8. A; DOK Level: 1; Content Topic: P.b.2; **Practices:** SP.1.a, SP.1.b, SP.1.c, SP.7.a
The arrows representing the two forces are the same length and point in opposite directions, so they are balanced forces. If the forces were unbalanced, the arrows would be of differing sizes. If the upward force were stronger, the arrow pointing upward would be larger than the one pointing downward. If the downward force were stronger, the arrow pointing downward would be bigger than the one pointing upward.

9. **D**; **DOK Level:** 1; **Content Topic:** P.b.2; **Practices:** SP.1.a, SP.1.b, SP.1.c, SP.7.a

If the wagon is moving to the right, the pulling force must be greater than the frictional force. So of the pairs of forces listed, only a pulling force of 20 N and a friction force of 15 N will cause the wagon to move. In the incorrect answer choices, the pulling force is less than the force of friction.

10. **B**; **DOK Level:** 2; **Content Topic:** P.b.2; **Practices:** SP.1.a, SP.1.b, SP.1.c, SP.7.a

You can reason that the different size vector arrows represent forces because force is the only variable that can differ in the scenario described. Both meteors have the same acceleration, 1.6 m/s²; therefore, their respective velocities are changing at the same rate as well. Mass has no directional component, so it would not be depicted with a vector arrow.

11. **C**; **DOK Level:** 2; **Content Topic:** P.b.2; **Practices:** SP.1.a, SP.1.b, SP.1.c, SP.7.a, SP.7.b

Force equals mass times acceleration. Acceleration is the same for both meteors: 1.6 m/s². Their masses are different, however, so the force with which they will strike the moon is different. That is, the meteor with more mass will strike with more force; because their acceleration is the same, both will strike at the same time.

12. **D**; **DOK Level:** 3; **Content Topic:** P.b.2; **Practices:** SP.1.a, SP.1.b, SP.1.c, SP.7.a

Before the box can move, it has to be acted on by an unbalanced force. Forces A and B will always be equal, according to Newton's third law. The same can be said of forces C and D. However, if the man pushes back harder on the floor with his foot, eventually force D will exceed force C, and the box will move.

LESSON 8, pp. 90–93

1. **A**; **DOK Level:** 2; **Content Topic:** P.b.2; **Practices:** SP.1.a, SP.1.b, SP.1.c, SP.7.a, SP.7.b, SP.8.b

The question requires that you find mass when weight is known by using the formula $w = mg$, where w equals 637 N, m is unknown, and g equals 9.8 m/s². So the equation is 637 N = x • 9.8 m/s². To solve for x, you use the equation x = (637 N)/(9.8 m/s²). Therefore, x, or mass, equals 65 kg. The incorrect answer choices may be reached through incorrect calculations or formula application.

2. **A**; **DOK Level:** 2; **Content Topic:** P.b.2; **Practices:** SP.1.a, SP.1.b, SP.1.c, SP.3.c, SP.7.a

The mass of an object never changes; only its weight does. Therefore, its mass is the same, regardless of the force of gravity. The incorrect answer choices might be reached through incorrect calculations or formula application.

3. **A**; **DOK Level:** 2; **Content Topics:** P.b.1, P.b.2; **Practices:** SP.1.a, SP.1.b, SP.1.c, SP.7.a, SP.7.b

The equation used to determine momentum is $p = mv$, and the equation used to determine the change in momentum is $Ft = mv$. Distance is not needed to determine momentum or the change in momentum. Looking at the equation for finding change in momentum, you can see that both the force applied to an object and the amount of time the force is applied are related to determining change in momentum. The mass of an object is not directly related to the change in momentum, but it is a variable needed to determine momentum.

4. **B**; **DOK Level:** 3; **Content Topic:** P.b.1; **Practices:** SP.1.a, SP.1.b, SP.1.c, SP.3.c, SP.7.a, SP.8.b

To determine an object's velocity in m/s when the size of the force, the amount of time over which the force is applied, and the object's mass are known, you can insert the known values in the formula $Ft = mv$. For the scenario described, the equation would be 20 × 5 = 20 × v. By dividing both sides of the equation by 20 and taking into account the direction of the movement of the object, you determine that v equals 5 m/s to the right. The incorrect answer choices might be reached through incorrect calculations or formula application.

5. **C**; **DOK Level:** 2; **Content Topic:** P.b.1; **Practices:** SP.1.a, SP.1.b, SP.1.c, SP.3.c, SP.7.a, SP.7.b, SP.8.b

To determine momentum, use the formula $p = mv$. For the scenario described, p equals 20 kg multiplied by 5 m/s, or 100 kg • m/s to the right. If the momentum were to the left, the result of the calculation would have been a negative number. The incorrect answer choices might be reached through incorrect calculations or formula application.

6. **B**; **DOK Level:** 2; **Content Topics:** P.b.1, P.b.2; **Practices:** SP.1.a, SP.1.b, SP.1.c, SP.3.c, SP.7.a, SP.7.b

The line on the graph indicates that when force has been applied to the object for 1 second, momentum is + 25 kg • m/s.

7. **D**; **DOK Level:** 2; **Content Topics:** P.b.1, P.b.2; **Practices:** SP.1.a, SP.1.b, SP.1.c, SP.3.c, SP.7.a, SP.7.b, SP.8.b

To determine velocity, use the equation $p = mv$. Fill in the values you know for momentum (from the graph) and for mass (given in the passage), and then solve for v to determine velocity. The incorrect answer choices might be reached through incorrect calculations or formula application or by misreading the graph.

8. **A**; **DOK Level:** 2; **Content Topics:** P.b.1, P.b.2; **Practices:** SP.1.a, SP.1.b, SP.1.c, SP.7.a

Impulse is the change in momentum over time. The graph shows how momentum changes over time; therefore, the line represents impulse. The line does not represent force, which equals mass times acceleration. The y-axis, not the line, represents momentum, and the x-axis, not the line, represents time.

9. **C**; **DOK Level:** 2; **Content Topics:** P.b.1, P.b.2; **Practices:** SP.1.a, SP.1.b, SP.1.c, SP.7.a, SP.7.b, SP.8.b

The final momentum must equal the initial momentum. The initial momentum is zero. Therefore, the total final momentum of the system also must be zero. The incorrect answer choices might be reached through misunderstanding of the concept of momentum conservation.

10. **D**; **DOK Level:** 2; **Content Topics:** P.b.1, P.b.2; **Practices:** SP.1.a, SP.1.b, SP.1.c, SP.7.a, SP.7.b, SP.8.b

The initial momentum is zero. Therefore, the total final momentum of the system, that is, the momentum of the ball plus the momentum of the person and skateboard, must also be zero. If the momentum of the ball is −20 kg • m/s, then the momentum of the person and skateboard must be equal and opposite: +20 kg • m/s. The incorrect answer choices might be reached through incorrect calculations.

Answer Key

UNIT 2 (continued)

11. A; DOK Level: 2; **Content Topics:** P.b.1, P.b.2;
Practices: SP.1.a, SP.1.b, SP.1.c, SP.7.a, SP.7.b, SP.8.b
To determine velocity, use the formula $p = mv$. In this
scenario, p equals +20 kg • m/s, and m equals 40 kg, so
you use the equation +20 kg • m/s = 40 kg • x. Divide each
side by 40 kg to arrive at the equation +0.5 m/s = v. The
incorrect answer choices might be reached through incorrect
calculations or formula application.

12. B; DOK Level: 2; **Content Topic:** P.b.2; **Practices:**
SP.1.a, SP.1.b, SP.1.c, SP.7.a, SP.7.b, SP.8.b
The mass of each object does not change. The passage
states that the total mass of the system (both packages)
after the collision is 10 kg. The diagram shows that the
mass of Package A is 8 kg; therefore, Package B has a
mass of 2 kg (10 minus 8). The incorrect answer choices
might be reached through incorrect calculations.

13. D; DOK Level: 3; **Content Topic:** P.b.2; **Practices:**
SP.1.a, SP.1.b, SP.1.c, SP.7.a, SP.7.b, SP.8.b
You determine the velocity of Package B by using the
formula $p = mv$. First, you use the information provided
in the passage and diagram to find the momentum of the
system: p equals 10 kg multiplied by 2.5 m/s, or 25 kg • m/s.
Next, you use what you know now to find the velocity of
Package B. You know that the mass of Package B is
2 kg and the momentum of the system is 25 kg • m/s.
By rearranging the formula $p = mv$ as $v = \frac{p}{m}$, you can
find the velocity of Package B by using this equation:
$x = \frac{25 \text{ kg} \cdot \text{m/s}}{2 \text{ kg}}$, or x = 12.5 m/s The incorrect answer choices
might be reached through incorrect calculations or formula
application.

14. D; DOK Level: 2; **Content Topic:** P.b.1; **Practices:**
SP.1.a, SP.1.b, SP.1.c, SP.7.a, SP.7.b, SP.8.b
To determine momentum, use the formula $p = mv$; in this
case, m equals 247 kg and v equals 21 m/s; therefore,
p equals 247 kg • 21 m/s, which equals 5,187 kg • m/s.
The incorrect answer choices might be reached through
incorrect calculations or formula application.

15. C; DOK Level: 2; **Content Topic:** P.b.1; **Practices:**
SP.1.a, SP.1.b, SP.1.c, SP.7.a, SP.7.b, SP.8.b
To determine average force, use the formula $F_{average} = \frac{mv}{t}$.
In this case m equals 247 kg, v equals 21 m/s, and t equals
0.05 s; therefore, $F_{average}$ equals $\frac{247 \text{ kg} \cdot 21 \text{ m/s}}{0.05 \text{ s}}$, which equals
103,740 N. The incorrect answer choices might be reached
through incorrect calculations or formula application.

16. A; DOK Level: 2; **Content Topic:** P.b.1; **Practices:**
SP.1.a, SP.1.b, SP.1.c, SP.7.a, SP.7.b, SP.8.b
Use the formula for momentum, $p = mv$, to determine
the momentum of the smaller motorcycle: p equals 105
kg • 50 m/s, or 5,250 kg • m/s. The momentum of the
smaller motorcycle is slightly greater than that of the larger
motorcycle (5,187 kg • m/s). The incorrect answer choices
might be reached through incorrect calculations or formula
application.

17. A; DOK Level: 2; **Content Topic:** P.b.1; **Practices:**
SP.1.a, SP.1.b, SP.7.a, SP.7.b, SP.8.b
To find average force in this scenario, use the formula
$F_{average} = \frac{mv}{t}$, where m equals 60 kg, v equals 25 m/s, and
t equals 0.5 s, to arrive at the equation $F_{average} = \frac{60 \text{ kg} \cdot 25 \text{ m/s}}{0.5 \text{ s}}$.
Then solve the equation to determine that average force
equals 3,000 N. The incorrect answer choices might
be reached through incorrect calculations or formula
application.

18. C; DOK Level: 2; **Content Topics:** P.b.1, P.b.2;
Practices: SP.1.a, SP.1.b, SP.1.c, SP.7.a, SP.7.b, SP.8.b
To find average force in this scenario, use the formula
$F_{average} = \frac{mv}{t}$, where m = 60 kg, v = 25 m/s, and t = 0.002 s, to
arrive at the equation $F_{average} = \frac{60 \text{ kg} \cdot 25 \text{ m/s}}{0.002 \text{ s}}$. Then solve the
equation to determine that average force equals 750,000 N.
The incorrect answer choices might be reached through
incorrect calculations or formula application.

19. B; DOK Level: 2; **Content Topics:** P.b.1, P.b.2;
Practices: SP.1.a, SP.1.b, SP.1.c, SP.3.a, SP.7.a, SP.7.b,
SP.8.b
The only difference between the two equations is the value
of t. Part of the effectiveness of driver restraint is that it
lengthens the time over which the force is applied; that is, a
longer time interval decreases the average force.

LESSON 9, pp. 94–97

1. D; DOK Level: 2; **Content Topic:** P.b.3; **Practices:**
SP.1.a, SP.1.b, SP.1.c
Based on your experience with using a hammer to remove
a nail from a board (or experience with other levers) along
with the information provided, you can determine that the
load, or object to be moved, is the nail. The hand of the user
moves to apply the input force. When a claw hammer is
used to pull a nail from a board, the handle and the claw of
the hammer work as the lever arm, and the fulcrum is the
top of the hammer head that rests against the wood.

2. C; DOK Level: 2; **Content Topic:** P.b.3; **Practices:**
SP.1.a, SP.1.b, SP.1.c
Based on your experience with using a hammer to remove
a nail from a board (or experience with other levers) along
with the information provided, you can determine that the
hammer makes work easier by reducing the force that
needs to be applied to remove the nail. The force needed is
reduced because the lesser force is applied over a greater
distance.

3. B; DOK Level: 2; **Content Topic:** P.b.3; **Practices:**
SP.1.a, SP.1.b, SP.7.b
The passage states that power is calculated by dividing
the amount of work done by the time used to do the work.
You can use your knowledge of math to determine that
Machine A exerts 800 watts of power (8,000 divided by 10)
and Machine B exerts 3,200 watts of power (16,000 divided
by 5). So Machine A exerts less power than Machine B. The
other answer choices might be reached through incorrect
calculations or formula application.

4. B; DOK Level: 2; **Content Topic:** P.b.3; **Practices:** SP.1.a, SP.1.b, SP.1.c, SP.7.b

The passage states that mechanical advantage is a ratio of the size of the output force to the size of the input force. You can use your understanding of ratios and knowledge of math to calculate the mechanical advantage of each machine and then use the skill of comparing and contrasting to arrive at the correct answer. Machine B has a mechanical advantage of 10 (150 divided by 15), which is the highest mechanical advantage among the four machines. The mechanical advantage of Machine A is 3 (900 divided by 300). The mechanical advantage of Machine C is 2 (10 divided by 5). Machine D has the greatest output force but a mechanical advantage of only 1.25 (1,000 divided by 800).

5. C; DOK Level: 2; **Content Topic:** P.b.3; **Practices:** SP.1.a, SP.1.b, SP.1.c, SP.3.b

By using your knowledge of forces and mass and the equation for work, you can determine that an accurate statement about using ramps is that because a ramp reduces the amount of force needed to lift an object, it can be used to raise an object that is too heavy to lift straight up. The equation for work indicates that pushing objects up shorter ramps requires more force than pushing objects up longer ramps. Raising an object that is lightweight does not require much force, so there is no reason to use a ramp to lift a lightweight object. Using a simple machine does not change the amount of work done, so pushing an object up a ramp does not require any less work than lifting the object.

6. A; DOK Level: 2; **Content Topic:** P.b.3; **Practices:** SP.1.a, SP.1.b, SP.1.c, SP.3.b, SP.7.b

By using your knowledge of the equation for work, you can determine that if the distance of the force is decreased, the size of the force will be increased. So if the length of the ramp is shortened, more force, not less force, will be needed to move the box. The amount of work done will not change; only the size of the force used to do the work will change.

7. C; DOK Level: 3; **Content Topic:** P.b.3; **Practices:** SP.1.a, SP.1.b, SP.1.c, SP.3.b

By using your experience with the common objects listed and what you have learned about simple machines, you can determine that a ladder is used as an inclined plane when it is leaned against a wall. Because of their shapes and purposes, claw hammers, rolling pins, and garden spades are not likely to be used as inclined planes.

8. A; DOK Level: 2; **Content Topic:** P.b.3; **Practices:** SP.1.a, SP.1.b, SP.1.c, SP.3.b

By using your knowledge of simple machines and the equation for work, you can determine that because using a pulley decreases the size of the force needed to move an object but increases its distance, pulleys do not change the amount of work done. Any simple machine makes work easier by changing the size or direction of the force required to move an object. When a simple machine makes work easier by changing the size of the force needed to move an object, it decreases the size of that force. Amount of work done is not related to how long it takes to do the work.

9. D; DOK Level: 2; **Content Topic:** P.b.3; **Practices:** SP.1.a, SP.1.b, SP.1.c, SP.3.b

Your experience with pulleys, such as flagpole or window-blind mechanisms, along with the information provided, tells you that a pulley system that changes a downward force into an upward force allows you to pull downward with your weight and use the resulting force to lift an object. You know that simple machines can make work easier by changing the size or direction of the applied force, so you can conclude that pulleys do not always change the size of the applied force. The passage states that a movable pulley is part of a block-and-tackle pulley, not vice versa. One way in which simple machines, including pulleys, can make work easier is by changing the direction of the applied force.

10. D; DOK Level: 2; **Content Topic:** P.b.3; **Practices:** SP.1.a, SP.1.b, SP.1.c, SP.3.b

Based on your experience with wheels and axles, such as use of a screwdriver to move a screw into wood, along with information provided, you can determine that wheels and axles are used when a force is required to rotate an object.

11. A; DOK Level: 1; **Content Topic:** P.b.3; **Practices:** SP.1.a, SP.1.b, SP.1.c, SP.7.b

By using your knowledge of math and the equation for work, you can calculate that if a person uses 5 newtons of force to push a box 5 meters, the amount of work done is 25 joules (5 multiplied by 5). The other answer choices might be reached through incorrect calculations or formula application.

12. B; DOK Level: 1; **Content Topic:** P.b.3; **Practices:** SP.1.a, SP.1.b, SP.1.c, SP.3.b

Your knowledge of simple machines and the concept of mechanical advantage tells you that any machine that provides a mechanical advantage makes work easier. So all the machines listed in the table make doing work easier. It is incorrect to interpret the information in the table to mean that all simple machines have a mechanical advantage of at least 1.5 just because the lowest mechanical advantage among the machines listed in the table is 1.5. It is incorrect to use the information in the table to make a generalization about one type of simple machine making work easier than another; moreover, the table shows that of the wedges listed, only Wedge B makes work easier than the pulley listed. It is incorrect to use the information in the table to assume that only the machines listed have a mechanical advantage; the purpose of a machine is to make work easier, and mechanical advantage is the amount by which a machine makes work easier, so you may presume that all machines have a mechanical advantage.

13. D; DOK Level: 1; **Content Topic:** P.b.3; **Practices:** SP.1.a, SP.1.b, SP.1.c, SP.7.b

By using your knowledge of math and the equation for mechanical advantage, you can calculate that the ramp was used if the input force was 5 and the output force was 12.5 (12.5 divided by 5 equals 2.5, the mechanical advantage of the ramp). The other answer choices might be reached through incorrect calculations or formula application.

Answer Key

UNIT 2 *(continued)*

14. A; **DOK Level:** 2; **Content Topic:** P.b.3; **Practices:** SP.1.a, SP.1.b, SP.1.c, SP.3.b
Based on your experience with bicycles, your knowledge about how various simple machines work, and the locations of the simple machines shown in the diagram, you can determine that the pulleys and wheels and axles that move the bicycle chain are the simple machines that cause the bicycle to move forward. The levers shown in the diagram are involved in operating the bicycle's brakes and, therefore, are not involved in making the bicycle move forward.

15. D; **DOK Level:** 2; **Content Topic:** P.b.3; **Practices:** SP.1.a, SP.1.b, SP.1.c, SP.3.b
By using your experience with bicycles and information from the diagram, you can determine that the levers shown in the diagram are involved in operating the bicycle's brakes and, therefore, are involved in making the bicycle stop moving. They are not used to make the bicycle start moving, move faster, or move more easily uphill.

16. C; **DOK Level:** 3; **Content Topic:** P.b.3; **Practices:** SP.1.a, SP.1.b, SP.1.c, SP.3.b
By using your knowledge of simple machines and experience with the common objects listed along with the information about compound machines provided in the passage, you can determine that a pair of scissors is made up of four simple machines—two levers (the arms) and two wedges (the blades). Drill bits and boat ramps are simple machines—screws and ramps, respectively. A wagon wheel can be part of the simple machine wheel and axle.

LESSON 10, *pp. 98–101*

1. C; **DOK Level:** 2; **Content Topic:** P.a.1; **Practices:** SP.1.a, SP.1.b, SP.1.c, SP.3.c, SP.7.a
Because the thermometer is warmer than the substance, the flow of thermal energy is from the thermometer to the substance. So the substance gets slightly warmer as the materials in the thermometer get cooler. The particles in the substance will gain energy and begin to move faster; that is, they will gain kinetic energy until both the thermometer and the substance have the same temperature, or reach equilibrium. The substance will not lose kinetic energy, and its kinetic energy will not fluctuate.

2. A; **DOK Level:** 2; **Content Topic:** P.a.1; **Practices:** SP.1.a, SP.1.b, SP.1.c, SP.3.c, SP.7.a
Because the thermometer is warmer than the substance, the flow of thermal energy is from the thermometer to the substance. So the thermometer gets slightly cooler and the substance gets slightly warmer. The particles in the thermometer will lose energy and move more slowly; that is, they will lose kinetic energy until both the thermometer and the substance have the same temperature, or reach equilibrium. The thermometer will not gain kinetic energy, and its kinetic energy will not fluctuate.

3. C; **DOK Level:** 2; **Content Topics:** P.a.1, P.a.3; **Practices:** SP.1.a, SP.1.b, SP.1.c, SP.3.b, SP.7.a
Microscopic events are those that are too small to be observed with one's senses. The transfer of energy from the flames to the water cannot be observed; therefore, it is a microscopic event in the system. The movement of the piston, the expansion of the water, and the changing of the steam back to water are all observable events and are, therefore, macroscopic, not microscopic.

4. D; **DOK Level:** 3; **Content Topics:** P.a.1, P.a.3; **Practices:** SP.1.a, SP.1.b, SP.1.c, SP.3.c, SP.7.a
If the gas molecules were forced into a smaller space, they would move faster and collide more often with one another, the sides of the cylinder, and the bottom of the piston. All this movement and colliding would raise the kinetic energy of the gas, causing a rise in temperature. So the gas would heat up, not cool down. Less volume would mean an increase in pressure, which would result in a rise in the temperature of the gas.

5. A; **DOK Level:** 2; **Content Topics:** P.a.1, P.a.5; **Practices:** SP.1.a, SP.1.b, SP.1.c, SP.3.b, SP.7.a
Conduction occurs when a warmer object is in physical contact with a cooler object, as with the solid objects in the diagram. Radiation, on the other hand, is thermal energy carried by waves across space; no contact between objects occurs. Convection does not occur in solid objects. Particles do not move from one object to the other; only thermal energy is moving.

6. B; **DOK Level:** 2; **Content Topics:** P.a.1, P.a.5; **Practices:** SP.1.a, SP.1.b, SP.1.c, SP.3.b, SP.7.a
The aluminum's shiny surface would reflect the radiation, meaning that the grill cooks mostly by conduction (where the grate touches the food) and convection (where energy is transferred throughout the grill by means of currents). The incorrect answer choices fail to describe accurately the role of at least one form of energy transfer.

7. D; **DOK Level:** 2; **Content Topics:** P.a.1, P.a.5; **Practices:** SP.1.a, SP.1.b, SP.1.c, SP.3.b, SP.7.a
Conduction transfers energy through solids, so conduction is transferring energy through the solid material of the mug as well as where the mug is in contact with the solid table. Convection transfers energy through gases and liquids; therefore, convection is moving energy through the coffee and the air. Radiation transfers energy through space by waves and is emitted by all warm objects, from warmer objects or areas to cooler; therefore, radiation is transferring energy from the outside surface of the mug. The incorrect answer choices fail to describe accurately the role of at least one form of energy transfer.

8. D; **DOK Level:** 3; **Content Topics:** P.a.1, P.a.5; **Practices:** SP.1.a, SP.1.b, SP.1.c, SP.3.b, SP.4.a, SP.7.a
The diagram shows that energy is transferred to Earth's surface by radiation emitted by the sun. Air molecules in direct contact with Earth's surface are warmed by conduction. The warmer air molecules rise, displacing cooler ones and setting up a convection current. Radiation does not depend on a medium and so passes through the atmosphere to Earth's surface. Conduction relies on two objects being in contact with each other, and Earth's atmosphere is not in contact with the surface of the sun. In addition, energy is transferred through the atmosphere by convection because the atmosphere is made up of gases and liquids.

LESSON 11, pp. 102–105

1. C; DOK Level: 2; **Content Topic:** P.a.3; **Practices:** SP.1.a, SP.1.b, SP.1.c, SP.7.a

At all points on the graph, the sum of potential energy and kinetic energy equals 10 J. At all times, the total energy of a system equals the sum of its potential energy and kinetic energy, so the only time that a system's total energy would equal twice its kinetic energy is when the potential energy and the kinetic energy are exactly equal. The total energy in the system does not change; it changes from one form to another. Although the kinetic energy equals 0 J at 0 seconds, and potential energy equals 0 J at 50 seconds, the total energy of the system is never 0 J; it is always 10 J.

2. D; DOK Level: 2; **Content Topic:** P.a.3; **Practices:** SP.1.a, SP.1.b, SP.1.c, SP.7.a

At 50 seconds, the line representing kinetic energy is at 0 J and the line representing potential energy is at its highest point in the graph; therefore, all the energy in the system has completely changed into potential energy. Kinetic energy cannot be both at 0 J and at maximum at the same point in time. The total amount of energy is the sum of kinetic energy and potential energy; therefore, the kinetic energy cannot be greater than the total energy of the system. The two forms of energy are equal where the two lines intersect, which is at about 15 seconds and 85 seconds.

3. B; DOK Level: 2; **Content Topic:** P.a.3; **Practices:** SP.1.a, SP.1.b, SP.1.c, SP.7.a

The graph shows that the bars representing potential energy get shorter over time and the bars representing kinetic energy get taller over time. Therefore, as potential energy is decreasing, kinetic energy is increasing. The bar representing the kinetic energy at the end of the investigation is shorter than that representing the potential energy at the start of the investigation. The toy car has less total energy at the bottom of the slope than at the top because some of its energy changes to thermal energy as it overcomes the force of friction on the ramp's surface. Energy is conserved, even if all the potential energy is not changed to kinetic energy. The car has less energy at the bottom of the ramp because some of its energy is "lost" as thermal energy to the ramp's surface.

4. A; DOK Level: 2; **Content Topic:** P.a.3; **Practices:** SP.1.a, SP.1.b, SP.1.c, SP.3.b, SP.7.a

The graph shows that the total mechanical energy (kinetic energy plus potential energy) of the car was about 1.5 J lower at the end of the investigation than it was at the beginning. Because energy cannot be destroyed, the difference resulted because energy was lost to heat; that is, energy was changed into thermal energy.

5. C; DOK Level: 2; **Content Topic:** P.a.3; **Practices:** SP.1.a, SP.1.b, SP.1.c, SP.3.a, SP.7.a

The passage explains that voltage of a battery is a measure of the potential energy stored in the battery; therefore, the data points on the graph showing that the voltage of the non-rechargeable battery is 1.6 and the voltage of the rechargeable battery is less than 1.4 at zero hours support the interpretation that the non-rechargeable battery has more potential energy when the batteries are new. The facts that the voltage of the non-rechargeable battery decreases more rapidly and reaches 0.2 first support the interpretation that its stored energy is transformed to other types of energy more quickly and do not relate to the amount of stored energy the batteries have when new. The fact that the voltage of the non-rechargeable battery is greater at two hours does not relate to the amount of stored energy the batteries have when new.

6. A; DOK Level: 2; **Content Topic:** P.a.3; **Practices:** SP.1.a, SP.1.b, SP.1.c, SP.7.a

The graph shows that the voltage of the rechargeable battery stays relatively constant from about one hour to about nine hours. It also shows that although the voltage of the non-rechargeable battery decreases quickly, it starts out with more voltage than the rechargeable battery. The voltage of the rechargeable battery begins to decrease rapidly at about nine hours. The graph shows the voltage of the non-rechargeable battery decreasing to zero about three hours before the voltage of the rechargeable battery does so.

7. DOK Level: 2; **Content Topic:** P.a.3; **Practices:** SP.1.a, SP.1.c, SP.7.a

Although the roller coaster car has its greatest potential energy at the tops of the hills, the first hill is the highest hill. Therefore, the car's potential energy is greatest **at the peak of the first hill**.

8. DOK Level: 2; **Content Topic:** P.a.3; **Practices:** SP.1.a, SP.1.c, SP.7.a

By the time the car reaches the bottom of a hill, all the potential energy has been changed to kinetic energy. As the car's momentum starts moving it up the next hill, kinetic energy starts to change back to potential energy. So the energy changes from kinetic to potential **at the bottom of each hill**.

9. B; DOK Level: 2; **Content Topic:** P.a.2; **Practices:** SP.1.a, SP.1.b, SP.3.b, SP.7.a

The chemical reaction that occurs in a cold pack absorbs thermal energy from the surroundings, making the cold pack feel cold because it is absorbing thermal energy from the user's body. If a reaction takes in energy, it is an endothermic reaction. The term *energetic* is not used to describe types of chemical reactions. Combustion produces heat and light; no heat or light is produced in this reaction. An exothermic reaction produces heat; therefore, an exothermic reaction would make the pack feel warm, not cold.

Answer Key

UNIT 2 (continued)

10. D; DOK Level: 2; **Content Topic:** P.a.2; **Practices:** SP.1.a, SP.1.b, SP.3.b, SP.7.a

The reaction is releasing thermal energy, meaning that it is exothermic. The term *energetic* is not used to describe types of chemical reactions. If it were an endothermic reaction, it would feel cold because it would be absorbing thermal energy from its surroundings, including the user's body. Combustion produces heat and light; no light is produced in this reaction.

11. A; DOK Level: 2; **Content Topic:** P.a.2; **Practices:** SP.1.a, SP.1.b, SP.7.a

In an exothermic reaction, the reactants have more, not less, energy than the products because the reaction releases energy. The incorrect answer choices are not supported by the data in the graph.

12. D; DOK Level: 2; **Content Topic:** P.a.2; **Practices:** SP.1.a, SP.1.b, SP.3.b, SP.7.a

An endothermic reaction absorbs thermal energy from its surroundings, including the student's hand. If the reaction is drawing thermal energy from the student's hand, the beaker will feel cold. If energy were going into the student's hand, the beaker would feel warm. Liquids can range in temperature and be cooler than their surroundings. Whether an electric charge is generated likely is unrelated to how cold the solution feels.

13. B; DOK Level: 3; **Content Topics:** P.a.2, P.a.3; **Practices:** SP.1.a, SP.1.b, SP.7.a

The equations show that the chemical reaction that occurs during photosynthesis absorbs, or takes in, light energy and the chemical reaction that occurs during respiration releases mechanical and thermal energy. So photosynthesis is endothermic, and respiration is exothermic.

14. A; DOK Level: 3; **Content Topics:** P.a.2, P.a.3; **Practices:** SP.1.a, SP.1.b, SP.3.b, SP.7.a

Although organisms do use water in their life processes, both carbon dioxide and water are considered waste products in this reaction because the cell is using respiration to extract energy from sugar, not to obtain water. Energy, therefore, is not a waste product. Oxygen is one of the reactants, not a product. That is, oxygen reacts with the sugar molecule to produce the products: carbon dioxide, water, and energy.

LESSON 12, pp. 106–109

1. A; DOK Level: 1; **Content Topic:** P.a.5; **Practices:** SP.1.a, SP.1.b, SP.1.c, SP.3.b

The passage and diagram indicate that waves in the electromagnetic spectrum are arranged in order of increasing energy and decreasing wavelength. Gamma rays have the shortest wavelengths and, therefore, the most energy. Radio waves have the longest wavelengths and, therefore, the least energy. Microwaves and visible light waves have wavelengths that are longer than those of gamma rays and shorter than those of radio waves.

2. D; DOK Level: 2; **Content Topic:** P.a.5; **Practices:** SP.1.a, SP.1.b, SP.1.c, SP.3.b

The passage and diagram indicate that the energy of the electromagnetic waves in the electromagnetic spectrum depends on their wavelengths and that waves with longer wavelengths have less energy than waves with shorter wavelengths. The diagram shows that microwaves have longer wavelengths than infrared waves. Therefore, microwaves have less energy than infrared waves. All waves of the electromagnetic spectrum, including radio waves, can travel through empty space. The diagram includes visible light, so visible light is part of the electromagnetic spectrum. Sound waves are not included in the diagram, so you can infer that they are not part of the electromagnetic spectrum.

3. D; DOK Level: 2; **Content Topic:** P.a.5; **Practices:** SP.1.a, SP.1.b, SP.1.c, SP.3.b, SP.7.a

The passage states that light waves are transverse waves, and the diagram indicates that transverse waves have crests and troughs. So light waves can be characterized by their crests and troughs. The diagram indicates that rarefactions are found in longitudinal waves, not transverse waves, and that compressions are the areas in longitudinal waves where particles are closest together, not farthest apart. Because light waves are transverse waves, not longitudinal waves, they do not have compressions and rarefactions.

4. D; DOK Level: 2; **Content Topic:** P.a.5; **Practices:** SP.1.a, SP.1.b, SP.1.c, SP.3.b, SP.7.a

The passage states that sound waves are longitudinal waves. Both the text and the diagram indicate that particles vibrate parallel to the direction that longitudinal waves travel. Sound waves are longitudinal, so they form compressions but not crests or troughs, and they cause particles to move parallel to the direction of wave movement.

5. A; DOK Level: 2; **Content Topic:** P.a.5; **Practices:** SP.1.a, SP.1.b, SP.1.c, SP.3.b, SP.7.a

The passage explains that longitudinal waves are those that cause particles to vibrate in the direction that the wave moves. The diagram shows that these waves form compressions and rarefactions. Transverse waves do not form compressions and rarefactions, and longitudinal waves do not form crests and troughs. Transverse waves form crests and troughs as particles vibrate perpendicular to the wave; however, the passage states that P waves cause particles to move parallel to the wave.

6. B; DOK Level: 2; **Content Topic:** P.a.5; **Practices:** SP.1.a, SP.1.b, SP.1.c, SP.3.b, SP.7.a

The diagram shows that Rayleigh waves move Earth's crust up and down in circular paths, so water waves would affect the leaf the same way.

7. A; **DOK Level:** 2; **Content Topic:** P.a.5; **Practices:** SP.1.a, SP.1.b, SP.1.c, SP.3.b, SP.7.a
The passage explains that a Rayleigh wave travels along the boundary between Earth's crust and air; trees grow in Earth's crust, so the Rayleigh wave moves the tree as it travels along Earth's crust. The diagram shows that the Rayleigh wave moves left to right; the other arrows in the diagram indicate the movement of Earth's crust caused by the Rayleigh wave. A Rayleigh wave travels along Earth's crust, not deep beneath its surface. Water waves, not Rayleigh waves, move along the boundary between water and air.

8. D; **DOK Level:** 2; **Content Topic:** P.a.5; **Practices:** SP.1.a, SP.1.b, SP.1.c, SP.7.a
The table shows that a jackhammer produces sound at a decibel level of 110, which is louder than a conversation, a vacuum cleaner, or a lawn mower.

9. A; **DOK Level:** 2; **Content Topic:** P.a.5; **Practices:** SP.1.a, SP.1.b, SP.1.c, SP.3.b, SP.7.a
The passage explains that volume is related to amplitude. Conversation has the lowest volume, so its sound waves have the smallest amplitude. A vacuum cleaner, a lawn mower, and a jackhammer all produce sounds louder than a conversation, so their sound waves have greater amplitudes.

10. C; **DOK Level:** 2; **Content Topic:** P.a.5; **Practices:** SP.1.a, SP.1.b, SP.1.c, SP.7.a
The passage states that hearing damage can result from sounds beginning at a level of 85 dB. The table shows that lawn mowers, jackhammers, and jet engines produce sounds above 85 dB.

11. B; **DOK Level:** 1; **Content Topic:** P.a.5; **Practices:** SP.1.a, SP.1.b, SP.1.c, SP.7.a
The diagram shows that the wavelength of the visible spectrum ranges from 400 nm to 700 nm. A wave with 500 nm would have to be that of the color green, based on its position in the spectrum. Violet light has a wavelength closer to 400 nm, and orange light and red light have wavelengths closer to 700 nm.

12. A; **DOK Level:** 2; **Content Topic:** P.a.5; **Practices:** SP.1.a, SP.1.b, SP.1.c, SP.7.a
The passage explains that frequency and wavelength determine the energy of a wave. The diagram shows that blue light has a shorter wavelength and higher frequency—and, therefore, higher energy—than orange light.

13. B; **DOK Level:** 3; **Content Topic:** P.a.5; **Practices:** SP.1.a, SP.1.b, SP.1.c, SP.3.b, SP.7.a
White light is composed of the waves of every color. Therefore, the wavelengths of the waves that make up white light range from 400 nm to 700 nm, the range of wavelengths of the colors in the visible spectrum. It is not possible to conclude the speed with which white light travels from the information provided. Because white light is made up of the waves of the various colors, the waves that make up white light have varying wavelengths and frequencies.

14. D; **DOK Level:** 2; **Content Topic:** P.a.5; **Practices:** SP.1.a, SP.1.b, SP.1.c, SP.7.a
The passage states that the speed of a wave can be determined by multiplying its frequency by its wavelength. Therefore, frequency of a wave can be determined by dividing its wavelength by its speed. By applying this formula, you can determine that the higher the speed of a sound wave, the higher its frequency. According to the table, sound waves traveling through rubber have higher speeds than those traveling through air, water, or lead. Therefore, sound waves traveling through rubber have higher frequencies than those traveling through air, water, or lead.

LESSON 13, *pp. 110–113*
1. B; **DOK Level:** 2; **Content Topic:** P.a.4; **Practices:** SP.1.a, SP.1.b, SP.1.c, SP.3.b, SP.5.a
The passage indicates that hydroelectric plants are a renewable energy source. The circle graph shows that renewable energy sources account for 9 percent of the total U.S. energy sources. Therefore, you can draw the conclusion that hydroelectric plants must contribute less than 9 percent of the total energy. It is possible that hydroelectric plants account for about 5 percent or at least 8 percent of total U.S. energy sources; however, not enough information is provided to draw these conclusions. Because renewable sources account for 9 percent of total U.S. energy sources, hydroelectric plants cannot account for more than 10 percent of that total.

2. D; **DOK Level:** 2; **Content Topic:** P.a.4; **Practices:** SP.1.a, SP.1.b, SP.1.c, SP.3.b, SP.5.a
The circle graph shows that coal, natural gas, and petroleum account for most U.S. energy consumption. These energy sources are all nonrenewable fossil fuels, so the United States does rely mostly on nonrenewable energy sources. Nothing in the graph or passage can be used to determine the amount of energy the United States uses per unit of time or how long energy supplies will last. Also, no data in the graph or passage can be used to make a comparison between the use of petroleum and natural gas by the United States as compared to use in any other country. Finally, the graph shows that the United States gets only 9 percent of its energy from renewable sources, which is much less than half.

3. D; **DOK Level:** 2; **Content Topic:** P.a.4; **Practices:** SP.1.b, SP.1.c, SP.3.b, SP.5.a, SP.7.a
The diagrams show that the process of making electricity in a hydroelectric plant does not produce waste gases, such as carbon dioxide, as in a coal-fired plant. Just as in other plants, the generator in a hydroelectric plant produces an electric current. The diagrams give no information to determine the relative cost of different types of electric power plants. Hydroelectric plants use the power of water only, not wind.

4. C; **DOK Level:** 2; **Content Topic:** P.a.4; **Practices:** SP.1.a, SP.1.b, SP.1.c, SP.3.b, SP.5.a, SP.7.a
Based on the passage and diagram, you can draw the conclusion that the energy products of fission are thermal energy and radiation. Although thermal energy is one product, it is not the only one. As subatomic particles, neutrons are matter, not energy.

UNIT 2 (continued)

5. C; DOK Level: 2; **Content Topic:** P.a.4; **Practices:** SP.1.a, SP.1.b, SP.1.c, SP.3.b, SP.5.a, SP.7.a
The fact that the energy source for nuclear fission is nonrenewable uranium means that the supply of this fuel is limited, although there is no indication that it will run out soon. There is no indication in the passage or diagram that neutrons stop the fission chain reaction. The passage states that a new nuclear plant is scheduled to open by 2017, so the construction of these plants has not stopped.

6. D; DOK Level: 2; **Content Topic:** P.a.4; **Practices:** SP.1.a, SP.1.b, SP.1.c, SP.3.b, SP.5.a
The maps' keys explain how the colors of the maps should be interpreted. They indicate that the areas with the most intense sunlight are in deep red and orange, followed by areas with the next most intense amounts of sunlight in yellow. Sunlight is least intense in areas of green and blue. Using this color key, you can draw the conclusion that the area of the country most suited to solar power is the Southwest.

7. B; DOK Level: 2; **Content Topic:** P.a.4; **Practices:** SP.1.a, SP.1.b, SP.1.c, SP.3.b, SP.5.a
Based on the information provided, refrigerators use the relatively highest amount of electricity. The pictograph indicates that using a smaller refrigerator will cut down on the use of electricity and contribute, even in a small way, to pollution prevention. Turning off the computer at night may save a little energy but is not the best option for reducing energy consumption. Recycling is a good idea for the shop because it conserves resources and reduces waste, but it does not directly affect air pollution. Turning down the thermostat in the summer to keep the shop cool results in greater use of electricity.

8. DOK Level: 3; **Content Topic:** P.a.4; **Practices:** SP.1.a, SP.1.b, SP.1.c, SP.3.a, SP.3.b, SP.5.a, SP.6.c
Possible answer:
Ⓐ The data on the graph show that global emissions of carbon dioxide have risen drastically since the 1960s. Ⓑ The passage explains that carbon dioxide is a greenhouse gas that helps retain Earth's thermal energy. Also, it states that the warmest 12-month periods between 1895 and 2012 have occurred since 2000—with five having occurred during the most recent years. Ⓒ With this information, the conclusion can be reached that the increase in carbon dioxide in the air, due in part to burning fossil fuels, has given Earth a greater capacity to hold in thermal energy and has made it a warmer planet.
Ⓐ The first sentence interprets the graph as providing proof of the increase in carbon dioxide in the air.
Ⓑ The next two sentences use information from the passage to relate carbon dioxide to data about Earth's temperature.
Ⓒ The last sentence identifies a conclusion that can be drawn from information in the passage and graph and related inferences.

LESSON 14, pp. 114–117

1. D; DOK Level: 2; **Content Topics:** P.c.1, P.c.3; **Practices:** SP.2.c, SP.3.b, SP.7.a
Although all aspects of investigation design are significant, analysis of results is the factor that supports or does not support a hypothesis. In Lavoisier's investigation, he caused a chemical reaction in which hydrogen and oxygen were the reactants and water was the product. The fact that the weight of the water equaled the combined weights of the hydrogen and oxygen supported the idea that the water was a compound made up of the hydrogen and the oxygen. The presence of other scientists at an investigation is irrelevant in supporting or refuting the hypothesis. The amounts of hydrogen and oxygen and the tools used were important parts of Lavoisier's investigation design, but they were not the factors that supported the hypothesis.

2. B; DOK Level: 2; **Content Topic:** P.c.2; **Practices:** SP.2.b, SP.2.d, SP.7.a
When an investigation yields unexpected results, especially results that fail to align with ideas based on existing evidence, scientists should analyze the investigation design to ensure that it is free from error. The periodic table of elements should not be modified unless scientists are certain of the discovery of a new element. Results of investigations cannot be modified; they can be reinterpreted, but the process used to obtain them should be analyzed first. Consulting experts may or may not be helpful; however, doing so is not a part of the scientific method.

3. D; DOK Level: 2; **Content Topic:** P.a.4; **Practices:** SP.3.d, SP.8.a, SP.8.b
Mean, or average, is determined by adding the values in a data set and then dividing by the number of values in the data set. The value 384 μR/h is the average of all the data points, rounded to the nearest whole number. The other answer choices might be reached through incorrect calculations or a misunderstanding of the concept of mean.

4. C; DOK Level: 3; **Content Topic:** P.a.4; **Practices:** SP.3.b, SP.3.d, SP.5.a, SP.8.a
The value for Sample 4 is an extreme outlier, so it is appropriate to conclude that a sampling, testing, or recording error has been made with that sample. It is not likely that all bodies of water except one would be contaminated; they have all been exposed to about the same level of radiation. Because the value for Sample 4 is an outlier, it should not be included in the results. The values of the other samples are close enough to one another that one outlier should not cast doubt on the sampling process.

5. A; DOK Level: 2; **Content Topic:** P.a.1; **Practices:** SP.2.e, SP.7.a
The variable to be observed is the variable that is affected by changing the shape of the container, or the rate of cooling. Therefore, the rate of cooling is the dependent variable. The shape of the container is the independent variable; that is, it is purposely being changed. The volume of water and the room temperature should be held constant.

6. **B**; **DOK Level:** 2; **Content Topic:** P.a.1; **Practices:** SP.2.e, SP.7.a

To determine whether container shape affects cooling, Mick must use different container shapes in the investigation. Therefore, the variable to be modified, or the independent variable, is shape of container. The rate of cooling is the dependent variable, or the one that will be affected by changing the independent variable. The volume of water and the room temperature should be held constant.

7. **A**; **DOK Level:** 2; **Content Topic:** P.a.1; **Practices:** SP.2.d, SP.7.a

Different volumes of water will cool at different rates, so volume of water should be held constant. If the temperature of the room is held constant, time of day is an irrelevant factor in this investigation. The rate of cooling is the dependent variable and cannot be held constant. The boiling point of water has already been established in science and will be the same for all samples.

8. **C**; **DOK Level:** 1; **Content Topic:** P.c.2; **Practices:** SP.2.d, SP.7.a

Properties of a substance can change in subtle to significant ways under certain conditions. For an investigation about changes in certain properties of a substance, recording the investigation with a video camera with narration would allow the researcher to record all parts of the investigation, including all changes to the properties in question, accurately. The practice of writing down observations after events occur—whether immediately after concluding a test or the next day—relies on human memory and, thus, is not as effective as writing down or recording comments about observations as events are occurring. Repeating the process the next day does not have anything to do with recording and capturing information about the events of the original investigation.

9. **D**; **DOK Level:** 1; **Content Topic:** P.b.1; **Practices:** SP.2.d, SP.7.a

Once an investigation has been conducted, the data must be analyzed and interpreted before any conclusions can be drawn or predictions can be made. The design of an investigation depends on the hypothesis, so forming a hypothesis happens before the investigation. A theory is developed only after multiple investigations validate a hypothesis. A researcher cannot make a prediction from an investigation without first analyzing the results and reaching a conclusion.

10. **B**; **DOK Level:** 3; **Content Topic:** P.c.4; **Practices:** SP.3.b, SP.3.c, SP.7.a

The investigation results indicate that solubility of CO_2 decreases as water temperature increases. So the researcher can predict that as oceans warm, less CO_2 will dissolve in them. The investigation results offer no support for the ideas that adding salt to water affects CO_2 solubility, solubility of CO_2 would differ in ocean water and distilled water, and adding distilled water to ocean water would affect CO_2 solubility.

11. **DOK Level:** 3; **Content Topic:** P.c.4; **Practices:** SP.2.d, SP.2.e, SP.6.c, SP.7.a
Possible answer:

Ⓐ Set a starting point and an ending point for the water temperature (for example, 20 °C and 90 °C), and control for the amount of water used; that is, maintain the same volume of water throughout the investigation. Next, slowly add salt to the water at the coolest temperature to determine the saturation point for the solution. Record the figure for the applicable amount of salt and the water temperature. Then raise the temperature of the water a predetermined increment, add the same amount of salt to the warmer water, and observe whether all the salt goes into solution. Continue the process until reaching a temperature at which all the salt does not go into solution. At that point, strain the precipitate out of the water and measure it to determine what percentage of the salt did not go into solution. The dependent variable is the amount of salt that dissolves before the saturation point is reached; the independent variable is the amount of increase in water temperature.
Ⓑ After the investigation, plot data on a line graph, graphing the relationship between saturation point and water temperature. Ⓒ If the investigation results demonstrate that warmer water dissolves less salt, the hypothesis is validated.
Ⓐ The response includes a complete description of the investigation, including identifying the dependent and independent variables and the controlled factor (volume of water).
Ⓑ It also includes a well-formulated data collection method—entering values for the amount of salt and water temperature in a table and then graphing the data points.
Ⓒ Finally, it explains how the results might or might not validate the hypothesis.

12. **B**; **DOK Level:** 2; **Content Topic:** P.c.1; **Practices:** SP.3.b, SP.5.a, SP.7.a

In the late 1800s, chemist J. J. Thomson conducted investigations that supported the hypothesis that atoms contain smaller, negatively charged particles, or electrons. It makes sense to conclude that this discovery of a smaller particle within an atom caused the scientific community to reject Dalton's assertion that an atom is a single solid particle. A theory proposed by John Jacob Berzelius in 1826 asserted that atoms have electrical charges and that atoms join in fixed proportions to form various compounds; however, these assertions did not negate the idea that an atom is a single solid particle and so did not cause scientists to reject Dalton's earlier notion. The model of atomic structure put forth by Niels Bohr in 1922 indicated that electrons are arranged in energy levels around an atom's nucleus, but Bohr's discovery came after the discovery that atoms contain electrons, so scientists already had rejected Dalton's idea that an atom is a single solid particle.

Answer Key

UNIT 2 (continued)

LESSON 15, pp. 118–121

1. C; DOK Level: 2; Content Topics: P.a.1, P.c.2;
Practices: SP.1.a, SP.1.b, SP.2.b, SP.4.a, SP.7.a
The investigation showed that copper is a better conductor of thermal energy than glass. This conclusion cannot be applied to all metals and nonmetals. The only metal tested in the investigation was copper, so there is no way of knowing whether it conducts thermal energy better than other metals. The only nonmetal tested was glass, so another nonmetal that is an even poorer conductor of thermal energy might exist.

2. A; DOK Level: 2; Content Topics: P.a.1, P.c.2; **Practices:** SP.1.a, SP.1.b, SP.2.a, SP.2.c, SP.4.a, SP.7.a
It would be prohibitively difficult to test thermal energy conductivity of all metals and nonmetals, so the hypothesis was too vague to be investigated validly. The investigation showed that at least one metal, copper, is a good thermal energy conductor. The investigation did include dependent and independent variables; the rate of heating was the dependent variable, and the material being heated was the independent variable. The passage makes no reference to recording of results, so it is possible this task was done properly.

3. D; DOK Level: 2; Content Topic: P.c.2; **Practices:** SP.1.a, SP.1.b, SP.1.c, SP.2.c, SP.7.a
The hypothesis is testable because it is possible to observe whether lowering pressure causes ice to sublimate rather than melt. All matter, not just CO_2, goes through different states. A chemistry textbook is usually a reliable source of information. Determining whether gas (water vapor) subjected to lower pressure would change state directly to ice is not a way to test the hypothesis.

4. B; DOK Level: 2; Content Topic: P.c.2; **Practices:** SP.1.a, SP.1.b, SP.1.c, SP.2.a, SP.3.b, SP.7.a
Running multiple tests tends to eliminate or at least reduce random errors in measuring, observation, calculation, and so on. A hypothesis cannot be validated or invalidated on the basis of one test. It is premature to revise a hypothesis, assume that a hypothesis is wrong, or consult with other researchers after only one test.

5. B; DOK Level: 3; Content Topics: P.a.3, P.b.1, P.b.2; **Practices:** SP.1.a, SP.1.b, SP.2.a, SP.2.c, SP.5.a, SP.7.a
The difference in the velocities is easily accounted for by the force of air resistance acting on the bullets. Although the test might have been improved by measuring and recording the mass of each bullet, the difference in their masses likely had little effect on the test. The test design called for the bullet to be fired straight up, so the angle is irrelevant. Furthermore, the type of bullet would not likely affect the test.

6. D; DOK Level: 2; Content Topic: P.b.2; **Practices:** SP.1.a, SP.1.b, SP.2.e, SP.7.a
The depth of the hole in the clay is the dependent variable because it is the variable being observed. The initial height is a controlled variable because Iona is using the same height for each trial. Iona is purposefully varying the mass of the ball; therefore, mass is the independent variable. Iona has not considered the size (or volume) of the ball bearing and has not counted it as a possible variable at all.

7. B; DOK Level: 2; Content Topic: P.b.2; **Practices:** SP.1.a, SP.1.b, SP.2.e, SP.7.a
Iona is varying the mass of the ball; therefore, mass is the independent variable. The initial height is a controlled factor because Iona is using the same height for each trial. Iona has not considered the size (or volume) of the ball bearing and has not counted it as a possible variable at all. The depth of the hole in the clay is the dependent variable.

8. C; DOK Level: 3; Content Topic: P.b.2; **Practices:** SP.1.a, SP.1.b, SP.2.a, SP.2.c, SP.3.b, SP.7.a
Iona has not considered the size (or volume) of the ball bearing, a factor that could affect hole depth, the dependent variable. She has measured the mass of each ball bearing, but a larger ball bearing will presumably make a wider hole, which will skew the test results. The initial height is a controlled factor in the investigation. Ball bearing mass is the independent variable, and hole depth is the dependent variable.

9. A; DOK Level: 2; Content Topic: P.c.3; **Practices:** SP.1.a, SP.4.a, SP.5.a, SP.7.a
New information based on sound investigation can invalidate a scientific theory or hypothesis. So if scientists were to conduct repeated controlled investigations showing that the quantity of matter in certain reactants is unequal to the quantity of matter in their products, the new information resulting from those investigations would call into question the validity of the theory of conservation of mass. On the other hand, circumstances that cannot invalidate a scientific theory include beliefs without support from scientific investigation and the inability of nonscientists to understand a theory. Moreover, the possibility that future scientific discoveries might suggest that a theory is incorrect do not invalidate the theory now; in fact, scientific theory by its very nature is subject to challenge and change as new evidence is discovered.

10. C; DOK Level: 2; Content Topics: P.c.2, P.c.3; **Practices:** SP.1.a, SP.7.a
A theory explains a wider range of observations, such as all observations related to conservation of mass, than a hypothesis. Both hypotheses and theories try to explain an observation or observations, and both can be challenged and refuted. Neither one relies on data but can be validated only by data gathered from a sound, repeatable test.

11. D; DOK Level: 2; Content Topic: P.a.5; **Practices:** SP.1.a, SP.1.b, SP.3.b, SP.7.a
The conjecture that an invisible, warmer area of energy lies next to the red light area is a testable hypothesis that aligns with the observation. The hypothesis was in fact tested and validated in the 1800s by William Herschel. Everyday experience should indicate that darker areas are not always warmer than lighter ones. The thermometers were able to measure the temperature of the different colors of light, indicating that special equipment is not required. Although all parts of the visible light spectrum have measurable temperatures, the temperature reading in question was outside the visible spectrum.

12. **A; DOK Level:** 2; **Content Topic:** P.b.2; **Practices:** SP.1.a, SP.1.b, SP.2.b, SP.2.c, SP.3.b, SP.7.a
Through the use of equipment such as telescopes and observation of patterns of bodies in space, scientists were able to demonstrate that Earth is a planet that revolves around the sun and, thereby, nullify the null hypothesis. The incorrect answer choices are valid statements but do not nullify the null hypothesis.

13. **C; DOK Level:** 2; **Content Topic:** P.c.3; **Practices:** SP.1.a, SP.1.b, SP.2.c, SP.3.b, SP.4.a, SP.5.a, SP.7.a
Lavoisier conducted a controlled, repeatable investigation that yielded evidence that conflicted with the earlier theory and led to the rejection of the theory of phlogiston. The theory of phlogiston did have popular support because it seemed to explain every observation. Proponents of the theory even developed chemical equations that seemed to support the theory. Most scientists at the time accepted the theory, whether they were influential or not.

UNIT 3 EARTH AND SPACE SCIENCE

LESSON 1, *pp. 122–125*
1. **B; DOK Level:** 1; **Content Topic:** ES.b.4; **Practices:** SP.1.a, SP.1.b, SP.7.a
Wegener's hypothesis was linked to his question about why some continents look as though they were once joined, so his hypothesis suggested the breaking apart and movement of the continents. Continents do have many different shapes, but that fact alone does not constitute Wegener's hypothesis. There is no indication in the material that today's continents will form another landmass such as Pangaea or that the continents of today are larger than those of the past.

2. **B; DOK Level:** 2; **Content Topic:** ES.b.4; **Practices:** SP.1.a, SP.1.b, SP.7.a
To present a theory that Earth's landmasses are different now than they were in the past because continents had moved, Wegener would have to present evidence that the continents had moved, although he would not necessarily need to provide an explanation of how they moved. Support from other scientists would not suffice without evidence. Building a new theory from an outdated theory would not succeed unless new evidence could be found.

3.1 **C**; 3.2 **B**; 3.3 **D**; 3.4 **A; DOK Level:** 2; **Content Topic:** ES.b.4; **Practices:** SP.1.a, SP.1.b, SP.1.c, SP.3.a, SP.7.a
3.1 The diagram indicates that the impetus for Wegener's research on continental drift was the fact that South America and Africa seem to fit together. They do not have the same shape. Wegener was looking at a map, so he was observing the shapes of the continents, not their compositions or climates.
3.2 Because the land masses seemed to fit together, Wegener hypothesized that they were once joined. The incorrect answer choices do not relate to his observation about their fitting together.
3.3 The continents are now separated by an ocean. If they were once joined, it is logical to hypothesize that they somehow moved from where they were to their present locations. It is not logical to hypothesize that they changed shape, formed at different times, or were Earth's only landmasses.

3.4 A theory relies on evidence. To propose a theory, Wegener had to obtain evidence to support his hypothesis through scientific investigation, not disprove other scientific laws. Wegener had to show only that the movement occurred, not that it continued. Acceptance of an idea by others comes from obtaining evidence; alone, it is not support of a theory.

4. **B; DOK Level:** 2; **Content Topic:** ES.c.1; **Practices:** SP.1.a, SP.1.b, SP.3.b, SP.4.a, SP.7.a
The passage identifies discoveries that explain that the explosiveness of the Big Bang would have spread cosmic radiation throughout the universe. There is no evidence presented that the radiation could be detected only from Earth. If the radiation is found throughout the universe, that situation would be unlikely. The existence of cosmic background radiation in and of itself does not offer information about the exact age of the universe. The passage states that radiation produced by the Big Bang would have cooled to become microwaves, not that the Big Bang produced only microwave radiation.

5. **B; DOK Level:** 2; **Content Topic:** ES.b.4; **Practices:** SP.1.a, SP.1.b, SP.1.c, SP.3.b, SP.4.a, SP.5.a, SP.7.a
If *Mesosaurus,* an aquatic creature, had been a poor long-distance swimmer, it would not have crossed the ocean. This line of reasoning supports the theory that the animal developed when the two landmasses were joined and survived on both continents when they split apart. If the fossils are common all over the world, there would be nothing remarkable about finding them in those specific areas of South America and Africa. The statement that there is a species today that descended from *Mesosaurus* does not indicate where it lives and, thus, would not help support Wegener's theory. If the fossils on the two continents came from two different species, they probably developed independently on the two different continents.

6. **A; DOK Level:** 3; **Content Topic:** ES.b.4; **Practices:** SP.1.a, SP.1.b, SP.1.c, SP.3.b, SP.5.a, SP.7.a
To support the theory, the fossils have to have been found on two landmasses that are not currently connected but could have been. South Africa and Antarctica are two landmasses that are across from each other but are now separated by ocean. The other options do not fit this description.

7. **C; DOK Level:** 2; **Content Topic:** ES.b.4; **Practices:** SP.1.a, SP.1.b, SP.1.c, SP.4.a, SP.5.a, SP.7.a
Remnants of an ancient land bridge now on the seafloor would provide evidence that the animals could have crossed between the two continents long ago, when the sea level was lower. A map showing how the land bridge would have looked would be merely another hypothesis, not evidence. Signed statements from other scientists are not a valid form of evidence. The presence of land bridges, even if they are all over the world today, does not prove that a land bridge existed between Africa and South America millions of years ago.

8. **C; DOK Level:** 2; **Content Topic:** ES.b.4; **Practices:** SP.1.a, SP.1.b, SP.1.c, SP.4.a, SP.7.a
Lines of evidence A, B, and C (not just A and B or A and C) support the idea that continents have moved. Line of evidence D is not relevant because the occurrence of earthquakes in certain areas of Earth's surface does not prove that continents have moved.

Answer Key

9. C; **DOK Level:** 2; **Content Topic:** ES.b.4; **Practices:** SP.1.a, SP.1.b, SP.1.c, SP.3.b, SP.4.a, SP.5.a, SP.7.a
If the seafloor is spreading evenly on both sides of a ridge, rock age would increase in seafloor farther away from the ridge. The youngest rocks would be closest to the ridge because that is where the new ocean floor is continually being formed. If the seafloor is spreading, continents on either side of a mid-ocean ridge are moving farther apart, not closer together. Also, if the seafloor is spreading evenly, rocks at equal distances from the ridge would be the same age. The presence or absence of fossils does not affect seafloor spreading.

10. A; **DOK Level:** 3; **Content Topic:** ES.b.4; **Practices:** SP.1.a, SP.1.b, SP.1.c, SP.4.a, SP.5.a, SP.7.a
The idea that the seafloor under the oceans that separate continents is spreading supports the theory that the continents are moving slowly away from each other. Seafloor spreading does not indicate that continents float. It also does not prove the existence of Pangaea millions of years ago. There is no evidence presented that oceans move and continents are stationary.

11. D; **DOK Level:** 2; **Content Topic:** ES.b.4; **Practices:** SP.1.a, SP.1.b, SP.1.c, SP.3.b, SP.4.a, SP.7.a
Based on the elements of the map identified in the key, the map shows that most earthquakes occur where there are plate boundaries. The map clearly shows that some earthquakes happen away from continent edges. It is also clear from the map that plate boundaries and continent boundaries are not the same. The information does not explain where earthquakes are most dangerous.

12. A; **DOK Level:** 2; **Content Topic:** ES.b.4; **Practices:** SP.1.a, SP.1.b, SP.1.c, SP.3.b, SP.4.a, SP.5.a, SP.7.a
The positioning of many earthquakes along plate boundaries supports the idea that the movement of plates has significant effects at plate boundaries. The locations of earthquakes alone do not prove that Earth's surface is composed of plates. Additional information would be needed to prove this suggestion. The locations of earthquakes prove nothing about what plates contain. Plates are composed of solid rock, but the locations of earthquakes do not prove this fact.

LESSON 2, *pp. 126–129*
1. D; **DOK Level:** 2; **Content Topic:** ES.c.1; **Practices:** SP.1.a, SP.1.b, SP.1.c, SP.7.a
An important detail of the passage is that nuclear fusion takes place in the sun's core, so a summary might include this detail. The incorrect answer choices represent inaccurate interpretations of the information in the passage.

2. B; **DOK Level:** 2; **Content Topic:** ES.c.1; **Practices:** SP.1.a, SP.1.b, SP.1.c, SP.7.a
The main idea of the passage and model is that atoms fuse during fusion and produce energy. Therefore, that information must be included in a summary. Information regarding the elements contained in the sun, the types of elements that fusion produces, and the comparison of fusion and fission as energy-producing processes are interesting details but are not essential to a summary.

3. C; **DOK Level:** 2; **Content Topic:** ES.c.1; **Practices:** SP.1.a, SP.1.b, SP.1.c, SP.7.a
The fact that stars more massive than the sun explode represents a key part of the main idea of the information, so it should be included in a summary of the information. The incorrect answer choices present facts that are not important enough to warrant inclusion in a summary of the information.

4. A; **DOK Level:** 2; **Content Topic:** ES.c.1; **Practices:** SP.1.a, SP.1.b, SP.1.c, SP.7.a
The main topic of the diagram and passage is how massive stars end, so a brief explanation of this process is an appropriate summary of the information. Nuclear fusion is mentioned, but it is not the main point of the passage. Massive stars do become very dense bodies, but this information represents just one supporting detail. The detail that stars are all born in the same way is not relevant to the topic of how stars die.

5. C; **DOK Level:** 2; **Content Topic:** ES.c.1; **Practices:** SP.1.a, SP.1.b, SP.7.a
The student's summary copies the language of the passage; a summary must be in the writer's own words. The student's summary does provide details about the Milky Way, although these details are too specific and too unrelated to the main point of the passage to be in the summary. Summaries should be shorter than the passages they summarize, so the length of the student's summary is not problematic. Also, summaries do not necessarily need to define terms.

6. DOK Level: 3; **Content Topic:** ES.c.1; **Practices:** SP.1.a, SP.1.b, SP.1.c, SP.6.c, SP.7.a
Possible answer:
Ⓐ The relationships among the traits of color, temperature, and brightness vary depending on the type of star. Ⓑ For example, main sequence stars range from cool, dim stars (represented in the bottom right corner of the diagram) to bright, hot stars (represented in the top left corner of the diagram). Blue giants are large, hot, and bright. Red giants are large, cool, and bright. White dwarfs are small, hot, and dim.
Ⓐ The summary begins with a statement of the main idea conveyed by the diagram.
Ⓑ The summary includes the most important details supporting the main idea.

7. D; **DOK Level:** 2; **Content Topic:** ES.c.1; **Practices:** SP.1.a, SP.1.b, SP.7.a
The passage explains that both neutron stars and black holes form at the end of the life cycles of large stars. Neutron stars form after a supernova, rather than before. Only black holes are so dense that light cannot escape them. The passage does not say or suggest that neutron stars and black holes are composed only of neutrons.

8. A; **DOK Level:** 2; **Content Topic:** ES.c.1; **Practices:** SP.1.a, SP.1.b, SP.1.c, SP.7.a
The timeline and passage provide information about what will occur at the end of the sun's life cycle, so a summary should identify the major stages of the sun at the end of its life cycle. Information about when the sun formed and how it will grow is important but omits the significant details about what will happen to the sun at the end of its life cycle. The statements about Earth's current life-forms being eliminated and nuclear fusion in the sun's core ending are true but do not capture the most important ideas of the passage.

LESSON 3, pp. 130–133

1. **D**; **DOK Level:** 1; **Content Topic:** ES.c.2; **Practices:** SP.1.a, SP.1.b, SP.1.c, SP.7.a
Any location in the northern hemisphere receives more energy during the summer, not any other season, because that is when the hemisphere is tilted toward the sun and the sun's energy is most direct.

2. **D**; **DOK Level:** 3; **Content Topic:** ES.c.2; **Practices:** SP.1.a, SP.1.b, SP.1.c, SP.3.b, SP.7.a
As the diagram indicates, the tilt of Earth on its axis is the most important factor that produces seasons on the planet. Earth's revolution by itself would not produce seasons if not for Earth's tilt. The ideas that there would be seasons that are the same but shorter and that there would be perpetual summer or winter are not supported by the information provided.

3. **C**; **DOK Level:** 2; **Content Topic:** ES.c.1; **Practices:** SP.1.a, SP.1.b, SP.1.c, SP.7.a
The passage indicates that the pattern of visible constellations changes throughout the year as Earth revolves around the sun. Although constellations do change their shape, this change occurs only over very long periods of time. Constellations have been observed since ancient times, so they exist for long periods. The passage provides no evidence that Earth's positioning during summer affects our ability to view constellations.

4. **A**; **DOK Level:** 3; **Content Topic:** ES.c.1; **Practices:** SP.1.a, SP.1.b, SP.1.c, SP.3.c, SP.7.a
Because stars move over time, a constellation will not look exactly as it does now in the future. So in 100,000 years, the constellations we see today would no longer be recognizable because they will not look the same. Therefore, they will not have the same shapes that they have today. There is no information in the passage to suggest which stars might be dimmer 100,000 years from now.

5. **C**; **DOK Level:** 1; **Content Topic:** ES.c.2; **Practices:** SP.1.a, SP.1.b, SP.1.c, SP.7.a
Based on information in the passage, it can be inferred that the dotted arrows on the diagram represent the wind direction if the Coriolis effect did not exist. The solid arrows represent wind direction under the Coriolis effect. No part of the map represents Earth's rotation. The dotted arrows are present throughout the map, so they do not represent only winds at the equator or poles.

6. **C**; **DOK Level:** 3; **Content Topic:** ES.c.2; **Practices:** SP.1.a, SP.1.b, SP.1.c, SP.7.a
The passage explains that the Coriolis effect causes the deflection of fluids, including wind, water, and surface ocean currents. The Coriolis effect keeps winds from blowing in a straight line. It does not cause high pressure areas on the planet or Earth's rotation.

7. **DOK Level:** 1; **Content Topic:** ES.c.2; **Practices:** SP.1.a, SP.1.b, SP.1.c, SP.6.c, SP.7.a
The passage explains that we see different parts of the moon's lit side because of its **revolution** around Earth. If the moon did not revolve around Earth, there would not be phases of the moon.

8. **DOK Level:** 2; **Content Topic:** ES.c.2; **Practices:** SP.1.a, SP.1.b, SP.1.c, SP.6.c, SP.7.a
The diagram shows that the phase that occurs when the moon is between Earth and the sun is a **new moon**. At new moon, the moon's lighted side faces the sun and Earth is faced by its unlit side, so new moon nights sometimes appear moonless.

9. **DOK Level:** 3; **Content Topic:** ES.c.2; **Practices:** SP.1.a, SP.1.b, SP.1.c, SP.6.c, SP.7.a
The circle of arrows in the diagram shows the direction of the changes in the appearance of the moon. During waxing phases, the lit side of the moon that we see appears to grow **larger** each night. During waning phases, the lit part of the moon we see appears to grow **smaller** each night.

10. **C**; **DOK Level:** 2; **Content Topic:** ES.c.2; **Practices:** SP.1.a, SP.1.b, SP.7.a
The passage states that Halley's comet completes its orbit every 76 years. Any comet follows an elliptical orbit around the sun, not Earth, and forms a tail as it draws closer to the sun, not when it is far away from the sun. The passage provides no support for the idea that Halley's comet follows the path of all other comets.

11. **B**; **DOK Level:** 2; **Content Topic:** ES.c.2; **Practices:** SP.1.a, SP.1.b, SP.1.c, SP.3.b, SP.7.a
The passage and diagram indicate that the moon moves in front of the sun during a solar eclipse. Therefore, it is the moon's orbit, or revolution around Earth, that is responsible for the event. The phenomena of the rotations of Earth and the moon and the production of energy in the sun do not cause eclipses.

12. **C**; **DOK Level:** 2; **Content Topics:** ES.c.1, ES.c.2; **Practices:** SP.1.a, SP.1.b, SP.1.c, SP.7.a
The passage states that Kepler identified information about patterns of movement of objects in our solar system. So his laws deal with planetary motion—and the motion of other bodies in the universe. They do not relate to the distances of planets from stars or explain how planets form. They also do not address the relationship between mass and motion.

LESSON 4, pp. 134–137

1. **D**; **DOK Level:** 2; **Content Topic:** ES.b.4; **Practices:** SP.1.a, SP.1.b, SP.1.c, SP.3.b
The diagram shows that the crust is the outermost layer of Earth and that it is proportionally much smaller than the other layers. The mantle cannot be seen from Earth's surface because it is underneath the crust. The diagram does not address density or temperature.

2. **C**; **DOK Level:** 2; **Content Topic:** ES.b.4; **Practices:** SP.1.a, SP.1.b, SP.1.c, SP.3.b
The diagram indicates that the crust is Earth's outermost layer and that Earth's other layers are made of flowing or liquid rock. Based on this information, the conclusion can be drawn that Earth's landforms are part of Earth's crust. The incorrect answer choices represent areas where Earth's landforms could not be.

3. **D**; **DOK Level:** 2; **Content Topic:** ES.b.4; **Practices:** SP.1.a, SP.1.b, SP.1.c, SP.7.a
The diagram shows that the epicenter is located on the surface of Earth, directly above the focus, which is under Earth's surface. The incorrect answer choices are inaccurate descriptions of the locations of the epicenter and focus.

Answer Key

UNIT 3 (continued)

4. A; DOK Level: 2; **Content Topic:** ES.b.4; **Practices:** SP.1.a, SP.1.b, SP.1.c, SP.7.a
The diagram shows that the waves produced by the rock shift radiate out in all directions from the focus, or location of the rock shift, and the passage states that they travel away from the break. They do not travel only along the fault, from the epicenter to the fault, or inward from the surface.

5. A; DOK Level: 2; **Content Topic:** ES.b.4; **Practices:** SP.1.a, SP.1.b, SP.1.c, SP.3.b, SP.7.a
The diagram text explains that the material that erupts from the volcano forms layers, building on itself. The passage states that volcanoes erupt lava and give off gases, ash, and rock fragments. Of these substances, only lava after it has cooled, rock fragments, and ash can build the layers of solid material needed to form a volcano. Gases do not make up any part of a volcano's surface. Rock is part of the material deposited on the surface of the volcano, but not all of it. Magma is melted rock below the surface, not material that makes up the layers of the volcano.

6. C; DOK Level: 2; **Content Topic:** ES.b.4; **Practices:** SP.1.a, SP.1.b, SP.1.c, SP.3.b, SP.7.a
The idea that volcanoes are smaller when they first form is supported by the fact that they grow larger as they build up layers over time. The presence of side vents indicates that lava does not always erupt from the main vent at the center of a volcano. The diagram text indicates that volcanoes do not erupt continuously by explaining that a volcano erupts when the magma chamber fills. The passage states that volcanoes erupt lava, rock fragments, gases, and ash. It does not say that these substances cannot issue from the volcano at the same time.

7. B; DOK Level: 2; **Content Topic:** ES.b.4; **Practices:** SP.1.a, SP.1.b, SP.1.c, SP.7.a
The diagram shows that the mountain became shorter after the eruption. There is no indication from the diagram that the volcano is narrower. The volcano still exists, so it was not destroyed. The diagram indicates that the volcano has grown shorter, not larger.

8. B; DOK Level: 2; **Content Topic:** ES.b.4; **Practices:** SP.1.a, SP.1.b, SP.1.c, SP.7.a
The volcano released rock from below its surface. The diagram indicates that the eruption also caused parts of the mountain to break free and fly through the air, so rock from below the surface as well as rock from the mountain was flung through the air during the eruption. The incorrect answer choices are too narrow in identifying what materials were involved in the eruption.

9. D; DOK Level: 2; **Content Topic:** ES.b.4; **Practices:** SP.1.a, SP.1.b, SP.1.c, SP.3.b, SP.7.a
The text and arrows in the diagram indicate that movement of rock in the mantle produces currents that cause the plates to move. Earthquakes are the result of plate movement, not the cause. Friction between plates does not cause movement; it would tend to slow movement or stop it. The moving rock that affects plate motion does not come from the core.

10. A; DOK Level: 2; **Content Topic:** ES.b.4; **Practices:** SP.1.a, SP.1.b, SP.1.c, SP.7.a
Studying the diagram reveals that the plates are located in the lithosphere, not in the lower mantle, the asthenosphere, or the outer core.

11. C; DOK Level: 2 **Content Topic:** ES.b.4; **Practices:** SP.1.a, SP.1.b, SP.1.c, SP.3.b, SP.7.a
The diagram shows that trenches form where two plates move together, with one being pushed under the other. A trench can occur at the edge of a plate, but it is not the edge itself. It is also not the surface of a plate. Ridges, not trenches, form where two plates move apart.

12. DOK Level: 2; **Content Topic:** ES.c.3; **Practices:** SP.1.a, SP.1.b, SP.1.c, SP.3.d, SP.7.a
According to the principles, in a sequence of rock layers, the lowest layer is the oldest and the top layer is the youngest. Also, if a feature cuts across another feature, the feature it cuts across formed first. In the diagram, Features B and C are layers above Feature D and Feature A cuts across Feature D. So Features **A**, **B**, and **C** are younger than Feature D.

13. D; DOK Level: 2; **Content Topic:** ES.b.4; **Practices:** SP.1.b, SP.1.c, SP.3.b, SP.7.a
The diagram text indicates that rock that becomes new crust originates as hot, flowing magma that comes from the mantle. It does not originate in the core, crust, or surface sediment.

14. B; DOK Level: 3; **Content Topic:** ES.b.4; **Practices:** SP.1.b, SP.1.c, SP.7.a
The diagram shows and explains that rock in the mantle melts and then rises to the surface, where it cools, so the conclusion can be reached that particles in the liquid rock move from the hotter mantle to Earth's cooler surface. The diagram indicates that the crust is cooler than the mantle because rock cools there, so thermal energy would not be transferred from the crust, a cooler area, to the mantle, a warmer area. The diagram provides no evidence that thermal energy transfer between tectonic plates occurs or that thermal energy transfer from ocean waters to the air above them occurs because such thermal energy transfer, if it does occur, is not directly related to crust formation.

LESSON 5, pp. 138–141

1. C; DOK Level: 2; **Content Topics:** ES.b.1, ES.b.2; **Practices:** SP.1.a, SP.1.b, SP.1.c, SP.3.b, SP.7.a
You have learned that energy from the sun warms Earth, including its land, air, and water. So the sun provides the energy that warms ocean waters. The atmosphere, nearby shores, and precipitation are not sources of energy.

2. A; DOK Level: 2; **Content Topics:** ES.b.1, ES.b.2, ES.b.3; **Practices:** SP.1.a, SP.1.b, SP.1.c, SP.3.b, SP.7.a
You have learned that thermal energy moves from warmer matter to cooler matter, so you can conclude that the Gulf Stream warms the atmosphere above it because the Gulf Stream waters are warmer than the air in the atmosphere. Although exothermic chemical reactions can produce thermal energy, the Gulf Stream warms the atmosphere because of thermal energy transfer, or an increase in the movement of particles in the atmosphere, not because of a chemical reaction. When particles in the air come in contact with Gulf Stream waters, their movement speeds up and thus raises the air temperature; if the particles slowed, the air temperature would lower. All matter, including ocean waters and Earth's atmosphere, has internal kinetic energy caused by the movement of molecules, atoms, and subatomic particles.

3.1 **D**; 3.2 **D**; 3.3 **C**; 3.4 **A**; 3.5 **B**; **DOK Level:** 2; **Content Topics:** ES.a.1, ES.b.1; **Practices:** SP.1.a, SP.1.b, SP.1.c, SP.3.b, SP.7.a

3.1 Based on concepts related to energy, you know that the sun is an energy source that warms Earth's waters. Clouds are the result of water vapor in the air releasing energy and changing from the gaseous to the liquid state. Wind results from unequal pressure on Earth's surface, due to unequal heating of the surface by the sun. Ozone is a form of oxygen that is most plentiful in the stratosphere.

3.2 Based on the concept of states of matter, you know that liquid water on Earth's surface that absorbs energy from the sun becomes gaseous water vapor during evaporation. In condensation, the opposite happens. Water loses energy and changes from the gaseous state to the liquid state. Deposition is the process in which matter changes from the gaseous state to the solid state without becoming a liquid first. Sublimation is the process in which matter changes from the solid state to the gaseous state without becoming a liquid first.

3.3 Based on the concept of changes in states of matter, you know that when water vapor in the atmosphere cools, it changes from a gas to a liquid. Water vapor would have to become even colder and freeze to become solid. It is already a gas, so it cannot change state to become a gas. Plasma is a fourth state of matter, formed by charged particles that behave somewhat like a gas. The sun is plasma. At no part of the water cycle is a substance changed into plasma.

3.4 Based on the concept of changes in states of matter, you know that precipitation that falls as ice and snow is frozen. Liquid water freezes when it cools to its freezing point. Condensation is the change of state from gas to liquid; melting is the change of state from solid to liquid; and vaporization is the change of state from liquid to gas. Snow and ice are solids (not liquids or gases), so the precipitation in the clouds does not condense, melt, or evaporate to become snow and ice.

3.5 Based on the concept of changes in states of matter, you know that snow and ice are water in the solid state. Snow and ice are not in the plasma state or gaseous state. *Slushy* describes partly melted snow or ice but not a state of matter.

4. **C**; **DOK Level:** 2; **Content Topic:** ES.b.2; **Practices:** SP.1.a, SP.1.b, SP.1.c, SP.3.b, SP.7.a

Solubility is the amount of solute that can be dissolved in a given amount of solvent at a specific temperature, so when the temperature of a solution changes, its solubility changes. The passage explains that salt remains (or goes out of solution) when the ocean water freezes, indicating that as the temperature of the ocean water decreases, its solubility decreases. Because ocean water is a solution, or homogeneous mixture, the molecules of the substances that make it up are distributed in the same proportions, so salt is distributed in the ocean water at the poles before the water freezes. If solubility were to increase as the temperature of ocean water decreases, salt would stay in solution, not go out of solution, when ocean water freezes. If ocean water were to become saturated at a temperature above its freezing point, salt would go out of solution before the ocean water freezes, not when it freezes.

5. **A**; **DOK Level:** 2; **Content Topic:** ES.b.2; **Practices:** SP.1.a, SP.1.b, SP.1.c, SP.7.a

Density is the ratio of mass to volume, so ocean water with higher salinity has a greater ratio of mass to volume than ocean water with lower salinity. Ocean water with a greater ratio of volume to mass would have lower salinity. The properties of mass and volume are dependent on sample size, so a larger quantity of ocean water would have more mass and volume than a smaller quantity of ocean water regardless of the levels of salinity of the two samples.

6. **B**; **DOK Level:** 2; **Content Topic:** ES.b.2; **Practices:** SP.1.a, SP.1.b, SP.3.b

The passage states that the oceans are becoming acidic. Because acids have values less than 7.0 and bases have values greater than 7.0 on the pH scale, a change from a pH of 8.0 to a pH of 6.0 indicates that a solution is changing from basic to acidic. A change from a pH of 7.0 to a pH of 9.0 or from a pH of 10.0 to a pH of 12.0 indicates that a solution is becoming more basic. A change from a pH of 12.0 to 10.0 indicates that a solution is becoming less basic; however, it is still basic, not acidic.

7. **A**; **DOK Level:** 2; **Content Topic:** ES.b.2; **Practices:** SP.1.a, SP.1.b, SP.3.b, SP.3.c, SP.7.a

The passage states that ocean acidification is occurring, so it makes sense to predict that the ocean will become more acidic.

8. **D**; **DOK Level:** 2; **Content Topics:** ES.b.1, ES.b.2; **Practices:** SP.1.a, SP.1.b, SP.1.c, SP.3.b, SP.7.a

Based on the concept of heat transfer, you know that conduction is the transfer of heat between adjacent molecules, so you can reason that heat is transferred by conduction from the warm ocean surface to the air adjacent to it. Radiation is the transfer of heat through space by electromagnetic waves. In convection, warm air rises, then cools and sinks to rise again. Convection would warm air high in the troposphere, not the air adjacent to the ocean surface. Saturation is not a type of heat transfer; it is the point at which no more solute can be dissolved in a solution at its current temperature.

9. **A**; **DOK Level:** 2; **Content Topics:** ES.b.1, ES.b.2; **Practices:** SP.1.a, SP.1.b, SP.1.c, SP.3.b, SP.7.a

Recall that convection is the transfer of heat through fluids, such as air and water. Warm air rises from Earth's surface into the atmosphere. Then it cools and sinks to rise again. Condensation is a change in state that occurs when heat is withdrawn from a gas, causing the gas to become a liquid. It is not a type of heat transfer. Radiation and conduction are not the types of heat transfer described. Radiation is the transfer of heat through space by electromagnetic waves. Conduction is heat transfer between objects that are in contact with one another.

UNIT 3 *(continued)*

10. C; **DOK Level:** 3; **Content Topics:** ES.b.1, ES.b.2; **Practices:** SP.1.a, SP.1.b, SP.1.c, SP.3.b, SP.7.a
The passage explains that during a hurricane, heat transferred from ocean waters warms air, causing it to rise. The diagram also shows how warm air rises during a hurricane. Therefore, the formation of a hurricane demonstrates the concept of convection, or warm air becoming less dense than the cooler air around it and rising. The prevailing westerly winds in middle latitudes have nothing to do with hurricane formation. In addition, as the passage states, hurricanes do not form in the middle latitudes. They form in the tropics. The density of ocean water also has nothing to do with the formation of hurricanes. The law of conservation of energy is not a major principle that explains hurricane formation.

11. C; **DOK Level:** 3; **Content Topic:** ES.b.2; **Practices:** SP.1.a, SP.1.b, SP.1.c, SP.3.a, SP.7.a
The underlying concept of the Coriolis effect—that it causes air and water to be deflected to the left or right due to Earth's rotation—explains how it helps determine the path of ocean currents. The path of ocean currents is not caused by Earth's revolution around the sun, the sun's gravitational pull on Earth, or weather changes.

LESSON 6, pp. 142–145

1. C; **DOK Level:** 2; **Content Topic:** ES.b.1; **Practices:** SP.1.a, SP.1.b, SP.1.c
The circle graph on the left shows that carbon dioxide represented 84 percent of the total U.S. greenhouse gas emissions in 2010. The incorrect answer choices are not supported by the graph.

2. D; **DOK Level:** 2; **Content Topic:** ES.b.1; **Practices:** SP.1.a, SP.1.b, SP.1.c
The circle graph on the right shows that electricity production accounted for 40 percent of carbon dioxide emissions in 2010, transportation accounted for 31 percent, and industry accounted for 14 percent. So these three sources combined accounted for 85 percent of carbon dioxide emissions in 2010. The incorrect answer choices each express the proportion that only one of these sources contributed.

3. D; **DOK Level:** 2; **Content Topic:** ES.b.1; **Practices:** SP.1.a, SP.1.b, SP.1.c
The diagram indicates that all people on Earth live within the troposphere and that commercial aircraft fly in the lower stratosphere, so people can be found in these layers but not in the other layers of the atmosphere.

4. B; **DOK Level:** 1; **Content Topic:** ES.b.1; **Practices:** SP.1.a, SP.1.b, SP.1.c
The diagram indicates that most weather and clouds are in the troposphere. The mesosphere, not the troposphere, is the coldest part of the atmosphere. Airplanes fly in the stratosphere as well as in the troposphere. The exosphere, not the troposphere, contains particles that are miles apart.

5. B; **DOK Level:** 2; **Content Topic:** ES.b.1; **Practices:** SP.1.a, SP.1.b, SP.1.c
Because the passage explains that AM radio signals stay closer to their transmitter during the day than at night and the black arrows are shorter in the "day" part of the diagram than in the "night" part of the diagram, you can infer that the arrows represent radio signals. The ionosphere contains charged particles as well as nitrogen molecules and oxygen atoms, but these objects are not what the arrows represent. If arrows representing radiation from the sun were included in the diagram, they would go from the sun toward Earth.

6. C; **DOK Level:** 2; **Content Topic:** ES.b.1; **Practices:** SP.1.a, SP.1.b, SP.1.c
Based on information from the passage and the diagram, radio waves bouncing off the F layer of the ionosphere at night help the transmissions go farther than they would in the day when the lower layers of the ionosphere absorb them. None of the information provided supports the statement that transmitters send out more powerful signals at night, the ionosphere boosts the energy of radio signals, or sunlight blocks radio signals in daylight hours.

7. DOK Level: 1; **Content Topics:** ES.b.1; ES.b.3; **Practices:** SP.1.a, SP.1.b, SP.1.c, SP.6.a, SP.6.c
On the basis of information in the passage, the diagram should be labeled as follows: **very strong acidic precipitation** at pH 3.0, **lower end of the range of most acid rain** at pH 5.0, **higher end of the range of most acid rain** at pH 5.5, **rainwater** at pH 5.6, **ocean water** at pH 8.0, **higher end of range of freshwater** at pH 9.0.

8. C; **DOK Level:** 2; **Content Topic:** ES.b.3; **Practices:** SP.1.a, SP.1.b, SP.5.a
The passage states that wind is the second-largest renewable energy source in the United States, so it is an important energy source. Data identified in the passage indicate that the use of wind as an energy source is increasing, not occurring less and less. Although the passage identifies disadvantages of wind power, the existence of controversy over wind power would not impact the effectiveness of wind power.

9. D; **DOK Level:** 2; **Content Topic:** ES.b.1; **Practices:** SP.1.a, SP.1.b, SP.1.c
The curve in the graph begins at a point of high altitude and low pressure. The slope of the line indicates that as altitude decreases, pressure increases, at first slightly and then more dramatically. The passage states that air pressure is greatest at sea level. Air pressure is a downward force, whereas distance from a mountain is a horizontal measurement, so air pressure is unrelated to distance from mountains. If air pressure were to increase as altitude increases, the curve in the graph would begin in the lower left corner and go to the upper right corner.

10. B; **DOK Level:** 3; **Content Topic:** ES.b.1; **Practices:** SP.1.a, SP.1.b, SP.1.c, SP.7.a
The model shows the chemical reactions by which chlorine in the atmosphere breaks down ozone. Chlorine atoms break down ozone molecules by bonding with them to produce chlorine monoxide (ClO) and oxygen molecules. Furthermore, chlorine monoxide molecules bond with oxygen atoms, making them unavailable for ozone production. The incorrect answers provide information about ozone but do not state the information expressed by the model.

LESSON 7, pp. 146–149

1. B; DOK Level: 2; **Topics:** ES.a.1, ES.a.3; **Practices:** SP.1.a, SP.1.b, SP.3.a, SP.3.b

The main idea of the first paragraph of the passage is that lack of access to clean water is a problem. The other problems identified in the passage—armed conflicts and unsuccessful projects—are details supporting the main idea. The fact that WHO/UNICEF reports on lack of access to clean water is not a problem.

2. D; DOK Level: 1; **Topics:** ES.a.1, ES.a.3; **Practices:** SP.1.a, SP.1.b, SP.3.a

The passage states that increasing access to piped-in water has solved the problem of access to clean drinking water for people in many parts of the world. Water conservation is not a solution to the problem of accessing clean water. Although improving projects and reducing armed conflicts might help, these ideas are not mentioned in the passage as possible solutions.

3. A; DOK Level: 3; **Content Topic:** ES.a.2; **Practices:** SP.1.a, SP.1.b, SP.1.c, SP.3.b

Based on the information provided, the idea of building barrier walls and raising structures higher off the ground could better protect homes and businesses. Building larger buildings does not make them better able to withstand hurricanes; hurricanes knock down very large structures. Building more bridges would allow people to escape more quickly but would do nothing about helping buildings withstand the storms. Causing the area to be less populated would keep storms from affecting as many people but would not help buildings withstand storms.

4. C; DOK Level: 2; **Content Topic:** ES.a.2; **Practices:** SP.1.a, SP.1.b, SP.1.c, SP.3.a, SP.3.b

The passage indicates that it is likely that storms will hit this area again at some point, so many of the homes rebuilt there could be destroyed again. Although houses typically are expensive at a shore, the information presented does not relate to expense of rebuilding. It is illogical to believe that most hurricanes will hit the same stretch of shore, and the passage does not support this idea. The passage indicates indirectly that some homes on the coast did withstand the storm.

5. C; DOK Level: 1; **Content Topic:** ES.a.2; **Practices:** SP.1.a, SP.1.b, SP.1.c

The passage indicates that a hurricane emergency kit solves the problem of lack of vital supplies after a hurricane. So the purpose of the kit is to provide such supplies, not to help people exit the area or to tell what actions to take when a hurricane is approaching. A hurricane kit does include food and water, but its purpose is broader than just ensuring that hurricane victims have these essentials.

6. D; DOK Level: 3; **Content Topic:** ES.a.2; **Practices:** SP.1.a, SP.1.b, SP.1.c, SP.3.b

Flashlights would be a useful light source if electricity were unavailable. If the power were out, fresh milk would be useless without refrigeration. Pots and pans would not be the most useful items because without cooking facilities, there would be little call for them. Electric blankets would not work without power.

7. C; DOK Level: 1; **Content Topics:** ES.a.1, ES.b.1; **Practices:** SP.1.a, SP.1.b, SP.1.c, SP.3.a

The passage states that animals and plants must use nitrogen, but not the elemental form found in the atmosphere. The passage also indicates that all plants and animals use nitrogen to form proteins and that most of Earth's atmosphere is nitrogen. Nothing in the passage or diagram suggests that nitrogen breaks down proteins.

8. D; DOK Level: 2; **Content Topics:** ES.a.1, ES.b.1; **Practices:** SP.1.a, SP.1.b, SP.1.c, SP.3.b

Without nitrogen, plants and animals would have no protein because as the passage states, nitrogen is needed to produce it. A lack of nitrogen, therefore, could not result in too much protein. Neither the passage nor the diagram supports the idea that a lack of nitrogen would cause infection by bacteria or eliminate bacteria in the soil.

9. C; DOK Level: 2; **Content Topics:** ES.a.1, ES.b.1; **Practices:** SP.1.a, SP.1.b, SP.1.c, SP.3.a

The diagram indicates that after nitric acid enters soil, bacteria break down nitric acid into a form of nitrogen that plants can use (nitrates). Plants' roots absorb nitrogen compounds from the soil, not the air. Neither the diagram nor the passage indicates that bacteria become nitrogen or that plant-eating animals break down nitrogen compounds.

10. B; DOK Level: 2; **Content Topic:** ES.a.2; **Practices:** SP.1.a, SP.1.b, SP.3.b

The passage explains that scientists use volcano monitoring to identify activity that signals a possible upcoming eruption, so volcano monitoring helps address the need to have early warnings of eruptions. Volcano monitoring cannot stop volcanoes from erupting or reduce the number of eruptions. Although volcano monitoring helps scientists understand volcanoes, lack of understanding of volcanoes is not the main problem that monitoring helps solve.

11. C; DOK Level: 1; **Content Topic:** ES.a.2; **Practices:** SP.1.a, SP.1.b, SP.1.c, SP.3.a

The passage explains that earthquake-resistant design allows structures to resist forces that cause collapse, or destruction. Earthquake-resistant design does not have any effect on earthquakes themselves. The passage does not provide information about the cost of earthquake-resistant design. Whether buildings are attractive depends on an observer's judgment.

12. C; DOK Level: 2; **Content Topic:** ES.a.2; **Practices:** SP.1.a, SP.1.b, SP.1.c, SP.3.b

The passage suggests that knowing where and when a tornado will form is important in reducing deaths from tornadoes, so it can be inferred that the National Weather Service created tornado alerts to help people know when a tornado is in their area. Development of the system of watches and warnings did not help explain how tornadoes form or help people get services after a tornado. Although the system of alerts does relate to forecasting and tracking tornadoes, its purpose is to warn people of an approaching tornado or conditions conducive to formation of a tornado.

13. B; DOK Level: 2; **Content Topic:** ES.a.2; **Practices:** SP.1.a, SP.1.b, SP.1.c, SP.3.b

It can be inferred from the information presented that knowing how to respond when tornado conditions are present is vital to people's safety, so the best thing the store owner can do is ensure that all employees know what to do and where to go in case of a tornado warning. Reading a book about tornadoes will not necessarily help someone prepare for tornado season. It would be unreasonable to close the shop each time there is a severe thunderstorm because tornadoes do not always occur in the presence of thunderstorms. No part of the watch and warning system tells the public to phone the National Weather Service. The watches and warnings are enough information to allow people to take cover.

LESSON 8, *pp. 150–153*

1. D; DOK Level: 2; **Content Topics:** ES.a.1, ES.a.3; **Practices:** SP.1.a, SP.1.c, SP.3.a, SP.3.b, SP.4.a

The passage and the graph could be used to make a good case for designing vehicles that get better gas mileage. Because so much of the oil imported is used in transportation, a reduction in the need for oil in transportation would have a large impact in reducing dependence on oil. By stating that the United States *must* import oil, the passage infers that this situation is not ideal, so the passage does not support the argument to increase oil imports. The information presented is related to energy conservation, not pollution caused by energy sources. Also, the information does not relate to energy prices; moreover, importers cannot set the prices of imported goods.

2. C; DOK Level: 2; **Content Topics:** ES.a.1, ES.a.3; **Practices:** SP.1.a, SP.1.c, SP.3.a, SP.3.b, SP.4.a

The fact that energy consumption continues to trend upward is the best argument to support the development and use of renewable energy sources because nonrenewable energy sources eventually will run out. The statement that adequate supplies of nonrenewable sources exist is not a strong argument for using renewable energy sources because it contradicts the urgency of the idea that supplies will run out. How energy is used is irrelevant in supporting the argument for renewable energy sources. The fact that energy production is increasing is not the most compelling argument to support the use of renewable energy sources because increased energy production merely reflects the law of supply and demand with relation to energy consumption.

3. D; DOK Level: 2; **Content Topics:** ES.a.1, ES.a.3; **Practices:** SP.1.a, SP.3.a, SP.3.b, SP.4.a

The least biased source would be the U.S. Department of Energy. Although government agencies can introduce their own biases into information, federal government agencies are generally known for reliable, factual information. The names of the other organizations listed show that each has an obvious connection to a cause surrounding the issue of the pipeline.

4. C; DOK Level: 2; **Content Topics:** ES.a.1, ES.a.3; **Practices:** SP.1.a, SP.3.a, SP.3.b, SP.4.a

Given the huge amount of oil needed to supply the United States on a daily basis, the fact that the pipeline could bring large amounts of oil in from a friendly neighboring country is a strong argument in its favor. The fact that petroleum can be obtained from tar sands explains the purpose of the pipeline but does not offer a persuasive reason to build it rather than meet energy needs in another way. The statement that safeguards are likely to prevent leaks in the pipeline helps the argument in favor of the pipeline, but it is more a prediction than an actual fact; therefore, it is not the strongest supporting statement. The fact that the United States uses 20 million barrels of oil each day might be an explanation for why the United States needs to import so much oil, but it does not support any particular source of imported oil, including this pipeline.

5. A; DOK Level: 2; **Content Topics:** ES.a.1, ES.a.3; **Practices:** SP.1.a, SP.3.a, SP.3.b, SP.4.a

The fact that a leak in the pipeline could pollute the aquifer is the strongest argument against the pipeline. The makeup of the tar sands is not relevant to an argument against the pipeline. The fact that the aquifer is a major water supply is significant only if that water supply becomes contaminated. The statement that the United States imports so much oil would help make a case in favor of the pipeline, not against it.

6. B; DOK Level: 2; **Content Topic:** ES.a.1; **Practices:** SP.1.a, SP.1.c, SP.3.a, SP.3.b, SP.4.a

The contrast between the two photos shows that the glacier shrunk between 1913 and 2005, thus supporting the argument for global warming. The photos give no indication of how large the glacier was in 1913. However, it is clear that it was larger in 1913 than in 2005. The fact that the glacier is in a rocky area is unrelated to global warming. The photographs give no evidence that the glacier is moving downhill. However, glaciers do move slowly downhill under the influence of gravity, and such movement would happen regardless of any warming of Earth.

7. C; DOK Level: 2; **Content Topic:** ES.a.1; **Practices:** SP.1.a, SP.1.c, SP.3.a, SP.3.b, SP.4.a

The absence of the glacier in 2020 would indicate that the glacier had continued to shrink until it completely melted away. This change would support the argument for the idea that climate change is occurring in the form of Earth's warming. The crumbling of mountains cannot be attributed to climate change. The appearance of sand dunes would suggest erosion but not necessarily climate change. The glacier's maintaining its same size until 2015 would support an argument against the idea that climate change is occurring rather than for it.

8. A; DOK Level: 2; Content Topics: ES.a.1, ES.a.3; **Practices:** SP.1.a, SP.1.c, SP.3.a

An entry in the "Against" row of the table states that some people believe that the real problem is unrelated to drilling in ANWR and is instead the fact that U.S. oil consumption is too high. No one would logically argue that few uses for oil exist in the United States today because oil is used in numerous ways, including in heating buildings, producing fuel for motor vehicles, and manufacturing products such as plastics. The United States does depend greatly on foreign oil, and extraction can disturb environments, but these factors are results of the base problem of a high level of oil consumption in the United States.

9. B; DOK Level: 2; Content Topics: ES.a.1, ES.a.3; **Practices:** SP.1.a, SP.1.c, SP.3.b

The table indicates that drilling in ANWR will create some jobs and will affect only a small part of the refuge, so people who prioritize job creation over protection of the environment probably would support drilling in spite of any impact it might have on the environment. Foreign oil producers likely would prefer that the United States have fewer, not more, domestic oil sources. Environmentalists likely would be concerned about any impact on the environment, regardless of how small. People concerned about oil prices would not necessarily view drilling in ANWR as beneficial because doing so is unlikely to lower oil prices, according to the information presented.

10. A; DOK Level: 2; Content Topic: ES.a.3; **Practices:** SP.1.a, SP.1.c, SP.3.b, SP.4.a

The passage states that construction of hydroelectric dams affects wildlife, including salmon, and changes environmental conditions downstream, so a valid argument against the construction of a hydroelectric dam is that it can threaten aquatic environments downstream. The passage states that hydropower produces no air or water pollution, not too much pollution. The fuel to run a hydroelectric plant is water, which is basically free. Hydroelectric dams can be built only where there is a source of running or falling water, usually a river that can be dammed to produce a reservoir or lake.

11. C; DOK Level: 2; Content Topic: ES.a.3; **Practices:** SP.1.a, SP.1.c, SP.3.a, SP.4.a

The passage states that hydropower does not produce air or water pollution, a fact that would be a valid argument for construction of hydroelectric dams. Hydroelectric dams can be built only where a source of running or falling water exists, not anywhere. The information provided does not address the cost of maintaining hydroelectric dams, but costly maintenance would be an argument against, not for, the construction of these dams. Hydroelectric dams do pose threats to wildlife, a factor that helps support a case against their construction, not for it.

12. A; DOK Level: 2; Content Topics: ES.a.1, ES.a.3; **Practices:** SP.1.a, SP.1.c, SP.3.a, SP.3.b, SP.4.a

The large size of U.S. coal reserves supports the idea that the United States should continue to rely on coal—at least for a while longer. Increasing the use of oil would make no sense because the United States has very small oil reserves. China has smaller coal reserves than the United States and is probably drawing down its own reserves; therefore, it is unlikely that the United States would rely on China for coal. Based on reserves alone and not on environmental concerns, the United States has much larger reserves of coal than natural gas. Therefore, the use of coal would be more sustainable, in terms of supply.

13. B; DOK Level: 2; Content Topics: ES.a.1, ES.a.3; **Practices:** SP.1.a, SP.1.c, SP.3.a, SP.3.b, SP.4.a

The graph shows that the European Union is the area of the world with the smallest reserves of fossil fuels, thus giving it the greatest incentive to switch to renewable energy sources.

14. D; DOK Level: 3; Content Topics: ES.a.1, ES.a.3; **Practices:** SP.1.a, SP.1.c, SP.3.a, SP.3.b, SP.4.a

The passage explains that as countries with large populations develop, they will use more energy; in the short term, at least, this population growth will mean greater use of fossil fuels. The information given does not suggest that current estimates may be wrong. It is also highly unlikely that fossil fuels will be the only energy sources in the future, especially because they are nonrenewable fuels. Based on current trends, developed countries likely will not decrease their use of fossil fuels, at least in the foreseeable future.

15. A; DOK Level: 3; Content Topic: ES.a.3; **Practices:** SP.1.a, SP.1.c, SP.3.a, SP.3.b, SP.4.a

According to the graph on the right, most freshwater is used for irrigation. Raising crops in areas where they can survive on rainfall alone would eliminate the need for irrigation, thus saving a lot of water. The act of drinking water is a domestic use of water, and according to the same graph, domestic use represents the least significant use of freshwater. Consequently, production of more drinking water would have less of an impact than reducing irrigation. Use of water for industry is also significantly less than use of water for irrigation, so restricting use in factories also would have less of an effect than changing farming methods to use less water. Expanding irrigated land would increase water use, and there is no reason to think that this expansion would force people and businesses to conserve water.

Index

A

Acceleration, 85, 89–90
Acidic solutions, 80
Acid precipitation, 144
Acids, 73, 78–80
Acquired immune deficiency syndrome (AIDS), 21
Adaptation
  to climatic conditions, 58
  extinction and, 61
  of microbes, 60
  speciation, 59
Adenosine triphosphate, 5
Aerobic respiration, 5
Agricultural practices, 35
AIDS, 21
Alkali metals, 70
Alkalinity, 73
Alkanes, 77
Alleles, 42–44, 48
Allergies, 17
Alligator holes, 29
Alloys, 81
Altitude, 143, 145
Aluminum, 72
Amalgams, 81
Amplitude, 108
Anaerobic respiration, 5
Anaphase, 40
Animals
  adaptations to climate, 58
  artificial selection, 57
  carrying capacity, 31
  cells of, 4
  as consumers, 23, 25
  effects of human activities, 33–34
  as eukaryotes, 39
  evolutionary theory, 50–53
  eyes of burrowing animals, 54
  eye structures, 53
  feeding relationships, 22–25
  food web disruption, 36
  keystone species, 36
  mitochondria in cells of, 5
  symbiotic relationships, 26–29
  threatened species, 31, 33–34
Antibodies, 16
Antigens, 16
Anus, 7
Arctic National Wildlife Refuge, 152
Arguments
  analyzing and presenting, 150–153
  evaluating, 146
Arrows
  in chemical equations, 74, 79
  in diagrams, 22
  in illustrations, 2
  in vector diagrams, 86–89
Artificial selection, 57
Association neurons, 8
Asthenosphere, 136
Asthma, 17
Atmosphere, 143
Atomic mass, 72

B

Atomic number, 70, 71, 72
Atomic radius, 72
Atomic theory, 117
Atomic weight, 70, 71, 72
Atoms
  covalent bonding, 63, 68
  ionic bonding, 64, 68
  ions, 63–64
  as matter, 62
  structure of, 62, 63, 117
Average force, 93
Average kinetic energy, 98
Average speed, 82–84
Axes of graphs, 18

Bacteria
  adaptation to environment, 60
  cells, 4
  as decomposers, 25
  in deep-ocean ecosystems, 25
  as prokaryotes, 39
  role in nitrogen cycle, 148
  role in plagues, 19
Balanced chemical equations, 74–75
Balanced forces, 86, 88–89
Bar graphs, 34
Barracuda, 28
Base isolation, 149
Bases, 73, 78, 80
Batteries, 103
Behavioral adaptations, 58
Big Bang theory, 123
Biomass energy sources, 110
Bison, 33
Black Death, 19
Black dwarf stars, 127, 129
Black hole, 127, 129
Block-and-tackle pulley, 96
Blood, 7, 16
Blood pressure, 15
Blood vessels, 7
Body systems, 6–9
Boiling point, 68
Bonding
  covalent, 63, 68
  ionic, 64, 68
Brain, 8, 14
Breeding, 57
Brightness, 128
Bullet velocity, 119
Butane, 77

C

Calcium, 11
Calcium carbonate, 140
Calculations, 82–85, 90
Callouts in diagrams, 134
Caloric intake, 10
Calories, 10, 12–13

Captions, 126
Carbon, 13, 63, 68
Carbon dioxide
  covalent bonding, 63
  as greenhouse gas, 113
  ocean acidification and, 140
  in photosynthesis, 4, 105
  produced by fossil fuel burning, 113, 140
  as product of burning alkanes, 77
  released in respiration, 5
  in soda, 80
  solubility of, 116
  sublimation of, 69, 119
Carbon monoxide, 72
Cardiac muscle, 7
Carriers, 44
Carrying capacity, 31–32
Categorizing and classifying, 26–29
Cause and effect, identifying, 14–17
Cell membrane, 2–5
Cells
  animal, 4
  bacteria, 4
  differentiation of, 39
  division of, 38–41
  DNA in, 38, 40
  DNA replication, 40
  epithelial cells, 39
  eukaryotic, 39
  levels of organization, 6
  meiosis, 3, 41, 46
  membrane of, 2–5
  mitochondria, 5
  mitosis, 3, 38, 40–41
  muscle cells, 7
  neurons (nerve cells), 8, 39
  nucleus of cell, 3–4, 38–40
  photosynthesis in, 4
  prokaryotic, 39
  reproduction of, 3
  respiration in, 5, 105
  specialization, 6
Cellular respiration, 5, 105
Centromere, 38
Changes of state
  of carbon dioxide, 69
  effects of temperature and pressure, 66
  properties of matter and, 67
  sublimation, 69
  of tert-butyl alcohol, 69
  of water, 69
Cheetahs, 34
Chemical bonds, 104
Chemical changes, 73, 77
Chemical energy, 4, 103–105, 113
Chemical equations, understanding, 74–78
Chemical formulas, 65, 68, 74
Chemical properties, 72–73
Chemical reactions
  cellular respiration, 105
  chemical changes, 73
  chemical equations for, 74–77
  endothermic and exothermic, 104–105

photosynthesis, 105
types of, 75
Chloride ion, 64
Chlorine, 64
Chlorofluorocarbons, 145
Chlorophyll, 4
Chloroplasts, 4
Chromatids, 38, 40–41
Chromatin, 38
Chromosomes
genetic recombination, 41, 46
in mitosis, 38, 40
replication of, 3, 38, 40, 41, 46
Circle graphs, 18, 142
Circulatory system, 7
Citric acid cycle, 5
Cladograms, 50, 52
Classifying, categorizing and, 26–29
Cleaning fish, 28
Climate
adaptations to, 58
changes in, 36, 117, 140, 147, 151
effect of Gulf Stream, 138
extinction due to changes in, 61
Coal, 110–111, 150, 153
Coal-fired power plants, 111
Coefficients, 74, 76
Collisions, 92–93
Colors of stars, 128
Columns
in periodic table, 72
in tables, 10, 26, 70
Combustion, 104
Comets, 132
Commensalism, 26–27, 29
Common ancestry, 50–53
Comparing and contrasting, 34–37
Complex material, summarizing, 126–129
Complex tables, interpreting, 70–73
Complex visuals, interpreting, 66–69
Compound machines, 97
Compounds, 63–65, 68
Compressions, 107
Conclusions, drawing, 58–61, 110–113
Condensation, 66–67
Conduction, 98, 100–101
Conservation of energy, law of, 102–103
Conservation of mass, law of, 74, 76, 120–121
Constellations, 131
Consumers, 23, 25
Content-based tools
chemical equations, 74
cladograms, 50, 52
Hertzsprung-Russell (H-R) diagram, 128
pedigree charts, 44
periodic table, 71–72
phase diagrams, 66, 119
Punnett squares, 42, 45
scientific models, 62, 65
understanding, 42–45
vector diagrams, 86
Content Practices
determining probability of events, 42
evaluating scientific information, 118
reasoning to conclusions, 110

understanding nontextual scientific
presentations, 38
Content Topics, skin as organ, 6
Content from varied formats, linking, 106–109
Context clues, using, 46–49
Continental drift theory, 122–124
Contrasting, comparing and, 34–37
Convection, 100–101
Core of Earth, 134, 136
Coriolis effect, 131, 141
Corn, 57
Cosmic background radiation, 123
Covalent bonds, 63
Covalent compounds, 63
Crests of waves, 107
Crop-improvement technology, 57
Crust of Earth, 134, 136
Cuticle, 4
Cystic fibrosis, 44
Cytokinesis, 40

D

Dalton, John, 117
Dams, 152
Darwin, Charles, 52, 54, 56
Data
analysis and interpretation of, 114–115
display in tables, 10
making predictions from, 78
as numerical expression of scientific information, 142
recording of, 116
as support for arguments, 150
Daughter cells, 3, 40–41, 46
Deceleration, 85
Decibels, 108
Decomposers, 25
Decomposition reactions, 75
Deep ocean currents, 141
Deep-ocean ecosystems, 25
Deletion mutations, 47
Density, 72, 129, 140, 145
Dental amalgam, 81
Deoxyribonucleic acid (DNA)
in cells, 38
development of new alleles, 48
epigenome and, 49
manufacture of proteins, 53
mutations, 47–48
replication in mitosis, 38–40
sequences of, 53
Dependent variable, 115, 118
Deposition, 66, 67
Desalination, 153
Desert ecosystems, 23
Desertification, 35
Deserts, 58
Details, supporting, 6
Detritivores, 25
Diagrams
cladograms, 50, 52

context clues in, 46
depicting patterns, 130
dot diagram, 85
drawing conclusions from, 110
Hertzsprung-Russell (H-R) diagram, 128
interpreting, 22–25, 66, 82, 86–89, 119, 134–137
numerical data in, 82
pedigree charts, 44
periodic table, 71–72
phase diagrams, 66, 119
Punnett squares, 42, 45
relating to text, 106
scientific models, 62, 65
three-dimensional diagrams, 134
understanding, 42–45
vector diagrams, 86
Digestion, 2, 7
Digestive system, 7
Direction
of forces, 86
of movement, 83–85
Diseases
AIDS, 21
asthma, 17
cystic fibrosis, 44
environmental influences and, 47
hepatitis C, 20
influenza, 18
plague, 19
polio, 20
tracking inheritable diseases, 44
Displacement, 83
Distance, 82–83
DNA
in cells, 38
development of new alleles, 48
epigenome and, 49
manufacture of proteins, 53
mutations, 47–48
replication in mitosis, 38–40
sequences of, 53
Dogs, 57
Dominant alleles, 42–44
Dot diagram, 85
Double displacement reactions, 75
Drinking water, 19
Droughts, 35
Drug resistance, 60
Dry ice, 69, 119

E

Earthquake-resistant buildings, 149
Earthquakes, 108, 125, 135, 149
Earth
layers, 134
revolution around sun, 130
tilt, 130
Earthworms, 25
Eclipses, 133
Ecosystems
carrying capacity, 30–32
deep-ocean ecosystems, 25

INDEX

Index

desert ecosystems, 23, 58
desertification, 35
effects of dams, 152
effects of human activities, 31, 33
energy transfer in, 23, 24
feeding relationships in, 22–25
food web disruption, 36
grassland ecosystems, 22, 24
invasive species, 37
nonliving things in, 32
populations, 30, 33
role of decomposers and detritivores, 25
symbiotic relationships, 26–29
temperate deciduous forest
   ecosystems, 58
threatened species, 31, 33–34
trophic levels, 23
tundra ecosystems, 58
Effect, identifying cause and, 14–17
Effector neurons, 8
Egg, 3, 39, 41
Electrical charge
in ionosphere, 143
of ions, 63–64
of subatomic particles, 62
in water molecules, 65
Electrical current, 143
Electrical energy, 103
Electricity
conduction of, 70
generation, 111–112, 152
Electromagnetic spectrum,
   106, 109
Electromagnetic waves, 100–101,
   106, 109
Electron cloud, 62
Electrons, 62–64, 143
Elements, 63–65, 70–72, 127
Embryonic development, 39
Emergency kits, 147
Endangered species. See **Threatened
   species**
Endangered Species Act (1973), 31
Endocrine system, 9
Endothermic reactions, 104–105
Energy
chemical energy, 4, 103–105, 113
in chemical reactions, 104–105
conservation of, 102–103
dwindling resources, 153
electrical energy, 103
heat transfer, 98, 100–101
hydroelectric power, 110–111, 152
kinetic energy, 98–100, 102–104
mechanical energy, 104–105
from nuclear fission, 111
from nuclear fusion, 126
potential energy, 102–104
production in the United States, 150
released by mitochondria, 5
solar energy, 110, 112
sources of, 5, 12, 23, 25, 99, 110–113,
   138, 141, 144, 150–153
thermal energy, 99–101, 103, 105
transfer in ecosystems, 22–25
transformation, 102–105

trophic levels, 23
use in United States, 150
of waves, 109
wind power, 110, 144
Environment
acidity of ocean waters, 140
adaptations to climate, 58
changes leading to extinction, 61
climate change and, 151
desertification, 35
effect on traits, 47, 55–56
effects of change in on survival, 55
effects of human activities, 35–36
factors causing speciation, 59
gene expression related to, 49
interaction with genes, 47
microbes' adaptation to, 60
risks of oil drilling, 152
Enzymes, 2
Epicenter, 135
Epigenetic drugs, 49
Epigenetics, 49
Epigenome, 49
Epithelial cells, 39
Equations. See **Formulas**
Erosion, 35, 37
Estrogen, 9
Eukaryotes, 39
Evidence, scientific, 51–53, 122–124
Evolutionary theory
adaptation, 54, 56, 58–60
cladograms, 50, 52
common ancestry, 50–53
DNA sequence comparisons, 53
extinction, 61
fossil record, 51–52
natural selection, 55–56, 59–60
speciation, 59
vestigial structures, 51
whale evolution, 51
Excretory system, 7
Exosphere, 143
Exothermic reactions, 104–105
Expansion of matter, 99
Extinction, 61

F

Facts
applying concepts to, 138
drawing conclusions from, 58
Faults, 135
Feces, 7
**Federal Emergency Management
   Agency**, 147
Feedback loops, 9, 14
Feeding relationships, 22–25
Fermentation, 5
Fertilized egg, 39
Finches, beaks of, 56
First quarter moon, 132
Fleas, 19
Focus of earthquake, 135
Folic acid, 11

Food
absorption in body, 7
Calories in, 12
nutrients in, 11
plant production of, 105
transfer of energy from, 5, 23
Food chains, 22
Food and Drug Administration, 49
Food groups, 12–13
Food vacuoles, 2
Food webs, 22
Forces
balanced and unbalanced forces,
   86–89
equal and opposite, 89
friction, 88, 103–104
gravity, 85, 88–90, 104, 119–120, 129,
   145
magnetism, 87
momentum and, 91–93
Newton's laws of motion and, 86,
   89–90, 93
power and, 95
simple machines, 94–97
as vectors, 86–89
work and, 94–97
Forest ecosystems, 24
Formulas
acceleration, 85
average force, 93
change in momentum, 91
density, 72
distance, 82
force, 89–90, 93
frictional force, 88
momentum, 91–92
speed, 82, 84
time of travel, 82
velocity, 85
weight, 90
Fossil fuels
burning of, 113, 140, 142, 144, 151
coal, 110–111, 150, 153
natural gas, 68, 77, 110, 150, 153
oil, 110, 150–151, 153
petroleum, 110
in tar sands, 151
Fossils, 51–52, 124
**Frame of reference for relative
   motion**, 84
Frameshift mutations, 47
Freckles, 43
Free fall, 85
Freezing, 66–67
Frequency, 109
Friction, 88, 103–104
Fulcrum, 94
Full moon, 132
Fungi, 25, 39, 60

G

Galápagos Island finches, 56
Galaxies, 127

Gametes, 3, 41, 46
Gamma rays, 106, 129
Gases, 66–69, 72
Gasoline, 72, 77
GED® Journeys, ix
GED® Science Test, x
GED® Test
　alignment to content practices, v
　alignment to content topics, v
　alignment to Depth of Knowledge
　　(DOK) levels, iv–v
　calculator, xii–xiii
　on computer, vi–vii
　question types, iv–v
　study skills, xv
　subject areas, iv–v
　tips for taking, xiv
Gene expression, 39, 49
Generalizing, 30–33
Generators, 111
Genes
　alleles, 42–44, 48
　DNA sequences, 53
　interaction with environment, 47
　mutations, 47–48
　replication in meiosis, 3, 41, 46
　replication in mitosis, 3, 38–41
Gene switches, 48
Genetic engineering, 57
Genetic material, 3–4
Genetic mutations, 47–48
Genetic recombination, 41, 46
Genome, 53
Genotype, 42, 43, 45
**Genotypic and phenotypic
　ratios**, 45
Germ line cells, 48
Glands, 9
Global conveyer belt, 140
Global warming, 61, 113, 142,
　151
Glucose, 3–5
Glycolysis, 5
Graphics. See **Visuals**
Graphs
　bar graphs, 18, 102
　circle graphs, 18, 142
　drawing conclusions from, 110
　generalizing from, 30
　line graphs, 18, 102
　phase diagrams as, 66
　relating to text, 102
　as support for arguments, 150
Grassland ecosystems, 22, 24
Gravity
　acceleration in free fall, 85
　collapse of stars due to, 129
　effect on air pressure, 145
　effect on bullet shot in air, 119
　force of, 89
　relationship to weight, 90
　roller coasters' use of, 104
Gray wolves, 31
Greenhouse gases, 113, 142
Growth hormone, 9
Gulf Stream, 138

H

Halley's comet, 132
Hares, 32
Headings
　of table columns, 10
　of visuals, 6
Heart, 7
Heat
　absorption by water, 65
　Calories as units of, 12
　in chemical reactions, 104–105
　as result of molecular movement, 98
　transfer of, 98, 100–101
　See also **Temperature; Thermal energy**
Hepatitis C, 20
Heredity
　development of new alleles, 48
　DNA, 38
　environmental effects on gene
　　expression, 49
　genetic recombination, 41, 46
　genotype, 42–45
　meiosis, 3, 41, 46
　mitosis, 3, 38–41
　mutations, 47–48
　pedigree charts, 44
　phenotype, 43, 45
　Punnett squares, 42–43, 45
Hertz, 109
**Hertzsprung-Russell (H-R)
　diagram**, 128
Heterozygous genotype, 43, 45
Histones, 38
HIV, 21
Homeostasis, 15
Homologous chromosomes, 41
Homozygous genotype, 43–45
Hormones, 9
Human activities
　artificial selection, 57
　desertification caused by, 35
　effects on other populations, 33
　extinction due to, 61
　food web disruption, 36
　genetic engineering, 57
　release of greenhouse gases, 142
Human body
　balanced meals and, 13
　circulatory system, 7
　digestive system, 7
　diseases, 18–21, 44
　endocrine system, 9
　excretory system, 7
　homeostasis, 15
　immune system, 16–17
　micronutrients and macronutrients
　　needed, 13
　muscular system, 7
　nervous system, 8
　organization of cells, 6
　recommended daily allowance of food
　　groups, 12
　recommended daily caloric intake, 10
　respiratory system, 7

　skin, 6
　skin color, 56
　somatic cells of, 41
　specialization of cells, 39
　systems working together, 7
　temperature regulation, 14
　transport of oxygen, 7
　vitamins and minerals needed, 11
Hurricanes, 141, 147
Hydrocarbons, 68, 77
Hydrochloric acid, 80
Hydroelectric plants, 110–111
Hydroelectric power, 152
Hydrogen
　chemical formula of, 65
　density of, 72
　in human body, 13
　as product of acid-metal reaction, 77
　in sun, 126
　in water, 65
Hydrogen ions, 73, 78–80
Hydrogen molecule, 64
Hydrogen peroxide, 65
Hydroxide ions, 80
Hypothalamus, 9, 14
Hypothermia, 14
Hypotheses
　evaluation of, 121
　forming and proving, 78, 114–115,
　　117–120, 122–125
　null hypotheses, 121
　theories compared to, 120

I

Ice, 72
Illustrations
　interpreting, 2–5
　relating to text, 38
　as scientific models, 62
Immune system, 16–17, 21
Impulse, 91
Inclined plane, 95
Independent variable, 115, 118
Inferences
　drawing conclusions from, 58
　making and identifying, 54–57, 74,
　　110
Influenza vaccines, 18
Infrared light, 106
Inner core of Earth, 136
Input force, 94–95
Insertion mutations, 47
Integrator neurons, 15
Interphase, 40
Invalid generalizations, 30
Invasive species, 37
**Investigation techniques,
　understanding**, 114–117
Involuntary muscles, 7
Iodine, 13
Ionic bonds, 64, 68
Ionic compounds, 64, 68
Ionization, 78–80

INDEX

Index

Ionosphere, 143
Ions, 63–64, 143
Iron, 11, 75, 127
Irrigation, 153

J

Joule, 95, 102

K

Kepler, Johannes, 133
Kepler's laws of planetary motion, 133
Keys
    for graphs, 18
    for tables, 10, 70
Keystone species, 36
Kinetic energy, 98–100, 102–104, 119
Kudzu vine, 37

L

Labels
    on diagrams, 134
    on illustrations, 2, 38
    on visuals, 126
Lactate, 5
Landforms, 125, 137
Large intestine, 7
Last quarter moon, 132
Lava, 135, 148
Lavoisier, Antoine, 121
Lead, 72
Leopards, 34
Lever, 94, 97
Light
    electromagnetic waves, 106
    plants' use in photosynthesis, 4, 105
    speed of, 109
    visible light, 106, 109
Lightning, 148
Light waves, 107
Line graphs, 18, 102
Lions, 34
Lipids, 3
Liquefaction, 68
Liquids, 66–67
Lithosphere, 136
Liver, 39
Living things, 26–28. *See also* **Animals; Bacteria; Fungi; Plants**
Load, 94
Longitudinal waves, 107
Lower epidermis, 4
Lunar eclipses, 133
Lungs, 7
Lynxes, 32, 34
Lysosomes, 2

M

Macronutrients, 13
Macroscopic events, 98–101
Magma, 125, 135–136, 148
Magma chamber, 135
Magnesium, 127
Magnetism, 87
Magnitudes of stars, 128
Main idea and details, identifying, 6–9, 126
Main sequence stars, 127
Main vent of volcano, 135
Making Assumptions
    applying known concepts to new situations, 86
    based on data in tables, 10
    interpreting diagrams, 134
    labels on axes of graphs, 18
    model labels, 62
    numerical data in tables, 70
    using prior knowledge, 26
Mammals, 51
Mantle, 134, 136–137
Maps, interpreting graphs and, 18–21
Mass
    average force, 93
    calculating, 72
    conservation of, 74, 76, 120–121
    definition, 90
    momentum and, 91
    relationship to force and acceleration, 89
Mathematical equations as scientific models, 62
Mathematical formulas. *See* **Formulas**
Matter
    chemical changes, 73, 77
    chemical reactions, 73–77
    conservation of mass, 74, 76, 120–121
    expansion of, 99
    mass of, 72, 90
    physical changes, 73, 77
    properties of, 67–68, 72
    states of, 66–69
Meal planning, 13
Mean, 115
Mechanical advantage, 95
Mechanical energy, 104–105
Median, 115
Meiosis, 3, 41, 46
Melting, 66–67
Melting point, 70
Mendel, Gregor, 43
Mendeleev, Dmitri, 72
Mercury, 72, 81
Mesophyll, 4
Mesosaurus **fossils**, 124
Mesosphere, 143
Metals, 70, 77, 81, 118
Metaphase, 40
Methane, 77
Microbes, 60
Micronutrients, 13

Microscopic and observable events, linking, 98–101
Microwaves, 106, 123
Mid-ocean ridge, 125, 137
Migration, 58
Milky Way, 127
Millipedes, 25
Minerals
    human body's need of, 11
    recommended daily values, 11
Mitochondria, 5
Mitosis, 3, 38–41
Molecular genetics, 47
Molecules, 63–66
Momentum
    average force, 93
    change in, 91, 93
    law of conservation of, 91
    third law of motion and, 92
Moon
    eclipses, 133
    phases of, 132
Moths, 55
Motion of objects
    acceleration, 85, 89–90
    changing momentum, 91
    displacement, 83
    forces and vectors, 86–89
    Kepler's laws of planetary motion, 133
    law of momentum conservation, 91
    momentum, 91–92
    Newton's laws of motion, 86, 89–91, 120
    relative motion, 84
    speed, 82–83
    vector diagrams, 86–89
    velocity, 83, 85
    work, 94, 95, 97
Motorcycle physics, 93
Motor neurons, 8
Mount St. Helens, 136
Movable pulley, 96
Movement, of human body, 7
Multicellular organisms, 4, 39. *See also* **Animals; Fungi; Human body; Plants**
Muscle, 7
Muscular system, 7
Mutations
    in gene switches, 48
    in germ line cells, 48
    types of, 47
Mutualism, 26–29

N

National Oceanic and Atmospheric Administration, 151
National Weather Service, 149
Natural gas
    composition of, 68, 77
    as source of energy, 110, 150
    states of, 68
Natural selection, 54–56, 58, 60
Nervous system, 8
Net force, 86, 88

INDEX

Neurons, 8, 39
Neutralization of acids, 80
Neutrons, 62–63, 111
Neutron star, 127, 129
New moon, 132
Newton, 86, 88, 90
Newton's laws of motion
    first law, 86, 91
    second law, 89–90, 93
    third law, 89
Nitrogen, 13, 72, 148
Nitrogen cycle, 148
Nonliving things, 32
Nonrenewable energy, 110–111, 153
Nuclear envelope, 4
Nuclear fission, 111, 126
Nuclear fusion, 126–127
Nuclear power plants, 111
Nucleolus, 4
Nucleotides, 47
Nucleus of atom, 62
Nucleus of cell, 3, 4, 38–40
Null hypotheses, 121
Nutrients
    absorption in body, 7
    flow through ecosystems,
        22, 25
    vitamins and minerals, 11

O

Obesity, 49
Observable events, linking to
    microscopic events, 98–101
Observations
    drawing conclusions from, 58
    inferences based on, 54
    interpreting, 102–105
    making predictions from, 78
    as part of scientific method, 114
    scientific laws based on, 90
Ocean currents, 138, 140–141
Oceans
    acidification of, 140
    crust formation, 137
    formation of hurricanes, 141
    increasing temperatures, 36
Octane, 77
Offspring, 42, 45
Ogallala Aquifer, 151
Oil, 150–152
Opinions, 150
Orbits
    of comets, 132
    of Earth and moon, 132
Orca whales, 36
Organisms as level in ecosystems, 6
Organs, 6–7
Outcomes
    calculating to interpret, 82–85
    predicting, 78–81
Outer core of Earth, 136
Outliers, 115
Output force, 94–95
Overfishing, 36

Over-generalization, 58
Overgrazing, 35
Ovum, 41
Oxidation, 75
Oxpecker birds, 28
Oxygen
    in human body, 13
    movement across cell membranes, 3
    oxidation reactions, 75
    produced by stars, 127
    as product of photosynthesis, 4, 105
    in respiration, 5
    transport of in body, 7
    in water, 65
Ozone, 65
Ozone layer, 145

P

Pakicetus skeleton, 51
Parasites, 27
Parasitism, 26–27
Parent cells, 3, 40–41, 46
Partial eclipse, 133
Particles, 66–67, 98–100
Patterns in science, understanding,
    130–133
Pea plants, 42–43
Pedigree charts, 42, 44
Penumbra, 133
Periodicity, 72
Periodic table, 71–72
Permian Period, 124
Perspiration, 14
Petroleum, 110
Phase diagrams, 66, 119
Phases of matter, 66
Phenotype, 43, 45
Phloem, 4
Phlogiston, theory of, 121
pH of ocean waters, 140
Photosynthesis, 4, 105
Photovoltaic systems, 112
pH scale, 73, 144
Physical adaptations, 58
Physical changes, 73, 77
Physical properties, 72
Piston, 99
Pituitary gland, 9
Pivot point, 94
Plagues, 19
Planets
    formation of, 127
    Kepler's laws of planetary motion, 133
Plants
    adaptations to climate, 58
    artificial selection, 57
    as eukaryotes, 39
    invasive species versus native plants,
        37
    leaf structure, 4
    photosynthesis, 4, 105
    as producers, 23–25
    symbiotic relationships, 26, 29
Plate tectonic theory, 124–125, 136

Polar bodies, 41
Poles of magnets, 87
Polio vaccine, 20
Pollution, 144–145
Populations
    of big cats, 34
    carrying capacity, 31–32
    exponential growth of, 33
Pore in cell nucleus, 4
Potassium, 13
Potential energy, 102–104
Power, 95
Predation, 26–27, 32
Predator-prey relationships,
    26–27, 32
Predators, 26–27, 32
Predictions, making, 78
Pressure
    changes of state affected by, 66
    effect on solubility, 80, 116
Prey, 26–27, 32
Primary consumers, 23
Prior knowledge, accessing,
    94–97
Problem and solution, identifying,
    146–149
Producers, 23, 25
Products, 74
Prokaryotes, 39
Prophase, 40, 46
Protein channel, 3
Proteins
    antibodies, 16
    in cell membranes, 3
    production of in cells, 39
Protons, 62–63
Protozoans, 60
Pseudoscience, 118
Pulley, 96–97
Punnett squares, 42–43, 45

Q

Questions, asking, 114, 122

R

Rabbits, running speed of, 55
Radiation, 100–101
Radiation levels, 115
Radioactive waste, 111
Radiometric dating, 137
Radio signals, 143
Radio waves, 106
Rainfall, 32, 58
Rarefactions, 107
Rats, 19
Rayleigh waves, 108
Reactants, 74
Receptor neurons, 8, 15
Recessive alleles, 42, 44–45
Recommended Daily Allowance, 12
Rectum, 7

INDEX

Index

Red giant stars, 127–129
Red supergiant stars, 127–128
Relative motion, 84
Renewable energy, 110, 144, 152–153
Reproduction
    meiosis, 3, 41, 46
    mitosis, 3, 38–41
Reservoirs, 152
Resistance, 88, 94
Respiration, cellular, 5, 105
Respiratory system, 7
Rhinoceroses, 28
Ridge, 136
Rock
    finding relative age of, 137
    layers of, 137
Roller coasters, 104
Rows
    in periodic table, 72
    in tables, 70

S

Salinity, 140
Salk, Jonas, 20
Salts, 64, 77–78, 80, 117
Sandy, Hurricane, 147
Sanitation, 19
Saturated solutions, 79
Schizophrenia, 47
Science concepts, applying, 138–141
Scientific evidence, understanding, 50–53
Scientific information
    evaluating, 118–121
    expressing, 142–145
Scientific investigation
    evaluation of, 118
    organization of, 116
    proving or disproving hypotheses, 122
    scientific laws based on, 90
    scientific method, 114
    use of statistics for analysis of
        results, 115
    variables in, 115
Scientific laws, 74, 76, 86, 89–93, 102–103, 120–121, 133
Scientific laws, applying, 90–93
Scientific method, 114
Scientific models
    for chemical equations, 75
    understanding, 62–65
Scientific theories, understanding, 122–125
Scientific theory, 121–125. *See also* **Atomic theory; Big Bang theory; Continental drift theory; Evolutionary theory; Phlogiston, theory of; Plate tectonic theory; Scientific theories, understanding**
Screw, 97
Screwdrivers, 96
Scurvy, 11
Seafloor spreading, 125

Sea lions, 36
Seals, 36
Sea otter, 36
Seasons, 130
Seat belts, 93
Secondary consumers, 23
Seismographs, 148
Senses, 8, 102
Sensory neurons, 8
Sex cells, 41
Sexual reproduction, 3
Siamese cats, 49
Side vent of volcano, 135
Silicon, 127
Simple machines, 94–97
Single-celled organisms, 4
Single displacement reactions, 75
Single fixed pulley, 96
Skeletal muscle, 7
Skin, 6
Skin color, 56
Small intestine, 7
Smooth muscle, 7
Sodium, 11, 13, 64
Sodium ion, 64
Soil, 25
Soil conservation, 35
Solar eclipses, 133
Solar energy, 110, 112
Solar system, 127, 133
Solids, 66–67, 81, 99
Solubility, 79–81, 116
Solute, 78–81, 116
Solution, identifying problem and, 146–149
Solutions, 78–81, 117
Solvent, 78–81
Somatic cells, 41, 48
Sound
    speed of, 84, 109
    volume, 108
Sound waves, 84, 107–109
Source line in tables, 10
Speciation, 59, 61
Speed
    distance and, 82
    of light, 109
    of sound, 84, 109
    velocity and, 83
Sperm, 3, 41
Spinal cord, 8
Spotlighted Items
    drag-and-drop, 35–37, 40, 52, 65, 144
    drop-down, 15–17, 21, 24, 87, 123, 139
    fill-in-the-blank, 27–29, 76, 84, 132
    hot spot, 43–45, 104, 137
    short answer, 59–61, 79, 113, 117, 128
Stars
    constellations, 131
    death of, 127, 129
    elements produced by, 127
    traits of, 128
States of matter, 66–68
Statistics, 115
Stimulus, 15
St. Matthew Island reindeer, 30
Stratosphere, 143

Subatomic particles, 62–63
Sublimation, 66–67, 69, 119
Substitution mutations, 47
Sugars, 5, 105
Sun
    brightness and temperature of, 128
    eclipse of, 133
    life cycle of, 129
    nuclear fusion in, 126
    as source of energy, 110, 112
Sunlight
    amount in ecosystems, 32
    plants' use in photosynthesis, 4, 105
Supernovas, 127, 129
Supporting details, 6
Surface ocean currents, 141
Surface waves, 108
Symbiotic relationships, 26–29, 32
Symbols
    for dominant and recessive alleles, 42
    as models, 62
    for elements, 65, 71
    in tables, 70
Synthesis reactions, 75
Systems of human body, 6–9

T

Tables
    categorizing and classifying with, 26
    complex tables, 70
    interpreting, 10–13, 70–73
    relating to text, 38
Tar sands, 151
Tectonic plates, 124–125, 136
Telomere, 38
Telophase, 40
Temperate deciduous forests, 58
Temperature
    as average kinetic energy, 98
    changes of state, 66
    driving global conveyer belt, 140
    in ecosystems, 32
    effect on solubility, 79, 116–117
    heat transfer, 98–99
    measurement of, 98
    regulation in human body, 14
    of stars, 128
    See also **Heat; Thermal energy**
Teosinte, 57
Tert-butyl alcohol, 69
Tertiary consumers, 23
Testosterone, 9
Test-Taking Tech
    computer skills, 2
    highlighting feature, 30
    using a calculator, 90
Test-Taking Tips, xiv
    identifying inferences, 54
    identifying problem and solution, 146
    interpreting complex visuals, 66
    multiple-choice questions, 58, 106, 122
    performing operations on equations, 82
    responding to short answer questions, 58
    summarizing, 126

INDEX

using context clues to determine meaning, 46
Text, relating to visuals, 38–41, 102, 106
Thermal energy
  Calories as units of, 12
  in chemical reactions, 104–105
  energy changed to by friction, 103
  in gases, 99
  transfer of, 98, 100–101
  See also **Heat; Temperature**
Thermal equilibrium, 98
Thermometer, 98
Thermosphere, 143
Threatened species, 31, 33–34
Three-dimensional diagrams, interpreting, 134–137
Time, 82–83, 85
Tissues, 6
Tornado watches/warnings, 149
Traits
  adaptations, 55–58
  artificial selection, 57
  eyes of burrowing animals, 54
  genotype, 43
  interaction of genes with environment, 47
  modification over time, 54–56
  natural selection of, 55–56
  phenotype, 43
  prediction of, 42
  tracking in families, 44
Transverse waves, 107
Trench, 136
Trophic levels, 23
Troposphere, 143
Troughs of waves, 107
Tumor-blocking genes, 49
Tundras, 58
Turbines, 111

U

Ultraviolet light, 106
Umbra, 133
Unbalanced forces, 86–88
UNICEF, 146
United Nations Millennium Development Goals, 19
Unsaturated solutions, 79
Upper epidermis, 4
Uranium-235, 111
U.S. Department of Agriculture, 12
Using Logic
  answers supporting arguments, 150
  applying concepts, 138
  comparing and contrasting, 34
  effect of Earth's tilt, 130
  identifying hypotheses, 114
  interpreting diagrams, 22
  interpreting trends in graphs, 102
  looking for patterns, 78
  making predictions, 98
  sequence of cause and effect, 14

subscripts and coefficients, 74
understanding cladograms, 50
using content from visuals to express information, 142
using prior knowledge, 94

V

Vaccines, 18, 20
Valid generalizations, 30
Vaporization, 66–67
Variables, 115, 118
Vector diagrams, understanding, 86–89, 90–92
Vectors, 86–89
Velocity
  acceleration and, 85
  average force, 93
  change in, 85
  momentum and, 91
  speed and, 83
Vertebrates, 53
Vestigial structures, 51
Viruses, 20–21, 60
Visible light, 106, 109
Visuals
  cladograms, 50, 52
  complex tables, 70
  complex visuals, 66
  content-based tools, 42
  diagrams, 22, 34, 85
  food chains, 22
  food webs, 22
  graphs, 18, 30, 66, 102, 142, 150
  illustrations, 2, 38
  interpreting, 2, 10, 18, 22, 42, 62, 66, 70, 86, 134
  maps, 5
  pedigree charts, 42, 44
  phase diagrams, 66, 119
  Punnett squares, 42, 45
  relating to text, 38–41, 102, 106
  scientific models, 62, 65
  tables, 10, 26, 38, 70
  vector diagrams, 86, 90
Vitamin C deficiency, 11
Vitamin D, 56
Vitamins, 11, 56
Volcanoes, 125, 135–136, 148
Voltage, 103
Volume, 72
Volume of sound, 108

W

Waning crescent moon, 132
Waning gibbous moon, 132
Waste products, 105
Water
  access to clean water, 146
  chemical equation for production of, 76

density of, 72
in ecosystems, 32
molecular structure of, 65
movement across cell membranes, 3
as a natural resource, 153
in photosynthesis, 4, 105
as product of burning alkanes, 77
as product of neutralization, 80
as source of energy, 110
use in respiration, 5
Water conservation, 35
Water cycle, 139
Water waves, 108
Watt, 95
Wavelength, 106, 109
Waves
  amplitude, 108
  electromagnetic, 106, 109
  frequency, 109
  light and sound, 107
  longitudinal, 107
  Rayleigh waves, 108
  surface, 108, 135
  transverse, 107
  wavelength, 106
Waxing crescent moon, 132
Waxing gibbous moon, 132
Wedge, 97
Wegener, Alfred, 122
Weight, 90
Whale evolution, 51
Wheel and axle, 96–97
White dwarf stars, 127–129
Wind
  ocean currents and, 141
  patterns of, 131
  as source of energy, 110, 144
  in tornadoes, 149
Work
  definition, 94, 97
  expansion of matter and, 99
  mechanical advantage, 95
  mechanical energy and, 104
  power and, 95
World Health Organization, 146

X

X-rays, 106, 129
Xylem, 4

Y

Yellowstone National Park, 31
Yersinia pestis, 19

Z

Zinc, 13

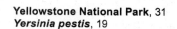